# MEDIEVAL RELIGIOUS HOUSES
## SCOTLAND

# MEDIEVAL RELIGIOUS HOUSES

## SCOTLAND

*With an Appendix on the*
*Houses in the Isle of Man*

*By*

### D. E. EASSON

*With a Foreword by*
### DAVID KNOWLES

*and Maps by*
### R. NEVILLE HADCOCK

## LONGMANS, GREEN AND CO
### LONDON ❖ NEW YORK ❖ TORONTO

LONGMANS, GREEN AND CO LTD
6 & 7 CLIFFORD STREET LONDON W I

THIBAULT HOUSE THIBAULT SQUARE CAPE TOWN
605–611 LONSDALE STREET MELBOURNE C I

LONGMANS, GREEN AND CO INC
55 FIFTH AVENUE NEW YORK 3

LONGMANS, GREEN AND CO
20 CRANFIELD ROAD TORONTO 16

ORIENT LONGMANS PRIVATE LTD
CALCUTTA BOMBAY MADRAS
DELHI HYDERABAD DACCA

*First published 1957*

PRINTED IN GREAT BRITAIN
BY WESTERN PRINTING SERVICES LTD BRISTOL

# FOREWORD

DR EASSON's learned and in many respects pioneer work needs no herald to proclaim its importance, and he has himself provided, in his introductory essays, a review of the work of earlier historians and antiquaries and a survey of the development of the religious orders in Scotland. There may be room, however, in the few pages that I have been asked to write, for a glance at the position of Scotland on the wider canvas of north-western Europe during the five centuries in which her religious life was closely integrated into that of the compact medieval Church, which was itself coincident with an intellectual and cultural republic of ideas and sentiments, linked by a common system of education and a common literary language.

Within the area of north-western Europe there were, in the tenth century, roughly speaking three regions in the matter of religion: that covered by the organized Church, connected with Rome by bonds of varying strength; that of Celtic Christianity embracing Ireland, Scotland and (though less definitely) Wales; and that of the pagan north, in which the first seeds of Christianity were being planted by the Irish and the Anglo-Saxon missionaries. Monasticism was common to the whole of western Christendom, but whereas in the organized Church it was the life of individual communities, entirely separate from the clergy and hierarchy, in the Celtic lands it contained within itself the priesthood and even the episcopate, and was indeed the only powerful religious and cultural force in the land. In form, too, the monastic body differed greatly in the two regions. In the organized Church it was now almost entirely dominated by the Rule of St Benedict and a common set of liturgical and disciplinary customs, while the more austere and individualistic monachism of the Celtic lands had never aimed at or attained more than a loose kind of union or uniformity.

In the late tenth century these differences were greatly accentuated. The missionary achievements and the golden age of Celtic monasticism lay in the distant past, and in Ireland, Wales and Scotland alike what had been a class of great social and intellectual importance had now become a scattering of small groups and individuals living a solitary, or at least an isolated, existence. In continental Europe, on the other hand, the great expansion of Western civilization had begun, helped rather than hindered in the long run by the migrations of the Northmen and the Normans. Scandinavia and its island dependencies, hitherto almost virgin soil, received Christianity from England and Germany along with all its contemporary developments, as every new institution gradually made its way to the frontier. The Celtic lands had various fortunes. Wales, within easy reach of England, became, by a mixture of conquest and peaceful penetration, at least superficially similar in church matters to England. Ireland, a prey to disorder for many centuries before the Norman Conquest, remained throughout the Middle Ages as a shifting sand beneath a surface of the familiar western pattern artificially imposed upon it. Scotland's religious history was determined by the racial affinities of its Celtic west and Nordic east, by its relationship, at first friendly, but later hostile, with England, and by the gradual emergence of a national spirit and character.

Scotland, unlike England, had in the eleventh century no past traditions of the monastic life as one of the elements of its national greatness, and no associations in the past history of great and wealthy abbeys, and of notable monk-bishops and reformers. Her many Celtic saints were revered as holy individuals and as figures of legend rather than of history. The Culdees, the last representatives of Celtic monasticism, had neither the strength nor the organization to resist or to influence the newcomers; they were gradually absorbed into the new system, or disappeared before it. Scotland, therefore, which in the mid-eleventh century had for the first time attained something like political unity, was more potentially receptive of external influences than at any time since her first conversion to Christianity. With Celtic Christianity losing its shape and force she was in many respects a *tabula rasa*, like the Scandinavian lands, but with the possession of Christian faith and practice she was more open to religious influences.

It was at this very moment in the history of Europe that the vast multiplication and proliferation of the monastic life began. Starting with the reforms and developments of the traditional Benedictine or "black" monks, of which the most spectacular example was the growth of the "order" of Cluny, it continued with the emergence of powerful new monastic and canonical bodies, of which the greatest by far were the Cistercian (or "white") monks and the Premonstratensian (or "white") canons, and after producing in the four chief orders of friars the most characteristic creation of the later Middle Ages, dwindled to its last manifestation, a shadow of its old self, in the collegiate church of the fifteenth century. These waves, issuing from France and Italy, swept outwards across Europe and normally reached Scotland late, but as with tides, so with human movements, an obstacle or a free passage can change rhythms and seasons, and personal or political accidents could on occasion bring to Scotland a religious family that had not yet arrived in England, or perhaps never was to arrive.

It is generally acknowledged that the infiltration of what Scottish historians are agreed in calling Roman monastic life was directly due to the influence of Queen Margaret, daughter of Edward the Atheling, who became the second wife of King Malcolm III in 1069. The moment was propitious, for in England also a great stirring and development was on the point of taking place. Margaret had chosen as her somewhat remote spiritual director the new Italian archbishop of Canterbury, and when she had thoughts of introducing monks to Scotland it was to him she turned. Lanfranc met her request by sending three of his Canterbury monks, and they formed the nucleus of the house that was afforced fifty years later by another colony from Christ Church and became to the Scottish monarchy something of what Westminster and St Denis were in England and France. Dunfermline became wealthy and its abbot was a person of distinction, but it remained the only sizeable independent house of the Benedictines.

Dunfermline owed its splendour to Margaret's son, King David I, and in his long reign the monastic map of Scotland was firmly blocked in. David, half English in blood through his mother, and earl of Huntingdon and Northampton by his marriage with Maude, daughter of the earl Waltheof who had been beheaded by the Conqueror, had many personal and feudal connections with England, where he had spent much of his youth. At that time the border between England and Scotland was still fluid: Cumberland, Northumberland and Durham were not yet finally part of either country, and communications between them and Teviotdale and Lothian were open and free. David, at home in England and Scotland alike, turned naturally, as did his Norman vassals, both to England and the Continent for help in his task of religious plantation. Thus the Augustinian houses of Holyrood, Scone (under Alexander I) and perhaps St Andrews were founded from Merton (Surrey) and Nostell (Yorks), while the first Premonstratensian abbey at Dryburgh was a daughter of Alnwick (Northumberland). Still more striking was the filiation of the Cistercians. Melrose, the first Scottish house, had as its founding abbot the king's stepson, St Waldef. Waldef was a monk of Rievaulx, and the whole family of eleven Cistercian abbeys in Scotland, the most compact and in some ways the most remarkable group of monasteries in the country, was derived at one remove or more from Rievaulx, either through Melrose or through another daughter, yet another of the king's foundations, Dundrennan in Kirkcudbrightshire. King David, however, was catholic in his choice and went further than England to find what he needed. Thus for

Cambuskenneth and Jedburgh he summoned canons from Arrouaise and Beauvais, while for Selkirk (later Kelso) he introduced into Scotland an order all but unknown in England, the monks of the reform of Tiron in Brittany, and it is probable that he visited Tiron itself to secure his purpose. Kelso in its early maturity was probably the most populous abbey in Scotland, while Arbroath, another Tironian house founded in Angus by William the Lion, was the wealthiest. Whether judged by their number, their size, their wide distribution or the variety of their rule, the foundations of David I must rank as the most remarkable of any Scottish monarch, or indeed of any monarch of the age.

The monastic family continued to grow in Scotland for half-a-century or so after expansion had ceased in England. While some orders, such as those of Grandmont and Fontevrault, never came so far north, and others, such as the Carthusians and Gilbertines, either came late or failed to make a lasting stay, the chief families of men were well represented. Nunneries were always few, and relatively small and poor, and Scotland lacked almost entirely the galaxy of small priories and cells that covered the face of medieval England. By far the greater number of these were "alien priories", the lesser Cluniac dependencies and the small establishments set up by Norman and French abbeys on their English estates, often simply as a *pied-à-terre* or centre of economic administration. By the time of King David, the high tide of this expansion had passed, and the number of small monastic establishments in Scotland in his day barely exceeded half-a-dozen. This was no loss; indeed, it eliminated one great source of religious weakness and one great temptation for the confiscator.

The friars, who needed neither abbey nor benefaction nor even a summons to attract them, reached Scotland within a few years of arriving in London, and the country soon had its quota. All four orders were represented, but the Augustinian friars had only a single house and the splinter-orders barely reached the north. On the other hand, an order of canons, the Trinitarians, sometimes known as "red friars", was relatively strong, and there were three houses of a family unknown to England, that of the Valliscaulians, a minor monastic group not unlike the Cistercians. The friars reached the north through England, and during the whole of the thirteenth century the bonds of religious and intellectual unity were stronger than the forces of separation throughout Europe; at the dawn of the century Adam of Dryburgh sought the Carthusian solitude at Witham in Somerset, and at its close John Duns the Scotsman gave lustre to Oxford.[1]

With the fourteenth century, a time of change throughout Europe, the break came also in Scotland. Henceforth the Border was not only a real barrier, but also an area of destruction in which the Scottish abbeys fared worse than the English, for in England there were no rich houses north of Durham and Carlisle, which were never overrun, whereas in Scotland a group of the fairest and wealthiest abbeys lay to hand unprotected in the basin of the Tweed. These and other houses near the Firth of Forth had to suffer again and again a fate that no English abbey endured between the Conquest and the Dissolution—fire and ruin at the hands of a merciless enemy.

The pattern of the religious life in Scotland deviates most markedly from that of any other part of the British Isles in the fifteenth and early sixteenth centuries. Whereas in England, Wales and Ireland, though in different ways, the rhythm of life becomes universally slower, and scarcely any new feature appears until the abrupt end, in Scotland development and deterioration continue side by side. While England was absorbed in the French war and internal disputes, Scotland maintained its continental associations; in consequence, the new reform of the Franciscans, that of the Observants, found entry half-a-century before it came to England, and provided a body of friars, small in number but influential in an age of waning fervour. Similarly,

[1] I should perhaps warn the reader that Dr Easson considers the Scottish provenance of Duns not proven.

the solitary Scottish Charterhouse of Perth, though probably owing its conception to the English memories of Jane Beaufort, drew its first community from the Continent. A further development was that of the secular colleges. Whereas in England the great extension of numbers took place before 1450, in Scotland foundations were made with the greatest frequency throughout the period 1440–1540. In one of the earliest, St Mary's at St Andrews, a lingering group of Culdees was transformed; of the remainder, a certain number were parish churches of which the revenue had been augmented and parcelled into prebends, but more than a third were "chantry" colleges or incorporations of chaplains. A type almost peculiar to Scotland was that of the large burgh church, with a number of endowed altars, which became (or was on the way to becoming) collegiate, and was the centre of all kinds of civic activity.

Alongside of these developments the decline of observance in the monasteries was hastened by their occupation by lay "abbots". The system of commendam, common on the Continent but unknown in England, was introduced into Scotland in the last decades of the fifteenth century. The abbey and title of abbot was given to a commendator, often a bishop or court official or high-born cleric, who enjoyed the revenues and allowed the monks their "portions"; in later years he was often a layman who installed himself, as at Melrose, in a house adjacent to the abbey. Simultaneously, the feuing of monastic lands and the allotment of individual incomes to the religious were destroying both the property and the spirit of the communities. In addition, the houses near the Border and the Forth experienced the brutality of the disgraceful expedition of the Earl of Hertford in 1544. Nevertheless, the end came far more slowly in Scotland than in England, and it was both more violent and more gentle in different houses. As neither James V nor the Earl of Arran took the forthright advice of Henry VIII to imitate his own successful action, the religious houses were never confiscated *en bloc* at the Reformation. While the urban houses, especially those of the friars, were sacked by the lawless element among the reformers, the abbeys held or controlled by the great lairds continued to exist, with the community gradually losing every vestige of traditional monastic routine, until their annexation to the Crown in 1587, and even then in many cases did not legally come to an end till they almost insensibly became lay property at the turn of the century, when they were irrevocably secularized by a crown charter and an act of parliament.

Owing to the late introduction of regular monasticism to Scotland, when the "Benedictine centuries" were about to end, the country owed little of its artistic or literary capital, and none of its religious tradition, to the black monks. There were no centres of manuscript illumination and literary composition comparable to St Albans, Canterbury and Durham. Similarly, the age of saints was passing, and after the death of St Waldef at Melrose it is difficult to name a monk or friar of outstanding sanctity or reputation. There were relatively few monk-bishops, and the monks came too late to provide a creative statesman of the type of Lanfranc or Suger.

The monastic map of Scotland is for the most part sparsely covered, and much of its area is entirely barren of houses. If a line is drawn from Inverness to Perth, and thence to Glasgow, the only sizable house north and west of this is the revived abbey of Iona. Most of this area is indeed mountain or moorland, but it may seem at first surprising that the Cistercians and Premonstratensians, who penetrated to the Alps and the Pyrenees, never sought out the fertile glens and islands of the west. Possibly the Celtic temperament and system of clans were not susceptible of a life ordered upon the needs and habits of Latin lands; possibly those in search of "noble wild prospects" could find them to hand without crossing the Highland line.

Though a few abbeys were well-endowed and populous, no Scottish house was great or inordinately wealthy by continental or even by English standards, nor were their buildings of any great complexity or architectural distinction, save in the region between Forth and Tay, and, above all, in the wide basin of the Tweed. There, more than anywhere else, at Jedburgh, Dryburgh and Melrose, a regional version of Gothic architecture was produced which resembled that of Yorkshire, but had an idiom of its own. Melrose is a particular jewel in the treasury of the Middle Ages, just as, by Solway Firth, Dundrennan and Sweetheart, for all their conformity to strict Cistercian planning, have a colour and texture of their own.

DAVID KNOWLES

# CONTENTS

# MAPS

*Following page* 204

HOUSES OF MONKS, REGULAR CANONS, ETC., AND NUNS IN SCOTLAND

HOUSES OF THE FRIARS IN SCOTLAND

THE CATHEDRALS, COLLEGIATE CHURCHES AND HOSPITALS IN SCOTLAND BEFORE THE REFORMATION

*The maps are based on the Ordnance Survey Map of Monastic Britain (North Sheet), by permission of the Director General*

xvii

# PREFACE

THE present work, as a companion volume to *Medieval Religious Houses: England and Wales*, follows in its general arrangement the lines adopted by Professor Knowles and Mr Hadcock in that publication. The religious foundations are listed according to orders or in other appropriate categories and each list is accompanied by notes on the individual houses. But in a number of respects it differs—necessarily—from the English volume. The lists are primarily inclusive of houses accepted as authentic, while in each section a subsidiary list of doubtful and unauthentic foundations is appended. This procedure has been deemed advisable because, in certain cases, e.g. the Trinitarians and Dominicans, the number of unauthentic houses mentioned is considerable and these, if included with the houses which have been verified, would have formed a disproportionate as well as a confusing element in the lists. Again, because reliable works on Scottish religious foundations are lamentably few, the lists and notes are based to a large extent on material drawn from original sources, These sources, it is hoped, are sufficiently indicated on pp. 40ff., where the somewhat lengthy note of abbreviations may also serve in some measure as a bibliography. The lists include a properly computed statement of the incomes of the religious houses and other foundations in 1561, i.e. at the Reformation, so far as these incomes can be ascertained from existing records. These revenues purport to be set forth in various works which allude to the Scottish monasteries (e.g. Keith, *History of the Affairs of Church and State in Scotland*, Book III, Appendix); but, as a rule, the figures given cover only the money income and no attempt has hitherto been made to assess and include their victual revenues and thus to arrive at their total resources. We are indebted to Dr Gordon Donaldson not only for making this

xix

computation but for supplying a valuable note explaining its sources and basis.[1] A column showing where possible the founder(s) of each house has been added to the lists. "Dissolution" and "suppression" are terms which cannot be applied to the Scottish houses in the sense in which they are applicable to the English monasteries. Those houses which became extinct before the Reformation are noted as "dissolved" or, in some cases where the term is appropriate, "suppressed". But in the case of the communities which continued till the Reformation the column recording their extinction is headed "secularized"; and the date there given is generally that of the formal erection of the abbey or priory into a temporal lordship. Such an erection was usually made in terms of a crown charter and an act of parliament and the date which is listed is that on which the erection is first recorded. In the case of the hospitals, the more non-committal heading "terminated" is used. The difficulties involved in making an estimate of the monastic population of Scotland have deterred the writer from attempting that task. Only in the sixteenth century do we find in feu-charters some indication of the number of monks. But these figures are by no means complete; their investigation is a matter of considerable research; and it is questionable how far their interpretation can attain confident results.

The period covered by this work is approximately 1050 to 1560; and an effort has been made to ensure that all the religious houses, as well as colleges, hospitals, etc., which are mentioned within these five centuries are included in it. It should, however, be pointed out that while 1560 is the terminal date for foundations, the date of extinction is often much later (and well beyond the Reformation) as the secularization of a considerable number of Scottish monasteries did not take place, finally, until the seventeenth century.

No apology is needed for including among Scottish foundations those at Berwick-on-Tweed. A writer in the *Downside*

[1] *V.* Appendix II *infra.*

*Review*, commenting on the omission in *Medieval Religious Houses: England and Wales* of the Franciscan and Dominican houses at Berwick "presumably because these are to be included in the Scottish volume", cites Dr Little, *Franciscan Papers*, p. 22, to the effect that "the Berwick Franciscans were established in 1231 and in the custody of Newcastle"; and this is not disputed, though it should be pointed out that all the Scottish Franciscan houses were at first in that custody. But the statement that "later political changes moved them to the vicarate [*sic*] of Scotland" is hardly an adequate summary of the complicated series of events which occupies eleven pages of Moir Bryce's *Scottish Greyfriars* (I, 6–17); and the further contention that "they have a better right to the English connection and are so treated by Dr Little, *v.* Studies, p. 6, n. 1" is one which (*pace* Dr Little) the present writer cannot accept of this order or any of the orders represented at Berwick. The religious houses and hospitals at Berwick were founded within the period when it was indisputably a Scottish burgh and situated in the diocese of St Andrews. Again, the Cistercian nunnery and the Dominican priory were founded by Scottish kings; the Trinitarian house was the foundation of a Scottish countess; the house of Segden is specifically described as Scottish; and, in 1333, Edward III gave orders for the removal of the Scottish friars from the four friaries. After 1482, when Berwick finally passed from Scottish possession, its monastic history virtually ceases. The case for the inclusion of the houses at Berwick in this volume seems sufficiently obvious.

As the houses of the Isle of Man do not appear in the English volume, it has been thought desirable to include them in the present work. The listing and annotation of the Manx foundations will, it is hoped, suffice without special commentary to illustrate the main features of their history.

It should be mentioned that customary Scottish terminology has been retained. Thus "Augustinian" is preferred to "Austin" as a designation of regular canons and friars. On the other hand, although the Trinitarians are sometimes described by writers (but not in medieval records) as "Red friars", this term is avoided as inaccurate—the Trinitarians were not, strictly speaking, friars. "Collegiate church" is employed, in accordance with the usage of Scottish records and writers, as signifying a college of secular priests; the term "provostry", often used in the same sense, is only admitted where sources which are cited make use of it. Scottish writers, legal and ecclesiastical, do not speak of "peculiars". "Lazar house" is not found; the usual term is "leper house". "Teinds" are the Scottish equivalent of "tithes" and, except in references to English records, "sasine" appears instead of "seisin".

Attention may be drawn to the maps which illustrate the distribution of (*a*) the houses of monks, regular canons, etc., and nuns, (*b*) the houses of friars, and (*c*) the cathedrals, collegiate churches and hospitals in the late fifteenth and the sixteenth centuries. These maps are the contribution of Mr R. Neville Hadcock, of whose skill and ingenuity in devising their details warm appreciation should be expressed.

In the compilation of the present work, I have been placed under great obligation for generous and ready help accorded me at every stage of my task. Dr C. T. McInnes, Curator of Historical Records, H.M. General Register House, Edinburgh, whose good offices have been constantly at my disposal, facilitated the consultation of records and answered innumerable queries; Dr Gordon Donaldson has provided information not only on monastic incomes but on many other matters; Dr Annie I. Dunlop made available for this work her most recent transcripts from the Vatican archives; Colonel L. Nowosilski gave much help in tracing lists of religious foundations; Mr A. A. M. Duncan lent notes on the priory of May; Mr B. R. S. Megaw rendered valuable assistance in the investigation of the houses in Man; Mr G. W. S. Barrow was very profitably consulted on Celtic foundations; Dr A. O. Anderson kindly elucidated problems referred to him; the Rev. Dr W. E. K. Rankin contributed information on St Andrews and Mr R. C. Reid on

Galloway; and Mr D. J. Withrington participated in the computation of monastic incomes. It is a pleasure likewise to mention the varied and valued services of the Rev. W. J. Anderson, Librarian at St Mary's College, Blairs; of Mr W. Park, Keeper of MSS., National Library of Scotland, Edinburgh; of Dr C. A. Malcolm, Librarian of the Signet Library, Edinburgh; of Mr T. R. Harley and other members of Edinburgh University Library staff; and, last but not least, of the staff of the Brotherton Library, Leeds. Throughout, I have had the very helpful cooperation and encouragement of the authors of the corresponding English volume, Professor David Knowles and Mr R. Neville Hadcock. To all these and to others who have lightened my labours I tender my most sincere thanks.

Finally, I desire to record my indebtedness to the Roman Catholic bishops of Scotland for their permission to make use of the Brockie MSS. for the purposes of this work. I have likewise been enabled to quote certain publications through the permission extended to me by the Controller of H.M. Stationery Office (for an extract from *The Letters of James V*), Messrs Thomas Nelson and Sons, Ltd. (for passages in *A Source Book of Scottish History*), Columbia University Press (for a passage in Kenney, *Sources for the Early History of Ireland*), the Scottish Text Society, the Historical Association of Scotland, Professor W. Stanford Reid, Dr A. O. Anderson and Dr I. F. Grant. Of these facilities grateful acknowledgment is duly made.

D.E.E.

Scholes, near Leeds
*May* 1956

# RES MONASTICAE

A RELIABLE account of the Scottish religious foundations of the Middle Ages has long been a *desideratum*; but there are good reasons for regarding with diffidence even the attempt to compile a preliminary catalogue. The field of investigation is considerably smaller than the corresponding field in England and Wales—for the latter had approximately eight times as many foundations as Scotland could show. But even within this limited range comparatively little pioneer work of any worth has been done. Scotland has produced assiduous collectors of records and some notable record scholars, but no Dugdale or Dodsworth to essay a synoptic account of the monasteries on the basis of surviving archives. Beside these compilers of the classic *Monasticon* the Scottish Spottiswoode takes a lowly place. It is true that his small work, despite its imperfections and blunders, is one of the few efforts of the kind that can be regarded with some respect; and he is quoted more often than any other writer on Scottish monastic antiquities. Yet it is significant that for two centuries, in which more and more sources have become available, no adequate attempt has been made to revise and amplify his account of the Scottish foundations.

In the introduction to a volume published in 1899,[1] the late Professor David Masson wrote these words:

> The preparation of a list of the old Scottish religious houses that should wholly supersede Spottiswood's [*sic*] would be a work requiring prolonged, varied and minute research and the exercise of much critical, not to say sceptical, sagacity.

This statement would be little more than a truism but for the particular case to which it applies. Any discussion of the work that has been done on the formation of a catalogue of Scottish

[1] *Register of the Privy Council of Scotland*, 2nd Series, I, cviii *n*.

religious houses must make it plain that research, properly so-called, in this direction has been largely wanting and that, while lists of a sort abound, criticism has hardly touched them. Scepticism (to follow out Masson's statement) has not been an outstanding characteristic of writers on Scottish monastic antiquities. On the contrary, they have been apt to display an inert and careless credulity. If we take almost at random any of the lists which appear from the seventeenth to the nineteenth (and indeed to the twentieth) century, we may expect to find the same assumptions and blunders blithely repeated; and to these "chronic" errors others from time to time have been added, so that some nineteenth-century lists are much less trustworthy than those in circulation three hundred years before. Thus, ere the critical historian can venture to lay the foundation of a Scottish Monasticon, he has an accumulation of *débris* to clear away.

Scottish religious foundations were catalogued more than once during the Middle Ages. The earliest lists are given in the writings of English chroniclers, one in the *Mappa Mundi* of Gervase of Canterbury, a work which has been dated *c.* 1207 or -1216, and another appended to the Chronicle of Henry of Silgrave, *c.* 1272. These lists have considerable similarities, but the latter is the more accurate. The first list of Scottish *provenance* appears in the addition to the *Scotichronicon* which purports to be the composition of Robert Scot. On his own statement, Scot completed this supplement in May 1510; but internal evidence suggests that the list which it incorporates belongs to the latter part of the preceding century.[1] That this list was the prototype of many later compilations of a similar nature can hardly be doubted; for they often reproduce its arrangement— the grouping of entries under abbeys, priories, houses of friars and of lesser orders, secular colleges (which are called "praefecturae" or "praepositurae") and nunneries, though not

---

[1] Cf. the reference to the contemporary building of the collegiate churches of Roslin and Dunglass.

invariably in that sequence; while its idiosyncrasies, e.g. its reference to St Columba as the founder of the houses in Iona, its mention of the mysterious Trinitarian foundation of "Crennach", and its inclusion of the apocryphal nunneries of Gullane and Elbottle become stock features of post-Reformation lists. A less complete list of slightly later date (1523–41(?)) occurs in "Law's MS." in Edinburgh University Library (MS. Dc. 7. 63).

Catalogues of two main types emerge in the seventeenth century: (1) MS. lists, under such a heading as "Nomina monasteriorum", which contain entries of foundations grouped after the fashion of the *Scotichronicon* list[1] (from which they very probably derive), but often with the addition of a section giving the names of "chori oppidani" ("town choirs", i.e. burgh churches with a quasi-collegiate organization). The usual though not invariable entry, in the case of the abbeys, priories, nunneries and colleges, has the name of the house, its location, its order and its founder, with an occasional note of the date of foundation. In the sections dealing with the houses of friars and of the smaller orders, no details beyond the names of these are given. There was undoubtedly something like a *textus receptus* of these lists, which, as with the analogous lists of kings, were copied again and again. Examples are found in MS. collections in the National Library of Scotland (e.g. MSS. 22.1.14, 33.2.12) and in an Edinburgh University Library MS. (Db. 6.19)[2]. A list of like character appears in Thomas Dempster's *Apparatus ad historiam Scoticam* (1622). This writer may have had before him the *Scotichronicon* (or a similar) list, though he introduces some dubious items of his own.[3] (2) Lists which give a more discursive account of the religious houses and are independent of the *Scotichronicon* list. Such a compilation is included in Habukkuk

---

[1] It is convenient to refer to it thus, though it is later in date than the *Scotichronicon*, because it is included in Goodall's edition of that work.

[2] One of the best specimens among lists of this type belonged to the late William Saunders, Edinburgh, who lent it to the present writer for transcription. It is cited *infra* as "MS. Saunders".

[3] Dempster is an unreliable writer whose blunders and inventions cannot be justified by the suggestion (cf. Backmund, *Monast. Praemon.*, ii. 112 *n*) that he made use of sources no longer available.

Bisset's *Rolment of Courtis* (1626(?)) and, taking a different form, in the *De Scotorum Fortitudine, Doctrina et Pietate* (1631) of David Camerarius (Chambers). These lists, although the former has a few points of interest, are confused and rambling performances, with an admixture of legendary matter. Of the lists emanating from this period it cannot be said that they show any advance on the catalogue appended to the *Scotichronicon*.

A curious feature of one of the foregoing lists (in National Library of Scotland MS. 22.1.14) is that the scribe appears to have blundered by including under the Friars Preachers items which properly belong to, and elsewhere are placed in, the section on "chori oppidani". This confusion reappears in the list of religious houses, attributed to Thomas Middleton, which is appended to the 1677 edition of archbishop Spottiswoode's *History of the Church of Scotland*, and, whether through dependence on Middleton or otherwise, has misled other writers. Hence the number of Dominican foundations has sometimes been falsified and exaggerated.

The eighteenth century saw the preparation of catalogues of religious houses on a more ambitious scale. Thus, Fr Richard Augustine Hay's Scotia Sacra (1700), which exists in MS. in the National Library of Scotland, is an *omnium gatherum*, dealing at length with Scottish foundations and including also much material of a biographical and hagiographical character. Hay is a voluminous but by no means critical writer. In the same library is his Diplomatum Veterum Collectio, a collection of transcripts which also comprises an elaborated catalogue of Scottish Trinitarian houses. The latter, unfortunately, is of no historical value. Hay's interest in records, as manifested by his collections, is not matched by the use he made of them; he was a hagiographer rather than a historian. More significant is the work of John Spottiswoode (a layman, to be distinguished from his kinsman the archbishop) which, under the title *An account of all the Religious Houses that were in Scotland at the time of the Reformation*, was published in 1734 as an appendix to Hope's *Minor Practicks* and in 1755 as part of Keith's *Historical Catalogue of Scottish Bishops*. This treatise covers the houses, under their orders, of monks, friars, and nuns with an account of the secular colleges and, for the first time, of the hospitals. Though it has manifest inaccuracies and misinterpretations and borrows too much that is legendary from previous writers (e.g. Hay), Spottiswoode's production is more comprehensive and more systematically constructed than any preceding catalogue; moreover, it makes considerable reference to records.[1] That this work has long maintained its ground is due to its unquestionable (though not outstanding) merits. William Maitland, who included a list of religious houses in his *History and Antiquities of Scotland* (1757), closely follows Spottiswoode (to the extent of faithfully reproducing his errors), though he adds details of the revenues in money and victual of the various houses. The same period saw the composition by Fr Marianus Brockie of his monumental Monasticon Scoticum, the MS. of which is preserved in St Mary's College, Blairs, near Aberdeen. Brockie's collection of transcripts and *notitiae* is in the tradition of Hay. Comparatively little use of this material has been made by subsequent writers[2] and its historical value has not been rated highly, though an estimate based on a critical survey of the collection remains to be undertaken. Brockie was a most assiduous but uncritical compiler of monastic data. His relation to other workers in the same field (e.g. Spottiswoode and Hay) is a complex question. It is evident that a number of fresh errors came into circulation in the later seventeenth and earlier eighteenth centuries. How these errors originated is often difficult to ascertain, but as there was a good deal of dependence of one writer on another, mistaken statements were apt to be repeated and expanded.

In the later part of the eighteenth century, George Henry

---

[1] It is unnecessary to investigate here the question of how far these were due to his own researches. Spottiswoode wrote mainly on legal subjects and his *Religious Houses*, as appears *supra*, was originally a contribution to a legal treatise.

[2] It was used by Gordon, with not too happy results, for his *Monasticon* (1875). A few Coupar Angus items from this source appear in *Rental Bk. of the Cist. Abbey of Cupar-Angus* (Grampian Club), ii. 284 ff. (1880).

Hutton (†1827), an English artillery officer who rose to be a lieutenant-general, became, while stationed in Scotland, deeply interested in its monastic antiquities, pursuing his inquiries by an extensive correspondence and collecting copies of records and drawings. In the *Dictionary of National Biography*, Hutton is stated to have gathered these materials "with a view to compiling a 'Monasticon Scotiae'". If this was the case, he did not carry out his intention. But his Collections, covering much of the country, are deposited in the National Library of Scotland. By its nature, this miscellany of letters, notes and transcripts varies in value. Hutton's correspondents too often reveal the limitations of contemporary knowledge of monastic institutions and history.

Reference is not uncommonly made by writers on the Scottish monasteries to George Chalmers's *Caledonia* (originally published in three volumes, 1807, 1811, 1824; later in eight volumes, 1887–1902). This is not a Monasticon nor yet a catalogue of religious houses—it is described as "a historical and topographical account of North Britain from the most ancient to the present time"; but it has much to say on Scottish religious foundations. The vogue of this work has been out of all proportion to its worth. Of Chalmers Cosmo Innes declares: "He laboured under the disadvantage of defective scholarship of which he was quite unconscious. . . . In charter study . . . he worked with faulty copies."[1] Chalmers is in no sense an authority on monastic history. His work may well be discarded as unreliable and out of date.

With the earlier nineteenth century came a recrudescence of interest in the discovery and publication of records which seemed propitious for the more exact study of monasticism in Scotland. The Bannatyne and Maitland Clubs, precursors of many other historical and antiquarian societies, were founded respectively in 1823 and 1828 and among the volumes issued

---

[1] *Scotch Legal Antiquities*, 17. Cf. Somerville, *My Own Life and Times* (Edinburgh, 1861), 312–13.

under their auspices monastic chartularies took a prominent place; thus a valuable and growing contribution was made to the sources readily available for an account of the Scottish religious houses. This was recognized e.g. by W. B. D. D. Turnbull, an enthusiast rather than a scholar, whose anonymous *Fragmenta Scoto-Monastica* (1842) has as its sub-title "Memoir of what has been already done, and what materials exist towards the formation of a Scotish [*sic*] Monasticon". That these newly accessible materials were not utilized at the time to the best advantage, though they have since become indispensable to the student of Scottish monastic history, was due in large measure to the fact that they were regarded from an antiquarian rather than a historical standpoint. They were an addition to the lore of what was quaint and curious. It was the age of Scott—himself a prominent member of the Bannatyne Club—who was not exempt from the foibles of his own Monkbarns.

Among those who were well aware of the significance for the historian of the new publications was Cosmo Innes, professor of constitutional law and history at the University of Edinburgh (1846–74), who edited many of the Bannatyne volumes and whose works *Scotland in the Middle Ages* (1860), *Sketches of Early Scotch History* (1861) and *Scotch Legal Antiquities* (1872) were, at the time, epoch-making for the study of Scottish medieval history. In 1851 and 1854–5 appeared as one of the publications of the Bannatyne Club *Origines Parochiales Scotiae*, for the editing of which Innes was largely responsible. How marked an advance this work displayed is seen by comparing its historical standard with that of other works which, to a certain extent, cover the same ground, e.g. the *Statistical Account of Scotland* (in twenty-one volumes, 1791–9) and the *New Statistical Account of Scotland* (in fifteen volumes, 1845). These were made up of contributions (answers to something like a questionnaire) on all the parishes in Scotland, supplied by the parish ministers and concerned primarily with contemporary social and ecclesiastical conditions; but local antiquities are also designedly mentioned and, with a few exceptions, dealt with ineptly—ruins, to take a common instance, are much too readily identified as "monasteries".[1] *Origines Parochiales* is on a different level. Here we find carefully prepared and adequately documented accounts of the religious foundations which occur in the parishes included in this work. It is noticeable that, in their anxiety to omit no details, the editors sometimes admit unsatisfactory statements from the *Statistical Accounts* and conjectural interpretations of place-names. But, on the whole, *Origines Parochiales* is a sound and useful compilation. Unfortunately, it is incomplete; the editors did not carry it beyond the dioceses of Glasgow, Argyll, the Isles, Ross and Caithness.

So far the nineteenth century had passed without a specific attempt to construct a Monasticon, although the materials for such a work were accumulating. Besides the publications of the historical clubs and James Raine's *History and Antiquities of North Durham* (1852), with its important appendix of Coldingham charters, the Acts of Parliament and certain of the public records of Scotland, as well as English records like *Rotuli Scotiae*, had been published; while Augustinus Theiner's *Vetera Monumenta Hibernorum et Scotorum historiam illustrantia* (1864) for the first time provided from the Vatican archives an extensive collection of records bearing on Scottish ecclesiastical history. It is a sad anti-climax to mention, in this promising period, the *Scoti-Monasticon* (otherwise *The Ancient Church in Scotland*) (1874) of Mackenzie Walcott, precentor of Chichester; for, so far as this egregious writer was concerned, these accumulations of valuable source-material might never have been made. Depending on secondary sources often of poor quality, Walcott used these quite uncritically and to their errors added, through his gross carelessness and ignorance both of Scotland and of Scottish history, a

[1] For a good example, *v.* Fintray, p. 60 *infra*. In this connection may be mentioned the description by Robert Louis Stevenson of the farm at Swanston, in the neighbourhood of Edinburgh: "It was first a grange of Whitekirk abbey, tilled and inhabited by rosy friars" (Edinburgh, *Picturesque Notes* (Tusitala ed.), 193). It is enough to say of this ludicrous statement that no such abbey existed. This type of identification is not extinct. Cf. the fanciful statement regarding the church of Durrisdeer in Dumfriesshire that "the oldest part was a monastery" (*Scotsman*, 2 August 1954).

number of choice blunders of his own.[1] It is unfortunate that this slipshod work, *faute de mieux*, has been so frequently quoted. Another *Monasticon*, the compilation of J. F. S. Gordon, an Episcopalian clergyman, appeared in 1875. This is in no sense a product of research; it is incomplete and it borrows its statements (and errors) from earlier writers, notably Brockie. Lists of religious houses appear in various subsequent publications, but they are of no authority and as often as not are derived from Walcott or Gordon.

If a survey of the work which has so far been done on Scottish monastic antiquities and history is on the whole depressing and a record largely of shortcomings and failures, the explanation of the ill-success of many of the efforts which have been narrated is not far to seek. We do not expect to find in the majority of these catalogues and treatises an anticipation of the historical outlook and methods of the twentieth century; yet it is fair to say that the general reason for the defects of these accounts, over a considerable period, was a lack of reference to primary sources. That these were often inaccessible to writers who embarked on the making of a Monasticon (or catalogue of foundations) goes without saying. But the want of them did not sufficiently act as a deterrent; and it made for the uncritical repetition of the statements of other compilers, encouraged too ready a resort to tradition and legend, and opened a wide door to conjecture and improvised opinions. The "Scot Abroad", intent on glorifying the past of his country (like Camerarius) or his Church (like Dempster or Brockie) was beset with a tendency to overdraw the picture. The Scot in his own country, unfamiliar with but attracted to its monastic past, romanticized it, read into it ideas which were fanciful, ill-informed, unhistorical.

The sources available for the making of a Monasticon have greatly multiplied since collections of monastic charters began to be published in the early nineteenth century. Surviving

---

[1] One instance will suffice. Writing on the Carmelite friary at Aberdeen, Walcott declares: "In 1560, the church was sacked by the Covenanters" (*Scoti-Monasticon*, 336).

C

chartularies and collections of monastic charters have now in the main been edited. But while considerable material exists for the history of the religious foundations of the south-eastern, central and eastern Lowlands, the monastic (as well as the episcopal) records of Galloway are missing; not a single chartulary of the notable group of religious houses in that region is known to be extant. There is likewise a dearth of sources for the history of the monasteries situated in the western and northern Highlands and the Hebrides; while the foundations in Orkney and Shetland raise problems of peculiar difficulty. On the other hand, much that is important for Scottish monastic history has come to light in the Vatican records and especially in recent years through the distinguished researches of Dr Annie I. Dunlop. In the present century, useful work has been done on the history of individual orders in Scotland. Dr W. Moir Bryce's volumes, *The Scottish Greyfriars*, supply a well-documented study of the Franciscans. More recently, Fr Norbert Backmund, in *Monasticon Praemonstratense*, II (1952), has dealt in detail with the Scottish houses of white canons. This admirably industrious writer is at times somewhat uncritical in his use of sources (at this time of day no one takes Dempster seriously) and his acquaintance with Scottish ecclesiastical history and topography has limitations; but his work makes a valuable contribution to our knowledge of the development of Premonstratensian organization in Scotland. The late Professor R. K. Hannay did much to shed light on the later history of the medieval church in Scotland and the publication of the *Letters of James IV* (1953) and the *Letters of James V* (1954), which he was responsible for collecting, makes available material which is highly significant for the last half century (or thereby) of the monasteries' career.

The difficulty of locating houses which are mentioned under different names is not encountered to any great extent in Scotland. It is well known that Holywood Abbey is sometimes called Dercongal; the religious house of Liddel is recognizable as Canonbie; and the abbot of Roxburgh, to whom there are a number of references, is evidently the abbot of Kelso under an alternative designation. Through a change of site, the priory of May becomes known as the priory of Pittenweem; and the priory of Loch Leven is latterly mentioned as the priory of Portmoak. The problem of identification mainly arises in connection with a few of the hospitals.[1]

In the case of the religious houses of Scotland, as elsewhere, the determination of the date of foundation is frequently beset with problems. Instances of the foundation antedating the foundation charter are fairly numerous. Again, existing foundation charters call for careful scrutiny, as spurious examples of such documents are not entirely uncommon;[2] and in a number of cases, record evidence concerning the foundation is wanting. Where doubt arises the various dates are given and discussed in the notes.

The main purpose of the present work is positive, viz., to list and annotate the houses of which the existence can be verified; and in the notes an attempt is made to indicate the significant features of their history, so far as these are ascertainable. To set forth all the erroneous statements that have figured in lists and other accounts of the Scottish foundations would be an impossible and, in any case, an invidious and somewhat unprofitable task. But an effort has been made to include the typical and recurring errors (which, as regards certain orders, are numerous) so that at least no pretext is provided for their reappearance.

In its scope this work is similar to the volume on the English religious houses. It comprises the cathedrals, secular colleges and hospitals as well as the Celtic establishments which survived beyond 1050. If any justification, beyond the conventional

---

[1] The cases are: Dalhousie-Lasswade-Polton (St Leonard's); Hebnisden-Helmsdale; Horndean-Upsettlington; Legerwood-Adniston; St Leonard's, Ayr-Doonslee.

[2] A detailed and critical study of Scottish foundation charters would be of great value. But it may be noted here that a number of dubious charters emanate from seventeenth- and eighteenth-century collections. It does not come within the scope of this work to deal in detail with collections other than those specifically supplying the material for a Monasticon, e.g. those of Sir James Balfour, to whom the survival of a number of original monastic records is due but whose transcripts of monastic charters—even when they bear the statement "concordat cum autographo"—are by no means exempt from critical examination.

arrangement of a Monasticon, is necessary for thus extending the range of the volume, it lies in the fact that these foundations stand much in need of listing and annotation.

The author is conscious that the contents of this volume are open to many criticisms and that, through inadvertence or misinterpretation, errors are certain to have found their way into it. He can only plead that this is a pioneer attempt, subject to amendment and amplification. Its results, indeed, cannot be regarded as other than provisional, since at many points Scottish monastic history awaits clarification. Much work in this field remains to be done and not least on sources "furth of Scotland" which have not as yet been explored or which are worthy of further exploration.

# THE DEVELOPMENT OF MONASTICISM IN SCOTLAND

## (i)

IT is impossible to say with certainty when monasticism was first introduced into Scotland. The traditional account of St Ninian's settlement in the late fourth century at Whithorn, as given by Bede and later elaborated by Ailred, has been taken as pointing to the establishment in Galloway of an outpost of Martinian monasticism, since these writers associate Candida Casa and its founder with the founder of Marmoutier and bishop of Tours. But recent years have seen much discussion of the Ninianic mission,[1] with the result that its traditional chronology has been challenged and the connection of St Ninian with St Martin disputed. Historians are not as yet in sight of confident conclusions on these topics. A more definite landmark in the monastic history of Scotland is the founding of a Celtic monastery at Iona, following the arrival in that island of St Columba and his companions from Ireland in 563. Iona came to play an important part in the christianizing of considerable tracts of Scotland and ultimately, through its daughter-house at Lindesfarne, of the north and east of England. Until the eleventh century, Scotland knew no other form of monasticism than that exemplified by the Celtic clergy. Much obscurity attends the history of Celtic Christianity in Scotland, but the indications are that its institutions and organization had been considerably transformed by the eleventh century as the result of Anglo-Roman influence —a salient instance is the institution of a Celtic bishopric at St Andrews and perhaps at other sites which in the course of time

---

[1] V. A. O. Anderson, "Ninian and the Southern Picts", *SHR*, xxvii (1948). 25–47; *Trans. Dumfriesshire and Galloway N.H. and Antiq. Socy.*, 3rd Ser., xxvii (1950), which contains a series of articles on this subject and which gives an account, *inter alia*, of recent excavations at Whithorn; these have brought to light masonry which, it is claimed, may be part of the "White House".

became medieval sees. What remained of Celtic monasticism in 1050? Despite the ravages of the Danes, Iona appears to have continued, though not without interruption, as the seat of a Celtic community and probably maintained that character until the foundation of the Benedictine monastery in the island in 1203. It is possible that Celtic monasticism persisted also at such places as Deer and Turriff.[1] But there can be little doubt that many Celtic settlements had disappeared. This is attested by the occurrence in medieval charters of the word *abthane* as a place-name; these *abthanes* are held to have been the sites of defunct Celtic communities. Likewise, we find "abbots", e.g. at Abernethy and Brechin, who are laymen and whose designation indicates an office—the headship of a Celtic monastery—which has become secularized. The most characteristic representatives of Celtic Christianity whose communities survived into the medieval period were the *Célidé*, the *Keledei* of medieval records, commonly known as the Culdees.

The assumption that the Celtic clergy could be inclusively designated Culdees was at one time common and is still not entirely unknown. But while this assumption is evidently unwarranted, the differentiation of the Culdees has provided a difficult and much discussed problem. Dr A. O. Anderson has pointed out that

> while queen Margaret, like Lanfranc, sought to suppress monastic houses that had no rule, she nevertheless favoured and endowed monasteries of the Irish tradition. These monasteries appear as the homes of *Kelidei* or célidé; and we may therefore assume that the célidé were in Margaret's time regarded as monks who lived according to rule.[2]

Although no specific rule for Scottish Culdees is extant, it seems indisputable that they formed, in some sort, communities of regular clergy; the Celtic church was, in any case, essentially monastic and knew nothing of a distinguishable class of secular clergy. Mr G. W. S. Barrow, who has made a special study of the

---

[1] *V.* pp. 190, 192–3 *infra.*          [2] *Early Sources*, ii. 73 *n.*

Culdees, suggests that they may have regarded themselves as an *élite*;[1] and this would explain their original differentiation, though it is likely that if their claim to distinctiveness was founded upon their strict observance of a rule—which, in terms of Celtic monasticism, would mean the practice of exceptional austerity— that claim had been deprived of much of its force by the eleventh century. The identity of the Scottish Culdees came to be lost, before the end of the thirteenth century, in various ways: thus, they disappeared at Monifieth and Muthill; they were replaced by or became assimilated to Augustinian canons at Loch Leven, Monymusk, Abernethy; they were transformed into a chapter of secular canons at Brechin; they were converted into a secular college at St Andrews.

In addition to the Culdees, who lived in community, the Celtic church was represented within the medieval period by hermits who perpetuated its ascetic tradition. Of this type, it would seem, were the "very many men,[2] shut up in cells apart, in various places in the district of the Scots" of Turgot's account, who, according to the same writer, "led the life of angels upon earth" and were held in respect and visited by Queen Margaret.[3] Such also, we may suppose, was the solitary of the island of Inchcolm, who, it is narrated in the *Scotichronicon*, succoured King Alexander I and his companions; and—to cite medieval charters—it is probable that John the hermit, who, in the later twelfth century, was granted an island in the loch of "Lunnin" by William the Lion, and Gillemichel, "the late hermit", whose hermitage was bestowed, in the early thirteenth century, upon Coupar Angus abbey, were followers of a pre-medieval tradition.

---

[1] In correspondence. This suggestion is in line with Dr Kenney's conclusions in regard to the Irish Culdees: "It seems certain that they owed their origin as a distinct institution to the reform movement of the eighth century. . . . The most satisfying hypothesis seems to be that the Céli Dé were the communities of religious who gathered around the reform leaders . . . [and] that their aim was to revive the ancient zeal and discipline of the monastic churches" (*Sources for the Early Hist. of Ireland*, i. Ecclesiastical (1929), 470, *q.v.*). The same writer speaks of them as, in certain places, "constituting a community of 'stricter observance' in the midst of the older, larger and laxer organization" (*ibid.*, 471).

[2] We may allow here for some exaggeration.

[3] A. O. Anderson, *Early Sources*, ii. 76.

(ii)

It was with the coming to Scotland of the Saxon princess, Margaret, Edward Aetheling's daughter, who, in 1068-9, married Malcolm III [Canmore], that the way was opened for the introduction of monasticism of the medieval type in the northern kingdom. Not infrequently Margaret has been described as the instigator of a "new order" within the ecclesiastical sphere in Scotland. This, however, is an exaggeration. Ere her time, Roman[1] influences had, almost inevitably, been infiltrating into Scotland; and her "innovations", significant as they may have been for the future, were modest contributions towards the alignment of Scottish ecclesiastical institutions with those of Western Christendom. The saintly queen "initiated no reforms in the administration or organization of the church"[2] and set herself rather to rectify certain of its prevailing customs and usages. So far from showing antagonism to the Celtic clergy, Margaret and her husband maintained towards them the benevolent policy of their predecessors. Thus Margaret and Malcolm are found bestowing a benefaction upon the Culdees of Loch Leven; and it is said by Ordericus Vitalis that the queen rebuilt the monastery of Iona and "gave monks fitting revenues for the work of the Lord".[3] But it is of much significance that, before 1089, Lanfranc, at Queen Margaret's request, sent Goldwin and two other "brethren" to Scotland. Little enough is known of this settlement of Benedictine monks, presumably at Dunfermline, the first of its kind in Scottish territory. But it is clear that, in bringing them into her realm, Margaret was not reviving Benedictinism, as it was revived in England. By this step, the queen inaugurated the policy of encouraging the establishment of the monastic orders in Scotland, a policy which was to be greatly developed by her sons and successors. The Crown, in the next two

---

[1] "Roman" is used here as implying a contrast with "Celtic".
[2] *A Source Book of Scottish History*, i (1952), 42.
[3] *Patr. Lat.*, 188, col. 620. If the chronicler's statement is reliable, it is difficult to suppose that these could have been other than Celtic monks.

centuries, was to play a leading part in fostering the spread of monasticism.

Three younger sons of Margaret in turn held the throne of Scotland. In the reign of Edgar (1097–1106/7) took place the foundation at Coldingham which developed into a second Benedictine monastery, a priory linked with Durham.[1] With Alexander I (1106/7–1124), Augustinian canons were brought to Scone—it is said, from Nostell. In 1113, Earl David, Margaret's sixth son, introduced at Selkirk Benedictines of Tiron and thus signalized the outstanding favour he was later to show, as king of Scotland, towards the religious orders. His reign, as David I (1124–53), is justly described as "one of the most momentous in all Scots history".[2] The elements of far-reaching changes were present in Scotland when he came to the throne; David of set policy expedited these developments. The characteristic features of his reign were the settlement of Normans, with royal encouragement, in the country and their acquisition of lands; the steady extension of feudal administration in the kingdom; and, as the counterpart of these secular movements, the marked expansion of the organization and institutions of the medieval church.

More especially, this reign is notable for the planting of religious houses on a scale unmatched in any other period of Scottish history. The new abbeys were, in many cases, of David's own foundation and endowment—to an extent which evoked the jibe attributed to James I that David was a "sair sanct for the croun"—and their first inhabitants came from England or, in some cases, from France. A few years after his accession, David appears to have secured for Dunfermline the status of a Benedictine abbey, having brought the first abbot and a fresh influx of monks from Canterbury. From Rievaulx came the Cistercians who colonized the first Scottish house of that order, the abbey

---

[1] A letter of Anselm, archbishop of Canterbury to Alexander I, in 1107, mentions "our brothers whom we have sent into Scotland according to the desire of your brother [King Edgar]" (*ESC*, no. xxv). If the reference is to monks sent from Canterbury, it remains incapable of explanation.

[2] I. F. Grant, *Social and Economic Development of Scotland* (1930), 13.

which the king had founded at Melrose (1136), parent-house of at least five abbeys among which Newbattle (1140) and Kinloss (1150 or 1151) were likewise of David's foundation. Another community from Rievaulx went to the abbey of Dundrennan (1142) which David had instituted and which became the mother-house of two later abbeys in Galloway. To the king also were due the Augustinian foundations of Holyrood (1128), a daughter-house of Merton; of Jedburgh (c. 1138), whose canons were derived from Beauvais; and of Cambuskenneth (c. 1140), an offshoot of Arrouaise. In addition to these royal foundations, the Augustinian priory of St Andrews (1144) was established by the bishop of that see; and the first house of Premonstratensians in Scotland—at Dryburgh (1150)—had as its founder, Hugh de Moreville, constable of Scotland, the canons being brought from Alnwick, King David, again, founded the Benedictine priories of Urquhart (c. 1136) and the Isle of May (–1153), the priory of Lesmahagow (1144) of the order of Tiron and the earliest Scottish Cistercian nunnery—at Berwick-on-Tweed (–1153). It is possible that he introduced the military orders, the Knights Templars and the Hospitallers. David's foundations were widely distributed—from the Borders to the Moray Firth, from Lothian to Galloway.

(iii)

Succeeding rulers followed King David's example. Thus, Malcolm IV (1153–65) had founded by 1164 the abbey of white monks at Coupar Angus, the Cistercian nunnery of Manuel and the Augustinian hospital of Soutra. Only second to the Crown in their promotion of religious foundations were the Scoto-Norman magnates and it was Walter FitzAlan, Steward of Scotland, who, for the first time, brought Cluniac monks (from Wenlock) to Scotland and settled them at Paisley (c. 1163); while Hugh de Moreville endowed a house of the order of Tiron at Kilwinning (–1162). Of the two or more Cistercian nunneries founded during Malcolm's reign, Haddington (–1159), the largest of the Scottish houses of women, owed its inception to the king's mother, the countess Ada, who, like her son, is said to have been influenced by St Waltheof, in showing favour to this order. Two Tironensian houses arose in the reign of Malcolm's brother and successor, William the Lion (1165–1214)—the great abbey of Arbroath, dedicated to St. Thomas of Canterbury, which the king himself founded in 1178; and the abbey of Lindores (1191), founded by David, earl of Huntingdon, his younger brother.

It may be noted that, in the period covered by these reigns, religious foundations took place in outlying parts of the kingdom through the initiative of local potentates who, in a scarcely homogeneous Scotland, were the virtual rulers of these regions. Successive lords of Galloway—Fergus, Roland, Alan—established the Premonstratensians at Soulseat (–1175) (and perhaps Whithorn (*c.* 1175)) as well as at Tongland (1218) and the Cistercians at Glenluce (1191/2), while the Benedictine nunnery of Lincluden (–1174) is said to have been founded by Uchtred, son of Fergus of Galloway. Again, the Benedictine abbey (–1203) and the Augustinian nunnery (–1208) of Iona and the Cistercian house of Saddell (–1207) in Kintyre had as their founder Reginald, son of Somerled, lord of the Isles. These groups of foundations were mainly situated in dioceses—Galloway (Candida Casa) and Sodor—which, until the fifteenth century, were in a position extraneous to the diocesan structure of the church in Scotland, since the former was under the jurisdiction of York and the latter under the jurisdiction of Nidaros in Norway.

The reign of Alexander II (1214–49) has some features important for Scottish monastic history. Three further Cistercian foundations—at Culross (–1217), Deer (1219) and Balmerino (*c.* 1227)—took place, the last of these effected by the king and his mother, Queen Ermengarde. A projected establishment of Gilbertines at Dalmilling in Ayrshire, the only attempt to extend this order beyond England, forms an interesting episode in the years between 1221 and 1238; the project, however, was abandoned.

But, in the third decade of this century, an order which is not represented in England came to occupy three Scottish houses. This was the order of Val de Choux (Vallis Caulium), which was instituted at the place of that name in the diocese of Langres in Burgundy by Viard, a former *conversus* of the Carthusian monastery of Louvigny, towards the end of the twelfth century. Its rule, confirmed by Pope Innocent III, in 1205, has affinities with the rules of the Cistercians and the Carthusians. In 1230, the order was introduced into Scotland; for this, it is said, William de Malvoisin, bishop of St Andrews, was responsible; and the king founded for its monks the priory of Pluscarden (1230 or 1231). The Valliscaulian houses were placed in isolated regions in the north and west of Scotland. A significant feature of the same decade is the arrival of the friars. In 1230, the Blackfriars appear at Edinburgh; and their coming to Scotland is said to have been due, once more, to Bishop de Malvoisin. Of the nine Dominican houses which came into being in this reign all, save one, were royal foundations. The Greyfriars were established at Berwick in 1231 and friaries at Roxburgh and Haddington followed. It is uncertain whether the Trinitarians settled in Scotland as early as the reign of William the Lion, though he is stated to have provided for a house at Aberdeen. But, towards the middle of the thirteenth century, they had been placed at Berwick and Dunbar.

It remains to add that the reign of Alexander III (1249–1285/6) saw the foundation of the first Scottish house of Carmelites at Tullilum near Perth (1262). Franciscan foundations increased and for a short time the Friars of the Sack were housed at Berwick. We may note also the latest of the Cistercian plantations—the abbey of Sweetheart, which Devorgilla de Balliol founded in 1273.

## (iv)

As the end of the thirteenth century marks an epoch in the history of the religious orders in Scotland, it is appropriate to comment at this point on the first and most important stage of the development of monasticism in Scotland which we have rapidly surveyed. Before 1300, all the greater orders, if we except the Carthusians, were present in the kingdom. Of these the most conspicuous were the orders of Cîteaux and Tiron and the Augustinian canons. The Cistercians had six houses established between 1136 and 1164; thereafter, until 1273, foundations of this order occur at longer intervals, a slowing-down which was probably the belated effect of the act of the General Chapter of 1152, forbidding new plantations. As early as 1157, Scottish abbots were given the concession of attending at Cîteaux only once in four years. But Scottish Cistercian affairs are the subject of statutes of the General Chapter from time to time until 1282, when there is a significant and protracted break in the record of the relations of the Scottish abbeys with the mother-house of the order. From the Chronicle of Melrose we learn of the crisis that overtook the Scottish Cistercians in 1216–18, when the monks were involved in a struggle with the legate, Gualo, in defence of their privileges. But the white monks stood high in the favour of the royal house and the feudal lords and such was their vogue that, *c.* 1240, it appeared possible that the Cluniacs of Paisley, at that time the one Scottish community of that order, might be superseded by Cistercians.[1] Of the original Benedictine monasteries only two were major foundations—Dunfermline abbey and Coldingham priory; but to these the Benedictines of the order of Tiron, who were relatively stronger in Scotland than in England, added four abbeys, including the important foundations of Kelso and Arbroath. Among the houses of Augustinian canons were the prominent abbeys of Scone, Holyrood, Jedburgh and Cambuskenneth, but their chief foundation was the priory of St Andrews whose canons formed the chapter of the cathedral. The Premonstratensians also contributed a monastic chapter at Whithorn. Again, the three orders of friars, Dominican, Franciscan and Carmelite, had become well established; and

[1] *V.* p. 57 *infra.*

the older orders of nuns, Benedictine, Cistercian, Augustinian, were now represented in Scotland. By the end of Alexander III's reign, the tale of monastic establishments in Scotland was relatively complete. A number of mendicant houses were yet to be founded and the Carthusians do not appear till the fifteenth century. But all the greater monastic foundations had been made.

The geographical distribution of the monasteries was uneven. Although they spread into the Hebrides and perhaps as far as the Orkneys, the great majority were situated in central and southern Scotland. Of the larger houses a number were located in Lothian and the proximity of the Border, advantageously, if only for their economic development, in time of peace, but precariously, as the later centuries of their history would show, in days of war and invasion.

In this period which witnessed the settlement and extension of the religious orders, we detect the signs of tensions which were to become accentuated by the worsening relations of Scotland and her neighbour. Thus, priories which were sited within Scottish territory but affiliated to English houses came to occupy the invidious position vividly displayed in the later, contentious history of Coldingham. Already in the reign of Alexander III, an attempt was made—and, in the end, successfully—to sever the priory of May from its mother-house at Reading and to associate it with the priory of St Andrews. Again, as the orders present in Scotland had in many cases been brought originally from England, they were not infrequently within the sphere of jurisdiction of English authorities. In the thirteenth century, the first movement was made—by the Greyfriars—to secure independence of English control. The Scottish friars, whose earlier foundations were included in the custody of Newcastle (though for a short time they had the name if not the reality of a province) enlisted the aid of King Alexander III to obtain for themselves, through the good offices of the Pope, a Provincial Minister; and, although this request was rejected by the Franciscan Chapter at

Narbonne in 1260, there is, according to Moir Bryce, "a strong presumption that they enjoyed a *de facto* autonomy".[1] A Scottish vicariate was ultimately formed in 1329.

## (v)

From the eleventh to the thirteenth centuries, few conspicuous names appear in the annals of the Scottish monasteries. In 1148, St Waltheof, who had been a canon of Nostell and prior of Kirkham and later a monk at Wardon and Rievaulx, crossed the Border to become abbot of Melrose and ruled that abbey till his death in 1159. Clement, who, as the able bishop of Dunblane (1233–1256 or 1258), was responsible for the revival of that decrepit see, is said to have been a Dominican, though the legend that he was appointed by St Dominic to bring the first colony of Blackfriars into Scotland must be regarded as doubtful. Two more notable figures have a brief and somewhat uncertain association with the orders in Scotland. Adam "the Scot", author of *On the Tripartite Tabernacle*, homilies on *The Order, Habit and Profession of Premonstratensian Canons* and other contemplative works, and also known as Adam of Dryburgh, was, in all likelihood, a canon of the Premonstratensian abbey of that name, rather than of the priory of that order at Whithorn, where he has sometimes been located; he eventually joined the Carthusians at Witham, *c.* 1189. Still more elusive is the association both with Scotland and with Scottish monasticism of the *Doctor Subtilis*, John Duns Scotus. It is true that in 1929,[2] and with greater detail, in 1931,[3] the announcement was made that, as the result of the discovery of new material in a Scottish Franciscan

---

[1] *Scottish Greyfriars*, i. 11. It may be noted that W. Mackay Mackenzie ("A Prelude to the War of Independence", *SHR*, xxvii. 110–11) and A. G. Little (*Franciscan Papers, etc.*, 222) accept the statement that, in 1278, the guardians of the Scottish Franciscan houses, at the king's behest and with the consent of the Minister General of the order, decreed that they should no longer be under the custody of Newcastle but be ruled by a Vicar General and elected Elias Duns (reputed uncle of John Duns). This statement comes from the so-called "Register" (Brockie MS. transcript, 9778; original, 1425), cited *AFH*, xxiv. 315–16. The present writer is not convinced of the reliability of this source. *V. infra.*

[2] *AFH*, xxii. 588–9.

[3] *Ibid.*, xxiv. 311 ff.

"Register"[1] among the Brockie MSS. at St Mary's College, Blairs, the problems of the nationality and early career of Duns Scotus were at last solved. For, according to this source, John Duns was the son of Ninian Duns of Littledean (identified as the place of that name in the parish of Maxton in Roxburghshire[2]), had his schooling at Haddington and having been brought to Dumfries, in 1278, by his uncle, Elias Duns, warden of the Grey-friars in that town, received the Franciscan habit there. This account, which purports to be derived from the MS. of William Tweedie, who, it is said, drew upon Scottish Franciscan records at Haddington, was accepted by Dr Mackay Mackenzie in Scotland and Dr A. G. Little in England, but their somewhat hasty confidence in it is not shared by the present writer. Good reasons in fact can be adduced for hesitating to accept it *au pied de la lettre*: (1) its statements find little or no support in existing records;[3] (2) other material in the Brockie MS. alleged to be derived from the same source[4] has been found unreliable and thus the account of Duns given by Brockie calls for closer scrutiny than has been given it; (3) the elements of this account appear (with some variants) in seventeenth-century writers, e.g. Dempster (1622) and Camerarius (1631)[5]—the material in the Brockie MS. looks like the elaboration of a tradition that Duns belonged to Scotland and entered religion at Dumfries. Thus, until the authenticity of Brockie's statements is substantiated, the problem of Duns's *origines* has not, it seems, been satisfactorily solved; it stands where it did—in the limbo of uncertainties.

[1] Actually the Brockie MS. is not a "Register" but a collection of transcripts and *notitiae* that includes material relating to other orders than the Friars Minor. The account of Duns Scotus is a lengthy *excursus* in which, *inter alia*, an attempt is made to prove that Duns was of Scottish, rather than English or Irish, origin.

[2] This identification is at best conjectural. Littledean in Maxton parish appears among the lands held at the Reformation by Dryburgh abbey (*Dryburgh*, 318 etc.).

[3] The existence of a family of Duns is vouched by records: Hugo de Duns appears –1153 (*Calchou*, no. 138); William de Duns, son of William of that ilk, 12 February 1437/8 (*HMC*, 12th Rep., App., Pt. VIII, 175); and Eustace de Duns, 20 June 1443 (*ibid.*, 176). But the various Dunses mentioned by Brockie have not been found elsewhere; and no evidence of a connection of this family with Littledean has so far been discovered.

[4] Neither William Tweedie, writer (*scriba*) in Haddington, nor the MS. attributed to him have as yet been traced.

[5] Hay, writing *c*, 1700, likewise mentions that John Duns Scotus assumed the habit at Dumfries (Scotia Sacra, 555).

## (vi)

In the troubled years of the late thirteenth century emerged the political situation which lasted more or less till the end of the medieval period; the relations of Scotland and England were uneasy, strained and often overtly hostile, while the Scots resorted to alliance and made common cause with France. This situation was primarily the outcome of the disputed succession which followed the death of "the Maid of Norway", the heiress to Alexander III's throne, and the opportunity it afforded Edward I of asserting overlordship of Scotland. How the War of Independence which developed out of the resistance movements of Wallace and Bruce affected the Scottish religious houses is too complicated a question to enter upon in detail here. It must suffice to note that warfare and occupation of the country did not leave the monasteries unscathed. This is seen more especially in the case of the abbey of Scone, from which, in 1296, Edward I removed the Stone of Destiny on which the Scottish kings were crowned, while, in 1298, for some unexplained reason, but probably because of its connection with the Scottish dynasty, the abbey was sacked and destroyed. Neither Bruce's victory in 1314 nor the treaty of Northampton which officially ended hostilities in 1328, brought immunity from the effects of invasion to the religious houses in the south of Scotland. Kelso, Melrose, Dryburgh, Holyrood had suffered and would suffer again. Meanwhile, the attitude of Robert I towards the monasteries, once he had become effective ruler of Scotland, maintained the tradition of royal benevolence. Three small foundations, an Augustinian priory at Strathfillan (1317/18), a Carmelite house at Banff (1321–4) and a Franciscan house at Lanark (1328–9) were of his creating. But the considerable number of his charters to the religious houses, confirming their properties and granting them new endowments, suggests that the king who, in 1319, proclaimed his policy of protecting "holy church and holy religion" was concerned to succour the monasteries and revive them.

D

But a period of marked decline was now to overtake them; and the fourteenth century is, in the main, a bleak and undistinguished stage in their history. One of the last documents of King Robert's reign is a letter exhorting his son and successors to augment rather than diminish the grants he has made to Melrose abbey and to protect it against "invaders and enviers". The fulfilment of this counsel was, however, beyond the power of the weak kings who followed him; and the religious houses, in a period vexed with unstable government, insecurity and intermittent war, shared in the demoralization of the kingdom. Isolation likewise befell them; for their contacts with mother-houses beyond the Border and the general chapters of their orders in France were broken as a result of hostilities with England, the Hundred Years' War and, eventually, the schism in the Church. Favour also fell away from them; their prestige declined and the former profusion of endowments ceased. It is tempting to suppose that the Black Death, which devastated the English religious houses, must have added to the adversities of the Scottish monasteries. That pestilence came to Scotland in 1349 or 1350 and there were later visitations of plague in the same century. How far the monasteries were affected remains, however, uncertain; for on this subject, save for a reference in the *Scotichronicon* to the death from plague of twenty-four canons of St Andrews, records are surprisingly silent. Nor is there any clear indication of monasteries becoming defunct from this cause. The effect of war rather than of pestilence accounts for the extinction e.g. of the Cistercian nunnery at Berwick.

One point of interest, however, emerges in the fourteenth century. To what extent episcopal visitation of non-exempt houses was maintained in Scotland we have no means of knowing; for apart from such a record as appears in 1345 acknowledging that the bishops of Moray had visited the priory of Pluscarden since its foundation and that the monks of that house had no exemption or privilege to the contrary—from which no inference on the regularity of visitation can be drawn—evidence is almost entirely lacking. The only visitation records, two in number, come to us from the later part of this century. From them we learn that William de Landallis, bishop of St Andrews, visited the abbey of Scone in January 1365/6 and October 1369, and his ordinances on discipline and obedience are set forth in detail. There is no indication that the state of this abbey was such as to demand the special attention of the bishop. De Landallis, we may gather from these isolated records, was acting simply as a conscientious diocesan.

A few houses of friars were endowed in this period. But before the end of the fourteenth century, foundations non-monastic and of a type new to Scotland had begun—very sporadically—to appear. These were colleges of secular clergy, an innovation inasmuch as Scotland, unlike England, had, apart from cathedral chapters, no early incorporations of secular canons after the pattern of Ripon or Southwell to be revived in the later Middle Ages. The first of these collegiate bodies came into existence when, towards 1250, the Culdee community at St Andrews became dissociated with its property from the cathedral and was set up as a secular college which figures thereafter as the collegiate church of St Mary on the Rock and for some time as a chapel royal. Not till the first half of the next century was well advanced were further colleges inaugurated. In 1342 a college for a dean, archpriest and eight prebendaries was founded in the parish church of Dunbar, in its constitution unlike later Scottish collegiate churches and somewhat reminiscent of an Italian *pieve*. Again, at Abernethy, what had once been a Culdee house and was latterly a priory of Augustinian canons became a secular college before 1345. Towards the end of this century, a succession of collegiate foundations begins with Maybole (1383/4), Lincluden (a suppressed house of Benedictine nuns) (1389) and Bothwell (1397/8) and continues to the eve of the Reformation; the last of the Scottish colleges was founded at Biggar (1545/6). In general, these foundations come within two categories: a *collegium* might be instituted in a parish church of which the revenues were augmented to maintain a number of prebendaries or canons or chaplains (for the clergy of such churches are variously designated), with provision for the parochial cure of souls; or a group of chantry priests was incorporated to serve a church or chapel which had no parochial commitments. At the head of a secular college was a provost or, occasionally, a dean; but the most ambitious of these foundations, the Chapel Royal of Stirling, ultimately had a bishop and dean (i.e. a dean of episcopal status) and dignitaries after the pattern of a cathedral. Two of the academic foundations—St Salvator's College, St Andrews, and King's College, Aberdeen—were primarily collegiate churches. The founders of the secular colleges were in many cases barons or "lairds"; a few colleges were royal foundations. It is noteworthy that, in the sixteenth century, there was a marked tendency on the part of the more important Scottish burghs to secure for their parish churches, in which the numerous choir and chantry priests constituted a quasi-collegiate organization, formal collegiate status, with a provost or president. This development is seen at Peebles, Aberdeen, Haddington and Stirling. In progress elsewhere, it was halted by the Reformation.

(vii)

We may regard the reigns of the five Jameses, extending from 1406 to 1542, as covering approximately the last phase of the active history of the Scottish religious houses. It is convenient to note, first of all, the progress of monastic foundations in this their final period. In 1429, James I was responsible for introducing the Carthusians, belatedly, into Scotland; the Charterhouse at Perth, established in that year, was the most considerable foundation since the thirteenth century. During the reign of the second James, the Franciscans of the Observantine reform had their first Scottish settlement at Edinburgh (1455–8). Of the eight houses of that order which arose in the next half-century one—at Stirling (1494)—was a royal foundation; several, on the other hand, were due to the characteristic initiative of the burgesses in the burghs where they were placed. It is significant that Observant friars were settled in St Andrews (1458) by Bishop James Kennedy, who, eight years previously, by establishing his college of St Salvator, had manifested his desire to vitalize the first Scottish university. The presence of the university likewise induced the development of the Dominican house in that city; in 1516, the provincial chapter envisaged its enlargement for friars "engaged continually in the study of sacred letters". Of the four mendicant orders, the Augustinian friars (or hermits) are of least account in the monastic annals of Scotland. They are, indeed, represented only by a house at Berwick which appears in the earlier fourteenth century, when from it, as from the other Berwick friaries, Edward III ordered the Scottish friars to be removed and English friars substituted. Much later, this austere order commended itself to James IV, who, in 1506, made an ineffective attempt to displace the nuns of the Cistercian priory of Manuel and to introduce in their stead Augustinian friars; and *c.* 1511, the same king designed unsuccessfully the conversion of the hospital of St Laurence at Haddington into a house of this order. Three nunneries appear among these later foundations —small houses of Franciscan nuns at Aberdour (1486) and Dundee (1501/2) and the more imposing establishment of Dominican nuns at Sciennes, Edinburgh (1517). Latest among the Scottish foundations were a Dominican priory at Dundee (*c.* 1521), destined to be destroyed after a brief existence, and a Carmelite house at Greenside, Edinburgh (1520–5).

While foundations continued to be made until the third decade of the sixteenth century, the later Middle Ages saw a number of houses, mostly small and sometimes non-conventual, in straits which led to their extinction. In these, religious observance had ceased or was barely maintained; and they were commonly merged in larger foundations. Before 1423, the obscure Cistercian nunnery of St Evoca in Galloway, a foundation unknown until the evidence of Vatican records was forthcoming, had dwindled and expired; and, about 1434, the Augustinian nunnery of St Leonard at Perth was extinguished—its revenues were annexed to the Charterhouse. The Benedictine priory of Urquhart, in 1453/4, was united to the priory of Pluscarden, in which Benedictines had replaced the order of Val de Choux; while the once important house of that order at Coldingham, where the community is said, in 1461, to have been reduced to two monks, barely survived the unexampled vicissitudes of its later career; the long and tortuous struggle to dissever this priory from Durham and its varied exploitation by ecclesiastics and laymen make its history more tangled than that of any other Scottish monastery. In the fifteenth century, a house of Friars Preachers at Haddington is mentioned twice in records—and disappears. Again, in the beginning of the sixteenth century, the Cistercian abbey of Saddell, isolated in Kintyre, had fallen on evil days and was beyond revival; and about 1508, the priory of Fyvie of the order of Tiron was finally annexed to the abbey of Arbroath. In 1519, the Dominicans at Cupar were incorporated in the friary at St Andrews. Lastly, the Trinitarian house of Peebles, before the middle of that century, had absorbed the small defunct settlements of that order at Berwick, Dunbar and Houston.

The state of certain of the religious houses in the earlier fifteenth century, when Scotland had lately renounced the antipope Benedict XIII and adhered to Pope Martin V, is disclosed in a well-known document, the letter which James I directed, in 1425, to the abbots and priors of the Benedictine monks and the Augustinian canons. Thus early in his active reign, for only in the previous year had he returned from captivity, the first energetic ruler whom Scotland had seen for well nigh a century addressed himself to the condition of the monasteries. Deploring the decadence of monasticism in his realm, he urges upon these heads of religious houses the reformation of their orders, especially by the holding of general chapters,[1]

[1] The evidence concerning the holding of chapters in Scotland is almost nil. One of the few indications is in a record of 17 September 1326, whereby the abbot of Dunfermline, who is designated "conservator of the general chapter of monks of the order of St Bene-

lest through your negligence and idleness the munificence of kings, who formerly for their preservation and the salvation of their subjects notably endowed your monasteries in olden days and enriched them, may repent of having erected walls of marble.

The king enjoins the strengthening of discipline to "take away all these occasions of decay" and promises the monasteries, thus reinvigorated, his protection.[1] It may have been that King James was influenced by Henry V's concern for the failure of these orders in England to hold general chapters; but the cases of Coldingham and Inchaffray suggest that his remonstrance was not without some justification; and his almost contemporary foundation of the Perth Charterhouse amounted to a direct encouragement of strict religious observance. The veiled threat which we may read between the lines of his letter to the Benedictines and the Augustinians is not, however, to be ignored. James I may or may not have carped at the liberality of his ancestor, King David;[2] but the suggestion conveyed in the letter would seem to be that failure on the part of the orders to amend might be met by the withholding of their endowments. James did not go beyond this threat; but its implication—that as the Crown had endowed the monasteries, so it might also recall these endowments—was significant for their future history. Later rulers were to treat monastic wealth as virtually at the disposal of the Crown; and the annexation of the monasteries to the Crown, as yet a long way ahead, was enacted (in 1587) on the ground that the revenues granted to the abbeys "of auld" had been Crown property.

From Cistercian records we learn something of the state of this the most prominent order in Scotland, at the same period.

dict in the realm of Scotland", summons the abbot of Arbroath, in terms of the Lateran statute requiring a triennial general chapter in each kingdom or province, to attend a forthcoming chapter at Dunfermline abbey on 21 October (*Aberbrothoc*, ii. no. 356).

[1] *V. Source Bk. of Scottish History*, ii. 97-9.

[2] John Major's version is that James, "when he visited the tomb of David, is reputed to have said: 'There abide, king most pious, but likewise to Scotland's state and kings most unprofitable', meaning thereby that on the establishment of some very wealthy communities he had lavished more than was right of the royal revenues" (*Hist. of Greater Britain*, 135-6).

Before the end of the schism, relations between the Scottish abbeys and Cîteaux had been resumed;[1] and, in 1408, the abbot of Balmerino is found at the mother-house of the order, where, in consideration of the "lamentable desolation" of the abbey of Coupar Angus, he obtained release of that monastery from arrears and remission of part of its future dues. Forty years later, the same abbey was allowed by the General Chapter to compound for its dues in respect of its poverty. That the Cistercians were beset with economic problems need not surprise us, for even the recently endowed Carthusians were soon to find the times stringent and to have difficulty in paying their debts. How far the white monks had otherwise declined is by no means easy to say. Ferrerius speaks of the abbot of Pontigny, who came to Scotland in 1417, as an emissary of the General Chapter sent to restore monastic observance which had fallen away, but it appears that this was not the sole object of the abbot's visit. Again, a statute of 1433 mentions disorders prevalent in Scottish as well as English, Welsh and Irish houses which are attributed to the absence of the abbots of these regions from the Chapter because of wars and the dangers of travel, while, in 1445 and later, commissaries were appointed to deal with their reform. More specific evidence, however, does not become available till the following century.

### (viii)

We may credit James I with a sincere desire to restore the vitality of the Scottish religious houses. But the beginnings of a system which thwarted their revival were soon to appear; and already in King James's reign took place the first phases of a struggle which was fraught for them with unhappy consequences. The practice of granting an abbey or priory to an already bene-ficed churchman as a commend (*in commendam*) was originally designed as a temporary and exceptional measure, e.g. to provide for the administration of a house and its revenues during a

---

[1] It is said that a prior of Kinloss attended the General Chapter –1371 (*Kinlos*, xl).

vacancy in its government. But the system of granting commends in perpetuity, which eventually attained disastrous dimensions in Scotland, meant that these were apt to be little more than a source of emolument to their holders; it led increasingly to the exploitation and demoralization of the monasteries; and its development is closely bound up with the involved and long-drawn struggle between the Papacy and the Crown for the control of appointments to benefices. The source of tension between the Pope and the Scottish kings of the period lay in the growth and great extension of the custom of reserving for papal provision benefices which were otherwise elective. It has been observed that while, in the time of James I, "no serious controversy . . . about the progressive inclusion of Scottish monasteries" among such reserved benefices had taken place, the trouble began when, in the pontificates of Eugenius IV (1431–1447) and Nicholas V (1447–55), monasteries over a certain value were brought into this category.

The practice affected monasteries which had hitherto enjoyed what the Scots described as 'free election' and had never required more than the ordinary's confirmation. It was specially in the case of the exempt orders, Cluniacs, Cistercian and Premonstratensian, that the Papal intervention caused disturbance, by suspending the confirmatory rights vested in the mother houses. The general effect was to exclude the royal and baronial influence, formerly exerted with some ease over the confirming authority, and to take more money out of the country in promotion taxes.[1]

In 1439, the provision of the abbey of Scone to the bishop of St Andrews *in commendam*—though that prelate probably did not obtain possession, as an abbot elected by the convent appears to have held his ground—set an unfortunate precedent; and the grant of a pension from Paisley abbey, in 1459, to placate a rival claimant to the commend exemplified a practice which was to become too common. During the reign of James I, legislative

[1] R. K. Hannay, *The Scottish Crown and the Papacy, 1424–1560* (Hist. Assoc. of Scotland; March 1931), 7–8. I am considerably indebted to Professor Hannay's discussion of this complex subject.

restraints had been placed upon the export of money and upon
the quest of benefices or pensions by purchase and without royal
licence.[1] Now, in 1466, a statute of the Scottish Parliament forbade the holding of commends "of new nor aulde" and in-
hibited, under penalties, the purchasing of them. Still more
drastic legislation followed in 1471, when, in consideration of
the ill-effects on "religious places" and the common good of the
realm of the annexation of the former to bishoprics, it was
enacted (rendering the Scots statute into English):

> that no such abbeys nor other benefices which were never at the
> court of Rome before be purchased by no secular nor religious per-
> son but that the said places have free election of the same as use and
> custom has been in the said places.

No further annexations were to be permitted and those made
since the accession of the present sovereign (James III (1460–
1488)) were to be revoked; while any contravention of this statute
was to be accounted treason. Repeated legislation on the same
lines suggests that matters were by no means mended.

The concern for the maintenance of "free election", manifested in the acts of parliament of this period, is, however,
specious and misleading. For the course of events shows quite
clearly that the term was not intended to mean the unimpeded
exercise by the monks of the right to elect their head, subject,
in some cases, to the ratification of the bishop of the diocese and,
in others, to the confirmation of the mother-house. In practice,
it signified royal nomination without papal interference.[2] Bishop
Lesley, in one version of his *History*, leaves us in no doubt of
this. For he cites the case of Dunfermline, where the monks
elected an abbot only to have him superseded by James III's

---

[1] This constituted the punishable offence of "barratry".
[2] The royal notion of "free election" is illustrated in a communication (6 April 1530)
which the duke of Albany is to make to the Pope on behalf of James V. "Albany is to
request that henceforth by apostolic grant monks may be allowed . . . to elect a suitable
abbot or prior from the fraternity at the royal recommendation, or, if election cannot be
held, to nominate an abbot or prior, the persons thus elected . . . to be admitted, confirmed
and blessed by the ordinary, so that there may be no need for the Roman see to look into
the matter or send a representative" (*Letters of James V*, 175).

nominee, the former abbot of Paisley; and he adds that to Paisley, thus vacated, the king proceeded to nominate a secular priest, the rector of Minto. It is to these practices which, he notes, "the Pope allows . . . at the king's request", that he traces the mischief that soon befell the monasteries.

> From this proceeded the first and foul slander that after infected monasteries and monks through all Scotland; when secular persons were begun to have place in cloisters, and through the king's force, in a manner, and his authority, began to rule and have dominion in religious places. . . . Then in religious places crept idleness, deliciousness, and all bodily pleasure, fertility in worldly affairs; then God's service began to be neglected and cool; then hospitality . . . began to be contemned, and what cloisters respected most was worldly wealth. . . . The monks now elect not abbots who are most godly and devout, but kings choose abbots who are lustiest and most with them in favour. . . . [1]

Lesley's strictures are more applicable to the proceedings of James IV than to those of James III. Meanwhile, in the reign of the latter king, legislation against the "impetration" and purchase of benefices at Rome was renewed in 1482 and 1484. Eventually, in 1485, a petition to the Pope sought a delay of six months in provision to "prelacies or dignities elective" so that the king's supplication on behalf of recommended candidates might reach the Vatican; and, in 1487, an indult was granted to James III whereby Pope Innocent VIII consented to postpone for eight months appointments to cathedrals and monasteries whose income exceeded two hundred florins and await royal nominations. The indult was a concession given to King James, late in his reign, at the same time as other tokens of papal favour. Its interpretation, which had marked and serious consequences for the monasteries, lay with his successors.

---

[1] *Historie of Scotland* (Scottish Text Society, 1895), ii. 90–1. Cf. *ibid.* (Bannatyne Club, 1830), 39–40.

(ix)

We may pause to notice certain developments internal to the religious orders. The formation of units of monastic administration on a national basis originated, as we have seen, with the Franciscans, who secured the erection of a Scottish vicariate in 1329. Though this vicariate was suppressed by the General Chapter in 1359, the decree, as Dr Little suggests, may have been a dead letter, for a vicar-general is mentioned in 1375; and the ensuing schism, during which Scotland and England adopted different allegiances, contributed to perpetuate the separation of the Scottish Greyfriars from the English province. A Conventual province was apparently in existence before the end of the fifteenth century, while the General Chapter of the Observants sanctioned the erection of a Scottish province in 1467. In 1481, the petition of James III led to the creation of a province of Scotland by the Dominican General Chapter; and towards the end of this century, the acts of the Premonstratensian General Chapter refer to a *circaria* of Scotland as existing in its own right. The one Scottish Charterhouse, originally associated with the province of Further Picardy, was united, *c.* 1456, to the English province of the Carthusians; but, in 1460, at the request of the Scottish king, it was transferred to the province of Geneva. In the early sixteenth century, the General Chapters of the Cistercians and the Premonstratensians show an increasing concern for the visitation of Scottish houses of these orders and the same period provides the only indications of contact between the Valliscaulian priories, now only two in number, with the motherhouse of Val de Choux. In 1506, the prior of Beauly received directions on the visitation of the priory of Ardchattan, and, again, on the relations of his house with the bishop of Ross, with an admonition from the head of the order to attend the General Chapter, which his predecessor, despite the concession of appearing there only once in six years, had failed to do and, moreover, to send to Bruges or Valenciennes (whence it would be taken to Dijon) the fish "called salmon", which his predecessor had promised. It is unlikely that either behest was heeded. The contact was not maintained and, a few years later, Beauly became a Cistercian dependency.[1]

(x)

In the chronicle known as the *Diurnal of Occurrents*, there is a character-sketch of James IV which dwells on his foundation of "mony religious places" and his personal piety; it adds significantly that "without counsel of spiritual estate", he gave such benefices as became vacant in his time to his "familiars". With this king and still more with his successor appears the ambivalent royal policy which, on the one hand, added to the number of monasteries and showed an ostensible concern for monastic reform and, on the other, exploited and crippled the religious houses. James's foundation of friaries has been mentioned elsewhere. We find the Cistercian General Chapter empowering, in 1491, the abbots of Coupar Angus, Melrose and Culross to visit the Scottish houses of that order because it has been brought to the notice of the Chapter by letters of the Scottish king how much these houses stand in need of visitation and reform; and, in 1506, he writes to the Pope at length on the situation of the monastery of Melrose. Again, the king communicates more than once with the Prior-General of the Dominicans (1506) on the affairs of that order in Scotland; and, in 1506/7, he appeals to the Pope on behalf of the Observants. But, on the other hand, the assertion of royal control over nominations to the monasteries did not relax. The indult of 1487 was not explicitly renewed by Pope Innocent VIII's successors. But not only did the Scots act on the assumption that it was a perpetual privilege; it was held to apply not merely to benefices of a certain value but to all which were elective. Moreover, the desire to counteract the device of

---

[1] On the state of Ardchattan priory, which seems to have remained—at least nominally— a Valliscaulian house, *v. Letters of James V*, 345–6.

"resignation in favour"—by which the holder of a benefice transferred his title to a successor but retained a life-rent, thus precluding a vacancy and an occasion for the exercise of patronage—may well have prompted the act of parliament of 1496 which forbade resort to Rome without licence of the king or his chancellor. At the same time, the former indignation at the system of commends conveniently subsided; they were (in Hannay's phrase) "now no longer offensive when directed according to royal wish" and, in encouraging them, the Crown was the arch-offender. Thus, James Stewart, duke of Ross, the king's brother, who, in 1497, had been made administrator of the diocese of St Andrews at the age of eighteen, was given, in the same year, the commend of the abbey of Holyrood; three years later, that of the abbey of Dunfermline; and, in 1503, the commend of the abbey of Arbroath. The king exerted himself to have Tongland abbey bestowed upon the bishop of Galloway, Glenluce abbey upon a secular clerk who was his Lord High Treasurer, the abbey of Cambuskenneth upon his Secretary, the celebrated Patrick Panter, who was not even in priest's orders; and contrived the annexation of the priories of Restennet and Inchmahome to his new Chapel Royal at Stirling. From the later years of James IV, the hold of the commendatory system upon the Scottish monasteries became firmly established. Some abbeys—like Inchaffray, from 1495—were in the hands of commendators continuously for the rest of their career.

(xi)

In 1513, James IV fell at Flodden. His policy towards the monasteries was continued and extended by his successor. When he came to rule in person, James V, as his recently published *Letters* display, evinced a considerable interest in the affairs—and reform—of the religious houses. We find him, in 1524, protesting to the Pope against the granting of a pension from the church of Dunkeld to a Dominican as a proceeding unworthy of the Blackfriars. In 1530/1, he requests the abbot of Cîteaux and the *diffinitores* of the General Chapter, in view of the shortcomings of the order in Scotland, to provide an abbot to visit and reform it, promising his co-operation, and the abbot of Chaalis was duly sent. Professing his anxiety to do his best for the state of the religious in Scotland, he appeals to the Pope, in 1531/2, for the conservation of the rules and privileges of the Observants. In 1532, he vouches his support to the abbot of Soulseat, commissioned by the Premonstratensian General Chapter to visit the monasteries of that order; and five years later, gives the like undertaking in regard to the representative whom the Prior General of the Carmelites shall send, at his somewhat peremptory invitation, to report on the Scottish Whitefriars. Again, when Henry VIII sought to prevail upon the Scottish king to follow his example in dealing with the monasteries and the English emissary dwelt, in terms of his instructions, upon the misdemeanours of the monks, James is said to have proclaimed his ability to reform them. But there are reasons, as will presently appear, for discounting James's zeal for monastic reform. Meanwhile, insistence on the royal right of nomination was maintained. During James's minority, Pope Leo X, after some contention with the Governor, had confirmed the indult of 1487; and, in 1526, on the ground that there had been violations of the rule that when bishoprics or abbeys were vacant, the nomination belonged to the king and provision to the Pope, an act of parliament declared that any who entered upon possession of such benefices without the king's "command, letters or charges, or desire of the convents thereof" should "incur the crime of treason". But a new factor soon entered into the situation. The English Reformation had begun and the Scottish king could advance the price of his allegiance to the Pope; and, on 7 March 1534/5, James secured from Pope Paul III a bull explicitly recognizing the royal right of nomination and extending the period to twelve months, giving the king likewise the right to use the temporalities of vacant prelacies (including Cluniac, Cistercian and Premonstratensian abbeys) in the first year of a vacancy at his discretion.

The results for the monasteries of the increasing exploitation of vacancies were deplorable. Already during the king's minority when the Governor Albany exercised control of ecclesiastical affairs, we find such situations as that which appears at Glenluce, where, in 1516, there were three candidates with conflicting claims upon the abbey: the papal nominee, the Cardinal of St Eusebius; the royal nominee, David, bishop of Lismore; the monks' nominee, Alexander Cunningham, who had been elected by his brethren with the confirmation of the father-abbot and whose claim to the benefice brought upon him imprisonment.[1] Again, in 1523/4, the election of a monk of Coupar Angus as abbot by the convent, "made without advice of the Crown and contrary to its privileges", was quashed and the monks ordered to choose according to the Governor's nomination, the abbot of Melrose who had confirmed the election being forced to annul it. Worse was to follow. Between 1534 and 1541, five of the greater monasteries, Kelso, Melrose, St Andrews, Holyrood and Coldingham, were granted to three of the king's illegitimate children.

The deteriorating economic situation of the monasteries from the fifteenth century onwards is demonstrated by the increase in leases of their lands as well as by the difficulties and compromises which appear in their dealings with General Chapters regarding the payment of their dues. James V was now to add to their embarrassments by imposing upon them crippling financial demands. In vain Henry VIII had besought the king of Scots to adopt his ecclesiastical policy; James would not consent to extinguish the religious houses—but he would exact a price for their survival. Thus was inaugurated what Mr W. Stanford Reid has aptly called "the Scottish alternative to the dissolution of the monasteries". The king was able to extract from Pope

---

[1] The General Chapter, in 1518, protested against the supersession of the monks' choice (Canivez, *Statuta*, vi. 543–4).

Clement VII, in 1531, a bull sanctioning the taxation of the Church. The pretext was the obtaining of funds for the establishment of a College of Justice, but the primary aim was the replenishing of the royal treasury; and the subsidy for the College of Justice became a precedent for further demands, e.g. for the defence of the realm. The effect upon the monasteries of this repeated drain on their resources was not only that they frequently fell into arrears and abbots, on occasion, were distrained for debt; they were driven to raise money by the expedient of "feuing" their lands. Feu-holding, a usage peculiar to Scotland, has been described as "a heritable tenure,[1] granted in return for a fixed and single rent and for certain casualties".[2] It had hitherto been applied to Crown lands. Now its extension to the lands of the monasteries brought about a "rapid dissolution" of monastic property.

> . . . The real ownership of the Church's property passed from its hands. . . . Once the Church's power was broken, it was comparatively easy for the feuars to assume complete ownership. On the other hand, it was correspondingly difficult for the crown or parliament to get possession of the land, once it had passed into the hands of the feuars. Consequently church lands disbursed by the clergy to meet the demands of taxation never again left the hands of those to whom they were granted.[3]

The feuing of monastic lands led straight to their alienation.

The financial demands of the Crown were by no means the only factor which contributed to the secularization of monastic property. As the sixteenth century progressed, lay control of the monasteries' lands and possessions proceeded apace. From 1529 onwards, the farming of religious houses—Coupar Angus, Kilwinning, St Mary's Isle, Dundrennan, Inchaffray, Holyrood, Kelso, Melrose, Holywood—was in vogue. A commendator,

---

[1] As contrasted with a terminable lease or (*Scottice*) tack.
[2] I. F. Grant, *Social and Economic Development of Scotland*, 256.
[3] W. Stanford Reid, "Clerical Taxation; the Scottish alternative to the dissolution of the monasteries, 1530–1560", *Cath. Hist. Rev.*, xxxv (1948), 152. This is a valuable discussion of the subject. Cf. also R. K. Hannay, "Church Lands at the Reformation", *SHR*, xvi (1918–19); I. F. Grant, *op. cit.*, 269 ff.

E

even if he was a court official who, by holding a quasi-monastic office, drew a revenue from a monastery, was, in the earlier stages of the system, usually a secular priest who took the habit of the order to which his house belonged; but, in the course of the sixteenth century, laymen are mentioned as holding commends. In various ways, indeed, the "land-hungry nobility" (in the phrase of the editor of *The Letters of James V*) and lairds established a hold upon the monasteries which they were able, in many cases, to maintain until, during and after the Reformation. Thus a Colville, called rector of Dysart, but recommended as the king's "familiar" for his father's services to James IV and out of regard for his brother as a royal official, secured a family hold upon the abbey of Culross; an Erskine, who, according to James V was "a young noble with proved personal qualities and strong family connections", staked a claim for himself and his successors in the case of Dryburgh abbey, by obtaining the commend in 1541 —despite an attempt at the provision to that house of the blind theologian, Robert Wauchope; a Stewart, aged fourteen, but described as "a noble and studious youth", became titular abbot of Inchcolm in 1544, and paved the way for the Stewarts, Lords St Colm, who were to come after him. Again, at Glenluce, in the fourth decade of the century, the acquisitive rivalry of the earl of Cassillis and Gordon of Lochinvar led to the invasion of that abbey by both parties in turn, the molestation of the convent and the spoliation of its possessions. Before the Reformation lay encroachment upon the Scottish monasteries had gone far. The fact can merely be illustrated here. Only by a study of the records of the period can its extent and ramifications be realized.

(xii)

What of the internal life of the monasteries in this period of exploitation and inevitable decadence? The correspondence of the ambiguous monarch, James V, commonly adduces as a reason for nomination to monastic office the suitability of the candidate for restoring the *morale* of a monastery or for repairing its dilapidations. No doubt we may discount many of these protestations—the prevalence of royal nominees tended to debase rather than to enhance the quality of those who held office as abbots. Yet, in some cases, the royal recommendations were justified; and in certain fortunate monasteries, where the abbots were notable and conscientious rulers of their houses, we see definite attempts at reform. The conspicuous examples are Kinloss and Cambuskenneth. Thomas Chrystall, who held Kinloss from *c.* 1504 to 1535, not only exerted himself to recover the alienated patrimony of the monastery but sought to raise the standard of monastic life and education and added to the number of the monks. In 1528, the regress of the abbot's office was granted to Robert Reid, already a pluralist, who, on becoming bishop of Orkney in 1541, continued to hold Kinloss as well as the priory of Beauly *in commendam*. Reid, who was prominent in state affairs, and in this and other respects a typical churchman of his time, was exceptional in that he displayed a practical interest in the wellbeing of his commended monasteries. To Kinloss he brought the Italian scholar, Ferrerius, who spent a number of years in the instruction of the monks of that abbey as well as of the novices from Beauly and among whose writings is an account of the course of study pursued in the monastery. In 1516, Alexander Myln, who had been official of Dunkeld, was nominated by the duke of Albany, the Governor, for the abbey of Cambuskenneth, and, on taking up office, exhibited an assiduous interest in the reform of observance and education in his monastery; to this end, he proposed, in 1522, the sending of his novices to the abbey of St Victor at Paris. It was to this outstanding abbot that Robert Richardson (Richardinus), himself a canon of the same order and abbey, dedicated his *Commentary on the Rule of St Augustine*.[1] That the plans of Robert Reid and Alexander Myln for reviving education in their monasteries were by no

[1] Myln, like Reid, played a conspicuous part in state affairs and became the first president of the College of Justice.

means misplaced is shown by the tardy attempt of the Church in Scotland to promote reform in this direction by legislation. Thus, a provincial council in 1549 enacted, in order that "the study of the holy scriptures and the virtues pleasing to God Himself may, as in time past so now again, flourish in the monasteries", that there should be a theologian maintained in each house who should daily expound holy writ and preach; and, further, that in proportion to their revenues, monasteries should send one or two monks to the universities, there to spend at least four years in the study of theology and holy scripture.[1] The records of the university of St Andrews supply some instances of monks matriculating after this date, including, curiously enough, in 1545, the abbot of Glenluce, who had been the Governor's secretary and must have been from forty to fifty years of age. This remedy for monastic decline came too late to be effective. The fact, however, is significant that, in this period when the monasteries appear at a low ebb, men were still entering the religious life and there is no abrupt drop in the numbers of monastic *personnel*.

We have seen that James V professed his zeal for the reformation of certain orders and the opportunity was accordingly taken by their General Chapters to provide for the visitation of Scottish houses. It is somewhat intriguing to find the king claiming the countenance of his lieutenants for the abbot of Soulseat, who, in 1532, was about to undertake the visitation of the Premonstratensians

> howbeit he dredis that the . . . abbottis, prioris and religious personis wald nocht obey, bot be the contrary resist and withstand to the same, without our supple, help, mainteinance and assistance.

The abbot of Chaalis, who came to visit the Cistercian houses in 1531, appears to have raised more problems than he solved. There is extant a lengthy list of ordinances on the religious life sent by him from Coupar Angus to the abbey of Deer "to which we ourselves have not been able to go". It is doubtful if these

---

[1] Subjoined to this statute is a list showing the number of monks to be sent from each house, with a secular priest representing each of two nunneries.

were much more than counsels of perfection; yet he saw enough of Scottish Cistercianism to discover local irregularities—with which he dealt without *finesse*. According to King James's letters to the General Chapter (1 March 1531/2), the visitor "failed to ask himself whether he was dealing a blow at country and custom by his expedients hastily imposed to alter the immemorial manner of monastic life", "gave strange and unusual orders to the monks which they could not put into practice without mature consideration", and, having put the religious under ecclesiastical censures, departed from Scotland. What were the local customs of which the French abbot disapproved? It appears from the ensuing controversy that they were relaxations of the principle of corporate possession, instances of the "damnable vice of ownership" which the visitor, for once hitting the mark, had denounced in his communication to the monks of Deer. In 1534, the abbots of Coupar Angus and Glenluce, as visitors of the Scottish houses, dealt with the abbot of Melrose who is said to have been chiefly responsible for impeding the reform of the order in regard to this prevailing deviation; and it transpires that the monks of Melrose, as well as those of its daughter-houses, Newbattle and Balmerino, had been in the habit of holding private gardens, of treating their portions as individual possessions and of receiving sums of money for the purchase of clothing and other necessities. The monks of the three monasteries urged against the discontinuance of these relaxations that Scotland was less fertile and less abundant in the requisites of monastic life than France and other countries and that their predecessors from time immemorial had lived in this way. James V seems to have intervened in the controversy on the side of the Scottish monks; for, pointing out that the obstacles to reform were the geographical position of the country and the customs which the Scottish Cistercians had always observed, he asked Cîteaux (28 March 1534 or 1535) to permit "what the old superiors of the order observed without sacrificing its weal". We find the monks of Deer obtaining in 1537 a specific relaxation from the constitutions of the abbot of Chaalis "on account of the inconvenient situation of the place and the maliciousness of the times". Yet, in the same year, the abbot and convent of that monastery made a compact that they should henceforth lead a regular and reformed life and, after providing for the brethren and officers of the abbey, have its fruits and rents in common. Nor is this the only sign that the Cistercians, at the eleventh hour, were persuaded to take steps towards counteracting the "vice" to which the abbot of Chaalis had drawn attention. Thus, in 1553, the community at Coupar Angus resolved "to lead a regular life and to order our manners according to the reformers of the Cistercian order" and that the abbot and convent should possess and use in common the fruits, income and provision of the monastery. How far the communities carried out these reforms is impossible to tell; but the fact that after the Reformation surviving monks continued to receive their portions points to the perpetuation of the idea that these were personal perquisites.[1]

## (xiii)

To the monasteries in the area between Tay and Tweed, where many of the great houses were situated, came in the sixteenth century the devastating experience of repeated invasion. In 1523, damage was done by English armies to the Border abbeys of Kelso, Jedburgh and Dryburgh, and the last was to suffer again in 1542. But from 1544, when Hertford began his operations in Scotland, to 1549, the havoc wrought by the invaders was systematic and widespread.[2] The abbeys, nunneries, friaries and hospitals of the Borders, Lothian and the Merse underwent terrible destruction and the invaders carried their forays to the Firth of Tay, burning the abbey of Balmerino, the nunnery of Elcho and the friaries of Dundee. From these devastations the

---

[1] Monks' portions were treated as private property when, after the Reformation, they were secularized. Thus, in 1588, portions of deceased monks of Coupar Angus were granted to the children of the king's master-saddler (*Coupar Angus*, ii. no. cclxxxvi).

[2] A contemporary list of the buildings destroyed by Hertford's forces in September 1545 is given in *Source Bk. of Scottish History*, ii. 127–8.

religious houses had no chance of recovering. To the decade of the later English invasions belongs also the first display of popular hostility towards the monasteries—the attack by a mob upon the friars' houses of Dundee and the expulsion of the monks from Lindores abbey in 1543;[1] and, in 1546, an act of the Lords of Council, ratified by parliament, on the preamble that "it is dred and ferit" that evilly disposed persons will invade, destroy and cast down abbeys and other religious structures, institutes the severest penalties for those who are guilty of such destruction.

On the eve of the Reformation (1556), Cardinal Sermonetta presented to Pope Paul IV a gloomy picture of the state of the Scottish monasteries, dwelling on the alienation of their property to the nobles and deploring the condition of their buildings which, he declared, were "reduced to ruins by hostile inroads or through the avarice and neglect of those placed in charge . . . crumbling to decay".[2] It must suffice to remark that while secularization of the religious houses and their possessions had passed beyond ecclesiastical control, there was, after the death of James V in 1542, no strong ruler to resist the vested interests which laymen steadily established in monastic property; the Crown played no part in the disposal of the monasteries until a much later stage. When the Reformation came, the commendators remained. Now, however, their pretensions to monastic status mattered little and their virtual possession of monastic property counted for much. The annexation of the monasteries to the Crown, in 1587, a quarter of a century after they had ceased to function, came as a belated measure, an afterthought and its effect was restricted by the fact that by this date not a little of the monasteries' possessions had been alienated beyond recall. There followed the gradual disposal by the Crown of what remained—once the convents had ceased to exist—through the erection of abbeys into temporal lordships. The monks remaining in an abbey, it is to be noted, were not dislodged but were

---

[1] The expulsion of the monks in this case was temporary.
[2] *Papal Negotiations*, 529.

allowed to die out; thereafter the suppression of the monastery took place and it became irrevocably secularized. Contrary to a common notion, there was no concerted destruction of monastic fabrics.

### (xiv)

One modification of the foregoing statement falls to be made. Although, as in England, the friars continued, in the sixteenth century, to receive small bequests, e.g. they are often mentioned in wills, and although, within that century, houses of friars were still being founded, there are unmistakable evidences of their unpopularity; and from the time of the mob-attack upon the friaries in Dundee (1543), many of their houses were damaged or destroyed. The houses of friars, indeed, rather than the greater monasteries, were the objects of violence at the Reformation. It is not easy to account for this, though the fact that friaries were situated in towns and were of little interest to the gentry who had established a hold upon the abbeys may partly explain it. Some, as at Aberdeen, Elgin, Inverness and Glasgow, are mentioned in 1561/2 as "undemolished"; it was, in fact, left to twentieth-century vandalism to erase the church of the Aberdeen Greyfriars. In general, the friars' properties passed to the possession of the burghs where they were located.

Religious foundations for women in Scotland were only fifteen in number and of these four expired before the Reformation. Most of the Scottish nunneries were small—the largest seem to have been those of Haddington and North Berwick—and none ranked higher than a priory. Their history is in many respects obscure. Nine are described as of the Cistercian order; two were Augustinian; one (Lincluden) is called Benedictine. There were also three late foundations of the mendicant orders: two small houses of Franciscan nuns and one larger house of Dominican sisters. These designations, however, raise some problems. The so-called Cistercian houses, which formed the majority of the Scottish nunneries, were in a somewhat anomalous position in regard to the order; and it is impossible to say how they stood towards each other. We find the nuns of North Berwick denied recognition as Cistercian because they did not wear the habit of the order;[1] and no mention of the Scottish Cistercian nunneries occurs in the records of the General Chapter till 1530, when the seven remaining houses are listed for assessment by the commissary of the Chapter in Scotland.[2] It is noteworthy that an earlier attempt (*c.* 1516) to include the Scottish nunneries among the houses to be visited by a Cistercian commissary concerned with the levying of contributions to the order was challenged by the archbishop of St. Andrews, who claimed an immemorial right to visit them; and the appointment by the General Chapter of the abbot of Glenluce, in 1530, for a similar purpose was met, at the instigation of the archbishop, by resolutions of the Lords of Council (31 January 1530/1; 23 July 1531) inhibiting him from visiting nunneries, because the archbishop and his predecessors had always had that right.

Though evidence is forthcoming that Scottish nuns exercised the right of electing their prioresses in the sixteenth century—the communities at Haddington (1517) and Coldstream (1537/8) furnish instances—there was a marked tendency at this period for a nunnery to become "the perquisite of some noble house", with the consequence that "as it passed from member to member, the revenues were alienated to their kinsfolk".[3] Thus, North Berwick nunnery became virtually the family benefice of the Humes of Polwarth, and Haddington of the Hepburns (though these were later displaced by the Maitlands). It may be added that the situation of most of the nunneries in the south-east of Scotland made them particularly vulnerable to destruction and spoliation in times of war.

So far in this account little mention has been made of the medieval hospitals of Scotland. These were of the types familiar in England and elsewhere—for the sick, lepers, the poor,

---

[1] *V.* p. 124 *infra.*    [2] Their names, presumably, were supplied by the commissary.
[3] G. Donaldson, "The Cistercian Nunnery of St Mary, Haddington", *Trans. of East Lothian Antiq. Socy.*, v (1952), 14.

travellers and pilgrims. Sometimes these types overlapped; occasionally, the original type of a hospital in course of time was changed. Some hospitals were in the hands of religious orders; thus, St Germains was a house of Bethlehemites, a congregation rarely exemplified in Britain; Soutra and Segden were Augustinian; St Anthony's, Leith, belonged to the order of St Anthony of Vienne, and was specially intended for sufferers from erysipelas. Of the hospitals originally maintained by religious only St Anthony's survived till the Reformation. A number of hospitals were attached to colleges of secular canons and formed, with their bedesmen, as at Trinity College, Edinburgh, an integral part of such foundations. Among the secular hospitals are some rarely mentioned and probably short-lived.

The state of the hospitals in the fifteenth century was such that by an act of parliament of 12 March 1424/5—early in the reign of James I—it was enacted that those which had been founded by the Crown for the poor and the sick were to be visited by the chancellor, "as has been done in the king's progenitors' times" —the usage has English parallels; while those founded by bishops and other spiritual and temporal lords were to have visitation of the diocesan bishop, in order (in both cases) to reform them in accordance with their original foundations. The specific defects prevailing in the hospitals are not disclosed; nor does any remedial action seem to have been taken. But a further act of 9 October 1466 for the reformation of the hospitals provided that their holders should be warned to produce the foundation charters for the perusal of the bishop and chancellor, so that these institutions might be "reducit [brought back] to thare first fundacione". Where such a document could not be exhibited, the income of the hospital was to be allocated to "poor and miserable" persons according to the extent of the endowments. Again, on 20 November 1469, the king's almoner-general is empowered by another act to put into operation the statute of 1466. The one known instance of the almoner's activity in this regard is his framing of a new constitution for St Laurence's hospital at Haddington—the solitary example of a constitution devised for a Scottish medieval hospital. But the reform, in this case, was only on paper and took no effect. It is, indeed, more than doubtful whether any reformation of the hospitals resulted from the acts of parliament. The hospitals tended to become mere benefices and sinecures. Yet some there were which maintained their services to the ailing and the poor and persisted not only to the Reformation but long after it.[1]

## (xv)

It is fair to state, in conclusion, that any account of the medieval religious houses in Scotland must be partial and incomplete because a reconstruction of their development is based on imperfect knowledge. Not only are there great gaps in the available records. Existing documents may enable us in some degree to recognize the external aspects of monasticism in the five centuries of its existence in Scotland. But the information conveyed to us regarding the domestic life of the Scottish monasteries is sparse, fragmentary and seldom intimate. Only in the sixteenth century do we find such items as the record which shows that the monks of Newbattle had gone on strike, since the abbot had refused to grant them larger portions;[2] and the recital of the involved dispute in the priory of Monymusk, where the canons were at odds with the prior and the formal Latin is relieved with an account of the sentence passed on one of the brethren couched in the robust Scots of the period.[3] Much that we would wish to know—and not least of the devotional life of the monasteries—eludes us. But if so many points remain "greatly dark", their obscurity serves to temper our judgments; on the other hand, such knowledge as we can attain of a great religious and social institution deserves to be frankly set forth, not without anticipation of shortcomings and blunders, but also in the hope that it may be amended and augmented.

---

[1] This was particularly so in the north-eastern counties (Aberdeen and Banff).
[2] *Formulare*, i. no. 261.   [3] *Illust. of Topog. and Antiqs. of Aberdeen and Banff*, iii. 490–1.

## GENERAL ABBREVIATIONS, ETC., USED IN THE
## FOLLOWING LISTS

(1) Symbols to left of name, denoting remains of site:

    \*   In charge of the Ministry of Works or the National Trust.

    ¶   Scheduled as an Ancient Monument.

    ‡   Church, or part(s) of Church, in ecclesiastical use.

    §   Remains of importance, in private hands and not necessarily open to the public.

(2) Under "Date":

| | |
|---|---|
| Fd. | Founded or established. |
| D. | Dissolved (usually by union to another house) before the Reformation. |
| Sec. | Secularized (usually by erection as a temporal lordship). |
| Supp. | Suppressed before the Reformation. |
| Term. | Terminated. |

    *c.* before date    about.            + after date     after that year.

    c. after figure    century.           † before date    died in.

    – before date    before that year.

(3) Abbreviations for MS. and printed sources and other references cited in the notes:

| | |
|---|---|
| *Aberbrothoc* | *Liber S. Thome de Aberbrothoc* (Bannatyne Club). 1848, 1856. |
| *Abredoniae Utriusque Descriptio* | *Abredoniae utriusque descriptio: A description of both towns of Aberdeen* (Spalding Club). 1842. |
| *Abstracts of Chs. in Chartulary of Torphichen* | *Abstracts of charters and other papers recorded in the chartulary of Torphichen from 1581 to 1596.* Edinburgh, 1830. |
| *AF; Aberdeen Friars* | *Aberdeen Friars; Red, Black, White, Grey* (Aberdeen University Studies). 1909. |
| ADC | Acta Dominorum Concilii (MS. in H.M. General Register House, Edinburgh). |
| *AFH* | *V. Arch. Francisc. Hist.* |
| *ALC, 1501–54* | *Acts of the Lords of Council in Public Affairs, 1501–1554.* 1932. |
| *Analecta F.P.* | *Analecta sacri ordinis Fratrum Praedicatorum.* |
| *Antiqs. Aberd. and Banff* | *Illustrations of the topography and antiquities of the shires of Aberdeen and Banff* (Spalding Club), i. 1869; ii. 1847; iii. 1857; iv. 1862. |
| A. O. Anderson, *Early Sources* | A. O. Anderson, *Early Sources of Scottish History,* Edinburgh, 1922. |
| A. O. Anderson, *Scottish Annals* | A. O. Anderson, *Scottish Annals from English Chroniclers.* London, 1908. |
| *APS* | *Acts of the Parliaments of Scotland.* i. 1844; ii–. 1814–. |
| *Arch. Francisc. Hist.* | *Archivum Franciscanum Historicum.* |
| *Archaeol. Aeliana* | *Archaeologia Aeliana.* |
| *Archaeol. Collns. rel. to Ayrshire and Galloway* | *Archaeological and historical collections relating to Ayrshire and Galloway* (Ayrshire and Galloway Archaeological Association). |
| *AS* | *Acta Sanctorum.* |
| *Balmorinach* | *Liber Sancte Marie de Balmorinach* in *the Chartularies of Balmerino and Lindores* (Abbotsford Club). 1841. |
| *Bamff Chs.* | *Bamff Charters, A.D. 1232–1703.* 1915. |
| *Bannatyne Misc.* | Miscellany volume of the Bannatyne Club. |
| *Beauly* | *Charters of the Priory of Beauly, with notices of the Priories of Pluscardine and Ardchattan* (Grampian Club). 1877. |
| *Berwickshire Nat. Club* | *Berwickshire Naturalists' Club* (Publications of). |

| | |
|---|---|
| Beveridge, BR of Dunf. | Erskine Beveridge, *The Burgh Records of Dunfermline*. Edinburgh, 1917. |
| Bk. of Arran | *The Book of Arran* (Arran Society of Glasgow). 1910–14. |
| Bk. of Pluscarden | *Liber Pluscardensis* (Historians of Scotland). Edinburgh, 1877. Translation in same series, 1880. |
| Brady, *Episc. Succession* | W. M. Brady, *The Episcopal Succession in England, Scotland and Ireland, A.D. 1400 to 1875*. |
| Breviarium | *V. Cupar.* |
| Brockie | MS. collections of Fr Marianus Brockie, in St Mary's College, Blairs. |
| Cal. Close Rolls | (*Calendar of*) *Close Rolls.* |
| Cal. Inquis. | *Calendar of Inquisitions Post Mortem.* |
| Cal of State Papers rel. to Scotland | *Calendar of the State Papers relating to Scotland.* 1858. |
| Cal. Pat. Rolls | *Calendar of the Patent Rolls.* |
| Cal. Scottish Papers | *Calendar of the State Papers relating to Scotland and Mary Queen of Scots, 1547–1603*. 1898. |
| Cal. of Writs of Munro of Foulis | *Calendar of Writs of Munro of Foulis* (Scottish Record Society). 1940. |
| Calchou | *Liber S. Marie de Calchou* (Bannatyne Club). 1846. |
| Cambuskenneth | *Registrum monasterii S. Marie de Cambuskenneth* (Grampian Club). 1872. |

Camerarius, *De Scotorum Fortitudine, Doctrina et Pietate*. Paris, 1631.

| | |
|---|---|
| Canivez, *Statuta* | *Statuta Capitulorum Generalium Ordinis Cisterciensis*, 1116– (ed. J. M. Canivez). 1933–. |
| Carnegies, Earls of Southesk | *History of the Carnegies, Earls of Southesk*. Edinburgh, 1867. |
| Cart. S. Nich. | *Cartularium ecclesiae Sancti Nicholai Aberdonensis* (New Spalding Club). 1888, 1892. |
| Cath. Hist. Rev. | *Catholic Historical Review.* |
| CCM | *Registrum domus de Soltre, necnon ecclesie collegiate S. Trinitatis prope Edinburgh, etc.; Charters of the Hospital of Soltre, of Trinity College, Edinburgh, and other collegiate churches in Midlothian* (Bannatyne Club). 1861. |
| CDS | *Calendar of Documents relating to Scotland.* 1881–8. |
| Chron. Holyrood | *The Chronicle of Holyrood* (Scottish History Society). 1938. |
| Chron. Lanercost | *Chronicon de Lanercost* (Bannatyne Club). 1839. |
| Chron. Mailros | *Chronica de Mailros* (Bannatyne Club). 1835. |
| Chron. Man | *The Chronicle of Man and the Sudreys* (ed. Munch). 1860. |
| Chrons. of Frasers | *Chronicles of the Frasers; the Wardlaw Manuscript, etc.* (Scottish History Society). 1905. |
| Chrons. of Stephen, etc. | *Chronicles of the reigns of Stephen, Henry II and Richard I* (Rolls Series). |
| Chs. and Docs. rel. to Glasgow | *Charters and other documents relating to the City of Glasgow* (Scottish Burgh Records Society). 1897–1906. |
| Chs. and Docs. rel. to Peebles | *Charters and documents relating to the Burgh of Peebles* (Scottish Burgh Records Society). 1872. |
| Chs. F.P. Ayr | *Munimenta fratrum predicatorum de Are; Charters of the Friars Preachers of Ayr* (Ayrshire and Galloway Archaeological Association). 1881. |

| | |
|---|---|
| Chs. etc. of Burgh of Dundee | Charters, writs, etc., of the Royal Burgh of Dundee. Dundee. 1880. |
| Chs. rel. to Stirling | Charters and other documents relating to the Royal Burgh of Stirling, 1124–1705. Glasgow, 1884. |
| Chs. Trin. College | Charters and documents relating to the Collegiate Church and Hospital of the Holy Trinity, Edinburgh (Scottish Burgh Records Society). 1871. |
| Cluny | Recueil des chartes de l'abbaye de Cluny (ed. Bruel) (Collection des documents inédits). Paris. 1876–1903. |
| Coldstream | Charters of the Cistercian Priory of Coldstream (Grampian Club). 1879. |
| Collns. Aberd. and Banff | Collections for a history of the shires of Aberdeen and Banff (Spalding Club). 1843. |
| Copiale | Copiale Prioratus Sanctiandree (St Andrews University Publications). 1930. |
| Coupar Angus | Charters of the Abbey of Coupar Angus (Scottish History Society). 1947. |

Court Book of the Barony of Carnwath (Scottish History Society). 1937.

| | |
|---|---|
| CPR | Calendar of entries in the Papal Registers. Letters, 1893– ; Petitions 1896. The sheets of the unpublished volumes xiii and xiv have been consulted (volume xiii is now published). |
| Cramond, Recs. of Elgin | Records of Elgin, 1234–1800 (ed. Cramond) (New Spalding Club). 1903. |
| Crosraguel | Charters of the Abbey of Crosraguel (Ayrshire and Galloway Archaeological Association). 1886. |
| Culdees | W. Reeves, The Culdees of the British Islands. Dublin, 1864. |
| Cupar | Rental Book of the Cistercian Abbey of Cupar [sic] Angus, with the breviary of the Register (Grampian Club). 1879–80. |
| Dempster, Apparatus | T. Dempster, Apparatus ad historiam Scoticam. Bologna, 1622. |
| Diurnal | A diurnal of remarkable occurrents . . . since the death of King James the Fourth till the year MDLXXV (Bannatyne and Maitland Clubs). 1833. |
| Docs. Illust. of Hist. of Scotland | Documents illustrative of the history of Scotland, MCCLXXXVI–MCCCVI. 1870. |
| Douglas Bk. | The Douglas Book. 1885. |
| Dowden, Bishops | J. Dowden, The Bishops of Scotland. Glasgow, 1912. |
| Dowden, Med. Ch. in Scotland | J. Dowden, The Medieval Church in Scotland. Glasgow, 1910. |
| Dryburgh | Liber S. Marie de Dryburgh (Bannatyne Club). 1847. |
| Dundas Chs. | Dundas Charters (uncatalogued) in National Library of Scotland. |
| Dundas of Dundas | Royal letters and other historical documents selected from the family papers of Dundas of Dundas. Edinburgh, 1897. |
| Dunfermelyn | Registrum de Dunfermelyn (Bannatyne Club). 1842. |
| Eadmer, Hist. Nov. Angl. | Eadmer, Historia Novorum in Anglia (Rolls Series). London. 1884. |
| Earls of Cromartie | The Earls of Cromartie. Edinburgh, 1876. |
| Earls of Haddington | Memorials of the Earls of Haddington. Edinburgh. 1889. |
| East Lothian Deeds | Deeds relating to East Lothian (ed. Wallace-James). Haddington, 1899. |

| | |
|---|---|
| *EBR; Edin. BR* | *Extracts from the records of the Burgh of Edinburgh* (Scottish Burgh Records Society). 1869–. |
| *Epp. Reg. Scot.* | *Epistolae Regum Scottorum* (ed. Ruddiman). 1722–4. |
| *ER* | *The Exchequer Rolls of Scotland.* |
| *ESC* | *V.* Lawrie, *ESC.* |
| EU. MS. | Manuscript in Edinburgh University Library. |
| *Extracta* | *Extracta ex variis cronicis Scocie* (Abbotsford Club). 1842. |
| *Extracts from Recs. of Lanark* | *Extracts from the records of the Royal Burgh of Lanark, 1150–1722.* Glasgow, 1893. |
| *Fasti Aberd.* | *Fasti Aberdonenses; Selections from the records of the University and King's College of Aberdeen, 1494–1854* (Spalding Club). 1854. |
| Ferrerius, *Hist. Abbatum Kynlos* | *Ferrerii historia abbatum de Kynlos* (Bannatyne Club). 1839. |
| Fittis, *Eccles. Annals of Perth* | R. S. Fittis, *Ecclesiastical Annals of Perth.* Edinburgh and Perth, 1885. |
| *Formulare* | *St Andrews Formulare* (Stair Society). 1942–4. |
| *Fraser Papers* | *Papers from the collection of Sir William Fraser* (Scottish History Society). 1924. |
| *Furness Coucher Book* | *The Coucher Book of Furness Abbey* (Cheetham Society). 1886–. |
| GRH. Chs. | Calendar of charters in H.M. General Register House, Edinburgh. |
| GRH. Vat. Trans. | Vatican Transcripts in H.M. General Register House, Edinburgh. |
| Haddan and Stubbs, *Councils* | *Councils and Ecclesiastical Documents relating to Great Britain and Ireland* (ed. Haddan and Stubbs). 1869–78. |
| *Hamilton Papers* | *The Hamilton Papers.* 1890–2. |
| Hay. Dipl. Vet. Coll. | Father R. A. Hay, Diplomatum Veterum Collectio. MS. 34.1.10 in National Library of Scotland, Edinburgh. |
| Hay, *Genealogie* | Father R. A. Hay, *Genealogie of the Sainte Claires of Rosslyn.* Edinburgh, 1835. |
| Hay of Park MSS. | In H.M. General Register House, Edinburgh. |
| Hay, Scotia Sacra | Father R. A. Hay, Scotia Sacra. MS. 34.1.18 in National Library of Scotland, Edinburgh. |
| Herkless and Hannay, *Archbps. of St Ands.* | Herkless and Hannay, *The Archbishops of St Andrews.* Edinburgh and London, 1907–15. |
| Hermans, *Ann. can. reg. S. Aug. ord. S. Crucis* | C. R. Hermans, *Annales canonicorum regularium S. Augustini ordinis S. Crucis,* i–iii. Bois-le-Duc. 1858. |
| *Highland Papers* | *Highland Papers* (Scottish History Society), i. 1914; ii. 1916; iii. 1920; iv. 1934. |
| *Hist. C.R. of Scotland* | *History of the Chapel Royal of Scotland* (Grampian Club). 1882. |
| *Hist. Mon. Comm. Rep.* | Report of the Royal Commission on the Ancient and Historical Monuments and Constructions of Scotland. |
| *Hist. Papers and Letters from Northern Regs.* | *Historical Papers and Letters from the Northern Registers* (Rolls Series). 1875. |
| *HMC. Rep.* | Report of the Royal Commission on Historical Manuscripts. |

| | |
|---|---|
| Hutton's Collns. | Hutton's Collections in National Library of Scotland, Edinburgh. |
| *H. VIII SP* | *State Papers of Henry VIII.* |
| *Inchaffray* | *Charters, etc., relating to the abbey of Inchaffray* (Scottish History Society). 1908. |
| *Inchcolm* | *Charters of the Abbey of Inchcolm* (Scottish History Society). 1938. |
| Janauschek, Orig. Cist. | Leopoldus Janauschek, *Originum Cisterciensium.* 1877. |
| *JBAA* | *Journal of the British Archaeological Association.* |
| *JEH* | *Journal of Ecclesiastical History.* |
| Kinlos | *Records of the Monastery of Kinlos* (Publications of the Society of Antiquaries of Scotland). 1872. |
| Knox, *History* | John Knox, *History of the Reformation in Scotland* in *Works* (ed. Laing), i–ii. 1846–8. |
| *L. & P. H. VIII* | *Letters and Papers of Henry VIII.* |
| Laing Chs. | *Calendar of Laing Charters.* Edinburgh, 1899. |
| Lawrie, *Annals* | Sir A. C. Lawrie, *Annals of the Reigns of Malcolm and William Kings of Scotland.* Glasgow, 1910. |
| Lawrie, *ESC* | Sir A. C. Lawrie, *Early Scottish Charters prior to A.D. 1153.* Glasgow, 1905. |
| *Lennox* | *V. The Lennox.* |
| Le Paige, *Bibliotheca Praem. Ord.* | Le Paige, *Bibliotheca Praemonstratensis Ordinis.* Paris, 1633. |
| Lesley, *De Origine* | John Lesley, *De Origine Moribus et Rebus Gestis Scotorum.* Rome, 1578. |
| Lesley, *History* | John Lesley, *The History of Scotland from the death of King James I, etc.* (Bannatyne Club). 1830; also in another version (Scottish Text Society). 1888, 1895. |
| *Letters of James IV* | *The Letters of James the Fourth* (Scottish History Society). 1953. |
| *Letters of James V* | *The Letters of James V* (H.M. Stationery Office). 1954. |
| *Letters of Sir Walter Scott.* | *The Letters of Sir Walter Scott* (ed. Grierson). London, 1932–7. |
| *LHT Accts.* | *Accounts of the Lord High Treasurer of Scotland.* 1877–. |
| *Lib. Coll. Nostre Domine.* | *Liber collegii nostre Domine* (Maitland Club). 1846. |
| *Lib. Ins. Missarum* | *Liber Insule Missarum* (Bannatyne Club). 1847. |
| *Lib. S. Crucis* | *Liber cartarum Sancte Crucis* (Bannatyne Club). 1840. |
| *Lib. S. Kath. Senen.* | *Liber conventus S. Katherine Senensis prope Edinburgum* (Abbotsford Club). 1841. |
| *Lindores* | *Chartulary of the Abbey of Lindores* (Scottish History Society). 1903. |
| *Macfarlane's Geneal. Collns.* | *Genealogical collections concerning Families in Scotland made by Walter Macfarlane* (Scottish History Society). 1900. |
| *Macfarlane's Geog. Collns.* | *Geographical collections relating to Scotland made by Walter Macfarlane* (Scottish History Society). 1906–7. |
| MacGibbon and Ross, *Eccles. Archit.* | D. MacGibbon and T. Ross, *The Ecclesiastical Architecture of Scotland.* Edinburgh, 1896–7. |
| Mackinlay, *Dedications* | J. M. Mackinlay, *Ancient Church Dedications in Scotland.* Scriptural, 1910; non-Scriptural, 1914. |

| | |
|---|---|
| Mackinlay, *Place Names* | J. M. Mackinlay. *The Influence of the pre-Reformation Church on Scottish Place Names.* Edinburgh and London, 1904. |
| Macphail, *Pluscardyn.* | S. R. Macphail, *The Religious House of Pluscardyn.* Edinburgh, 1881. |
| McPherson, *The Kirk's Care of the Poor* | J. M. McPherson, *The Kirk's Care of the Poor.* Aberdeen, n.d. |
| Maitland, *History* | W. Maitland, *The History and Antiquities of Scotland.* London, 1757. |
| Major, *Hist. of Greater Britain* | John Major, *History of Greater Britain* (Scottish History Society). 1928. |
| *Manx Society* | Publications of the Manx Society. |
| Martine, *Reliquiae Divi Andreae.* St Andrews, 1797. | |
| Matthew of Westminster, *Flores Historiarum* | *Flores Historiarum per Mattheum Westmonasteriensem collecti.* Frankfurt, 1601. |
| Maxwell, *Old Dundee* | A. Maxwell, *Old Dundee, ecclesiastical, burghal, and social, prior to the Reformation.* Dundee, 1891. |
| *May* | *Records of the Priory of the Isle of May* (Publications of the Society of Antiquaries of Scotland). 1868. |
| *Melros* | *Liber Sancte Marie de Melros* (Bannatyne Club). 1837. |
| *Mem. de Parl.* | *Memoranda de Parliamento* (Rolls Series). 1893. |
| *Menteith* | *The Red Book of Menteith.* 1880. |
| *MB.*; Moir Bryce, *Greyfriars.* | W. Moir Bryce, *The Scottish Greyfriars,* n.d. |
| *Migne* | *V. Patr. Lat.* |
| *Mon. ord. F.P. Hist.* | *Monumenta ordinis Fratrum Praedicatorum Historica.* 1898–. |
| Monro, *Western Isles* | D. Monro, *Description of the Western Isles called Hybrides* (1549). 1884. |
| Morton, *Monastic Annals* | J. Morton, *The monastic annals of Teviotdale.* Edinburgh, 1832. |
| MS. Saunders | MS. in the possession of the late William Saunders, Esq., Edinburgh. |
| *Mun. F.P. Glasgu* | *Liber collegii nostre Domine . . . accedunt Munimenta Fratrum Predicatorum de Glasgu* (Maitland Club). 1846. |
| Myln, *Vitae* | *Vitae Dunkeldensis ecclesiae episcoporum . . . ab Alexandro Myln . . . conscriptae* (Bannatyne Club). 1831. |
| *N. Berwic* | *Carte monialium de Northberwic* (Bannatyne Club). 1847. |
| *N. Durham* | *History and Antiquities of North Durham* (ed. J. Raine). 1852. (An appendix contains the charters of Coldingham Priory.) |
| *Neubotle* | *Registrum S. Marie de Neubotle* (Bannatyne Club). 1849. |
| NLS. MS. | Manuscript in the National Library of Scotland, Edinburgh. |
| *NSA*; *New Stat. Acct.* | *The New Statistical Account of Scotland.* Edinburgh, 1845. |
| *Oliphants* | *The Oliphants in Scotland with . . . original documents from the Charter Chest at Gask.* Edinburgh. 1879. |
| *OPS* | *Origines parochiales Scotiae* (Bannatyne Club). 1851–5. |
| *Papal Negotiations* | *Papal Negotiations with Mary Queen of Scots during her reign in Scotland, 1561–1567* (Scottish History Society). 1901. |
| *Passelet* | *Registrum monasterii de Passelet* (Maitland Club). 1832. |

F

| | |
|---|---|
| Patr. Lat. | Migne, *Patrologia Latina*. |
| PCR | *Register of the Privy Council of Scotland.* 1877–. |
| Pitscottie, Cronicles | *The historie and cronicles of Scotland . . . by Robert Lindsay of Pitscottie* (Scottish Text Society). 1899–. |
| Priory of Colding-ham. | *The Priory of Coldingham* (Surtees Society). 1841. |
| PRO | Public Record Office (documents in). |
| Prot. Bk. of John Foular | *Protocol Book of John Foular* (Scottish Record Society). 1930–44. |
| Prot. Bk. of Gilbert Grote | *Protocol Book of Gilbert Grote* (Scottish Record Society). 1914. |
| Prot. Bk. of Thomas Ireland | Protocol Book of Thomas Ireland, in archives of the city of Dundee. |
| Prot. Bk. of Thomas Johnsoun | *Protocol Book of Thomas Johnsoun* (Scottish Record Society). 1920. |
| Prot. Bk. of Thomas Steven | Protocol Book of Thomas Steven, in Haddington burgh records (now in H.M. General Register House, Edinburgh). |
| Prot. Bk. of Nicol Thounis | *Protocol Book of Nicol Thounis* (Scottish Record Society). 1926. |
| Prot. Bk. of James Young | *Protocol Book of James Young* (Scottish Record Society). 1941–52. |
| PSAS | *Proceedings of the Society of Antiquaries of Scotland.* |
| REA | *Registrum episcopatus Aberdonensis* (Spalding and Maitland Clubs). 1845. |
| REB | *Registrum episcopatus Brechinensis* (Bannatyne Club). 1856. |
| Recs. of Prestwick | *Records of the Burgh of Prestwick* (Maitland Club). 1834. |
| REG | *Registrum episcopatus Glasguensis* (Bannatyne and Maitland Clubs). 1843. |
| Reg. Coll. Ch. of Crail | *Register of the Collegiate Church of Crail* (Grampian Club). 1877. |
| Reg. C.R. Striv. | *Registrum Capellae Regiae Strivelinensis. V. Hist. C.R. of Scotland.* |
| Reg. Hon. de Morton | *Registrum Honoris de Morton* (Bannatyne Club). 1853. |
| Reg. of Walter Gray, archbp. of York | *Register of Walter Gray, archbishop of York* (Surtees Society). 1870–2. |
| Reg. Panmure | *Registrum de Panmure.* 1874. |
| Reg. S. Bees | *Register of the Priory of St Bees* (Surtees Society), 1915. |
| Reg. S. Egid. | *Registrum cartarum ecclesie S. Egidii de Edinburgh* (Bannatyne Club). 1859. |
| REM | *Registrum episcopatus Moraviensis* (Bannatyne Club). 1837. |
| Rentale Dunkeldense | *Rentale Dunkeldense* (Scottish History Society). 1915. |
| Rentale S. And. | *Rentale Sancti Andree* (Scottish History Society). 1913. |
| Rep. on State of Certain Parishes | *Reports on the state of certain parishes in Scotland . . . MDCXXVII* (Maitland Club). 1835. |
| Retours | *Inquisitionum ad capellam domini regis retornatarum . . . abbrevatio* (Record Commissioners). 1811–16. |
| RMS | *Registrum magni sigilli regum Scotorum.* i. 1912; ii–. 1882–. |
| Rose of Kilravock | *A genealogical deduction of the Family of Rose of Kilravock* (Spalding Club). 1848. |
| Ross Estate Muni-ments. | In H.M. General Register House, Edinburgh. |

| | |
|---|---|
| *Rot. Scot.* | *Rotuli Scotiae* (Record Commissioners). 1814–19. |
| *RPSA* | (*Registrum sive*) *Liber cartarum prioratus Sancti Andree in Scotia* (Bannatyne Club). 1841. |
| *RSS* | *Registrum secreti sigilli regum Scotorum.* 1908–. |
| *Scalacronica* | *Scalacronica: By Sir Thomas Gray of Heton Knight.* (Maitland Club). 1836. |
| *Scon* | *Liber ecclesie de Scon* (Bannatyne Club). 1843. |
| *Scotichronicon* | *Joannis de Fordun Scotichronicon cum supplementis et continuatione Walteri Boweri* (ed. W. Goodall). 1759. |
| *Scottish Benefices* | *The Apostolic Camera and Scottish Benefices* (ed. A. I. Cameron) (St Andrews University Publications). 1934. |
| *Scottish Corresp. of Mary of Lorraine* | *The Scottish Correspondence of Mary of Lorraine* (Scottish History Society). 1927. |
| *Scotts of Buccleuch* | *The Scotts of Buccleuch.* Edinburgh, 1878. |
| *SHR* | *Scottish Historical Review.* |
| *SHS. Misc.* | *Miscellany volume of the Scottish History Society.* |
| Smith, *Strathendrick* | J. G. Smith, *Strathendrick and its inhabitants.* Glasgow, 1896. |
| *SP* | *The Scots Peerage.* 1904–14. |
| *Spalding Club Misc.* | Miscellany volume of the Spalding Club. |
| Spottiswoode | J. Spottiswoode, *An Account of all the Religious Houses that were in Scotland at the time of the Reformation*; included in R. Keith, *An Historical Catalogue of the Scottish Bishops.* Edinburgh, 1824. |
| Spottiswoode, *Hist. of the Ch. of Scotland* | [Archbishop] J. Spottiswoode, *The History of the Church of Scotland.* The edition of this work published in 1677 has an appendix containing lists of religious houses. This appendix is also found as a separate publication—*An Appendix to the History of the Church of Scotland.* London, 1677. It is anonymous but attributed to T. Middleton. |
| *Spottiswoode Socy. Misc.* | Miscellany volume of the Spottiswoode Society. |
| St Andrews Chs. | Charters of the city of St Andrews (notes supplied by the Rev. W. E. K. Rankin, D.D.). |
| *Stirling Burgh Recs.* | *Extracts from the records of the Royal Burgh of Stirling, 1519–1666.* Glasgow, 1887. |
| *Supplics.* | *Calendar of Scottish Supplications to Rome, 1418–1422* (Scottish History Society). 1934. |
| Symeon of Durham, *Hist. Dunelm. Eccl.* | Symeon of Durham, *Historia Dunelmensis Ecclesiae* (Rolls Series). 1882. |
| Symeon of Durham, *Hist. Regum* | Symeon of Durham, *Historia Regum* (Rolls Series). 1885. |
| *Templaria* | *Templaria; Papers relative to the history of the Scottish Knights Templars and . . . the Knights of St John.* 1828. |
| *Thanes of Cawdor* | *The book of the Thanes of Cawdor* (Spalding Club). 1859. |
| *The Lennox* | *The Lennox* (Edinburgh). 1874. |
| Theiner, *Vet. Mon.* | *Vetera Monumenta Hibernorum et Scotorum Historiam illustrantia* (ed. A. Theiner). 1864. |
| *Thirds of Benefices* | *Accounts of the Collectors of the Thirds of Benefices, 1561–1572* (Scottish History Society). 1949. |
| Thomson, *Lauder and Lauderdale* | A. Thomson, *Lauder and Lauderdale.* Galashiels. 1904. |

| | |
|---|---|
| *Trans. Aberdeen Ecclesiol. Socy.* | *Transactions of the Aberdeen Ecclesiological Society.* |
| *Trans. BNC* | *Transactions of the Berwickshire Naturalists' Club.* |
| *Trans. Dumfries and Galloway Nat. Hist. and Antiq. Socy.* | *Transactions of the Dumfriesshire and Galloway Natural History and Antiquarian Society.* |
| *Trans. East Lothian Antiq. Socy.* | *Transactions of the East Lothian Antiquarian and Field Naturalists' Society.* |
| *Trans. Glasgow Archaeol. Socy.* | *Transactions of Glasgow Archaeological Society.* |
| *Trans. Hawick Archaeol. Socy.* | *Transactions of Hawick Archaeological Society.* |
| *Trans. RHS* | *Transactions of the Royal Historical Society.* |
| *Trans. SES* | *Transactions of the Scottish Ecclesiological Society.* |
| *Trans. Stirling Nat. Hist. and Archaeol. Socy.* | *Transactions of the Stirling Natural History and Archaeological Society.* |
| Tyninghame Letter Bk. | Tyninghame Letter Book; abstracts in H.M. General Register House, Edinburgh. |
| *Univ. Comm. Rep.* | *Universities Commission Report (St Andrews), 1837.* (Evidence . . . taken . . . by the Commissioners . . . for visiting the Universities of Scotland, III). |
| Vat. Reg. | Vatican Register. |
| Vat. Reg. Supp. | Vatican Register of Supplications. |
| Vat. Reg. Supp. (D) | Vatican Register of Supplications (notes supplied by Dr Annie I. Dunlop). |
| Wallace-James's Notebooks | MS. Notebooks of Dr J. G. Wallace-James (in H.M. General Register House Edinburgh). |
| Webster and Duncan, *Regality of Dunf. Court Bk.* | J. M. Webster, and A. A. M. Duncan, *Regality of Dunfermline Court Book, 1531–1538* (Carnegie Dunfermline Trust). 1935. |
| *Wemyss* | *Memorials of the Family of Wemyss of Wemyss.* Edinburgh, 1888. |
| Wyntoun, *Oryg. Cron.* | Wyntoun, *Orygynale Cronykil.* |
| *Yester Writs* | *Calendar of Writs preserved at Yester House* (Scottish Record Society). 1916–30. |

Fuller details of many of the above sources can be found in C. S. Terry, *A Catalogue of the Publications of Scottish Historical and Kindred Clubs and Societies and of the volumes relative to Scottish History issued by H.M. Stationery Office* (Glasgow, 1909) and C. Matheson's work under a similar title (Aberdeen, 1928).

(4) In the lists and notes, MS. sources appear in roman letters, printed sources in italics. Figures in brackets after a personal name (e.g. Spottiswoode) indicate a page reference to a work which is frequently cited (This is used only where a writer has one work to which repeated reference is made.)

## THE BENEDICTINE MONKS

Included in the list of the Benedictine houses is the priory of May, frequently regarded as Cluniac, as well as the more doubtful foundation of Rindalgros (Rhynd). These are taken as following the development of the abbey of Reading (of which they were dependencies), which, originating as in some sort a Cluniac foundation, appears from the thirteenth century onwards as a Benedictine house (*v.* Hurry, *Reading Abbey*, p. 65; *Medieval Religious Houses: England and Wales*, p. 74).

| Name | County | Rank | Minimum Income (1561) | Founder | Fd. | Date D. or Sec. | Dependent on |
|---|---|---|---|---|---|---|---|
| ABERDEEN | Aberdeen | Abbey | | | -1231 | ? | |
| ¶† COLDINGHAM | Berwick | Priory | £2600(?) | *V.* notes | -1139 | 1606 | Durham; later Dunfermline |

ABERDEEN. On 3 April 1231, Pope Gregory IX granted to the Benedictine abbot and convent "de Aberdono" leave to convert the church of "Culcdedono" to their own uses for maintaining hospitality (Theiner, *Vet. Mon.*, no. lxviii). "Aberdono" is taken by A. O. Anderson (*Early Sources*, ii. 479 *n.*) as Aberdeen. Again, two "monks of Aberdeen" appear as witnesses of an episcopal charter, 1239-42 (*REA*, i. 272). These references seem to point to the existence of a Benedictine community here in the thirteenth century, though its career must have been brief.

COLDINGHAM. Spottiswoode's statement (p. 465) that King Edgar rebuilt the Celtic monastery burned by the Danes, *c.* 870, cannot be substantiated. About 1098, Edgar granted Coldingham, with "all the lands which they have in Lothian", to the monks of Durham (*N. Durham*, App., no. ix). A church, not yet monastic, was built and Edgar was present at its dedication, *c.* 1100 (*Ibid.*, App., no. iv). But Edgar can hardly be regarded as the founder of the monastery. "Coldingham priory", it has been said, "cannot be assigned to a single founder though it grew from Edgar's gift" (Barrow, "Scottish Rulers and the Relig. Orders", *Trans. RHS*, iii (1953). 81). Lawrie, founding on the mention of a prior, 1147-50 (*Dunfermelyn*, no. 4), declares categorically that there was no priory at Coldingham before 1147 (*ESC*, p. 251). Yet a single monk of Coldingham appears, -1136 (*Ibid.*, no. clxxxiv); and in 1139 and *c.* 1141, charters of David I and Earl Henry, his son, refer to the monks serving the church of St Mary and St Cuthbert of Coldingham (*N. Durham*, App., nos. xx, ciii). *V.* Barrow, *loc. cit.* In January (?), 1215/16, the priory was plundered by King John's forces (*Chron. Mailros*, p. 122; *Chron. Lanercost*, p. 18). During the fourteenth and fifteenth centuries, a series of attempts were made to separate it from Durham and to annex it to Dunfermline abbey; and its history becomes extremely complicated. It is said that, "King Robert" granted the priory to Dunfermline (*Bk. of Pluscarden*, p. 149), a statement which must refer to Robert II; English monks were still present in it in 1323 (*Priory of Coldingham*, no. ix). In 1442, a papal letter refers to the assertion, made in a petition of Dunfermline, that about sixty years earlier, Robert II expelled the monks, deprived the chapter of Durham of the patronage of the priory and transferred it to Dunfermline, so that the presentation of the prior should belong to that abbey (*CPR*, ix. 298). It appears that, in 1378, that king issued a charter withdrawing Coldingham from Durham (Hay, Dipl. Vet. Coll., i. 380); there are complaints in this period of the intrusion of a monk of Dunfermline into the priory (*Priory of Coldingham*, no. xlviii ff.); and in 1379 (Swinton Chs., no. 3), 1380/1 (*Dunfermelyn*, no. 392) and later, the abbot of Dunfermline figures as superior of Coldingham, which is described as a dependency or cell of Dunfermline, in 1390 (*CPR*, Pet., i. 575) and in 1419 (*Supplics.*, p. 123). On the other hand, it is said, in 1380, that Robert II is willing conditionally to restore the priory to Durham (*CDS*, iv. no. 291); and the possessions of the priory were confirmed by Robert III's charter, 26 January 1391/2 (*RMS*, i. no. 839). In 1424, this house is described as destroyed by the English (although this could only have been partial), a precept being given by the Scottish king to the (English) prior for its repair (*RMS*, ii. no. 2; *APS*, ii. 25). The contention of rival claimants to the priory came to a head with the appearance of the formidable Patrick Hume, archdeacon of Teviotdale, representing the interest of a powerful Border family (*v. Priory of Coldingham*, no. clviii ff.), who obtained the priory *in commendam*, in 1461 (*CPR*, xi. 425–6), when, it is stated, the monks were only two in number (although the priory was founded for eighteen) and the Pope appointed mandatories to deprive the English prior and to separate the priory in perpetuity from Durham. On 6 April 1472, when the priory is called non-conventual, the Pope consented to its annexation to the collegiate church of St Mary (the Chapel Royal), St Andrews (*CPR*, xiii. 14, 16; *Scottish Benefices*, p. 170); and, on 3 April 1473, a bull of Pope Sixtus IV provided, at the king's request, for the allocation of the priory's revenues (in what proportion is not clear) to that church and for the erection of the priory (apparently from the residue of its property) into a collegiate church, to be called the Chapel Royal of Coldingham (Theiner, *Vet. Mon.*, no. dccclvii). In 1485, the Scottish parliament enacted that this proposition should be made anew at the Vatican (*APS*, ii. 171); and in 1487, Pope Innocent VIII issued a bull suppressing the priory and granting one-half of its revenues for the upkeep of the Chapel Royal and the other half for the erection of a collegiate church at Coldingham (*N. Durham*, App., no. ccccxlv). But the projected college was not established. About December 1509, in a letter to Pope Julius II, James IV states that while, one hundred and thirty years before, the Scottish council [*sic*] decided that the priory should be united to Dunfermline, it had latterly ceased to be under that abbey's control; and goes on to request that the priory, now vacant, should be annexed to Dunfermline, which is held *in commendam* by his son, the archbishop of St Andrews, or given to the archbishop for his lifetime (*Letters of James IV*, no. 287). The request was successful; Archbishop Alexander Stewart appears as commendator of Coldingham and Dunfermline (Herkless and Hannay, *Archbps. of St Ands.*, i. 245). In the sixteenth century, the priory suffered severely during invasions and was garrisoned both by Scottish and English forces. Coldingham was burned in October 1532, though the priory is not specifically mentioned (*L. & P. H. VIII*, v. no. 1460; *Diurnal*, p. 16). In November 1542, Coldingham, "with the abbey", appears in a list of places burned by Hertford's army (*L. & P. H. VIII*, xvii. nos. 1086, 1197); while, on 17 June 1544, the priory buildings, except the church, suffered a similar fate (*Ibid.*, xix[1], no. 762). They were being "held for the [English] king's use", November–February 1544/5 (*Ibid.*, xix[2]. no. 625; xx[1]. no. 129); and the Scots, in the same period, were besieging the garrisoned "abbey and steeple" (*RSS*, iii. nos. 990, 1013, etc.). The priory underwent further destruction in Hertford's invasion, August 1545 (*L. & P. H. VIII*, xx[2]. no. 494); and in October 1547, it was proposed to be razed (*Cal. Scottish Papers*, i. no. 57). On 4 February 1551/2, it is stated that "the priorie hes bene wastit be the weiris [wars] thir yeiris bigane, mekle of the place and kirk brint [burned] and distroyit" (*ALC, 1501–54*, p. 614). This priory along with the abbey of Jedburgh, was erected into a temporal lordship for Alexander, Lord Home, in parliament, 1606 (*APS*, iv. 360–1), and by charter, 1610 (*RMS*, vii. no. 290). In 1648, most of the remaining buildings were destroyed by Cromwell.

## THE BENEDICTINE MONKS

| Name | County | Rank | Minimum Income (1561) | Founder | Fd. | Date D. or Sec. | Dependent on |
|------|--------|------|------------------------|---------|-----|------------------|--------------|
| *‡ DUNFERMLINE | Fife | Priory | | Queen Margaret | c. 1070 | | |
| | | Abbey | £9630 | David I | 1128 | 1593 | |

DUNFERMLINE. The charter purporting to record the foundation of the abbey by Malcolm III, 1070–93 (*Dunfermelyn*, p. 417) is spurious (Lawrie, *ESC*, p. 237). According to Turgot, Queen Margaret, after her marriage to Malcolm, 1068–9, built a church here in honour of the Holy Trinity (A. O. Anderson, *Early Sources*, ii. 64–5), in which a priory was apparently established; a letter of Lanfranc, archbishop of Canterbury, announces the sending of Goldwin and other two brethren, at the queen's request (*Scalacronica*, p. 222) and a "monk and prior" of the church of Dunfermline is mentioned *s.a.* 1120 (Eadmer, *Hist. Nov. Angl.*, p. 279). In 1128, Geoffrey, prior of Canterbury, is said to have been sent, by desire of David I, to be the (first) abbot of Dunfermline (John of Worcester in A. O. Anderson, *Scottish Annals*, p. 166); and the statement is made (e.g. *Chron. Holyrood*, p. 121 n.) that King David, in that year, refounded the monastery as a Benedictine abbey. But is it necessary to assume a refoundation? The indications are that the original foundation was for Benedictine monks. If this was a priory, did it not simply become an abbey in or *c.* 1128? The source of the idea of refoundation is evidently the assertion of the *Scotichronicon* (lib. v, cap. xlviii (i. 301)) that David I brought thirteen monks as a convent from Canterbury. But King David's charter, *c.* 1128, if we accept it as genuine, grants anew to the church of Dunfermline lands bestowed by his parents [Malcolm III and Margaret] (*Dunfermelyn*, no. 1); and the *Scotichronicon* (lib. v, cap. xliv (i. 297)) speaks of that church as "first founded by [King David's] father and mother, augmented in possessions and buildings by his brother [Alexander I], while he himself enriched it, as now built, with more abundant gifts and honours". These references, with the dedication to the Holy Trinity, point to the continuity of the original foundation. The abbey church was dedicated in 1150 (*Chron. Holyrood*, p. 121). On 24 April 1245, Pope Innocent IV granted the abbot the use of the mitre (Theiner, *Vet. Mon.*, no. cxiii). The abbey, except for the church, was largely destroyed by Edward I's forces in 1303 (Matthew of Westminster, *Flores Historiarum*, p. 446). Part of the buildings were demolished by the Reforming lords, 26 March 1560 (Pitscottie, *Cronicles*, ii. 168). The lordship of Dunfermline, with its lands, etc., north of the Forth, was granted to Queen Anne, consort of James VI, 24 November 1589 (*APS*, iv. 24). From *c.* 1587, other portions of the abbey lands were separately erected: the lordship of Musselburghshire for Sir John Maitland, afterwards Lord Thirlestane (1587) (*Ibid.*, iii. 628–9); the barony of Burntisland for Sir Robert Melville (ratified, 1592) (*Ibid.*, iii. 601); the barony of Newburn for Andrew Wood of Largo (ratified 1592) (*Ibid.*, iii. 613); all of which were expressly excepted when the abbey was annexed to the Crown in 1593 (*Ibid.*, iv. 23). Alexander Seton, its hereditary bailie on the south side of the Forth (*Ibid.*, iv. 349–52), was created earl of Dunfermline, 4 March 1605 (*RMS*, vi. no. 1565).

Dependencies: Urquhart; Pluscarden (15–16 cs.); Coldingham (14–15 cs.).

## THE BENEDICTINE MONKS

| Name | County | Rank | Minimum Income (1561) | Founder | Fd. | Date D. or Sec. | Depen- dent on |
|---|---|---|---|---|---|---|---|
| ¶‡ Iona | Argyll | Abbey | ? | Reginald, son of Somerled, lord of the Isles | −1203 | 1587/8 (?) | |

Iona. Formerly a Celtic monastery. *V.* under Celtic Foundations. This house was founded by Reginald, son of Somerled, lord of the Isles (1164–1207) for black monks. (Bk. of Clanranald cited Skene, "Notes on the Hist. of the Ruins of Iona", *PSAS*, x (1875), 204; *Highland Papers*, i. 82). The foundation took place previous to 9 December 1203, when Pope Innocent III directed a letter to the abbot and convent taking the monastery under his protection and confirming its possessions (*Diplomatarium Norvegicum*, vii. 4–5, no. 4, cited A. O. Anderson, *Early Sources*, ii. 361 *n*). Spottiswoode (p. 414) includes Iona (Icolm-kill) under Cluniac houses; and it is described as "of the Cluniac order" in a charter, 8 August 1532 (*Thanes of Cawdor*, p. 156). But the papal letter of 1203 and other Vatican records, as well as the *Scotichronicon* (lib. ii, cap. x (i. 45) ) speak of it as Benedictine. Skene's attempt to demonstrate that it belonged to the order of Tiron (*PSAS*, x. 206–7) is uncon-vincing. On 22 April 1247, the Pope, on account of the distance of the abbey from Norway, gave the abbot the use of the mitre and ring and other episcopal privileges (*Dipl. Norveg.*, vii. 16, cited A. O. Anderson, *Early Sources*, ii. 361 *n*) and, on the same date, declared that the abbot and convent of Iona, in the diocese of Sodor, Norway, were not to be summoned to the general chapter of the Benedictines in Scotland (*CPR, Letters*, i. 231). Although the abbey was situated in the diocese of Sodor, we find the bishop of Dunkeld acting as its ordinary, e.g. in 1230, when that bishop confirmed the election of Finlay as its abbot (*Extracta*, p. 147) and in 1431, when the abbot made manual obedience to the bishop of that see (*Ibid.*, p. 233). In supplications granted 3, 5 and 17 December 1421, the abbey is described as impoverished and its buildings destroyed (*Highland Papers*, iv. 168–75). A letter to the Pope "for the erection of the Abbacy of Colmkyll in the bishoppis sete of the Ilis, quhil his principall kirk in the Ile of Man be recoverit fra Inglismen" is recorded 1 April 1498, the supplicant being the earl of Argyll (*RSS*, i. no. 184); and, on 15 June 1499, the Pope granted the abbey *in commendam* to the bishop of Sodor (*Highland Papers*, iv. 185). The abbey church, accordingly, came to serve as the cathedral of the diocese of the Isles; and the abbey became permanently attached to the bishopric. Thus, on 24 May 1530, Ferquhard, bishop of Sodor, has a precept of admission to the temporality of the bishop-ric and to the abbacy of Colmkill annexed to it (*RSS*, ii. no. 685). Besides the bishop-commendator, the prior and six monks attest a charter, 8 August 1532 (*Thanes of Cawdor*, p. 158). In 1551, the monastery had been occupied by master Patrick McLean and his brother, Hector McLean of Duart (later to obtain possession of the abbey) (*ALC, 1501-54*, pp. 610, 614). Hay (Scotia Sacra, p. 487) declares that in 1560 the monastery was destroyed and the monks driven away. This statement cannot be verified, but if destruction took place, it could only have been partial. On 6 June 1581, James VI constituted Alex-ander Campbell for his lifetime abbot and commendator of Icolmkill, granting him both the spirituality and the temporality, which the bishop had resigned (*RMS*, v. no. 208); and on 19 March 1587/8, the island, with the houses and other property formerly belonging to the monastery, was bestowed on Hector McLean, son of Lachlan McLean of Duart (*Ibid.*, v. no. 1491). The abbey was eventually annexed to the bishopric of the Isles, in 1615 (*APS*, iv. 654).

## THE BENEDICTINE MONKS

| Name | County | Rank | Minimum Income (1561) | Founder | Fd. | Date D. or Sec. | Dependent on |
|------|--------|------|------------------------|---------|-----|-----------------|--------------|
| MAY | Fife | Priory | *V.* Pittenweem | David I | −1153 | *V.* notes | Reading |

MAY. The history of this house abounds in problems and the account of the priory given by Stuart in *Records of the Priory of the Isle of May* is in many respects unsatisfactory. The following notes owe much to the help of Mr A. A. M. Duncan, who has made a special study of May records and given access to his transcripts and notes. It has generally been assumed, in accordance with statements made in records of 1292–3, that the priory was founded by David I, who is said to have granted it to Reading abbey for nine monks of that house (*May*, lxxxvi–lxxxviii). But the date of the foundation and that of the grant to Reading are alike difficult to ascertain. A prior of May is mentioned in one of King David's charters dated ?1144–?1147, by A. O. Anderson (*Early Sources* ii, 194); 1142–53, by Mr Duncan. The grant of the priory to Reading is assigned by Lawrie to a date probably after 1135, when Henry I, King David's brother-in-law, was buried at Reading (*ESC*, p. 387). The Isle of May, described as the gift of David I, was confirmed to Reading by Pope Alexander III (1159–81) (BM. Egerton MS., 67v–68r, 70v). In a charter of William the Lion, −1219, it is stated that the king confirms the priory's possessions "so that a convent of thirteen monks of the Cluniac order may be maintained there" (*May*, no. 12). It is described as Benedictine, 17 January 1257/8 (*CPR*, Letters, i. 340) and as Cluniac, on the following 25 February (*Ibid.*, i. 344). Cf. Reading, occasionally mentioned as Cluniac after it became specifically Benedictine (Hurry, *Reading Abbey*, p. 65). From *c.* 1270, the priory's history presents a series of complications and discrepancies. According to the *Scotichronicon* (lib. x, cap. xxvi (ii. 110–11) ), King Alexander III, in 1269, after a monk of Reading had been admitted as prior, was alarmed at the danger of English espionage and bought back the island, its purchase price (seven hundred marks) being paid by William Wishart, bishop of St Andrews, who conferred it upon St Andrews priory. But this account conflicts with record evidence. A grant by Reading to the countess of Warwick of ten marks yearly from the priory of May, 25 December 1284 (Hurry, *op. cit.*, p. 180) implies that at this date the priory was still in Reading's possession. According to the petition of the abbot of Reading to the Scottish king [John Balliol] and parliament in 1292–3, the priory of May was alienated by abbot Robert de Burghgate, who sold it to William [Fraser], bishop of St. Andrews, for £1,000. This transaction, it is stated, the bishop, as a guardian of the realm of Scotland (which was without a king) sworn to maintain the royal patrimony, had no right to carry through; while, in consequence of it, de Burghgate, who had acted without the assent of the majority of his convent, was deposed. The bishop is said to have paid only two hundred and fourteen marks of the purchase price and the procurators of Reading sought the arrears of the fruits for the four years previous to Palm Sunday (22 March 1292/3) (*May*, lxxxvi–lxxxvii). (It may be noted that they were asked if they were prepared to return to the bishop of St Andrews the sum of 1100 marks which he had paid to Reading (*Ibid.*, lxxxvi).) The sale of the priory to the bishop must have taken place between 2 April 1286, when Fraser was appointed a guardian, and −October 1288 (according to Mr Duncan's emendation of the date in *CDS*), when Edward I summoned Ralph de Broughton, *custos* of the monastery of Reading, to answer for connivance at the alienation of the priory of May from that abbey (*CDS*, iv. no. 1765) (Mr Duncan shows that de Broughton was appointed *custos* 16 March 1286/7, on the suspension of de Burghgate (BM. Harleian MS., 1708 (Chartulary of Reading) 232v) ). It is further stated that the abbot of Reading enfeoffed William Fresel [Fraser], bishop of St Andrews (†1297) in the priory of Pittenweem (which may be equivalent to May) and that Fraser in turn enfeoffed in it the church (i.e. the priory) of St Andrews (*Mem. de Parl.*, no. 317). From a writ of 24 March 1305/6, it appears that the Isle of May and its manor of Pittenweem were restored to Reading after the rebellion of John Balliol (1296) and that May was held as a cell of that abbey until the monks were ejected by Wallace (1297 or 1298) (*Cal. Close Rolls*, 1302–7, p. 249). But although, according to the same writ, Edward I ordered Reading to have seisin of May and Pittenweem "as before the commencement of the last war", we find that king writing to Aymer de Valence, 2 September 1306, regarding a complaint of the abbot of Reading that the bishop and prior of St Andrews had invaded the Isle of May and manor of Pittenweem, seized and taken away the monks' goods and beaten, wounded and ill-treated their men there (PRO. Ancient Corresp., xlvii/89). It is not possible to say precisely when St Andrews priory entered into possession of May or when the priory of May was finally transferred to Pittenweem. A petition, dated 1306–7 in *CDS*, is directed to Edward I by Thomas de Houburn, canon of St Andrews and liegeman of the English king, who is described as having been ousted by the Scots from his priory of Pittenweem (*CDS*, ii. no. 1964), but its significance is not clear; it may have been that St Andrews had taken possession of May and/or Pittenweem with the consent of Edward I, who had then intruded an English prior. There is a mention of a prior of May, 3 August 1313 (*Scon*, no. 148). Eventually, on 1 July 1318, a specific indication is given that the connection with Reading was at an end; for on that date, William de Lamberton, bishop of St Andrews, in virtue of the transference to the monastery of St Andrews of "all right of the monastery of Reading in England which it had in the priory of May and Pittenweem", granted to St Andrews priory the annual pension of sixteen marks formerly paid by May to Reading (*May*, xci–xcii). *V.* further Pittenweem under the Augustinian Canons. On 30 January 1549/50, the prior of Pittenweem granted a lease of the Isle of May, which is said to be now lying waste (*Ibid.*, xcvii).

## THE BENEDICTINE MONKS

| Name | County | Rank | Minimum Income (1561) | Founder | Fd. | Date D. or Sec. | Dependent on |
|---|---|---|---|---|---|---|---|
| ‡§ PLUSCARDEN | Moray | Priory | £3570 | | *V.* notes | 1587 | Dunfermline |
| RINDALGROS (RHYND) | Perth | ? | | | 1147–53(?) −1231 | | Reading *v.* notes |
| URQUHART | Moray | Priory | | David I | *c.* 1136 | 1453/4 (united to Pluscarden) | Dunfermline |

PLUSCARDEN. For the earlier history of this house *v.* under the Valliscaulian Monks. It was erected into a free barony for Alexander Seton, in parliament, 1587 (*APS*, iii. 485).

RINDALGROS or RINDELGROS (RHYND). David I granted Rindalgros (i.e. the lands) to Reading abbey, 1143–7, with the proviso that if the augmentation of his gift should enable a monastery to be maintained, that abbey should send a convent there (*May*, no. 1; *CDS*, ii. no. 1985 (1) ). Shortly after, i.e. 1147–53, the same king ordered his men of the sheriffdom of Perth to pay their teinds of grain and cheese, etc., to "the monks of Rindelgros" (*May*, no. 7; *CDS*, ii. no. 1985 (7) ); and a charter of Malcolm IV, 1153–62, bestows upon the monks of "Rindelcros" all the teind belonging to the church of that vill (*May*, no. 8; *CDS*, ii. no. 1985 (8) ). These statements have been taken to indicate that there was a religious house at this site. Lawrie, however, is probably right in his opinion that "no monastery was built at Rindalgros" (*ESC*, p. 390); and if monks were settled here, their stay must have been brief. In 1231, the monks of May appear as holding the parish church of Rhynd (*May*, no. 39); and the writ of 1307 which exemplifies a number of May charters describes Rindalgros as "a place of the . . . cell of May" (*Ibid.*, no. 7). There is, in fact, no further mention of a monastery.

URQUHART. David I, who makes a grant to the monks here, *c.* 1136 (*Dunfermelyn*, no. 34), is usually regarded as the founder of this priory. It appears as a dependency of Dunfermline abbey in King David's further charter of endowment, 1150–3 (*Ibid.*, no. 33; *REM*, no. 254). Spottiswoode (p. 404) dates this charter 1124, which is much too early. The Pope united this house to Pluscarden priory (*q.v.*), 12 March 1453/4 (*CPR*, x. 253–4).

### UNCERTAIN FOUNDATION

EYNHALLOW. For a discussion of the history of this Orcadian foundation *v. Hist. Mon. Comm. Rep.* (*Orkney & Shetland*), ii. 232–4, which gives reasons for abandoning the view that this was a Cistercian house and which notes the suggestion of Professor Johan Meyer that it was probably a Benedictine foundation from *c.* 1100. A "Description of Orkney" (*Macfarlane's Geog. Collns.*, iii. 306), said to be dated 1529, includes Eynhallow, but makes no mention of a monastery there. This may indicate that the monastery was extinct well before the sixteenth century; but nothing is known with certainty of its career.

### SUPPOSED FOUNDATION

*Kilconquhar.* Spottiswoode, *Hist. of the Ch. of Scotland* (1677 ed.), App., 20, gives under Benedictines: "the Monastery of Kilconquhar in Galloway, founded by Ethred (or rather Fergus), Lord of Galloway". There is no such place in Galloway and there was no such monastery. *V.* under Nunneries Kilconquhar in Fife, which is given erroneously as a nunnery.

## THE CLUNIAC MONKS

A detailed study of the Scottish Cluniac foundations is a *desideratum*. The two Scottish houses which may be properly regarded as of that order were abbeys, one attaining that status less than fifty years after its foundation and the other having it from the outset. It should be noted that the priory of the Isle of May, a dependency of the abbey of Reading and occasionally described as Cluniac, is listed among the Benedictine houses, for reasons which are given in that section.

| Name | County | Rank | Minimum Income (1561) | Founder | Date Fd. | Sec. | Dependent on |
|------|--------|------|------------------------|---------|----------|------|--------------|
| * CROSSRAGUEL | Ayr | Oratory | | Duncan of Carrick (later earl of Carrick) | −1214−16 | | |
| | | Abbey | £1860 | | −1286 | 1617 | Paisley |

CROSSRAGUEL. The date of foundation of this house cannot be fixed with precision and the circumstances which led up to that foundation are to some extent involved and obscure. These facts, however, can hardly be said to justify the reckless statements made by certain writers. Thus, it is asserted by Spottiswoode (pp. 413–4) that the abbey "was founded by Duncan, son of Gilbert earl of Carrick, in the year 1244, as we are informed by the chartulary of Paisley". Again, the editor of that chartulary declares: "It appears that Duncan, earl of Carric . . . founded and endowed the house of Crosraguel for monks of Paisley, and so richly that the new abbey aspired immediately to independence, while the mother house endeavoured to keep it as a cell or oratorium to be enjoyed by brethren of their convent and under their immediate control . . ." (*Passelet*, xviii). Lawrie is no less unsatisfactory; "[Duncan] granted to Paisley abbey Crossraguel . . . but because the abbot and monks of Paisley did not build a monastery, Duncan himself founded the abbey of Crossraguel and brought Cluniac monks there, to whom he gave the lands previously given to Paisley" (*Annals*, p. 327). Duncan, son of Gilbert, was made earl of Carrick, 1214–16 (A. O. Anderson, *Early Sources*, p. 331 *n*). Before that date, he had granted to the monks of Paisley "Crosragmol" (Crossraguel) and "Suthblan" a donation confirmed to Paisley abbey by Pope Honorius III, 23 January 1226/7 (*CPR*, Letters, i. 107) (1225, the date given for this bull in *Crosraguel* (i. no. 1) is erroneous), and, with three churches in Ayrshire given by Duncan, by King Alexander II, 25 August 1236 (*Crosraguel*, i. no. 2). In a later record (a bull of Pope Clement IV), it is said that after Duncan's endowment had been made, an oratory was built "in the said possessions" and Paisley had served it by some of its monks. The donor afterwards asserted that his benefaction had been given on condition that Paisley built a monastery on the lands and the consequent dispute between him and that abbey was remitted to the bishop of Glasgow (*Ibid.*, no. 4), whose judgment is recorded in a charter of 18 July 1244. This is to the effect that a "religious house of monks of the order of Paisley" shall be built at Crossraguel, the new house to be exempt from the jurisdiction of Paisley "save only in recognition of the order"; the abbot of Paisley will visit it yearly; the property in Carrick will be given up to the house of Crossraguel by Paisley, to which an annual tribute of ten marks will be paid (*Ibid.*, i. no. 3). After a lapse of about twenty years, Paisley had complained to the Pope against the bishop's ordinance as "redounding to its enormous hurt"; and on 11 June 1265 and 6 February 1265/6, Pope Clement VI appointed mandatories to investigate the case (*Ibid.*, i. no. 4), with what result is not known. Whether the abbey was in being by this date cannot be said with certainty. But some stage in its erection may have provided the occasion for the complaint to the Pope. The first abbot on record attests a charter, *c.* 1286 (*Ibid.*, i. no. 7). A visitation of the abbey, probably in 1405, shows that there were then ten monks (*Ibid.*, i. no. 23). Eight monks are named along with the abbot, in 1548 and 1552 (*Ibid.*, i. nos. 64, 66); and, in 1560, there were nine, besides the commendator and subprior (*Ibid.*, i. no. 68). Part of the abbey was "cast down" by Reformers, in 1561 (Knox, *History*, ii. 168). It was annexed to the bishopric of Dunblane in 1617 (*APS*, iv. 553).

Main 15 under Benedictine Houses.

## THE CLUNIAC MONKS

| Name | County | Rank | Minimum Income (1561) | Founder | Date Fd. | Date Sec. | Dependent on |
|------|--------|------|-----------------------|---------|---------|---------|--------------|
| ‡§ PAISLEY | Renfrew | Priory | | Walter, son of Alan, steward of Scotland | *c.* 1163 (Renfrew) –1165 (Paisley) | | (Wenlock) |
| | | Abbey | £6100 | | 1219 | 1587 | |

PAISLEY. A charter of Walter, son of Alan, steward of Scotland, 1161–4 (or, according to A. O. Anderson (*Early Sources*, ii. 251 *n*), probably 1163), declares his intention of founding within his land of Paisley a house of Cluniac monks, adding that he has available thirteen monks from Wenlock, one of whom will be chosen as prior (*Passelet*, pp. 1–2). According to a charter of Malcolm IV (†1165), the original settlement of the monks was at the church of St Mary and St James on the "inch" beside Renfrew (*Ibid.*, p. 249); and a charter of the founder, which is not earlier in date than 1165, refers to the "lands which the monks first inhabited" (*Ibid.*, p. 6). Under the year 1169, the Chronicle of Melrose has the statement: "Humbold the prior of Wenlock brought the convent to Paisley which is beside Renfrew" (*Chron. Mailros*, p. 81), and the *Scotichronicon* makes a similar assertion, adding that Walter the steward had founded the monastery at Paisley "a short time before" (lib. viii, cap. xiii (i. 460)). It is generally assumed that, at an early stage of its existence, the community was transferred from Renfrew to Paisley; but whether the Melrose chronicler's statement is intended to refer to this or whether it purports to indicate the first arrival of the monks (in which case the date is too late) it is impossible to say. On 15 July 1219, Pope Honorius III gave permission to the prior and convent to elect an abbot (*Passelet*, pp. 9–10), and the first abbot is mentioned, 3 May 1220 (*Ibid.*, p. 325). It is evident that the letter of the abbot and convent of Paisley to the abbey of Cluny regarding the appointment of an abbot (*Cluny*, vi. no. 4934) belongs to about this date rather than *c.* 1250, as given in *Cluny*. The relations of Paisley with Cluny were at first somewhat indeterminate. But, in March 1240/1 and later, the bishop of Glasgow took steps to regularize their relationship (*Ibid.*, vi. no. 4789; *Passelet*, pp. 15 ff). (The development of Paisley's relations with Cluny is too complex a topic to enter upon here; but it should be noted that the dating of some of the records of the period, both in *Passelet* and *Cluny*, is obviously wrong.) The bishop's intervention followed the attempt of Walter (II) the steward and others, sometime between 1232 and 1241, to transform Paisley into a Cistercian house (*Cluny*, vi. no. 4935). (A statute of the Cistercian general chapter of 1240 seems to suggest that there was a proposal to establish Cistercian nuns at Paisley. In terms of this enactment, the inspection of "the abbey of nuns which is called Passelet" is committed to the abbots of Dundrennan and Culross, who are personally to visit the site and the house is to be a daughter of "Nenbotis" (? Neubotle, i.e. Newbattle) (Canivez, *Statuta*, ii. 226)). The fixed number of monks is said to have been twenty-five (Duckett, *Visitn. of English Cluniac Foundns.*, p. 37). On 10 August 1395, the abbot was granted the mitre (*Passelet*, p. 429). In 1307, this house was burned by the English (*Scotich.*, lib. xii, cap. xiv (ii. 167)). It was again burned by Reformers in 1561 (Knox, *History*, ii. 167). On 29 July 1587 and 22 March 1591/2, it was erected into a temporal lordship for Lord Claud Hamilton (*RMS*, v. nos. 1320, 2070).

### SUPPOSED FOUNDATION

*Fail.* Called by Spottiswoode (p. 413) "Feale" and described by him as a cell or priory depending upon Paisley. Its alleged existence is due to the supposition (unfounded) that the Gilbertine house of Dalmulin (*q.v.*) became a dependency of Paisley and also to confusion with the Trinitarian house of Fail.

## MONKS OF THE ORDER OF TIRON

| Name | County | Rank | Minimum Income (1561) | Founder | Fd. | Date D. or Sec. | Dependent on |
|---|---|---|---|---|---|---|---|
| * ARBROATH | Angus | Abbey | £10924 | William the Lion | 1178 | 1606 | |
| FYVIE | Aberdeen | Priory | | Reginald le Chen | 1285 | 1508(?) | Arbroath abbey |

ARBROATH. The founder was William the Lion but his earliest extant charter to Arbroath abbey, in which he describes himself as having founded it, is to be dated 1211-14 (*Aberbrothoc*, i. no. 1). *Scotichronicon* (lib. viii, cap. xxv (i. 475) ) gives the date of foundation as 1178 and this is borne out by a charter of the abbot and convent of Kelso quitclaiming in that year the abbot-elect of Arbroath from subjection and obedience, indicating that monks had been provided from Kelso "for the building of that house" [Arbroath] and having King William, "who has founded that church in honour of St Thomas [i.e. Becket]" as a witness (*Aberbrothoc*, i. no. 2). The dedication of the church took place 8 May 1233 (*Chron. Mailros*, p. 143). On 11 May 1350, the church is said to have been damaged by assaults from English ships (*Aberbrothoc*, ii. no. 23); and on 11 February 1378/9, the church and monastery are stated to have suffered much havoc from English attacks (*Ibid.*, ii. no. 36). The church, in 1380, was ignited by lightning and during its repair the monks were temporarily removed to other places (*Extracta*, p. 194; *Supplics.*, p. 92 (*anno* 1419) ). On 26 June 1396 the abbot was given the mitre (Lawrie, *Annals*, p. 100). There were at least seventeen monks here besides the abbot and subprior in 1527 (*Laing Chs.*, no. 360), while the subprior and twenty monks attest a charter in 1546 (*REG*, ii. no. 508). We find conflicting accounts of the fate of the abbey in the sixteenth century. Thus, it is said to have been saved by Lord Ogilvy from destruction by Reformers in 1543 (*Diurnal*, p. 29). On the other hand, a letter of 5 September 1543 speaks of news that Ogilvy had sacked the abbey (*Hamilton Papers*, ii. no. 14). But the present state of the buildings shows that no serious damage was done to them. Held by a series of commendators from the end of the fifteenth century, the abbey was erected into a temporal lordship for the marquis of Hamilton, in parliament, 1606 (*APS*, iv. 321-3) and by charter, 1608 (*RMS*, vi. no. 2075).
Dependency: Fyvie.

FYVIE. Spottiswoode (p. 410) declares that this cell or priory of Arbroath was "founded with a parish church in honour of the Virgin Mary by Fergus, earl of Buchan, in 1179". (This somewhat clumsy statement seems to refer to the dedication of the *priory* church—it was dedicated to St Mary and All Saints (*Aberbrothoc*, i. no. [235]); the parish church, granted to Arbroath by William the Lion (*Ibid.*, i. no. 28), was dedicated to St Peter (*Ibid.*, i. no. [235]).) The foundation, however, took place in or somewhat before 1285. On 16 October of that year, Reginald le Chen [Cheyne] granted to Arbroath and the monks of that monastery "dwelling in the religious house built in the land of Ardlogy near the church . . . of Fyvie" the land of Ardlogy and Lethendy (*Ibid.*, i. no. [234]); and the confirmation charter of Henry, bishop of Aberdeen, 18 October 1285, specifically mentions Reginald as founder (*Ibid.*, i. no. [235]). The same charter grants the vicarage of Fyvie to the priory, the parish to be served by a chaplain. The head of this small house is frequently called "custos" and there are references to its "chapel" in 1325 and 1450 (*Ibid.*, i. no. 354; ii. no. 92). In 1325, the abbot of Arbroath instructed the "custos" to secure the observance of monastic discipline (*Ibid.*, i. no. 354); but a papal letter of 23 March 1450/1 describes this house as non-conventual, valued at no more than £12, while the prior was also parochial vicar (*CPR*, x. 578-9). On 21 August 1459, Pope Pius II, on the petition of the abbot and convent of Arbroath, united the priory to that abbey (*Ibid.*, xi. 405-6), but the union apparently did not take effect until 28 September 1508, after Pope Julius II had granted it to Arbroath in perpetuity and the last prior, who seems to have been a monk both of and at Arbroath, had resigned; the abbot on that date appointed a procurator to take possession of it on his behalf (*Aberbrothoc*, ii. no. 462). The priory lands were being leased in the latter half of the fifteenth century (*Ibid.*, ii. nos. 143, 144 (*anno* 1462), 368 (*anno* 1496/7) ). About 1546, the priory appears among the benefices taxed for the College of Justice; its contribution is assessed at £2 16s. (*Antiqs. Aberd. and Banff*, ii, 424 *n*). But this points merely to the survival of its revenues. There is little doubt that it was otherwise extinct.

## MONKS OF THE ORDER OF TIRON

| Name | County | Rank | Minimum Income (1561) | Founder | Fd. | Date D. or Sec. | Dependent on |
|---|---|---|---|---|---|---|---|
| * KELSO | Roxburgh | Abbey | £4830 (?) (with Lesmahagow) | Earl David (David I) | *c.* 1113 (at Selkirk) 1128 (at Kelso) | 1607 | |
| ¶‡ KILWINNING | Ayr | Abbey | £2560 | Hugh de Moreville | –1162 | 1592 | |
| LESMAHAGOW | Lanark | Priory | *V.* Kelso | David I | 1144 | 1607 | Kelso abbey |

KELSO. Founded first at Selkirk (*q.v.*) by Earl David (later David I). The *Scotichronicon* declares that "Herbert was made the third abbot of Selkirk and first of Kelso, because the monastery was transferred thither by King David I in the year of the Lord 1126 and two years after the transference of the community, he founded the church of Kelso"; and, at another point, the same chronicle states that in 1128 King David founded the monastery of Kelso (*op. cit.*, lib. v, capp. xxxvi, xliii (i. 286, 296)). Again, the church of Kelso is said to have been founded 3 May 1128 (*Chron. Mailros*, p. 69). Lawrie is of opinion that Abbot Herbert "persuaded the king to remove the monks to Kelso", *c.* 1128 (*ESC*, p. 275). The so-called foundation charter (*Calchou*, no. 2) is regarded by Lawrie as spurious (*ESC*, p. 411). Spottiswoode (p. 405) declares that the abbey was moved to Roxburgh and then to Kelso; but this is due to the misinterpretation of a phrase in the alleged foundation charter: "Because there was not a suitable site for the abbey at Roxburgh, I have transferred [the aforesaid monastery] to the church of the Blessed Virgin which is situated . . . in the place which is called Calkou". For some reason, however, Herbert, the first abbot, is designated, 1128–47, "abbot of Roxburgh" (*v. ESC, passim*); Arnold, his successor, appears as abbot of Kelso. In 1165, the abbot was granted the mitre, the first abbot of a Scottish house to be thus privileged (*Chron. Mailros*, p. 80; Lawrie, *Annals*, p. 100). In Edward I's parliament of 28 March 1305, the abbot sought remedy for the burning of the abbey's charters and muniments in the war (*Mem. de Parl.*, 188, no. 307); and the monastery is said, *c.* 1316, to have suffered so much spoliation and destruction during war that the monks were reduced to begging at other houses for food and clothing (*Calchou*, no. 309). Again, a supplication of 1420 refers to its precarious situation in the Borders, whence it is often severely damaged by hostile incursions (*Supplics.*, p. 177). The gatehouse tower was destroyed by Dacre, in 1523 (*L. & P. H. VIII*, iii[2]. nos. 3098, 3135). On 26 October 1542, the abbey was burned by the English (*Hamilton Papers*, i. 292; *L. & P. H. VIII*. xvii. nos. 996, 998); and again (probably) in 1544 (*L. & P. H. VIII*, xix[2]. no. 33) and in September 1545 (*Ibid.*, xx[2]. no. 456). The abbey was erected into a temporal lordship for Robert, earl of Roxburgh, 1607 (*APS*, iv. 399–400). This house is erroneously called Cistercian in a papal letter of 10 October 1331 (*CPR*, ii. 366) and in NLS. MS. 22.1.14, 152; and Premonstratensian in the list given *Scotichronicon*, ii. 538.

Dependency: Lesmahagow. *V.* Merchingley, *infra*.

KILWINNING. Founded by Hugh de Moreville (†1162). Spottiswoode (p. 407) gives the date of foundation as 1140, which is probably too early. Little is known of this abbey's history. The abbot was granted the mitre, 20 February 1409 (Lawrie, *Annals*, p. 100). In 1561 the abbey was "cast down" by Reformers (Knox, *History*, ii. 168). Its temporalities were erected into a free barony in favour of William Melville, 1592 (*RMS*, v. no. 2085; *APS*, iii. 599).

LESMAHAGOW. In 1144 David I granted the church and lands of Lesmahagow to Kelso abbey so that a prior and monks might be instituted in that church (*Calchou*, no. 8). The priory is said to have been burned in 1335 by troops under John of Eltham, brother of Edward III (Wyntoun, *Oryg. Cron.*, viii, 30 cited *OPS*, i. 111; *Scotich.*, lib. xiii, cap. xxxviii (ii, 323)). Five monks are mentioned in 1556 (*Calchou*, pp. 479–80). Spottiswoode (p. 407) appears to be the sole source of the statement that the priory was destroyed by Reformers in 1560. It was included in the erection of Kelso abbey for Robert, earl of Roxburgh, in 1607, but transferred to the marquis of Hamilton in 1623 (*PCR*, 2nd Ser., i. cxlv).

## MONKS OF THE ORDER OF TIRON

| Name | County | Rank | Minimum Income (1561) | Founder | Date Fd. D. or Sec. | | Dependent on |
|------|--------|------|----------|---------|------|------|------|
| ¶§ LINDORES | Fife | Abbey | £4790 | David, earl of Huntingdon | 1191 | 1600 | |
| SELKIRK | Selkirk | Abbey | | Earl David | c. 1113 | | (removed to Kelso, c. 1128) |

LINDORES. Founded by David, earl of Huntingdon. Dowden gives reasons for assigning the foundation to 1191 (*Lindores*, p. 302). The *Scotichronicon* (lib. viii, cap. xxv (i. 475)) assigns the foundation to 1178, but this may be regarded as too early. The same chronicle declares that at the time of the first abbot's death, i.e. in 1219, there were twenty-six monks in the monastery (*Ibid.*, lib. ix, cap. xxvii (ii. 34)). The abbot was granted the mitre, 19 September 1395 (Lawrie, *Annals*, p. 100). In 1543, Reformers sacked the abbey and expelled the monks (*Hamilton Papers*, ii. 15); and again in 1559, the altars were overthrown by Reformers, who burned statues, books and vestments (Lesley, *History*, p. 273; Knox, *History*, vi. 26). The abbey was erected into a temporal lordship for Patrick Leslie, created Lord Lindores, by charter 1600 (*RMS*, vi. no. 1032) and in parliament, 1606 (*APS*, iv. 355–6).

SELKIRK. Founded by Earl David (later David I). According to Symeon of Durham (*Hist. Regum*, ii. 247), the monks of Tiron came to Selkirk in 1113 and remained there for fifteen years, i.e. till 1128. A marginal note in the Chronicle of Melrose (A. O. Anderson, *Early Sources*, ii. 143), under the year 1109, states: "And Ralph sent from Tiron became first abbot of Selkirk"; and the coming of the monks to Selkirk is assigned to that year in the *Scotichronicon* (lib. v, cap. xxxvi (i. 286)). *V.* Barrow, "Scottish Rulers and the Religious Orders", *Trans. RHS*, 5th Ser., iii (1953), 87. The so-called foundation charter (*Calchou*, no. 1, on which *v.* Lawrie, *ESC*, p. 275) must be dated 1119–20. The monks removed to Kelso (*q.v.*) in or about 1128.

### SUPPOSED FOUNDATIONS

*Dull.* It is suggested by certain writers (e.g. Gordon, *Monasticon*, p. 438; MacEwen, *Hist of the Ch. in Scotland*, i. 197) that there was here a house of monks of the order of Tiron. This appears entirely erroneous. If we may judge from the mention of an abthane of Dull (*RPSA*, p. 296), this may have been at one time the site of a Celtic community. But there was no medieval monastery here. The parish church was granted to St Andrews priory by Malcolm, earl of Athole (*Ibid.*, p. 243).

*Fintray.* Under the "antiquities" of this parish (*NSA*, xii. 167–8), there is a reference to the "foundations of some buildings, supposed to have belonged to the Abbacy of Lindores . . . a branch of which is said to have stood where the principal burying ground of this parish now is. . . . The buildings (denominated the Northern Abbey) are supposed to have been erected about the year 1386, from a stone bearing that date . . . in the dike of the burying ground, which had probably been composed of fragments of the demolished abbey, whereof no vestige now remains above the surface of the ground." This abbey is entirely imaginary. The lands of Fintray were granted to Lindores abbey by its founder, David, earl of Huntingdon, 1198–9 (*Lindores*, no. ii), and the church likewise, 1202–3 (*Ibid.*, no. iii). But no priory or cell of Lindores is known to have existed and there was certainly none at Fintray.

*Iona.* Skene's suggestion that the abbey of Iona belonged to this order (*PSAS*, x. (1875), 206–7) is conjectural and unconvincing. *V.* p. 52.

### ADDITIONAL NOTE

*Merchingley* (*Mercheley*). According to a document in the Kelso chartulary, Walter de Bolbec gives to God and St Mary and brother William de Mercheley and his successors the hermitage called Merchingley, founded in his waste land beside Merchingburn, with the church of St Mary founded there (*Calchou*, no. 264). By another charter, Walter, son of Walter de Bolbec, grants this hermitage and church to William and Roger, monks of the order of Kelso, these to be succeeded by one or two monks of the like habit and order and no other (*Ibid.*, no. 265). A charter of this Walter de Bolbec in similar terms emphasizes that two and no more monks shall have "the aforesaid [grant in] alms of Mercheley" (*Ibid.*, no. 266). We find also a confirmation by Hugh de Balliol of a grant of land by his father, Eustace, to Roger, "monk of Merchingley" (*Ibid.*, no. 267). All these charters are dated *c.* 1280 by the editor of *Calchou*. But among the possessions confirmed to Kelso abbey by Pope Innocent IV (1243–54) is "in the bishopric of Durham the hermitage which is called Merchingley" (*Ibid.*, no. 460); and this reference indicates that the original grant must be dated considerably earlier than *c.* 1280; it also shows that Merchingley was situated in England. The assertion that this foundation was located on the Hermitage water in Liddesdale (e.g. Banks, *Scottish Border Country*, p. 84) is erroneous. On its probable site in Slaley or Riding parishes in Northumberland; *v.* Hodgson, *Hist. of Northumberland*, vi. 378. In 1296, the abbot of Kelso's lands of "Merthenley" appear among those sequestered by Edward I (*Docs. Illust. of Hist. of Scotland*, p. 48) and they were finally forfeited by Kelso in the reign of Edward II (Hodgson, *op. cit.*, p. 378). It is thus very probable that before or early in the fourteenth century, this site had no longer a monastic character. No trace of the hermitage or church remains.

G

## THE CISTERCIAN MONKS

The following list shows eleven abbeys of the Cistercian order; and it may be noted that, in 1516, when a commissary of Cîteaux proposed to visit the Scottish houses, their number is given as eleven (*RSS*, i. no. 2833).

| Name | County | Minimum Income (1561) | Founder | Date Fd. | D. or Sec. | Mother-house |
|------|--------|------------------------|---------|----------|------------|--------------|
| * Balmerino | Fife | £1773 | Ermengarde, widow of William the Lion, and Alexander II | *c.* 1227 | 1603 | Melrose |

BALMERINO (ST EDWARD). The founders were Ermengarde, widow of William the Lion and her son, Alexander II. A list of Cistercian foundations (*Kinlos*, p. 13) assigns the foundation to 1227; while the Chronicle of Melrose has the statement: "In the year of the Lord 1229, the abbey of St Edward of Balmerino was made by King Alexander and his mother; and the convent was sent to it from Melrose, on the day of St Lucy the virgin (13 December)" (*Chron. Mailros*, p. 141). The Balmerino chartulary (*Balmorinach*, nos. 4–7) supplies evidence that, from 1225, Queen Ermengarde was acquiring the land on which the monastery was built and which formed its first endowment; and the Cistercian General Chapter, in 1227, remitted the King of Scotland's petition for the building of an abbey of that order to the abbots of Rievaulx and Coupar Angus, who, if they were satisfied with the king's proposed endowment, were authorized to grant him a convent from the house of Melrose (Canivez, *Statuta*, ii. 63). It is also to be noted that the abbot of St Edward's is one of the seven Cistercian abbots who attest an indenture at Kinloss, 20 September 1229 (*Kinlos*, p. 119), i.e. before the date given by the Melrose Chronicle. That the foundation took place in or about 1227 seems a reasonable assumption. Again, it is remarked by A. O. Anderson (*Early Sources*, ii. 489) that King Alexander's foundation charter (*Balmorinach*, no. 1), which bears the date 3 February 1230/1, implies that it was granted after the death of his mother; but as Queen Ermengarde is said to have died on 11 February 1233/4 (*Chron. Mailros*, p. 143), the date of this charter must be advanced to 3 February 1234/5. The date of the queen's death, as given in the Chronicle of Melrose, raises, however, additional difficulties (*v.* Campbell, *Balmerino*, p. 122) and some uncertainty must remain regarding the date of the foundation charter. What seems clear is that the king's charter came at an interval after the foundation. The abbot and fourteen monks appear in 1537 (*Ibid.*, p. 247). In December 1547, the abbey was burned by the English (*Cal. of State Papers rel. to Scotland* (1858), i. 74). Reformers did some destruction at the abbey in June 1559 (Lesley, *History*, p. 273; *De Origine*, p. 507), but what this amounted to is difficult to say; the statement of Camerarius (*De Scotorum Fortitudine, etc.*, p. 271) that it was burned lacks confirmation. The abbey was erected into a temporal lordship for Sir James Elphinstone, created Lord Balmerino, in parliament, 1606 (*APS*, iv. 341–3) and by charters, 1603 and 1607 (*RMS*, vi. nos. 1411, 2001).

Dependency: Gadvan.

## THE CISTERCIAN MONKS

| Name | County | Minimum Income (1561) | Founder | Date Fd. | D. or Sec. | Mother-house |
|------|--------|----------------------|---------|----------|-----------|--------------|
| § Coupar Angus | Perth | £5590 | Malcolm IV | –1164 | 1606 | Melrose |
| *‡ Culross | Fife | £1600 | Malcolm, earl of Fife | –1217 | 1589 | Kinloss |
| * Deer | Aberdeen | £2300 | William Cumyn, earl of Buchan | 1219 (?–1219) | 1587 | Kinloss |

Coupar Angus. Writers and lists are unanimous that the founder was Malcolm IV and likewise give the date of foundation as 1164, one chronicle adding that it took place on 12 July (*Chron. Mailros*, p. 78). Janauschek (*Orig. Cist.*, p. 152) assigns the foundation to 1 July 1164. The alleged foundation charter (NLS. MS., 33.2.5, 9v) must, however, be dated 1161–2. This document is not entirely reliable; but it is possible that the foundation was projected somewhat earlier than 1164. The evidence that this was a daughter-house of Melrose is given *Coupar Angus*, i. xxvi–xxvii. The church was dedicated, 15 May 1233 (*Chron. Mailros*, p. 143). A petition of the abbot in Edward I's parliament of 28 February 1305 sought remedy for the burning of its granges and other damage (*Mem. de Parl.*, no. 355). The abbot became mitred 7 June 1464 (*Coupar Angus*, ii. no. clxxiv). According to one seventeenth-century writer—and there appears to be no other evidence—the abbey was burned by Reformers (Camerarius, *De Scotorum Fortitudine*, etc., p. 271); and in or c. 1622, it is described as ruinous (Bisset, *Rolment of Courtis*, ii. 194). It was erected into a temporal lordship for James Elphinstone, with the title of Lord Coupar, in parliament, 1606 (*APS*, iv, 340–1) and by charter 1607 (*RMS*, vi. no. 2002).

Culross. Founded by Malcolm, earl of Fife. The convent, it is said, was sent to Culross from Kinloss, 23 February 1217/18, along with Hugh, formerly prior of Kinloss, as first abbot of the new foundation; and they reached Culross on 18 March (*Chron. Mailros*, p. 129). A list of Cistercian foundations gives the date of foundation as 13 February 1217 (/18) (*Kinlos*, p. 13). That the foundation was contemplated before this date appears from a statute of the Cistercian General Chapter, in 1214, remitting a petition of Earl Malcolm to the abbots of Kinloss, Coupar Angus and Newbattle for inquiry into the suitability of the proposed site and the sufficiency of the endowment and for report to the following Chapter (Canivez, *Statuta*, i. 427). In 1540, besides the commendator and abbot, there were sixteen monks (*Laing Chs.*, no. 442). The abbey was erected into a temporal lordship for James Colville of Easter Wemyss, by charters 1589 and 1609 (*RMS*, v. no. 1675; vii. no. 9), the second charter creating him Lord Colville of Culross.

Deer. Founded by William Cumyn, earl of Buchan (*Chron. Mailros*, p. 144, which gives no date). The foundation took place in 1219 (A. O. Anderson, *Early Sources*, ii. 439 and *n*). This was a daughter-house of Kinloss, but Ferrerius's account of its foundation (*Hist. Abbatum Kynlos*, p. 24) is erroneous. A petition of Earl William was remitted by the General Chapter in 1214 to Scottish abbots for inquiry (as with Balmerino and Culross *supra*) (Canivez, *Statuta*, i. 427). This abbey was erected into a temporal lordship for Robert Keith, Lord Altrie, by charter 1587 (*RMS*, v. no. 1309).

## THE CISTERCIAN MONKS

| Name | County | Minimum Income (1561) | Founder | Fd. | Date D. or Sec. | Mother-house |
|---|---|---|---|---|---|---|
| * DUNDRENNAN | Kirkcud-bright | £500(?) | David I | 1142 | 1606 | Rievaulx |
| * GLENLUCE | Wigtown | £667 | Roland of Gallo-way | 1191/2 | 1602 | Dundren-nan |

DUNDRENNAN. Most writers and lists agree that this was a foundation of David I, but Spottiswoode (p. 417) and Lawrie (*ESC*, p. 362) attribute it to Fergus of Galloway. The date of foundation is also generally given as 1142—one list assigns it to 23 July of that year (A. O. Anderson, *Early Sources*, ii. 204 *n*); an exception is Smyth's Chronicle, which gives 1141 (*Kinlos*, p. 4). Spottiswoode (p. 417) declares that the monks were brought from Rievaulx. There is no record evidence that Rievaulx was the mother-house of this abbey (Dundrennan does not appear in the printed Rievaulx charters); but the abbot of Rievaulx is mentioned as in Galloway in 1164 (Lawrie, *Annals*, p. 90), and abbots of Dundrennan were elected to Rievaulx in 1167 and 1239 (*Chron. Mailros*, pp. 81, 149). In 1299, the convent sought compensation from the English king for loss by destruction and burning amounting to £8000 (*CDS*, ii. no. 1123); and again in 1328 they were seeking from Edward III the restoration of revenues in Ireland and of their lands in Meath from which they had been ejected (*Ibid.*, iii. nos. 967, 969; cf. no. 1157). The commendator, prior and nine monks attest a charter, 9 May 1545 (*Laing Chs.*, no. 497). The abbey was erected into a temporal lordship for John Murray, afterwards earl of Annandale, in parliament, 1606 (*APS*, iv. 326) and by charter, 1609 (*RMS*, vii. no. 35).

Daughter-houses: Glenluce and Sweetheart.

GLENLUCE. Said to have been founded by Roland of Galloway, constable of Scotland (*Scotich.*, ii. 538 and other lists; Spottiswoode, p. 421). A charter of regality, 31 May 1441, among the Hay of Park MSS. refers to charters granted to the abbey by Roland and other lords of Galloway. The date is generally given as 1190; but a list of Cistercian foundations (A. O. Anderson, *Early Sources*, ii. 328) has it as 21 January 1191/2. Spottiswoode (p. 421) asserts that the monks were brought from Melrose; but statutes of 1199 which refer to the abbot of Dundrennan as advising his "son-abbot" to absent himself from the General Chapter and to the abbot of Glenluce as, by the advice of his "father", staying away from it (Canivez, *Statuta*, i. 238), indicate that Glenluce was a daughter-house of Dundrennan. The abbey was molested in 1235, during a rebellion in Galloway (*Chron. Mailros*, p. 146). In the sixteenth century, the community suffered considerable disturbance and spoliation. Thus, in 1544, the abbot was expelled by the earl of Cassillis (*Hamilton Papers*, ii. 734); and, in 1545-6, the abbey was invaded both by his followers and those of Gordon of Lochinvar, who sought to obtain possession of it (*PCR*, 1st Ser., ii. 3, 4, 7, 8; *ALC*, 1501-54, p. 556). The institution of the last abbot, 29 September 1560, could not be held in the church, as Lochinvar had occupied the abbey and expelled the monks (*HMC*, 5th Rep., App., p. 615). In that year, a charter is signed by the abbot, prior, sub-prior and thirteen monks (*Archaeol. Collns. rel. to Ayrshire and Galloway* (1885), v. 161); and, in 1572, the commendator and five monks are left (*Ibid.*, v. 179). "The manor or place of Glenluce called of old the monastery of Glenluce" was granted to Lawrence Gordon, by charter, 1602 (*RMS*, vi. no. 1338), the grant being ratified in parliament, 1606 (*APS*, iv. 327-8). In 1619, the abbey was bestowed upon the bishop of Galloway (*Ibid.*, v. 72).

## THE CISTERCIAN MONKS

| Name | County | Minimum Income (1561) | Founder | Fd. | Date D. or Sec. | Mother-house |
|------|--------|------------------------|---------|-----|------------------|--------------|
| ¶ KINLOSS | Moray | £3480 | David I | 1150 or 1151 | 1601 | Melrose |
| * MELROSE | Roxburgh | £5180 | David I | 1136 | 1609 | Rievaulx |
| § NEWBATTLE | Midlothian | £1500 | David I | 1140 | 1587 | Melrose |

KINLOSS. Founded by David I. The unanimous statement of chroniclers and lists is confirmed by a reference to "the first foundation by the late king David of good memory" (*Kinlos*, p. 111). The date of foundation is given as 21 May 1150 (*Chron. Mailros*, p. 54). Smyth's Chronicle and an appended list of Cistercian foundations have this as 21 May 1151 (*Kinlos*, pp. 5, 13). The date 20 June 1151 (as given *Kinlos*, x) is probably erroneous; while 12 Kal. *Januarii*, the date mentioned by Spottiswoode (p. 418) is apparently an error for 12 Kal. *Junii*. Cistercian foundation lists also assign it to 1151 (A. O. Anderson, *Early Sources*, ii. 211). There seems no reason to query the statement of Spottiswoode (p. 419) that the monks came from Melrose. In 1229, there were twenty-three monks here, in addition to the abbot and prior (*Kinlos*, p. 119). A charter is attested, in 1537, by the abbot and nineteen monks (*Ibid.*, lxiv). The abbot was granted the mitre, 24 September 1395 (Lawrie, *Annals*, p. 100). The abbey was erected into a temporal lordship for Edward Bruce, erected Lord Kinloss, by charters, 1601 and 1608 (*RMS*, vi. nos. 1138, 2074).

MELROSE. Founded by David I. The date of foundation is generally given as 1136; but, according to the Chronicle of Melrose, the abbey was "created" 23 March 1136 (*Chron. Mailros*, p. 70), i.e. presumably 1136/7. *V.* also A. O. Anderson, *Early Sources*, ii. 195 *n*. The foundation charter (*Melros*, no. 1) is not earlier than 1143-4, though it incorporates a grant made previous to that date (*v.* Lawrie, *ESC*, p. 376). Melrose was colonized from Rievaulx (*Melros*, no. 1). The church was dedicated, 28 July 1146 (*Chron. Mailros*, p. 73). On 21 August 1391, the abbot was granted the mitre (Lawrie, *Annals*, p. 100). Twenty-six monks, besides the abbot, attest a charter, 20 December 1519 (*Scotts of Buccleuch*, ii. no. 126). The abbey suffered much damage from hostile action. Thus the monastic buildings seem to have been partially burned, 1300-7 (*CDS*, ii. no. 1982); and the English sacked it in 1322 (*Scotich.*, lib. xii, cap. iv (ii. 278)) and burned it in 1385 (*Ibid.*, lib. xiv, cap. 1 (ii. 401)). Again, Melrose was one of the religious houses burned and destroyed during Hertford's invasion, September 1545 (*L. & P. H. VIII*, xx². no. 456). With the exception of its lands of Kylesmuir in Ayrshire, separately erected for Lord Loudoun, in parliament, 1606 (*APS*, iv. 323-4) and by charter 1608 (*RMS*, vi. no. 2120), the abbey was erected into a temporal lordship for John Ramsay, Viscount Haddington, created Lord Melrose, in parliament, 1609 (*APS*, iv. 461).

Daughter-houses: Balmerino; Coupar Angus; Holmcultram; Kinloss; Newbattle.

NEWBATTLE. David I is usually regarded as the founder, but Mr Barrow ("Scottish Rulers and the Religious Orders", *Trans. RHS*, 5th Ser., iii (1953), 94-5) suggests that with the king was associated his son, Earl Henry. The date of the foundation is given as 1140 (*Chron. Mailros*, p. 71). A list of Cistercian foundations gives it as 1 November, 1140 (A. O. Anderson, *Early Sources*, ii. 202 *n*)—this is the date of King David's grant of Newbattle to the monks (*Neubotle*, no. 2). According to Spottiswoode (p. 417) the convent came from Melrose. The church was dedicated, 13 March 1233/4 (*Chron. Mailros*, p. 143). The abbey was burned by the English in 1385 (*Scotich.*, lib. xiv, cap. 1 (ii. 401)) and, again, on 15 May 1544 (*L. & P. H. VIII*, xix¹. no. 533) and in June 1548 (*Cal. of Scottish Papers*, i. no. 237). when, it is said, six of the monks were taken as prisoners to England (Canivez, *Statuta*, vii. 37). It was erected into a temporal lordship for Mark Ker by charter 1587 (*RMS*, v. no. 1307).

## THE CISTERCIAN MONKS

| Name | County | Minimum Income (1561) | Founder | Fd. | Date D. or Sec. | Mother-house |
|---|---|---|---|---|---|---|
| § Saddell | Argyll | | Reginald, son of Somerled, lord of the Isles | −1207 | *c.* 1507 | ? |
| * Sweetheart | Kirkcud-bright | £690 | Devorgilla de Balliol | 1273 | 1624 | Dundren-nan |

SADDELL. Founded by Reginald, son of Somerled, lord of the Isles (†1207) (*RMS*, ii. no. 3170; *Highland Papers*, iv. 147). He is stated to have founded at "Sagadul" a house of Greyfriars (Bk. of Clanranald cited *PSAS*, x (1875), 204). This, as it stands, is erroneous; but "Greyfriars" should probably be given as "grey monks" i.e. Cistercians (cf. *Chron. Man*, p. 116 *n*). A number of lists, e.g. *Scotichronicon*, ii, 538, have the founder's name as "Sorly Maclardy", i.e. Somerled, Reginald's father (†1164) (A. O. Anderson, *Early Sources*, ii. 244-5). The foundation is also attributed to Donald, lord of the Isles, Reginald's son (*Highland Papers*, i. 64; *Macfarlane's Geog. Collns.*, ii. 527). In a list of Cistercian foundations, the date of foundation of the abbey of "Scondale" (Sandale = Saddell) appears as 1160 (A. O. Anderson, *op. cit.*, ii. 247). *Origines Parochiales* (ii¹. 23) says "before the middle of the thirteenth century". Saddell is sometimes described as a daughter-house of Rushen, in Man; but this has not been verified. In 1507(?), James IV, in a letter to the Cardinal of St Mark, declares that the house of "Sadaguil", once Cistercian and founded by the king's ancestors[1] in the diocese of Lismore (Argyll), has within living memory seen no monastic life and has fallen to the use of laymen. There is no hope of reviving monastic life and the fruits are barely £9 sterling. James asks for a commission to the archbishop of Glasgow or some other prelate to investigate and with papal approval to unite the place in perpetuity to the bishopric of Lismore (*Letters of James IV*, no. 149). The abbey had been united to the bishopric −1 January 1507/8, on which date James IV erected its lands into the barony of Saddell (*RMS*, ii. no. 3170). On 22 April 1512, King James made the request to Pope Julius II that as the cathedral of Lismore had fallen into ruin and lay deserted, having neither bishop nor chapter nor safe access nor sufficient food, and since the suppressed monastery of "Sagadul" was united to the episcopal *mensa*, the see might be transferred to that site and a cathedral erected and endowed (*Letters of James IV*, no. 446). This proposal had no result.

SWEETHEART (NEW ABBEY). Founded by Devorgilla, widow of John de Balliol. The date of the foundation is usually given as 1275 (e.g. *Scotich.*, lib. x, cap. xxxvi (ii. 124) ). But a statute of the Cistercian General Chapter, in 1270, commissions the abbots of Furness and Rievaulx to inspect the site "in which the widow of John de Balliol intends to found an abbey of monks" (Canivez, *Statuta*, iii. 91); and, on 10 April 1273, Devorgilla granted a charter of endowment "to God and the church of St Mary of Sweetheart and the monks of the Cistercian order of the convent of Dundrennan, for the abbey to be built in honour of God . . ." (*Laing Chs.*, no. 46). A further statute of the General Chapter—in 1274—committed to the abbots of Holmcultram and Glenluce the inspection of the abbey "which, it is said, Devorgilla has founded"; and if they are satisfied, to incorporate it to the order and introduce the convent there. It is to be a daughter-house of Dundrennan (Canivez, *op. cit.*, iii. 138). In 1299 and 1308, the monks made complaint to the English king of damage amounting to more than £5000 through the burning of their granges and destruction of their goods in war (*CDS*, ii. nos. 1122, 1123; iii. no. 69); and, in 1397, the abbey buildings are said to have been set on fire by lightning and "totally burned" (Vat. Reg., 322, 440 v.), though this is no doubt an exaggeration. The abbot was made mitred, 4 July 1398 (Lawrie, *Annals*, p. 100). In 1624, the abbey was erected into a temporal lordship for Sir Robert Spottiswoode (*RMS*, viii. no. 572).

---

[1] This statement is rhetorical and inaccurate.

## THE CISTERCIAN MONKS

### Uncertain Foundations

*Soulseat.* According to St Bernard of Clairvaux's account of St Malachy (Maelmaedoic) of Armagh, that bishop "after a prosperous crossing (from Ireland) came to Scotland. On the third day he reached a place which is called *Viride Stagnum*, which he had caused to be prepared that he might establish an abbey there." The account goes on: "And leaving there some of his sons, our brothers, as a convent of monks and an abbot (for he had brought them with him for that purpose), he bade them farewell and set out . . ." (Vita S. Malachiae, in *Acta Sanctorum*, November, ii, Pt. I, 165a; *Patr. Lat.*, 182, col. 1113; *v.* A. O. Anderson, *Early Sources*, ii. 208; Lawlor, *Life of St Malachy of Armagh*, p. 120). At an earlier point in the narrative, St Bernard, having described the healing by St Malachy at Bangor of a clerk named Michael, declares of this man: "And from that moment he clave to God and to Malachy His servant . . . and at present, as we have heard, he presides over a monastery in the parts of Scotland; and this was the latest of all Malachy's foundations" (*AS*, November, ii. Pt. I, 140; *PL*, 182, col. 1083–4; Lawlor, *op. cit.*, p. 34). The points which emerge in these statements are: (1) This foundation, according to St Bernard's narrative, took place in the year of St Malachy's death, 1148; (2) it was, by implication, a house of Cistercians; (3) *Viride Stagnum* came to be identified with Soulseat, in Wigtownshire (perhaps, Dr A. O. Anderson suggests (in correspondence), because Soulseat Loch was regarded as the "Green Lake"). When this happened seems uncertain. Mr R. C. Reid has kindly given me a note of a Barnbarroch charter granted 19 June 1539, by the commendator of Soulseat (viridis stagni alias sedis animarum[1]) (cf. the reference to "Ecclesia Viridis Stagni alias Sanliesiete [*sic*]" (Le Paige, *Bibliotheca Praem. Ord.* (Paris, 1633), p. 333) ). Dr Anderson (*Early Sources*, ii. 208 *n.*) offers certain suggestions: (1) Maelmaedoic may have brought monks from Mellifont (founded for Cistercians in 1140) to Soulseat; in that case, the latter ceased shortly after to be a Cistercian house (Soulseat is not mentioned among the five daughter-houses of Mellifont (Lawlor, *St Malachy*, p. 76 *n.*) ); (2) this bishop may have founded a Cistercian house at Viride Lignum in Newry County (Dr Anderson now informs me of his view that while it might have been possible for the names Viride Lignum and Viride Stagnum to be confused, the only possible inference is that the two names stand for different places); (3) as Maelmaedoic had established an abbey of regular canons at Saul, "it would seem possible that the canons of Soulseat had been brought from Saul" (Soulseat was ultimately to be the site of a Praemonstratensian abbey). This would seem less plausible; but he goes on to state: "It is difficult to imagine that Bernard should have erred in his belief that the abbey founded in 1148 was Cistercian." Dr Anderson informs me that what he had in mind was that if the name "Saulseat" was derived from the Irish "Saball", it would have implied that the canons had gone there after their house at Saul had been dispersed. But he now suggests that there is probably no connection between the names and no evidence that Soulseat (Saulseat) had anything to do with Saul. I quote his words: "The one inference that I incline to make is that Cistercians occupied a place at Viride Stagnum; and Premonstratensians another place called Soulseat." It would appear that the identification of Viride Stagnum with Soulseat must remain unverified. That Maelmaedoic founded a Cistercian abbey at such a place in Scotland is by no means improbable. If so, there is no further evidence concerning it and its career must have been brief. Soulseat was founded for Premonstratensian canons somewhat later in the twelfth century. *V.* under Premonstratensian Canons.

---

[1] The name is commonly latinized in the latter form.

## CISTERCIAN DEPENDENCIES

| Name | County | Rank | Minimum Income (1561) | Founder | Date Fd. | D. or Sec. | Dependent on |
|---|---|---|---|---|---|---|---|
| BEAULY | Inverness | Priory | | *V*. p. 70 *infra* | | 1634 | Kinloss (16 c.) |
| GADVAN | Fife | Preceptory | ? | | −1486 | −1578 | Balmerino |
| *Mauchline* | Ayr | ? | | | | | Melrose |

BEAULY. For the previous history of this house *v.* the Valliscaulian monks (*infra*). From 1530 (according to Ferrerius), Robert Reid, abbot of the Cistercian house of Kinloss and later (1541) bishop of Orkney, held Beauly priory *in commendam* (*Beauly*, p. 218; *Kinlos*, p. 50). (That the foregoing date is, however, too early is indicated by a letter of James V to Pope Clement VII, requesting the ratification of Reid's exchange of another benefice for Beauly, as he is more suitable than a canon regular on whom that priory had been conferred; this letter is dated 1 August 1531 (*Letters of James V*, pp. 194–5, from Tyninghame Letter Bk.).) Reid's successors at Kinloss were also commendators of Beauly. There were six monks here in 1568 (*Beauly*, p. 256) and four in 1571 (*Ibid.*, p. 268). The erection of the priory into a temporal lordship in favour of Lord Hay of Sala is noted under 1612 in *APS* (iv. 522), but this is apparently an error (*v. Beauly*, p. 329; *RMS*, vii. no. 702). The priory was finally granted to the bishop of Ross by a crown charter, 20 October 1634 (*RMS*, ix. no. 227).

GADVAN. A cell of Balmerino abbey, situated in Dunbog parish. It is called, in 1630, a "preceptory or ministry" (*RMS*, viii. no. 1543). In a letter of James V to Pope Clement VII, 19 March 1529/30, it is described as "a monastic cell in a hamlet and . . . named Gadwyne, long wont to be governed by a Cistercian of Balmerino, with a second monk as his companion" (*Letters of James V*, p. 169; from Tyninghame Letter Bk.). This house was in existence −10 October 1486, when its head is called "prior of Dunbolg [Dunbog]" (*Aberbrothoc*, ii. no. 300); he is also designated "master of the place of Gadvan, annexed to the said monastery [Balmerino]", 25 January 1529/30 (*RMS*, iii. no. 898) and "preceptor", in 1603 (*Ibid.*, vi. no. 1492). Its chapel, manse and meadow are likewise mentioned in 1603 (*Ibid.*). This house and its property were secularized by 5 April 1578, when James Beaton of Creich held "the Gadvan and manor place thereof" (*Wemyss*, no. 226 (ii. 302) ); and a crown charter of Gadvan, with the manse and meadow (but excluding the chapel) and the lands of Johnstoun, "formerly held of the monastery [of Balmerino] and of the preceptors of the place of Gadvan annexed to the said monastery", was granted to him, 20 December 1603 (*RMS*, vi. no. 1492).

*Mauchline.* "Said to have been founded by David I", according to Spottiswoode (p. 426) and described as a "cell of Melrose" in lists (e.g. *Scotich.*, ii. 539; EU. MS. Db. 6.19; NLS. MSS. 22.1.14, 31.6.1; NLS. MS. 33.2.12 gives it erroneously as a "cell of Kelso"). According to Janauschek (*Orig. Cist.*, lxxx), it was not an abbey but a priory subject to Melrose. There is, however, no evidence that it was other than a grange (though its distance from Melrose may preclude this) or large landed property of Melrose abbey. Existing charters frequently mention the lands of Mauchline; but neither in the records of Melrose nor elsewhere is there any specific indication of a priory or religious house. The only relevant reference is in 1243, when Richard de Bigre, "then monk of Mauhelin", is mentioned (*Melros*, i. no. 191; verified from the original charter in General Register House). It is difficult to make a definite inference from the appearance of this solitary figure. The lands of Mauchline were granted to Melrose abbey by Walter, son of Alan, steward of Scotland, −1177 (*Ibid.*, i. no. 66), i.e. during the reign not of David I but of William the Lion. In this locality the only church seems to have been the church or chapel of St Michael mentioned 1204–31 (*Ibid.*, i. no. 73), which was given parochial status in 1315 (*Ibid.*, ii. nos. 407, 408). The surviving medieval buildings at Mauchline—the so-called "Castle"—are not in the strict sense ecclesiastical. They were probably erected *c.* 1450 and have been described as "a civil residence for ecclesiastics engaged in managing a large estate" (R. C. Reid, "Mauchline Castle", *Trans. Dumfriesshire and Galloway Nat. Hist. and Antiq. Socy.*, 3rd Ser., xvi (1931), 171). The office of the "mastership" of Mauchline, granted by the Pope to a monk of Melrose, 1 September 1487 (*Scottish Benefices*, p. 221) was probably connected with the administration of the abbey's lands in this area. These lands were erected separately into the lordship of Kylesmuir, 1606 and 1608. *V.* Melrose *supra*; also Mauchline *hospitium* (p. 164 *infra*).

## THE CISTERCIAN DEPENDENCIES

### SUPPOSED FOUNDATIONS

*Ancaria.* A place so named appears, in 1530, in a list of Scottish Cistercian monasteries which are to be assessed for contributions to the needs of the order (Canivez, *Statuta*, vi. 689–90). It cannot be identified.

*Dron.* It is stated in the *New Stat. Acct.* (x. 408) that this chapel, in the parish of Long-forgan, belonged to the abbey of Coupar Angus, though this is doubtful. The statement is also couched in terms which lend themselves to the suggestion that it was the site of a monastic community. This was not the case. The chapel was evidently secular and was probably intended to serve an outlying part of the parish.

*Forfar.* Adam, "abbot" of Forfar, who is mentioned in the Coupar Angus *Breviarium* (p. 42), is a mythical personage. The word "abbas" is apparently an error for "Albus". Likewise, the "monks" of Forfar who appear in the same document are mentioned in error for the monks of Coupar. *V. Coupar Angus*, i. lxviii, 24.

*Hichaten.* This name figures in the same list as "Ancaria" *supra*. It appears as "Hicha-ten vel Orcades"; but no place in Orkney can be identified with it.

*Lochkindeloch.* This was the parish in which Sweetheart abbey was situated. It had a parish church but no religious house other than the abbey existed in it.

*Roxburgh.* With reference to the exemption of the church of St James, Roxburgh (which was held by Kelso abbey) from synodals and episcopal aids, according to a declaration of the papal legate in 1201, A. O. Anderson (*Early Sources*, ii. 183 *n*.) declares: "It seems therefore to have been occupied by Cistercian monks at this time." This suggestion seems unfounded. There are no grounds for holding that monks were settled here or that these were Cistercians.

### ADDITIONAL NOTE

*Kerrara.* In an inventory of 1292 appears a letter of the abbot and convent of Coupar Angus by which they have obliged themselves to build a chapel at their own expense on the island of "Karnelay in Arkadia" and to find three monks to celebrate divine service for the soul of Alexander, late king of Scots, apparently in virtue of a sum of money which they had received "beforehand" from that king (*APS*, i. App. to Preface, 10). This island is Kerrara, off the coast of Argyll, where Alexander II died. There is no evidence that this foundation took place or that monks were placed in that island.

## THE VALLISCAULIAN MONKS

The order of Vallis Caulium (or Vallis Olerum) is said to have been introduced into Scotland in 1230 (*Chron. Mailros*, p. 142).

The principles of the rule of this order are given in a bull of Pope Innocent III (1205) (*REM*, no. 256). The Valliscaulian houses stood in a relation of direct dependence on the mother-house of Val de Choux, in the diocese of Langres, in France. The three Scottish priories of the order are sometimes called Cistercian, but Pluscarden was clearly a Valliscaulian house until it became Benedictine in 1454 and the prior of Val de Choux claimed jurisdiction over Beauly and Ardchattan until at least 1506. The former became Cistercian in 1510.

| Name | County | Rank | Minimum Income (1561) | Founder | Fd. | Date D. or Sec. | Depen-dent on |
|------|--------|------|------------------------|---------|-----|-----------------|----------------|
| * ARDCHATTAN | Argyll | | | Duncan McCowll | 1230 or 1231 | 1602 | |
| * BEAULY | Inverness | | £674 | John Byset and Alexander II(?) | c. 1230 | | V. notes |

ARDCHATTAN. Founded in 1230 or 1231 by Duncan McCowll (or McDougal) (*Extracta*, p. 93; MS. lists; *OPS*, ii¹. 149). Its prior swore fealty to Edward I in 1296 (*CDS*, ii. no. 823). This is apparently the monastery of St Mary and St John the Baptist in "Beandardaloch" [Benderloch], mentioned in 1425 (Vat. Reg. Supp., 190, 282v (D) ). Its history is largely obscure. Maitland (*History* i. 263) is among those who describe it as Cistercian, but, in 1506, in a commission for its visitation by the prior of Beauly, it is said to be immediately subject to Val de Choux (*Beauly*, p. 140), and there is no evidence that it became Cistercian. There were six monks, –1538 (*Letters of James V*, p. 346). This house was erected into a tenandry for Alexander Campbell, formerly its commendatory prior, in 1602 (*APS*, vii. 211); and annexed to the bishopric of the Isles by charter, 1615, and in parliament, 1617 (*Ibid.*, iv. 554).

BEAULY. The date of foundation of this house and the identity of the founder are alike difficult to ascertain. According to the Wardlaw MS., a late and not entirely reliable source (compiled by James Fraser, 1666–99+), John Byset founded and endowed it for Valliscaulian monks, 9 July 1223 (*Chrons. of Frasers*, p. 61). It is also asserted in that work that "these monks came out of France . . . *anno* 1222" (*Ibid.*, p. 63). If, however, the order was not introduced into Scotland until 1230, as is maintained by the Chronicle of Melrose (*v. supra*), these statements must be rejected. Spottiswoode (p. 427) assigns the foundation to *James* Byset and professes to quote the terms of the founder's charter. A bull of Pope Gregory IX, taking the monks and monastery under his protection as well as its possessions (including those bestowed by John Byset), is, in the existing version, imperfect, as the date is mainly left blank (*Beauly*, p. 14). But if it is identical with the bull mentioned by Spottiswoode (p. 428), it can be regarded as granted by Pope Gregory IX, 5 July 1230 (not 1231 as in *Beauly*, p. 15). In the Wardlaw MS., it is stated that the monks who "came out of France" in 1222 were six in number along with a prior. These "landed at Lovat and the country provided for them dureing the erection of the monastery; John Bisset in his time takeing care of that edifice, which afterwards was industriously carried on in Insula de Achinbady" (*Chrons. of Frasers*, p. 63).[1]   In another (and similar) account by the same writer, it is added that, in 1245, by a bull of Pope Innocent IV, the priory was "erected"

[1] It is pointed out (*Chrons. of Frasers*, p. 62, *n.* 1) that *insula* here is a translation of the Gaelic *innis*, which means not only "island" but "green pastureland" or "river meadow" (*Scotice*, "inch") This site, the "Inch of Achinbady", became known as Beauly (*beau lieu*), presumably because it was given that name by the monks.

for Valliscaulians, to whom Alexander II "mortified and confirmed . . . all the Lands of Strathalvay, the Monastry to be erected in Insuâ [Insula] de Ackinbady in Strathalvy, where stood a Chappel of St Michael, and John Bisset entrusted with the Erection . . ." (*Macfarlane's Geneal. Collns.*, ii. 87). This bull, however, if the description of it can be trusted, was evidently concerned with the confirmation of the monastery's endowments, including Alexander II's grant, rather than with its erection.[1] An entry in the Lovat writs which records that Alexander II, on 20 December, in the seventeenth year of his reign, i.e. 1230 (not 1231 as in *Beauly*, p. 17), confirmed a donation made to the priory (*Ibid.*), points to the existence of the monastery in that year. The foundation is attributed in some lists to John Byset (e.g. *Scotich.*, ii. 540; NLS. MS. 33.2.12) and in others to Alexander II and Byset (e.g. NLS. MS. 22.1.14; EU. MS. Db. 6.19; MS. Saunders). Beyond these alternatives record evidence (which is insufficient and ambiguous) does not permit us to go. The prior of Beauly was present at the parliament of Brigham, 17 March 1289/90 (*APS*, i. 85). In a bull of Pope Alexander VI, 25 February 1497/8, the monastery is described both as of the Cistercian order and as a dependency of the monastery of Val de Choux (*Beauly*, p. 106), as "of the Cistercian order under the rule of Vallis Caulium" in a form of oath sent to the prior on the same date (*Ibid.*, p. 111), and as of the Cistercian order in a writ of the bishop of Moray (which is also addressed to the abbot and convent of Vallis Caulium), 11 February 1500/1 (*Ibid.*, p. 113). Why it should be called Cistercian in these records is impossible to say; but, on 7 May 1506, the prior of Val de Choux commissions the prior of "our monastery" at Beauly to make a visitation of the monastery of Ardchattan (*Ibid.*, p. 140), and, on 18 December of the same year, the prior of Val de Choux as "head or general" of that order, writes to the prior and convent of Beauly on the question of episcopal visitation and summons him to the next general chapter of the order (*Ibid.*, pp. 157–9). We find, however, a bull of 10 May 1510, directed to the prior and convent of Beauly, extinguishing the order of Vallis Caulium there and instituting the Cistercian order (*L. & P. H. VIII*, i². 1522). For the further history of this house *v.* under Cistercian Dependencies.

---

[1] The foundation must have taken place prior to 1242, in which year Byset was banished. A charter of Andrew, bishop of Moray, confirming a donation made to the priory (*Beauly*, p. 38) was also granted not later than 1242.

## THE VALLISCAULIAN MONKS

| Name | County | Rank | Minimum Income (1561) | Founder | Fd. | Date D. or Sec. | Dependent on |
|------|--------|------|----------------------|---------|-----|-----------------|--------------|
| ‡§ PLUSCARDEN | Moray | | *V.* under Benedictine houses | Alexander II | 1230 or 1231 | 1454 (united to Urquhart) | *V.* under Benedictines |

PLUSCARDEN. Founded by Alexander II in 1230 (Spottiswoode, p. 427) or 1231 (*Bk. of Pluscarden*, p. 72). King Alexander is mentioned as founder in the confirmation-charter of Andrew, bishop of Moray, 1233 (Macphail, *Pluscardyn*, p. 201); and his charter of 7 April 1236 is concerned with the granting of endowments, privileges and protection to "the brethren of the order of Vallis Caulium serving . . . God in the house which we have founded in our forest of Elgin, in the place namely which is called the valley of St Andrew at Pluscarden" (*Ibid.*, p. 205). On 12 March 1453/4, Pope Nicholas V, on the petition of the Benedictine prior of Urquhart, containing that there were not more than six monks at Pluscarden and not more than two at Urquhart, consented to the separation of Pluscarden from Val de Choux, made it a dependency of Dunfermline and united it to Urquhart (*Ibid.*, pp. 223 ff; *CPR*, x. 253–4). The abbot of Dunfermline, on 8 November 1454, appointed a commissary to take possession of the priory in his name and to receive the profession as Benedictines of the monks (*Dunfermelyn*, no. 442). For its further history *v.* under Benedictine Monks. This house is erroneously described as of the order of Vallombrosa (Bisset, *Rolment of Courtis*, ii. 122) and as Cistercian (Maitland, *History*, p. 258).

### SUPPOSED FOUNDATION

*Dalvey.* The statement that Pluscarden had a cell at Dalvey, in the parish of Dyke (e.g in *Beauly*, p. 135) is based merely on conjecture. There is no evidence of such a cell.

## THE CARTHUSIAN MONKS

On the relations of the Scottish Carthusians with the order, *v.* E. M. Thompson, *The Carthusian Order in England*, pp. 247–8, whére it is shown that the one Carthusian house in Scotland was at first attached to the province of Picardy, about 1456 added to the English province, and in 1460 united to the province of Geneva.

| Name | County | Rank | Minimum Income (1561) | Founder | Fd. | Date D. or Sec. | Dependent on |
|------|--------|------|------------------------|---------|-----|-----------------|--------------|
| PERTH | Perth | Priory | £1680 | James I | 1429 | 1569 | |

PERTH. "Vale of Virtue". On 19 August 1426, the prior of the Grande Chartreuse, with the consent of the General Chapter and following on the proposition of James I, authorized the erection of a house near Perth for thirteen monks (Fittis, *Eccles. Annals of Perth*, pp. 216–17). King James, on 31 March 1429, by a charter in favour of the prior and convent of the monastery of Vallis Virtutis of the Carthusian order near Perth, bestowed upon this house extensive privileges (*Ibid.*, pp. 217–18); and it was incorporated by the General Chapter in 1430 (Thompson, *Carthus. Order in England*, p. 247). By 1434, the nunnery of St Leonard and the hospital of St Mary Magdalene had been annexed to it (Fittis, *op. cit.*, p. 222). The Charterhouse was sacked and destroyed in May 1559 by Reformers (Lesley, *History*, p. 272; Knox, *History*, i. 323; Pitscottie, *Cronicles*, ii. 146). The gardens, monastery and place belonging to the Charterhouse were included in the grant of the friars' lands to the burgh by James VI, 9 August 1569 (*RMS*, iv. no. 1874). Nevertheless, the Charterhouse was held by commendators till 1602 (by which date the convent was extinct), when the priory was finally suppressed (*Ibid.*, vi. nos. 851, 1276) and the Town Council apparently obtained effective possession of its property. The charter of 1569 was confirmed by James VI in 1600 (*Ibid.*, vi. no. 1098).

### PROPOSED FOUNDATION

On 5 June 1419, the Pope granted a petition of Archibald, earl of Douglas, who, out of his "singular devotion" to the order, had supplicated for licence to found a Carthusian house (*Supplics.*, p. 68); but the projected foundation was not made.

### SUPPOSED FOUNDATION

*Makerstoun.* It is asserted that "the priory of Charterhouse in the parish of Mackerston [*sic*], which is said to have been the abode of a small society of Carthusians, possessed half of the Midtoun and Mains of Sprouston" (*OPS*, i. 440, citing Morton, *Monastic Annals*, pp. 173, 321). There is a farm in this parish called Charterhouse, but no evidence of a priory is forthcoming. The lands in the neighbouring parish of Sprouston were bestowed upon the Charterhouse of *Perth* by Archibald, earl of Douglas, 2 February 1433/4 (*Douglas Bk.*, iii. no. 396; *HMC, 14th Rep.*, App., Pt. III, 24) and are mentioned in 1603 as "alleged holden" of the [Perth] Charterhouse (*PCR*, 1st Ser., vi. 812); the Mains of Sprouston is specifically described, 20 December 1607, as "belonging to the priory of Charterhouse" (*RMS*, vi. no. 2003), which must mean the Perth priory.

## THE AUGUSTINIAN CANONS

| Name | County | Rank | Minimum Income (1561) | Founder | Fd. | Date D. or Sec. | Dependent on |
|---|---|---|---|---|---|---|---|
| ABERNETHY | Perth | Priory | ? | | 1272 or 1273 | early 14 c. | |
| BLANTYRE | Lanark | Priory | £131 | Alexander II(?) | –1249 (?) | 1598/9 | Jedburgh abbey |
| * CAMBUSKENNETH | Stirling | Abbey | £3148 | David I | c. 1140 | 1604 | (Arrouaisian) |

ABERNETHY. Formerly a house of Culdees (*q.v.*). According to the *Scotichronicon* (lib. x, cap. xxxiii (ii. 120) ), "in this year [it is not clear whether the reference is to 1272 or 1273] the priory of Abernethy was made into regular canons, who formerly were Culdees." That the Culdees became regular canons is more likely to be true than the statement of Spottiswoode (p. 393): "At length it became a priory of canons brought from Inchaffray in the year 1273." There is, in any case, no evidence that canons were sent to Abernethy from that abbey. The priory appears in the taxation-roll of Baiamund for 1274-5 and the prior in the roll for 1275-6 (Theiner, *Vet. Mon.*, no. cclxiv; *SHS Misc.*, vi. 53, 71). This house was transformed into a college of secular canons in the earlier fourteenth century. *V.* under Secular Canons (II).

BLANTYRE. Said to have been founded by Alexander II (1214-49) (*OPS*, i. 59), but no mention of it occurs till 17 March 1289/90, when its prior was present in the parliament at Brigham (*APS*, i. 85). This house was a dependency of Jedburgh (*Scotich.*, ii. 539; *CPR*, Pet., i. 553). The reference to a "house or place assigned for regular canons of *Holyrood* . . . in the land of Blantar, Glasgow diocese" (*Scottish Benefices*, p. 184) is apparently an error. In the earlier sixteenth century (–24 March 1537/8, according to *RSS*, ii. no. 2475), this priory is described as "usually held by a canon of Jedburgh . . . non-conventual and . . . a dependent cell of Jedburgh" (*Formulare*, ii. no. 354). It was erected into a temporal lordship for Walter Stewart, who became Lord Blantyre, by charter, 18 January 1598/9 (*RMS*, vi. no. 833) and in parliament 1617 (*APS*, iv. 563).

CAMBUSKENNETH. David I's charter, 29 May–24 August 1147, usually taken as the foundation-charter, endows an already existing community of canons regular, serving the church of St Mary, Stirling (*Cambuskenneth*, no. 51; Lawrie, *ESC*, pp. 400–1). The bull of confirmation of Pope Eugenius III, 30 August 1147, addressed to the abbot, refers to the order of Arrouaise as having been set up in this church (*Cambuskenneth*, no. 23). Mr G. W. S. Barrow has adduced valuable additional evidence that this was a daughter-house of Arrouaise and indicates that it was in existence, *c.* 1140 ("Scottish Rulers and the Religious Orders", *Trans. RHS*, 5th Ser., iii (1953), 95–6). Among King David's endowments was the land of Cambuskenneth; and from 1201 the abbey was designated by that name (*v. Cambuskenneth*, no. 27). It is mentioned in 1350 as having been damaged by enemies (unspecified) (*Ibid.*, no. 61). The abbot was granted the mitre, 20 April 1406 (*Ibid.*, no. 32). For some unexplained reason, the dedication of the church, buildings and burial-ground did not take place till 11 July 1521 (*Ibid.*, no. 92). The abbey is said to have been "ruined and cast down" by the Reforming lords in 1559 (Spottiswoode, *Hist. of Ch. of Scotland*, i. 280); but this is not mentioned, e.g. by Lesley or Knox. It was erected, along with Dryburgh abbey and Inchmahome priory, into a temporal lordship for John, second earl of Mar, 1604 and 1606 (*APS*, iv. 343).

## THE AUGUSTINIAN CANONS

| Name | County | Rank | Minimum Income (1561) | Founder | Fd. | Date D. or Sec. | Depen- dent on |
|------|--------|------|------------------------|---------|-----|------------------|----------------|
| CANONBIE | Dumfries | Priory | included with Jedburgh | Turgot de Rosdale | –1220 | 1606 | Jedburgh |
| * HOLYROOD | Midlothian | Abbey | £5600 | David I | 1128 | 1606 | |
| § INCHAFFRAY | Perth | Priory | | Gilbert, earl of Strathearn | 1200 | | |
| | | Abbey | £667 | | 1220 or 1221 | 1609– 1669 (*V.* notes) | |

CANONBIE. A dependency of Jedburgh abbey (*Scotich.* ii. 539). First mentioned in 1220, when an agreement between the bishop of Glasgow and the abbot of Jedburgh refers to the chaplain serving in the church of Liddel and the prior residing there (*REG*, no. 114), A charter of Alexander II, 28 March 1229, confirming donations to Jedburgh abbey, includes the item: "From the gift of Turgot de Rosdale the religious house of Liddel with all the land adjoining it" (*RMS*, i. App. 1, no. 94). It is described, 1524–47, as "the place and cell of Canonbie" (*Formulare*, i. no. 291). Henry VIII took upon himself to give orders for the suppression of this priory (which was in the "Debatable land"), "as others have been suppressed in England", 30 November 1544 (*L. & P. H. VIII*, xix². no. 681). It was erected, along with Jedburgh abbey, into a temporal lordship for Alexander, Lord Home, in parliament, 1606 (*APS*, iv, 360–1) and by charter, 1610 (*RMS*, vii. no. 290). The buildings were demolished, –1620 (*Scotts of Buccleuch*, i. 252, 256; ii. 465–6).

HOLYROOD. According to *Chron. Mailros* (p. 68) and *Chron. Holyrood* (p. 116), "the church of Holyrood began to be founded" in 1128. A. O. Anderson shows that the theory that the canons were originally housed in Edinburgh Castle, first put forward by Father Hay in the seventeenth century, seems to be unwarranted (*Chron. Holyrood*, p. 117 *n.*). The founder was David I, whose "great charter" (*Lib. S. Crucis*, no. 1) is, however, later than 1128 (Lawrie, *ESC*, pp. 384, 386). Holyrood was a daughter-house of Merton, in Surrey (Dickinson, *Orig. of Austin Canons*, p. 118, *n.* 5). The abbot was granted the mitre 27 July 1379 (*Lib. S. Crucis*, p. 204). In 1322, the abbey was sacked by the English (*Scotich.*, lib. xii, cap. v (ii. 278) ) and burned by them, in 1385 (*Ibid.*, lib. xiv, cap. 1 (ii. 401 *n.*) ). It is said to have been rebuilt, *c.* 1460 (*Lib. S. Crucis*, xxxi). On 6 May 1544, it was burned by Hertford's forces (*Hamilton Papers*, ii. no. 233; *L. & P. H. VIII*, xix¹. nos. 533, 534; "the Late Expedicion in Scotlande" in Dalyell, *Fragments of Scottish Hist.*, p. 11); and again in 1547, during Somerset's expedition, when the abbey was found deserted of its monks and the lead and bells were removed (Patten, "The Expedicion into Scotlande", in Dalyell, *op. cit.*, p. 82). The Reformers appear to have destroyed the altars, in 1559 (Lesley, cited *Lib. S. Crucis*, lxxiv; Knox, *History*, i. 391). The abbey and certain of its properties were erected into a temporal lordship for John Bothwell, in parliament, 1606 (*APS*, iv. 330–2) and by charter, 1607 (*RMS*, vi. no. 2004). The church was afterwards used as the parish church of the Canongate.
Dependency: St Mary's Isle.

INCHAFFRAY. Originally the site of a Celtic community (*v.* under Celtic Foundations). Founded as a priory by Gilbert, earl of Strathearn in 1200 (*Inchaffray*, no. ix) and said to have been colonized from Scone (*Scotich.*, lib. viii, cap. lxxiii (i. 529) ). It became an abbey in 1220 or 1221 (*Inchaffray*, p. 250). On 11 June 1237, a bull of Pope Gregory IX contemplated the transference of the see of Dunblane to Inchaffray, the canons of which were to have the election of the bishop (Theiner, *Vet. Mon.*, no. xc), but this did not take place. From 1495 the abbey was in the hands of commendators (*Inchaffray*, pp. 255–9). It was erected into a temporal lordship in favour of James Drummond, as Lord Maddertie, 31 January 1609 (*Ibid.*, xciii). This, however, did not take effect; and the erection was not finally made until 15 February 1669, in favour of William Drummond, later Viscount Strathallan (*Ibid.*, p. 308).

## THE AUGUSTINIAN CANONS

| Name | County | Rank | Minimum Income (1561) | Founder | Fd. | Date D. or Sec. | Dependent on |
|---|---|---|---|---|---|---|---|
| * INCHCOLM | Fife | Priory | | Alexander I | c. 1123 | | |
| | | Abbey | £1240(?) | | 1235 | 1609 | |
| * INCHMAHOME | Perth | Priory | £1680 | Walter, earl of Menteith | 1238+ | 1604 | |

INCHCOLM. This island is said to have been the abode of a Celtic hermit (*Scotich.*, lib. v, cap. xxxvii (i. 287) ). Medieval writers as well as lists (both medieval and later) ascribe the foundation to Alexander I (†1124), and the *Scotichronicon* gives the date as c. 1123 (or, in certain versions, 1124) (*loc. cit.* (i. 286) ). But although a charter, c. 1180, speaks of the church of Aberdour as having been held by the canons of Inchcolm since the time of King Alexander (*Inchcolm*, no. v), the earliest extant charter of this house, 1162–9, represents Gregory, bishop of Dunkeld, as surrendering and quitclaiming to the canons the island and certain lands, of which, by precept of David I, he has had custody until the canons were settled in the island (*Ibid.*, no. 1). Since Bishop Gregory did not take office till late in the reign of David I (†1153), the indication is that the foundation was not complete till that time. One writer attributes the foundation to Murdoch, earl of Fife, and describes the community as Cistercian (Purves, *Revenue of the Scottish Crown* (1681), p. 105), but both these statements are inaccurate. This house, at first a priory, was erected into an abbey, 22 May 1235 (Theiner, *Vet. Mon.*, no. lxxviii). It is said that the abbey was attacked by the English in 1335 and 1385 (*Scotich.*, lib. xiii, cap. xxxiii (ii. 318); lib. xiv, cap. xlviii (ii. 398)) and that, "for fear of the English", the canons spent part of 1421 on the mainland (*Ibid.*, xv, cap. xxxviii (ii. 467) ). In 1547, the island was occupied by the English (*Inchcolm*, xxxix–xl) and by the French (*Ibid.*, xl). By 1564, the convent had finally removed from the island; and the convent had died out by 1578 (*Ibid.*). The abbey and its lands were erected into a temporal lordship for Henry Stewart, as Lord St Colme, in parliament, 1609 (*APS*, iv. 464) and by charter, 1611 (*RMS*, vii. no. 442).

INCHMAHOME. Before the erection of the priory, there was apparently a parish church on this island—a parson of "insula Macholem" is mentioned, c. 1210 (*Cambuskenneth*, no. 122). Soon after 1238, the priory was founded by Walter, earl of Menteith (*Lib. Ins. Missarum*, xxxi; *Menteith*, ii. no. 74). On 3 June 1508, it was annexed by Pope Julius II to the Chapel Royal of Stirling (GRH. Vat. Trans., iii. 168–9); but the union was dissolved before 27 October 1529 (*Letters of James V*, p. 161, from Tyninghame Letter Bk.). *V.* Stirling, Chapel Royal, under Secular Canons (II). On 22 April 1536, James V is found writing to the Cardinal of Ravenna resisting the union of this house, as a cell, to Jedburgh abbey (*Ibid.*). The priory, p. 317 with the abbeys of Dryburgh and Cambuskenneth, was erected into a temporal lordship for John, second earl of Mar, 1604 and 1606 (*APS*, iv. 343).

| Name | County | Rank | Minimum Income (1561) | Founder | Date Fd. | D. or Sec. | Dependent on |
|------|--------|------|------------------------|---------|----------|------------|--------------|
| * JEDBURGH | Roxburgh | Priory Abbey | £2480 (with Restennet and Canonbie) | David I | *c.* 1138 *c.* 1154 | 1606 | |

JEDBURGH. Egred, bishop of Lindesfarne (830–846), who, *c.* 830, granted the two vills, both called Jedworth, to the church of Lindesfarne (Symeon of Durham, *Hist. Dunelm. Eccl.*, i. 52–3; *Hist. Regum*, ii. 101) is said to have built a church in Jedburgh (*Annals of Lindesfarne*, cited A. O. Anderson, *Scottish Annals*, p. 60 *n.*). This church is mentioned, *c.* 1080 (Symeon of Durham, *Hist. Regum*, ii. 198). The inference that "Jedburgh was an ancient monastic church fallen into decay when David I revived it as a house of Austin canons" (M. Morgan, "Organisation of the Scottish Ch. in the Twelfth Cent.", *Trans. RHS*, 4th Ser., xxix (1947), 144) is possible but not certain—the church founded by Bishop Egred may have been at Old Jedburgh, about five miles from the site of the Augustinian foundation. David I founded this house, *c.* 1138 (Lawrie, *ESC*, no. clxxxix). The date, 1148, given in Smyth's Chronicle (*Kinlos*, p. 4) is too late. It is stated by John of Hexham that John, bishop of Glasgow, "was buried in the church of Jedburgh where he had himself established a convent of regular clergy" (A. O. Anderson, *Scottish Annals*, p. 221). This cannot be taken as a suggestion that the bishop was the founder; it must mean that he was instrumental in bringing the Augustinian canons to Jedburgh. The original foundation was a priory—a prior is mentioned in 1139 (Lawrie, *op. cit.*, no. cxxi). The canons were brought from Beauvais (*v.* Barrow, "Scottish Rulers and the Religious Orders", *Trans. RHS*, 5th Ser., iii (1953), 92–3). This house became an abbey, *c.* 1154 (Lawrie, *Annals*, no. xxxii). Morton (*Monastic Annals*, p. 11) declares that in the wars, 1297–1300, the abbey was plundered and destroyed, the lead stripped from the roof of the church and retained by Sir Richard Hastings, after its restoration had been ordered by the [English] king; and that the canons were reduced to such destitution that Edward I gave them asylum in England until their monastery should be repaired. This, apart from the removal of the lead, which happened *c.* 1305 (*CDS*, ii. no. 1727) is a travesty of the facts. In 1296, the election of a pro-English abbot was confirmed by Edward I (*Ibid.*, ii. nos. 836, 837, 839). The abbot and eleven canons left the abbey on 28 February 1312/3 (the day after the taking of Roxburgh Castle by the Scots), obviously because their pro-English activities had endangered their safety; they were housed at Thornton-on-Humber (*Ibid.*, iii. nos. 630 (1318–19), 894 (1314–26)), and refused re-admission to the abbey *c.* 1325 (*CPR*, ii. 245). The monastic buildings are described as ruinous, in 1502 (*ALC*, 1501–54, lx). On 24 September 1523, the abbey was burned by the English (*L. & P. H. VIII*, iii². no. 3360), and again 9 June 1544 (*Ibid.*, xix¹. no. 762; "the Late Expedicion", in Dalyell, *Fragments of Scottish Hist.*, p. 14) and in September 1545 (*H. VIII SP*, v. 518; *L. & P. H. VIII*, xx². no. 456). Along with Coldingham priory, it was erected into a temporal lordship for Alexander, Lord Home, in parliament, 1606 (*APS*, iv. 360 1) and by charter, 1610 (*RMS*, vii. no. 290). This house is erroneously called Cluniac (NLS. MS. 33.2.12, 2).

Dependencies: Blantyre; Canonbie; Restennet.

H

## THE AUGUSTINIAN CANONS

| Name | County | Rank | Minimum Income (1561) | Founder | Date Fd. | D. or Sec. | Mother House |
|------|--------|------|------------------------|---------|----------|------------|--------------|
| ¶ Loch Leven (Portmoak) | Kinross | Priory | £250 | Originally a house of Culdees | 1152/3 | 1580 | St Andrews priory |

May *v.* Pittenweem

Loch Leven, St Serf (Portmoak). Originally the site of a Culdee settlement (*v.* under Celtic Foundations). David I granted the *island* to the canons of St Andrews, *c.* 1150, with provision for expelling those Culdees who refused to become regular canons (*RPSA*, pp. 188–9). The *priory* of the island of Loch Leven is further granted to the priory of St Andrews by Robert, bishop of St Andrews, 1152–3 (*Ibid.*, p. 43). It is called the priory of St Serf's in Loch Leven, as late as 1 August 1562 (*RMS*, iv. no. 2934); but it is evidently identical with the priory of Portmoak. Thus, Walter Monypenny is designated prior of Loch Leven otherwise "Portmook", 22 September 1465 (*Scottish Benefices*, p. 150); there is a reference to the prior of St Serf's in Loch Leven or Portmoak, 9 October 1544 (*RMS*, v. no. 1146); and the priory is frequently described as of Portmoak in the fifteenth and sixteenth centuries. The use of this designation may mean that the canons ultimately resided there rather than on the island. The priory of Portmoak was granted by James VI to St Leonard's College, St Andrews, 29 July 1580 (*RMS*, v. no. 1; *APS*, iii. 278).

May. *V.* Pittenweem.

## THE AUGUSTINIAN CANONS

| Name | County | Rank | Minimum Income (1561) | Founder | Fd. | Date D. or Sec. | Dependent on |
|---|---|---|---|---|---|---|---|
| ‡§ MONYMUSK | Aberdeen | Priory | £400 | Gilchrist, earl of Mar | –1245 | 1617 | (St. Andrews) |
| ¶ ORONSAY | Argyll | Priory | ? | ? | ? | 1616 | |

MONYMUSK. Erroneously called "Monymaill in fyfe" (Bisset, *Rolment of Courtis*, ii. 123). This was originally a Culdee community; *v*. Celtic Foundations. There is a reference to the building of a monastery at Monymusk, about the end of the twelfth century, by Gilchrist, earl of Mar, "in the church of St Mary in which the Culdees formerly were" (*RPSA*, p. 374) (Gilchrist may be regarded as the founder rather than the (unnamed) bishop of St Andrews given as founder in the list appended to *Scotichronicon* (ii. 540) or Malcolm III (Canmore) (1080+) (*Collns. Aberd. and Banff*, i. 169; *ESC*, p. 235)). But as the result of a complaint by William de Malvoisin, bishop of St Andrews (who was not the diocesan bishop but who held the vill of Monymusk), that "certain *keledei* who profess to be canons . . . and certain others in the vill of Monymusk . . . do not fear to establish a kind of regular canonry in opposition to him . . . to the prejudice and hurt of his church", Pope Innocent III, on 23 March 1211, appointed commissioners who established an agreement between the bishop and the Culdees. In terms of this, the Culdees will have a refectory, a dormitory and an oratory, with burial rights in the cemetery of the parish church. There will be twelve Culdees, with a thirteenth as prior, on whose death or retirement they will choose three of their number from whom the bishop of St Andrews shall select a prior. Likewise, it shall not be lawful for the Culdees to adopt "the life or order of monks or canons regular" without the bishop's consent, nor to exceed their appointed number. The Culdees had confirmation of their lands and revenues and undertook to do nothing to the hurt of the parish church of Monymusk (*RPSA*, pp. 370–2). In charters of Duncan, earl of Mar, 1211–14, the brethren are designated "Culdees or canons" (*Ibid.*, p. 362) and also merely "canons" (*Ibid.*, p. 367). Dr Douglas Simpson regards the bull of Innocent IV, 19 May 1245, which is addressed to "the prior and convent of Monymusk of the order of St Augustine" (*Ibid.*, p. 372) as "marking the completed transformation of the Culdees into canons regular" (*PSAS*, lix (1925), 44). The history of this house until the sixteenth century is obscure. On 17 March 1548/9 and 9 December 1550, it is described as ruinous (*Collns. Aberd. and Banff*, pp. 179, 182); on 11 July 1554, it is mentioned as having through negligence of the prior and his servants, been burned (*Antiqs. Aberd. and Banff*, iv. 776–9); and on 27 March 1558, it is said of Monymusk that "the place and religion thereof [are] distroyit" (*Scottish Corresp. of Mary of Lorraine*, no. cclxxvi). The last surviving member of the convent appears on record, 13 August 1574 (*PCR*, 1st Ser., ii. 389–390) and *c*. 1584, Robert Forbes, the last prior (or commendator), considering that "the place and monastery . . . is now almost ruined and waste", granted to his kinsman, William Forbes of Monymusk, the dilapidated houses and buildings, with provision for their restoration and the institution of a school (*Collns. Aberd. and Banff*, p. 184). It is said, however, that the ruins supplied stone for the building of the Forbeses' castle of Monymusk (*Ibid.*, p. 171). The priory was annexed to the bishopric of Dunblane, in parliament, 1617 (*APS*, iv. 553–4). *V*. W. Douglas Simpson, "The Augustinian Priory and Parish Church of Monymusk", *PSAS*, lix (1925), 34–71. I am much indebted to this article.

ORONSAY. The history of this priory is obscure. It is said to have been the site of a Celtic monastery which was transformed by a lord of the Isles into a priory of canons regular brought from Holyrood (*Scotich.*, lib. i, cap. vi (i. 5)); but there is no mention of it in the Holyrood charters. That it was an Augustinian house is attested by references in the fifteenth century, e.g. in 1426 (*Scottish Benefices*, p. 92) and later. On 15 February 1616, James VI granted to the bishop of the Isles the island of Oronsay, along with land in Colonsay formerly belonging to the priory and other properties, all of which are incorporated in a tenandry of Oronsay (*RMS*, vii. no. 1386; *HMC 4th Rep.*, App., 479).

THE AUGUSTINIAN CANONS

| Name | County | Rank | Minimum Income (1561) | Founder | Fd. | Date D. or Sec. | Dependent on |
|------|--------|------|------------------------|---------|-----|-----------------|--------------|
| § PITTENWEEM | Fife | Priory | £1020 | *V.* notes | –1318 | 1606 | St Andrews |

PITTENWEEM. *V.* May under Benedictine Monks. The lands of Pittenweem were granted to the monks of May by David I, *c.* 1143 (*May*, no. 4; the date is given thus by Lawrie (*ESC*, no. clv)). While it is commonly assumed that the priory was established through the transference to Pittenweem of the community in the Isle of May during the late thirteenth or early fourteenth century, i.e. in the period within which the priory of May passed from the possession of the Benedictine abbey of Reading into the possession of the Augustinian priory of St Andrews, it is impossible to trace the precise course of events which led to this migration or to assign it a specific date. The available evidence presents an abundance of problems and discrepancies. Mr A. A. M. Duncan has drawn my attention to the mention of a prior of Pittenweem at the beginning of the thirteenth century—"H. prior de pethneweme" appears as a papal judge-delegate in a record of 1202+ (NLS. MS. 15.1.18, 18)—and suggests that he may be identified with Hugh de Mortimer, prior of May (–1206). If this identification is correct, it would seem to indicate that Pittenweem was used as an alternative designation of May before the priory was transferred from the island; this would explain the mention of a prior of Pittenweem, 25 October 1270 (*APS*, i. Preface, 92) and perhaps also certain later references to priors of this designation (e.g. *c.* 1300 (*Dryburgh*, nos. 291, 292)). In a petition of the prior and convent of St Andrews in Edward I's parliament of 1305 or 1306, it is stated that the abbot of Reading had enfeoffed William Fraser, bishop of St Andrews, in the priory of Pittenweem; and that he enfeoffed in it the church (i.e. the priory) of St Andrews (*v.* under May, where the sale of *May* to the bishop of St Andrews is shown to have taken place, 1286-8). The petitioners now seek remedy for their ejection by the abbot of Reading from the priory (*Mem. de Parl.*, no. 317). Another petition in the same parliament seeks remedy on behalf of the abbot of Reading for certain wrongs done to him and his men at Pittenweem (*Ibid.*, no. 318); and, on 2 September 1306, Edward I reported to Aymer de Valence a complaint of the abbey of Reading that the bishop and prior of St Andrews had invaded the Isle of May and the manor of Pittenweem, removed property and molested their men (PRO Ancient Corresp., xlvii/89). It is difficult to explain the facts that Thomas de Houburn, canon of St Andrews and liegeman of Edward I, describes himself in a petition to that king (dated in *CDS*, 1306-7) as ousted from the priory of Pittenweem by the Scots (*CDS*, ii. no. 1964) (*v.* May) and that, on 20 December 1309, Jordan, prior of Pittenweem, is mentioned as receiving supplies from the English (*Ibid.*, iii. no. 121). A prior of Pittenweem attended the Scots parliament 6 November 1314 (*APS*, i. 14); and by 1 July 1318, "all right of the monastery of Reading in England which it had in the priory of May and Pittenweem has been transferred entirely to the monastery of St Andrews". To the latter house, on that date, William de Lamberton, bishop of St Andrews, made payable the pension of sixteen marks, formerly paid to Reading by the priory of May (*May*, xci-xcii). Thereafter the priory is sometimes designated as of May, sometimes as of Pittenweem and May, though, by the sixteenth century, its more usual designation is of Pittenweem. It was held *in commendam* by a number of bishops and archbishops of St Andrews, beginning with James Kennedy, who obtained it, *c.* 1447 (A. I. Dunlop, *James Kennedy*, p. 82). To Kennedy's successor, Patrick Graham, who also held the commend and who became first archbishop of that see, the Pope granted that the priory should be united to the archbishopric, 22 December 1472 (Theiner, *Vet. Mon.*, no. dcccliii). But it appears to have been held *in commendam* rather than as specifically attached to the archbishopric by William Schevez (1477/8–1496/7), who, 26 June 1487, paid annates for the priory, "which was formerly united and is provided anew" (*Scottish Benefices*, p. 220); while Andrew Forman (1514–1520/1) had held it before becoming archbishop (Herkless and Hannay, *Archbps. of St Ands.*, ii. 12). On 22 April 1487, it is described as non-conventual (*CPR*, xiv. 157); but a charter of the prior of Pittenweem and May, 26 April 1542, is subscribed by nine canons (*Yester Writs*, no. 590). In 1593, James VI confirmed the grant of the monastic buildings to the magistrates and community of the burgh of Pittenweem (*RMS*, v. no. 2356). The lands of the priory were erected into a temporal lordship for Frederick Stewart, 1606 *APS*, iv. 361).

## THE AUGUSTINIAN CANONS

| Name | County | Rank | Minimum Income (1561) | Founder | Fd. | Date D. or Sec. | Depen-dent on |
|------|--------|------|----------------------|---------|-----|------------------|---------------|
| PORTMOAK *v.* LOCH LEVEN | | | | | | | |
| * RESTENNET | Angus | Priory | *v.* Jedburgh | Malcolm IV | −1153 or 1153–60 | 1606 | Jedburgh |

PORTMOAK *v.* LOCH LEVEN.

RESTENNET (RESTENNETH). Possibly the site of a Celtic foundation (*v.* Simpson, *Celtic Ch. in Scotland*, p. 112). Letters of Patrick, bishop of Brechin (dated 1 May 1361) testify to having seen a charter of David I relating to certain endowments of the prior and canons of Restennet (*HMC, 14th Rep.*, App., Pt. III, 187–8), which would suggest that the priory was founded −1153; some dubiety must attach to this, although the foundation may have been incomplete. At all events, Malcolm IV granted to Jedburgh abbey, 1153–60, the church of St Peter of Restennet, in which a prior and convent were to be placed (*Archaeologia Scotica*, v. 311–12; *Carnegies, Earls of Southesk*, ii. 475 (Charters, no. 22)); and the prior and "brethren" are mentioned as dependent on Jedburgh, 23 August 1242 (*HMC 14th Rep.*, App., Pt. III, 188). In 1305, the abbot of Jedburgh obtained from Edward I a writ for the supply of oaks for the repair of the church and houses "in great part destroyed and burned in the war" (*CDS*, ii. nos. 1428, 1704). It is recorded, 12 June 1476, that the priory had been united by apostolic authority to the abbatial *mensa* of Jedburgh (*HMC 14th Rep.*, App., Pt. III, 188). On 2 May 1501, the revenues, amounting to £120 annually, of this priory where, it is said, only two canons have been wont to reside, were granted by Pope Alexander VI to the Chapel Royal of Stirling, with the reservation of provision for six (regular) canons (*Reg. C.R. Striv.*, no. 1; (*Hist. C.R. of Scotland*, pp. 3, 13)). Following on a letter of James IV requesting its annexation, 1 March 1507/8 (*Letters of James IV*, no. 156), Pope Julius II again united the priory (along with the priory of Inchmahome and the provostry of Lincluden) to the Chapel Royal (*Hist. C.R. of Scotland*, cxlv; GRH. Vat. Trans., iii. 168–9). But it transpires, in letters of James IV, November 1508, that the annexation of Restennet to the Chapel Royal had not taken effect and the king now proposed that it should be incorporated into the *mensa* of the archbishop of St Andrews or disponed at the archbishop's discretion (*Letters of James IV*, nos. 195, 201). There is no evidence that either of these courses was followed; and the priory was still attached to Jedburgh at the Reformation (*v. Thirds of Benefices*, pp. 25, 159). Till 1591 the church was in use as a parish church (*Carnegies, Earls of Southesk*, i. x, n.). The priory was erected into a temporal lordship for Viscount Fenton, afterwards earl of Kellie, in parliament, 1606 (*APS*, iv. 357) and by charter, 1614 (*RMS*, vii. no. 1024). It may be noted that the editor of the *History of the Chapel Royal of Scotland* (e.g. xxxii, xxxiv), misled apparently by Hay, *Scotia Sacra*, p. 644, where it is stated that "Rosneth" was a priory of regular canons (cf. *Hist. C.R. Scotland*, xciii), confuses Restennet with Roseneath, which was not a monastic foundation (*v. infra*). I am also obliged to Mr R. Neville Hadcock for drawing my attention to an item (*CPR*, xiii, 625–6) regarding a monk of Dundrennan who petitions for permission to migrate to the monastery of St Peter, Ruthyn, described as of the institution of Bonshommes, O.S.A., 24 October 1478. The editor adds to the designation of the latter monastery: "In the diocese of St Andrews" and the index has "Ruthtyn, see Restennet". Both the location of "Ruthtyn" and its identification with Restennet are erroneous. The Bonshommes, in any case, are not found in Scotland. As Mr Hadcock has pointed out, this place is Ruthin, in the diocese of Bangor.

## THE AUGUSTINIAN CANONS

| Name | County | Rank | Minimum Income (1561) | Founder | Fd. | Date D. or Sec. | Dependent on |
|------|--------|------|------------------------|---------|-----|------------------|--------------|
| * St Andrews | Fife | Priory | £12500 | Robert, bishop of St Andrews | 1144 | 1592 | |
| St Mary's Isle (Trail) | Kirkcudbright | Priory | | ? | −1219/20 | 1608 | Holyrood |

St Andrews. The priory was eventually founded and endowed by Robert, bishop of St Andrews, in 1144 (*RPSA*, p. 122). *V.* Barrow, "Scottish Rulers and Relig. Orders", *Trans. RHS*, 5th Ser., iii (1953), 84. In 1147, Pope Eugenius III gave the rights of electing the bishop to the prior and canons instead of the Culdees (*RPSA*, p. 48). On the relations of the priory with the Culdees *v.* under Celtic Foundations. St Andrews was one of the two Scottish cathedrals whose clergy were regulars (the other was Whithorn which had Premonstratensian canons). The prior became mitred, 27 April 1418 (*Ibid.*, p. 412). There is no record of damage done to the priory buildings at the Reformation; but they are described as "decayit" in 1597 (*APS*, iv. 155). The priory was erected into a temporal lordship for Ludovic, duke of Lennox, in parliament, 1592 and 1606 (*APS*, iii. 589; iv. 353–5) and by charters, 1593 and 1611 (*RMS*, v. no. 2273; vii. no. 464).

Dependencies: Loch Leven; (Monymusk); (Pittenweem).

St Mary's Isle or The Isle of Trail. A fabulous account of the foundation of this priory attributes its erection to Fergus of Galloway (†1161) (*Bannatyne Misc.*, ii. 19 ff.). It is recorded that Fergus gave to the abbey of Holyrood the "island of Trail" (*Lib. S. Crucis*, pp. 24, 39). But there is no evidence that he founded the priory. The earliest indications of its existence are the mentions of a prior of the Isle in a papal letter, 22 February 1219/20 (Theiner, *Vet. Mon.*, no. xxxii) and of William, prior of the Isle, who is an emissary of Alan of Galloway to Henry III, −18 April 1220 (*CDS*, i. no. 754). David, prior of the Isle, witnesses the foundation charter of Sweetheart Abbey, 10 April 1273 (*Laing Chs.*, no. 46). On 1 August 1323, Robert I gave the tenth of the royal pleas between the rivers Cree and Nith to the abbot and convent of Holyrood for the support of the prior and canons of the Isle of St Mary (GRH. Chs., no. 274). A letter of James IV to the Cardinal of St Mark, 1 March 1511/12, describes this priory as a cell of Holyrood and indicates both that it has become virtually independent of that abbey and threatens to become ruinous. James asks that it should be reunited to Holyrood or granted to the abbot of that house *in commendam* (*Letters of James IV*, no. 426). On 23 October 1587, James VI granted certain lands of St Mary's Isle to James Lidderdale (to whom the most part of the priory lands had been leased) and incorporated these in a tenandry (*RMS*, v. no. 1397). The priory lands were finally granted to James Lidderdale and his son Thomas (the priory being suppressed) as a free tenandry, by charter, 10 February 1608 (*Ibid.*, vii. no. 2029).

## THE AUGUSTINIAN CANONS

| Name | County | Rank | Minimum Income (1561) | Founder | Date Fd. | D. or Sec. | Dependent on |
|------|--------|------|------------------------|---------|----------|------------|--------------|
| SCONE | Perth | Priory | | Alexander I | c. 1120 | | |
| | | Abbey | £5350 | | c. 1164 | 1606 | |
| STRATHFILLAN | Perth | Priory | £40(?) | Robert I | 1317/18 | 1607 | |
| TRAIL v. ST MARY'S ISLE | | | | | | | |

SCONE. Said to have been originally occupied by Culdees, though this cannot be verified (v. under Celtic Foundations). Scone was an ancient seat of the kings of Scotland. The foundation of this house as an Augustinian priory by Alexander I is ascribed to 1114 (*Scotich.*, lib. v, cap. xxxvi (i. 286); Edin. Univ. Chronicle cited A. O. Anderson, *Early Sources*, ii. 159 n.) and 1115 (*Chron. Mailros*, p. 65). Lawrie (*ESC*, pp. 280 ff.) contends that the so-called foundation charter, c. 1120 (*Scon*, no. 1) is spurious. He likewise seeks to controvert the statement made there and in the *Scotichronicon* that the king had canons sent to Scone from Nostell, on the ground that, in 1115, St Oswald's (Nostell) was not yet a house of regular canons (*ESC*, p. 286); and that Adelwald, prior of St Oswald's, who is said to have acceded to the king's request, did not hold that office till 1128 (*Ibid.*, p. 281). On the other hand, Wilson, while "leaving it to the reader's judgement" to say "whether Nostell . . . could have been famous enough to attract the notice of King Alexander so early as 1115", offers evidence to show that Adelwald was that king's contemporary and declares: "There can be now no hesitation in acknowledging Prior Adelwald's co-operation with him in establishing the Augustinians in Scotland" ("Foundation of the Austin Priories of Nostell and Scone", *SHR*, vii (1910). 156–7). The colonization of Scone from Nostell seems probable—it was accepted in the Middle Ages (cf. the reference to "the monastery of St Oswald in England from which our monastery of Scone took its origin" (4 February 1420/1) (*Copiale*, p. 103))—and the date of the foundation may be somewhat later than that given by *Chron. Mailros*. Barrow ("Scottish Rulers and the Relig. Orders", *Trans. RHS*, 5th Ser., iii (1953), 83) suggests c. 1120. The priory became an abbey, –5 December 1164 (*Scon*, no. 18; *Chron. Holyrood*, pp. 139, 140 n.); what is probably a genuine charter of Malcolm IV, 24 May 1163–23 May 1164, declares that after the church of Scone had been destroyed by fire, the king had constituted an abbot in it "for the stability and advancement" of that church (*Scon*, no. 5). The abbot became mitred, 12 September 1395 (*Ibid.*, no. 192). The abbey was pillaged and destroyed by an English army in 1298 (*Ibid.*, no. 124). In 1559 it was attacked and burned by Reformers (Lesley, *History*, p. 274; Knox, *History*, i. 359–61); the monastery, houses and church are said, in a charter of 28 August 1559 to be "now burned to the ground" (*Bamff Chs.*, no. 59). In 1581 the abbey was erected into a temporal lordship for the earl of Gowrie (*RMS*, v. no. 258), after whose forfeiture it was again erected for David Murray, Lord Scone and later Viscount Stormont, in parliament, 1606 (*APS*, iv. 328) and by charter, 1608 (*RMS*, vi. no. 2138).

STRATHFILLAN. On 26 February 1317/18, Robert I granted the patronage of the church of Killin to Inchaffray abbey so that this house might provide a canon to celebrate divine service in the church of Strathfillan (*Inchaffray*, no. cxxiii). The development of this foundation into a priory is seen in a charter, 28 October 1318, whereby William, bishop of Dunkeld, bestowed this church upon the abbot of Inchaffray and the canons of that monastery, who by appointment of the abbot shall serve in the chapel of St Fillan in Glendochart (provided that, according to the capabilities of the place, a sufficient number of canons should be settled there) "so that all the fruits and revenues of the said church [Killin] should be converted by the ordinance of the abbot to the use of the prior and canons dwelling at the said chapel for divine worship" (*Ibid.*, no. cxxvi). There is a record of a grant to the fabric of the church, in 1329 (*ER*, i. 214). Priors of this house appear on record from 2 October 1498 (*RMS*, ii. no. 2458). This was evidently a small and poor foundation; its rental is given, in 1573, as £40 (*Inchaffray*, xlvi). For an account of this house, v. *Inchaffray*, xliv–xlvi. Spottiswoode (p. 393) declares that it was bestowed on Campbell of Glenorchy; but the revenues of the priory were apparently granted to Archibald Campbell of Glencarradale by the Crown, 19 March 1607 (Gillies, *In Famed Breadalbane*, p. 239).

TRAIL, v. ST MARY'S ISLE.

## THE AUGUSTINIAN CANONS

### UNCERTAIN FOUNDATION

*Loch Tay.* Alexander I granted an island in Loch Tay to the canons of Scone "so that a church of God may be built there for me and for the soul of the late Sibilla (his queen) and that they may serve God there in religious habit" (*Scon*, no. 2). This charter must have been given between 13 July 1122 (the date of Queen Sibilla's death) and 23 April 1124 (the date of the king's death). *Scotichronicon* (lib. ii, cap. x (i. 46) ) mentions "Louch-Tay" as a "cell of canons of Scone". But while the island appears among the possessions of Scone in a charter of Malcolm IV, 1163–4 (*Scon*, no. 5) and bulls of 1164 and 1226/7 (*Ibid.*, nos. 18, 103), there is apparently no reference in records (including those of Scone) to a priory until 29 April 1612, when the "lands, castles, fisheries, etc., which belonged to the temporality of the priory of the island of Loch Tay" appear in a crown charter of confirmation granted to David, Lord Scone (*RMS*, vii. no. 645). A similar reference— to the lands, etc., belonging from of old to the temporality of the priory of Loch Tay— is found, 18 May 1642 (*Perth Retours*, no. 507). There is, however, no mention of such a priory in the acts of parliament of 1581 and 1606 erecting the abbey of Scone into a temporal lordship (*APS*, iii. 263; iv. 328); and neither the references to its properties (which are late, formal and exaggerated) nor the statement of Spottiswoode (p. 386) that in his time "the most part of the buildings" were still extant (since those to which he refers were very probably secular (*v.* Lawrie, *ESC*, p. 295) ) can be taken as proving unequivocally that the priory was established. Lawrie is not sure that the charter óf Alexander I is genuine and while admitting that "the story that a priory was built has been generally accepted", doubts the correctness of Spottiswoode's statements, e.g. that "Loch Tay . . . was a cell or priory belonging to Scone, founded by King Alexander in the year 1122" (*op. cit.*, pp. 294–5). The existence of this priory must be regarded as uncertain. Sir Walter Scott's description, in *The Fair Maid of Perth*, of a burial at this priory is picturesque but unhistorical and his statement, in a note to that novel, that the last inhabitants of it were three nuns is based on a fanciful explanation of the name of a local fair.

### SUPPOSED FOUNDATIONS

*Aberuthven.* The statement of MacGibbon and Ross that "this church was a cell of Inchaffray" (*Eccles. Archit.*, iii. 486) is utterly inaccurate. This church was granted to the "brethren" at Inchaffray, *c.* 1198 (*Inchaffray*, no. iii) and to the Augustinian canons there, *c.* 1200 (*Ibid.*, no. xiii). But it was a parish church and in no sense a "cell" of that abbey.

*Carinish.* "Scarinche" in Lewis [*sic*] is described as a cell of Inchaffray in the list appended to *Scotichronicon* (ii. 540) and by Spottiswoode (p. 393), who also attributes its foundation to "the Macleods of the Lewis". Dowden, however, shows that Inchaffray held the chapel and lands of "Karynch" in *Uist* (*Inchaffray*, xlvii–xlviii); there is no evidence of a priory. Monro mentions five parish churches in Uist (*Western Isles*, pp. 48–9) but no monastery, nor does he mention Scarinche in Lewis. This "cell" is apocryphal.

*Colonsay.* *Scotichronicon* (lib. ii, cap. x (i. 45) ) declares that there was an abbey of regular canons here and to this is added by Spottiswoode (p. 390) that it was founded by the lord of the Isles and colonized from Holyrood. Hay (Scotia Sacra, p. 458) elaborates this by stating that while the founder's name had been lost, there existed at the Vatican a letter addressed to the convent; and he gives alleged details of the first two abbots. Finally, *Origines Parochiales* (ii[1]. 281), having accepted the foregoing statements, goes on to make the (absurd) assertion that "it is traditionally believed that the abbey of Colonsay, which in all probability had been decayed after the retirement of the second abbot recorded by Father Hay, was that of which Oronsay was the priory". These accounts appear to be without foundation. There is no mention of Colonsay in the Holyrood charters. Monro's description (1549) mentions no monastery (*Western Isles*, p. 29); and it is impossible to believe that there were Augustinian foundations in both of the closely contiguous islands of Oronsay and Colonsay. According to a bull of 1203, the abbey of Iona held the church and island of Colonsay (*Highland Papers*, i. 83). Oronsay priory is also said, in the sixteenth century, to have held land in Colonsay (*HMC Rep.*, iv. App., 479).

*Crusay.* Mentioned by Spottiswoode (p. 390) as in the Western Isles, but the site is probably Crossaig in Kintyre, where there are some ecclesiastical remains. This alleged foundation appears also in seventeenth-century MS. lists; but no evidence of a priory here can be found.

## THE AUGUSTINIAN CANONS

*Kinkell.* This was simply a parish church, granted to Inchaffray abbey, *c.* 1200 (*Inchaffray*, no. xv). There is nothing to support the idea that it was a cell of that abbey.

*Rodel (Rowadill).* Monro describes it as "ane monastery with ane steipell . . . foundit and biggit by McCloyd of Harrey" (*Western Isles*, p. 61). It is included among Augustinian houses by Spottiswoode (p. 390), who also ascribes its foundation to MacLeod of Harris. Hay (Scotia Sacra, p. 644) calls it a monastery of canons regular. There is, however, no reason to regard this as other than a parish church or perhaps a chapel.

*Roslin.* Mentioned by Gervase of Canterbury as a priory of black canons (A. O. Anderson, *Scottish Annals*, p. 327). This is obviously an error for "Rostin[oth]", a form of the name Restennet (*v. supra*).

*Rosneath.* "It is said by some," declares Spottiswoode (p. 391), "that this place was a monastery of canons regular." He rightly adds: "It appears it was only a parish church." *V.* Restennet *supra* with which it has been confused.

*Roxburgh.* An Augustinian house is said to have existed here (A. O. Anderson, *Early Sources*, ii. 183 *n.*, 697). This is evidently due to confusion with the Franciscan friary (*q.v.*).

## THE PREMONSTRATENSIAN CANONS

The history of the houses of this order in Scotland is difficult to reconstruct, as the only surviving chartulary is that of the abbey of Dryburgh.

The development of the Scottish *circariae* and the question of the primacy of the abbey of Soulseat (*infra*) have been dealt with by Backmund, *Monasticon Praemonstratense*, ii, 94–6. On the latter point, it may be mentioned that a letter of James IV to the General of the Premonstratensians, 1 May 1507, states that the prior of Whithorn has extorted royal letters to the General asking that his house should be ranked first of the order in Scotland and that he should have the full jurisdiction in visitation and reformation which the abbot of Soulseat, despite his much inferior status, then held. The General complied. But King James referred the question to the archbishop of St Andrews, who found that Dryburgh, and not Soulseat or Whithorn, was at the head of the order. He accordingly besought the archbishop to put the matter right (*Letters of James IV*, no. 107). On the same date, the archbishop writes to the General asking that the old pre-eminence of Dryburgh should be revived.

| Name | County | Rank | Minimum Income (1561) | Founder | Fd. | Date D. or Sec. | (Mother-house) |
|------|--------|------|------------------------|---------|-----|------------------|----------------|
| * DRYBURGH | Berwick | Abbey | £2210 | Hugh de Moreville | 1150 | 1606 | (Alnwick) |

DRYBURGH. This house was founded 10 November 1150 and the convent came there 13 December 1152 (*Chron. Mailros*, p. 74). The founder was Hugh de Moreville (*Dryburgh*, no. 14); the alleged foundation charter (*Ibid.*, lxix), which attributes the foundation to David I is spurious (Lawrie, *ESC*, p. 436). On its pre-eminence in the order in Scotland, *v. supra*. On 9 March 1390/1, the abbey was granted the lands and possessions of South Berwick (i.e. Berwick-on-Tweed) nunnery (*RMS*, i. no. 832). It was burned by the English in 1322 (*Scotich.*, lib. xii, cap. iv (ii. 278)); in 1385 (*Ibid.*, lib. xiv, cap. 1 (ii. 401)); probably in 1523, since on 13 December of that year, the duke of Albany, writing to the cardinal of St Eusebius, speaks of the monastery having suffered loss and destruction through English raids and the need of an abbot who would revive monastic life and repair the buildings (*Letters of James V*, p. 95); and, again, except the church, in November 1544 (*L. & P. H. VIII*, xix². no. 625) and September 1545 (*Ibid.*, xx². no. 456). It was erected, along with Cambuskenneth abbey and Inchmahome priory, into the temporal lordship of Cardross in favour of John, earl of Mar, in parliament, 1604 and 1606 (*APS*, iv. 343 ff.) and by charter, 1610 and 1615 (*RMS*, vii. nos. 301, 1222).

## THE PREMONSTRATENSIAN CANONS

| Name | County | Rank | Minimum Income (1561) | Founder | Date Fd. D. or Sec. | | Mother House |
|------|--------|------|------------------------|---------|------|------|--------------|
| ‡§ FEARN | Ross | Abbey | £1010 | Ferquhard, earl of Ross | 1221–2 or *c.* 1227 (at Old Fearn) *c.* 1238 (at New Fearn) | 1609 | (Whithorn) |
| HOLYWOOD or DERCONGAL | Dumfries | Abbey | £880(?) | Not known | –1225 | 1609 | (Soulseat) |
| SOULSEAT | Wigtown | Abbey | £810(?) | Fergus of Galloway(?) | –1161(?) or –1175 | 1630 | (Prémontré) |

FEARN. Said to have been founded by Ferquhard, earl of Ross, at "Farne beside Kincardin in Stracharrin", 1221–2 or *c.* 1227, whence the abbey was transferred, *c.* 1238, to a site in the parish of Tarbat, after which it was called New Fearn. It is stated to have been rebuilt between 1338 and 1372 (*OPS*, ii². 435; *Beauly*, p. 313). In a letter of James V to Pope Paul III, 9 March 1540/1, this house is described as ruinous and neglected (*Letters of James V*, pp. 420–1). From the beginning of the sixteenth century it was mainly in the hands of commendators. On 1 February 1597/8, the manor of Fearn, "called of yore the monastery of Fearn", was granted in feu to Patrick Murray of Geanies (*RMS*, vi. no. 650; cf. *APS*, iv. 240 ff.). The abbey was annexed to the bishopric of Ross, in parliament, 1609 (*APS*, iv. 446).

HOLYWOOD or DERCONGAL. The identity of the founder and the date of foundation are unknown. One list (NLS. MS. 33.2.12) gives this house as Cistercian and the founder as Devorgilla, daughter of Alan of Galloway, but this is evidently due to confusion with Sweetheart abbey. An abbot of Dercongal is a papal mandatory, 18 December 1225 (*Passelet*, p. 320; this is the reference mentioned by Spottiswoode (p. 399) ). The history of this house is obscure. In 1609 it was erected, ineffectively, into a temporal lordship for Kirkpatrick of Closeburn (*APS*, iv. 464). It was finally erected for John Murray, afterwards earl of Annandale, in parliament, 1617 (*Ibid.*, iv. 575) and by charter, 1618 (*RMS*, viii, no. 1817).

SOULSEAT. Said to have been founded originally as a Cistercian abbey in 1148. *V.* under Cistercian Houses. The Obituary of Prémontré and the Necrology of Newhouse (cited Backmund, *Monasticon Praemonstratense*, ii. 109 *n.*) as well as lists of religious houses (e.g. *Scotich.*, ii. 538; EU. MS. Db. 6.19; NLS. MS. 22.1.14) (the two latter lists describe Soulseat as Cistercian) ascribe the foundation of this abbey to Fergus of Galloway (†12 May 1161). Backmund (*op. cit.*, ii. 109) seeks to argue from the fact that the Premonstratensian General Chapter gave the primacy in the (Scottish) *circaria* to Soulseat, that the latter abbey was presumably the first of the order in Scotland and anterior in foundation to Dryburgh, i.e. its foundation took place, –1150–2. (On the question of its primacy, *v.* p. 86 *supra*.) On the other hand, Radford (*Trans. Dumfriesshire and Galloway Nat. Hist. and Antiq. Socy.*, 3rd Ser., xxvii, 103–4) maintains that this abbey, like Whithorn, its daughter-house, must have been founded during the episcopate of Bishop Christian, 1154–86. The date can only be regarded as uncertain. It may be significant that this house is mentioned as a daughter-house of Prémontré (Le Paige, *Bibl. Praemonst. Ord.*, p. 333), though this may mean that its mother-house was not known. The history of this house is obscure. It was annexed, in 1630, to the parsonage of Portpatrick (*APS*, v. 132).

## THE PREMONSTRATENSIAN CANONS

| Name | County | Rank | Minimum Income (1561) | Founder | Fd. | Date D. or Sec. | (Mother-house) |
|------|--------|------|-----------------------|---------|-----|-----------------|----------------|
| TONGLAND | Kirkcud-bright | Abbey | | Alan of Galloway | 1218 | 1612 | (Cocker-sand) |
| * WHITHORN | Wigtown | Priory | £2540 | ? | c. 1175 | 1612 | (Soulseat) |

TONGLAND. This foundation is also ascribed in certain lists (e.g. *Scotich.*, ii. 538; NLS. MS. 33.2.12) to Fergus of Galloway (†1161). But other lists (EU. MS. Db. 6.19; NLS. MSS. 22.1.14, 31.6.1) give the founder as Alan of Galloway (†1234), and this is more probable. Backmund (*Mon. Praem.*, ii. 111) quotes the statement of the Catalogus Ninivensis (2): "In the diocese of Candida Casa, the daughter house of Cockersand, was founded in the year of grace 1218: Tongland." The prior and sacrist are said to have been killed during the insurrection in Galloway in 1235 (*Chron. Mailros*, p. 146). James IV, probably in 1509, requested Pope Julius II to bestow this abbey on David, bishop of Galloway, so that he may reform its discipline and repair its ruins (*Letters of James IV*, no. 289); and it was held *in commendam* by that bishop 1510–25 (GRH. Vat. Trans., iii. 246; Dowden, *Bishops*, p. 371). On 27 October 1529, when the abbey is described as ruinous, although a few monks remain, James V, in turn, writes to Pope Clement VII and the cardinal of Ancona seeking the annexation of Tongland to the bishopric of Galloway (*Letters of James V*, pp. 161–2); and this union was sanctioned by a bull of 14 January 1529/30 (Brady, *Episc. Succ.*, i. 209), while King James besought confirmation of it from Pope Paul III, 3 July 1541 (*Epp. Reg. Scot.*, ii. 115; *Letters of James V*, p. 425). *V. Trans. Dumfriesshire and Galloway Nat. Hist. and Antiq. Socy.*, 3rd Ser., xxvii, 128–9. Except for a period 1588–c. 1606, when the abbey was held by William Melville as commendator (*APS*, iv. 156, 308), it remained annexed to the bishopric. This annexation was confirmed in parliament, October 1612 (*RMS*, vii, no. 1238).

WHITHORN. The foundation is attributed in numerous lists to Fergus of Galloway (†1161), but Bishop Christian (1154–86) is said to have changed the canons regular of his cathedral church into Premonstratensians in 1177 (*Trans. Dumfriesshire and Galloway Nat. Hist. and Antiq. Socy.*, 3rd Ser., xxvii, 104) and further reasons for accepting a date *c.* 1175 are given (*Ibid.*, p. 105). The names of the prior and twenty canons are recorded, *c.* 1235 (*Reg. of Walter Gray, archbp. of York*, pp. 172–3). The priory was granted to the bishop of Galloway in 1605 (RSS, lxxiv. 405, cited *Trans. D. and G.* (*ut supra*), p. 129) and, in parliament, 1612 (*RMS*, vii. no. 1238). This house is erroneously described as for white monks by Gervase of Canterbury (A. O. Anderson, *Scottish Annals*, p. 328) and in lists (*Id., Early Sources*, ii. 700). *V.* Dr Gordon Donaldson's valuable article, "The Bishops and Priors of Whithorn", *Trans. Dumfriesshire and Galloway Nat. Hist. and Antiq. Socy.*, 3rd Ser., xxvii, 127 ff., to which I am considerably indebted.

### SUPPOSED FOUNDATION

*Fidra* (Elbottle). The island of Elbottle (now known as Fidra) was granted by William de Vaux to the canons of Dryburgh (*Dryburgh*, no. 105) and, *c.* 1220, canons of that abbey were serving the church of St Nicholas there (*Ibid.*, nos. 23, 25, 26, 104). Lawrie calls this a "cell" (*ESC*, p. 329), but that term exaggerates its status. About 1240, the foundation is specifically described as a "chantry" (a somewhat unusual term in Scottish charters) in a charter providing for its termination on the island. Instead, one canon is to celebrate at Stodfald (on the mainland) and another in the abbey of Dryburgh (*Dryburgh*, no. 289).

## THE GILBERTINES

The best account of the one evanescent Gilbertine foundation in Scotland is given by J. Edwards ("The Order of Sempringham and its connexion with the West of Scotland", *Trans. Glasgow Archaeol. Socy.*, ii (1908), 72–90).

| | | | Date | |
|---|---|---|---|---|
| Name | County | Founder | Fd. | D. |
| DALMILLING | Ayr | Walter II, son of Alan, steward of Scotland | 1221 | 1238 |

DALMILLING (DALMULIN). The Chartulary of Malton (BM. MS. Cotton, Claudius D, xi. 227) contains a letter from Walter II, son of Alan, steward of Scotland, to Roger, master of Sempringham, intimating his intention of founding a house of this order and the endowment he proposes to give it and seeking the master's approval. Dr Rose Graham (*St Gilbert and the Gilbertines*, p. 46) committed herself to the statement that the Steward's offer was refused. On the contrary, Walter proceeded to found and endow a house of the order "in the place which is called Dalmulin above Ayr" (*Passelet*, p. 12). Edwards dates his charter 1221 ("The Order of Sempringham, etc.", *Trans. Glasg. Archaeol. Socy.*, ii. 74). It is asserted by Spottiswoode (p. 433) that the nuns and canons were brought from "Sixle in Yorkshire", a statement which probably refers to Sixhills in Lincolnshire but has no direct evidence to support it. Edwards thinks it probable that no nuns were sent here (*art. cit.*, p. 78); and only two canons are mentioned (*v. infra*). The Gilbertines had resigned the lands and possessions granted them by Walter and these had been bestowed upon Paisley abbey before 29 November 1238, when the priors of Malton and St Andrew's, York, on behalf of the order, formally renounced all right to them, as did the master and chapter of Sempringham, delivering their charters to Paisley (*Passelet*, pp. 25–7); while the two canons at Dalmulin were instructed to hand over the properties to that abbey and to return to England (Chart. Malton, f. 227). In an undated charter, the Steward conveys to Paisley the possessions which the Gilbertines have resigned, with the proviso that Paisley should pay to them yearly at Dryburgh abbey a sum of forty marks (*Passelet*, p. 24). For the controversy and litigation that arose out of this obligation and continued for over a century, *v.* Edwards, *art. cit.*, pp. 82–90. Edwards (*art. cit.*, p. 90) accepts the view that Dalmilling became a cell or oratory of Paisley. Of this there is no evidence whatsoever. Spottiswoode (p. 434) declares that "the buildings or rather the ruins of this monastery subsisted (as I am informed) not long ago". This statement probably refers to the earlier eighteenth century, but it must be regarded with considerable dubiety. The charter of James VI, erecting the properties formerly belonging to Paisley abbey into a temporal lordship, 29 July 1587, has no mention of a religious house at this site but includes merely "the lands of Dalmelling with the mill" (*RMS*, v. no. 1320).

## THE TRINITARIANS

The number of Trinitarian houses in Scotland has frequently been exaggerated; and a considerable array of unauthentic foundations of this order appears in lists and works on Scottish religious houses. In the case of half the number of the genuine foundations, record evidence of their origin is wanting; and in only one instance—Scotlandwell—is the date of foundation precisely ascertainable.

A good, if incomplete, account of the Scottish houses of this order is given by Bain ("Notes on the Trinitarians or Red Friars in Scotland, etc.", *PSAS*, x (1887–8), 26–32).

The unpublished account of the Scottish Trinitarians given by Hay (Diplomatum Veterum Collectio (NLS. MS., 34.1.10), iii. 565 ff.) is historically worthless and the more detailed account (likewise unpublished) supplied by Brockie (Monasticon Scoticum, pp. 1065 ff.) is at many points unreliable. These are cited in the notes mainly with the negative purpose of exemplifying errors.

| Name | County | Minimum Income (1561) | Founder | Fd. | Date D. or Sec. |
|------|--------|------------------------|---------|-----|-----------------|
| ABERDEEN | Aberdeen | £54 | Uncertain | –1274 | 1561 |
| BERWICK | | | | –1240–8 –1488 | |

ABERDEEN. The date of foundation is uncertain. Hay gives it as 1181 (Scotia Sacra, p. 70). It is also said that, in 1211, William the Lion gave his royal residence at Aberdeen (regiam suam Aberdonensem) to two friars of the order sent to Scotland by Pope Innocent III (Boece, *Scotorum Historia*, p. 289 cited Hay, Dipl. Vet. Coll., iii. 571 (cf. *supra*) and *Aberdeen Friars*, p. 11). Bisset seems to indicate that this was a foundation of William and his queen, Ermengarde (*Rolment of Courtis*, ii. 116), in which case the date would be 1186–1214. Spottiswoode (p. 395) and Brockie (pp. 1170–1) assert that it was founded by King William and mention the lands, etc., with which that ruler endowed it. There is, however, no record evidence regarding the founder or date of foundation. Trinity friars here appear in Baiamund's taxation-roll for 1274–5 (Theiner, *Vet. Mon.*, no. cclxiv; *SHS Misc.*, vi. 42). This house is said to have been sacked in 1560 by the Reforming barons of the Mearns (Lesley, *De Origine*, p. 563). On 24 September 1561, sasine of the place or monastery of the Trinitarians, with the buildings, was granted to Gilbert Menzies of Cowlie (*Aberdeen Friars*, p. 98); and grants of these properties by the Crown appear in 1577 and 1589 (*Ibid.*, pp. 104, 110). The church is mentioned as still standing in the eighteenth century (*Collns. Aberd. and Banff*, p. 204).

BERWICK. Founded before 1240–8, when it was given custody of the new house at Dunbar (*Yester Writs*, no. 14). Brockie's statement (p. 1073) that it was founded by William the Lion in 1214 lacks confirmation. This house is described in 1447 as non-conventual (*CPR*, x. 287) and, in 1456, a papal commission was empowered to confer the ministry upon a monk of Coupar Angus (GRH. Vat. Trans., Dispensations, 1420–57, p. 321). Before 1488 its revenues were granted by James III to the Trinitarian house at Peebles (*RSS*, ii. no. 203). *V.* Berwick, St Edward under Hospitals.

## THE TRINITARIANS

| Name | County | Minimum Income (1561) | Founder | Fd. | Date D. or Sec. |
|------|--------|------|---------|-----|------|
| DIRLETON | East Lothian | | One of the family of Haliburton | 15 c.(?) | –1588 |
| DUNBAR | East Lothian | | Cristiana de Brus, countess of Dunbar | 1240–8 | 1529 |
| § FAIL | Ayr | £580 | | –1335 | 1561 (*v.* notes) |

DIRLETON. According to Bisset, the eighth foundation of the Trinitarians in Scotland (*Rolment of Courtis*, ii. 126); but this is not certain. The chapel of St Andrew, Dirleton, "founded by the predecessors of Patrick, Lord Haliburton [†6 December 1505]", is mentioned in 1507 as held by the Trinitarians (*RSS*, i. no. 1470). The friar lands which formed part of the temporality of the prior of Dirleton had been annexed to the Crown, –1 August 1588 (*RMS*, v. no. 1568).

DUNBAR. Hay (Dipl. Vet. Coll., iii. 575) and Spottiswoode (p. 396) give the date of foundation as 1218; Brockie (p. 1073) gives it as *c.* 1218. The first of these writers assigns the foundation to George, earl of March (a manifest inaccuracy) and the two latter (more plausibly) to Patrick, earl of Dunbar and March. Cristiana de Brus, countess of Dunbar, is, however, stated to have "biggit and foundit" this house (*RSS*, ii. no. 203); and the foundation probably took place, 1240–8, when the countess gave the cure and custody of the new house of Dunbar to the minister of the house of Berwick (*Yester Writs*, no. 14). It was a small house with one friar maintaining divine service (*RSS*, *loc. cit.*). On 8 March 1528/9, the priory was granted to a secular chaplain (*Ibid.*, i. no. 4110), but this was revoked 1 July 1529, when a letter under the privy seal confirmed the Trinitarians of Peebles in the possession of its revenues as included with those of the priory of Berwick (*Ibid.*, ii. no. 203).

FAIL or FAILFORD. The date of foundation is uncertain. This house does not seem to be mentioned before the fourteenth century, although Hay (Dipl. Vet. Mon., iii. 579) and Spottiswoode (p. 396) state that it was founded in 1252 (Brockie (p. 1078) says *c.* 1252). Hay and Brockie assign the foundation to Andrew Bruce. A charter was granted there in 1335 (*Melros*, no. 447) and on 7 January 1337/8, the minister and brethren were given the church of Tarbolton (GRH. Chs., no. 148). The burning of the monastery is mentioned in a charter of 21 July 1349 (*RMS*, i. App. 1, no. 145). On 3 November 1459, as the result of a petition of James IV and his queen, alleging the notorious decadence of the friars, the Pope appointed mandatories charged, if they found the accusations true, to remove the minister and friars to other Trinitarian houses, to suppress the order at this house and to appropriate it to the new royal foundation of Trinity College and Hospital, Edinburgh (*CPR*, xi. 403). No such steps were taken, but evidence of further retrogression appears in a letter of James IV to Pope Julius II, 2 July 1507, showing that this house had been held *in commendam* by the provincial of the Blackfriars, since whose death it had so far deteriorated that "the end must come unless there is succour". The king asks for the appointment of the new provincial as commendator, in the interests of restoring monastic discipline (*Letters of James IV*, no. 114; cf. no. 119). The house continued to exist till 1561, when it was "cast down" by Reformers (Knox, *History*, ii. 168). It seems, however, to have been virtually secularized from *c.* 1540 (*RSS*, ii. no. 2439; iii. no. 808).

## THE TRINITARIANS

| Name | County | Minimum Income (1561) | Founder | Fd. | Date D. or Sec. |
|---|---|---|---|---|---|
| HOUSTON | East Lothian | | Cristiana de Mubray | *c.* 1270 | 1531 |
| * PEEBLES | Peebles | £327 | | –1296 | 1560/1 |

HOUSTON. "The Grace of God." In East Lothian, though commonly (and erroneously) located at Houston in Renfrewshire. Hay (Dipl. Vet. Coll., iii. 576) and Spottiswoode (p. 396) give 1226 as the date of foundation. Brockie (p. 1074), who locates it in Renfrewshire, dates the foundation *c.* 1226, and ascribes it to Hugh, lord of Houston. This house was, however, founded by Cristiana, widow of Sir Roger Mubray, *c.* 1270 (Sir Roger died –20 January 1268/9; the foundation was confirmed by Alexander III, 26 January 1271/2) (Bain, "Notes on the Trinitarians or Red Friars", *PSAS*, x (1887–8), 27–8). In 1502, the minister of this house was provincial of the order in Scotland (*Prot. Bk. of James Young*, no. 1259). James V, on 2 December 1531, granted the ministry of Houston and its lands, which had been held by a commendator, to the house at Peebles (*RSS*, ii. no. 1069), following this up with a letter, 4 January 1531/2, to Pope Clement VII, in which he indicates that the house at Houston had for long been reduced to one member, the minister, usually non-resident and (during James's time) a secular, while its lands had been continuously leased to laymen. Having persuaded the minister to resign this for another benefice, the king asks for its annexation to Peebles (*Letters of James V*, pp. 204–5, from Tyninghame Letter Bk.). (In another letter of the same date, James declares that no one can remember more than a minister and a chapel at Houston and that for many years past there has been no monastic life there (*Ibid.*, p. 205).) The annexation was completed and confirmed by a crown charter, 8 January 1541/2 (*RMS*, iii. no. 2569). *V.* Houston under Hospitals.

PEEBLES. "Holy Cross." The master of this house swore fealty to Edward I, in 1296 (*CDS*, ii. no. 823); and this seems to be the earliest mention of it. In the *Scotichronicon* appears the story of the finding at Peebles, in 1261, of a cross and of what were said to be relics of "St Nicholas the bishop", whence Alexander III had a church built there in honour of the Holy Cross (lib. x, cap. xiv (ii. 96–7)). In this account the Trinitarians are not mentioned. Hay does not refer to the cross, but declares that King Alexander founded the monastery here on the occasion of the finding of the relics of "a certain St Nicholas" (Dipl. Vet. Coll., iii, 582–3). Spottiswoode (p. 397) says it was founded by Alexander III in 1257; while Brockie (pp. 1079–80), who refers both to the cross and the relics, also attributes it to this king. There is, however, no record evidence of the date of foundation nor of the identity of the founder. The houses at Berwick (with the hospital), Dunbar and Houston were later annexed to this house (*v. supra*). It is stated in a record of 1 June 1558 to have been burned by the English "during the last war" (*RMS*, iv. no. 3037); but the Privy Council, 7 December 1560, granted a petition of the burgesses and inhabitants that, since the parish church had been burned and destroyed by the English twelve years before, the Trinitarian friars' church, which "is as yet standand" should be taken over as the parish church (*Chs. and Docs. rel. to Peebles*, p. 264); and, on 27 January 1560/1, the minister of the Trinitarians surrendered the keys and ordered the brethren to disperse (*Ibid.*, pp. 269–70). The church was in use till 1784. On 3 February 1624, the lands formerly belonging to this house were erected into a barony for John, Lord Hay of Yester (*RMS*, viii. no. 570).

| Name | County | Minimum Income (1561) | Founder | Fd. | Date D. or Sec. |
|------|--------|----------------------|---------|-----|-----------------|
| SCOTLANDWELL | Kinross | £280 | | 1250/1 | –1591/2 |

SCOTLANDWELL. The original foundation was the hospital of St Mary (*q.v.* under Loch Leven). On 2 January 1250/1, David de Bernham, bishop of St Andrews, granted it to the Trinitarians (GRH. Chs., no. 48). The date 1249 given by Hay (Dipl. Vet. Coll., iii. 579) is incorrect. This grant evoked protest from St Andrews priory against the introduction of the Trinitarians within the bounds of its parishes without the canons' consent; and, on 2 July 1255, Pope Alexander IV appointed mandatories to deal with the priory's plea for their removal (NLS. MS., 15.1.19). Spottiswoode (p. 396) also mentions a bull of Pope Innocent IV, *c.* 1250, on this subject, but it has not been traced. From the record of the contention between rival claimants to the ministry, it appears that the family of Arnot had occupied the priory in 1543 and ejected the community (*ALC*, 1501–54, p. 531); and the house probably remained in their possession thereafter. It had become secularized by 11 February 1591/2, when lands forming part of the temporality were granted by James V to David, son of Andrew Arnot, minister (i.e. lay commendator) of Scotlandwell (*RMS*, v. no. 2056); and it is mentioned in 1606 as resigned in the king's hands (*APS*, iv. 334).

### SUPPOSED FOUNDATIONS

*Ancrum.* There is said to have been a house of Red Friars at Nether Ancrum (*Macfarlane's Geog. Collns.*, iii. 158). Of this no evidence is forthcoming and the statement is apparently unfounded.

*Barra.* *Scotichronicon* (lib. ii, cap. x (i. 46)) has an entry: "Barray and there a cell of the Holy Trinity." This statement may be based on the existence (unrecorded) of a church, perhaps of Celtic origin, dedicated to the Trinity. There is no evidence of Trinitarians here.

*Barry.* Hay refers to a house which he calls "domus Barensis", founded by William the Lion in 1212 for thirty-five friars (Dipl. Vet. Coll., iii. 573); and Brockie (p. 1074) locates this at Barry, in Angus, where, he declares, Alexander II erected and endowed a monastery *c.* 1224. This alleged house may have been suggested by the mention of Barra (Barray) (*supra*). It can be ruled out as fanciful.

*Brechin.* Spottiswoode (p. 397) includes this among the "places . . . mentioned in ancient charters and records, as houses belonging to this order"; but the fact that he does not cite these is suspicious. According to Hay, the founder was Edward, bishop of Brechin, in 1256 (Dipl. Vet. Coll., iii. 579). Brockie (p. 1081) makes a similar statement, but gives the date as *c.* 1258. There is, however, no bishop of that name—the contemporary bishop was Albin (Dowden, *Bishops*, p. 175). Maitland, who suggests David I as the founder (*History*, i. 251), seems to be led astray by the mention of abbots of Brechin (*v.* p. 190) and confuses the "college" (*v.* p. 187) with an entirely suppositious abbey. No reliable evidence of a Trinitarian house at Brechin can be found. There was, however, a "Trinity Church" at Brechin, viz., the cathedral, dedicated to the Holy Trinity; and this may be the source of the assertion that a Trinitarian monastery existed there.

*Brough of Birsay.* For the alleged connection of this site with the Red Friars, *v. Hist. Mon. Comm. Rep. (Orkney and Shetland)*, ii. 1, 3). (The statement made there that "the church and cloister . . . are considerably earlier than the date at which the friars arrived in Northern Europe, while the plan in no way suggests a house of friars" seems to assume unwarrantably that the Trinitarians formed one of the orders properly called friars). Record evidence regarding this monastery is, however, entirely wanting; and it has so far proved impossible to discover the order to which it belonged.

*Cara.* Hay (Scotia Sacra, p. 458) declares that in this island there was a cell of the Holy Trinity. But Monro (*Western Isles*, p. 17) calls Cara "ane little iyle [isle] with a Chapell in it"; and this chapel is no doubt the "cell" in question. This was not a Trinitarian site.

I

*Crenach.* A site so named is given by Spottiswoode (p. 397) and Brockie (p. 1082), who locate it at Cromarty—the latter appears to suggest that it was founded by Patrick Murray, *c.* 1271; and it figures in lists under various guises, e.g. Crennach (*Scotich.*, ii. 540; NLS. MS. 22.1.14); Crenwathe (NLS. MS. 33.2.12)—this may point to Carnwath, in Lanarkshire, but no religious house was situated there; Greenock (NLS. MS. 31.6.1, 33.5.11)—there is no evidence of a monastery either at Greenock, in Renfrewshire or in the part of Ayrshire where this place-name occurs. This alleged house cannot be identified; it is probably fictitious.

*Cromarty.* Mentioned by Spottiswoode (p. 397) and by him identified with Crenach (*supra*). Alleged references to the friars of Cromarty in the Lord High Treasurer's Accounts have been investigated with the result that the entries in this source have been found to refer to the "feriaris" [ferrymen] of Cromarty (*LHT Accts.*, i. 324, 363). No evidence of Trinitarians here is forthcoming.

*Cupar.* Hay gives a foundation here made by James, earl of Fife, in 1277 (Dipl. Vet. Coll., iii. 585). There was no such earl; and no such house.

*Dornoch.* Between 1127 and 1153, David I commanded Reinwald, earl of Orkney and others to respect the monks who live at Dornoch in Caithness (*Dunfermelyn*, no. 23). No record of a monastery here at that date is otherwise known, but the reference may be to Celtic monks; it cannot apply, in any case, to Trinitarians. It is stated by Spottiswoode (p. 397) that, in 1271, Sir Patrick Murray founded a house at "Dornock, in Sutherland" and that it was given the lands of the ministry of Berwick after that town passed into English possession. Brockie (p. 1083) declares that its foundation is attributed both to Patrick Murray and to the *reguli* of Sutherland, and suggests that Trinitarians were brought to Dornoch by William, "the younger earl of Sutherland", *c.* 1272. There appears to be no other evidence of such a foundation and it is missing from MS. lists. If Spottiswoode's phrase, "after the English had possessed themselves of that city" refers to the final capture of Berwick by the English in 1482, it can be shown that the revenues of the Trinitarian house there were made over to the house at Peebles (*v. supra*) before 1488. This foundation must be reckoned very doubtful.

*Dundee.* Maxwell (*Old Dundee*, pp. 64–5) assumes that there was a Trinitarian house here. But it is difficult to say that there was more than a hospital (*q.v.*) and no convent of this order is mentioned in the burgh charters. A Trinitarian foundation is said to have been made by Sir James Scrymgeour in 1283 (according to Brockie (p. 1085)) or 1285 (according to Hay (Dipl. Vet. Coll., iii. 587) ); but this is undoubtedly erroneous.

*Dunet (in Buchan).* This alleged site does not appear in any of the older lists. Hay (Dipl. Vet. Coll., iii. 585) gives the name of a house as "[coenobium] Dumeni", founded, he declares, in 1297. Brockie (p. 1086) mentions this as "Dunetum" or "Dumenum", locates it in Buchan and refers to its foundation in the above year. This writer (p. 1087) cites Keith's "History of the Reformation" (i.e. Keith's *History of the Affairs of Church and State in Scotland from the beginning of the Reformation to the year 1568*) as showing that "when the monks were driven out", the monasteries of Deer and Dunet were granted to the earl Marischal in 1567. Too much, however, is read by Brockie into Keith's statement, viz.: "Item, Deare, Dunet and Pillorth [Philorth] are given frie to the Erle of Marschell [and others]" (Keith, *op. cit.* (Spottiswoode Socy.), iii. 177). These places are in Buchan but they are not specified here as monasteries. Again, Brockie's account (which is badly paraphrased in Gordon, *Monasticon*, iii. 303) suggests a connection—sufficiently far-fetched—between Dunet and the hospitals at Newburgh and Turriff; his reference to a MS. supplement to Dempster's *Historia Ecclesiastica* as mentioning the connection of a certain William Keith with this monastery carries no weight in authenticating its existence; while his allusion to "Roger, prior of Dunet" as appearing during the reign of David I in the register of St Andrews [priory] is based on a misreading (the register does not give "Roger, prior of Dunet" but "Roger, prior of Dunfermline" (Rogero priore de Dunef[ermelyn]) (*RPSA*, p. 182)) and is, in any case, historically impossible. This cannot be regarded as a genuine foundation.

*Kettins.* This name appears in lists in various and sometimes misleading forms: Katnes (*Scotich.*, ii. 540); Katness (NLS. MS., 31.6.1); Kathness (NLS. MS., 35.3.11); Kattens (NLS. MS., 33.2.12); Ketnes (NLS. MS., 22.1.14). This place is Kettins, in Angus, which was not the site of a Trinitarian house, but the parish church was appropriated to the hospital of the bridge of Berwick (St Edward's) and thereafter to the Trinitarians. *V. Coupar Angus*, ii. 19 *n*.

*Lochfeal.* Mentioned by Spottiswoode (p. 397). There was no house of this designation. "Lochfeal" is simply Loch Fail or Failford Loch, which was in the close vicinity of the monastery of Fail, apart from which no other house existed in this region.

*Luffness.* Mentioned by Spottiswoode (p. 397), while Hay (Dipl. Vet. Coll., iii, 587) and Brockie (p. 1068) assign the foundation to 1285, the latter attributing it to one of the earls of Dunbar. This is an obvious confusion with the Carmelite house of Luffness.

*St Andrews.* Hay states that a Trinitarian monastery was founded here in 1247 (Dipl. Vet. Coll., iii. 579). This statement is entirely fictitious.

*Soutra.* On the statement (unfounded) as made by Brockie (p. 1084) that this was a Trinitarian foundation, *v.* Soutra under Hospitals.

Hay's list includes other foundations which are either fanciful or due to confusion with houses of other orders: [coenobium] "Benefici", "which is in the chief [town] of the province of Buchan" (Dipl. Vet. Coll., iii. 585); "monasterium Farnense", said to have been founded in 1293 (*Ibid.*, p. 585)—this may be a confusion with the Premonstratensian house of Fearn; Queensferry (*Ibid.*, p. 585)—confused with the Carmelite house there; "monasterium Ruthnae" (*Ibid.*, p. 587). All of these may be summarily rejected.

### THE DOMINICAN FRIARS

The Blackfriars are said to have entered Scotland for the first time in 1230 (*Chron. Mailros*, p. 142; *Scotich.*, lib. ix, cap. xlvii (ii. 58) ). The *Scotichronicon* says that they were induced to come there by Alexander II, who "appointed, provided for and founded" places for them; while Spottiswoode (p. 441) claims that they were brought to Scotland in that king's reign by William de Malvoisin, bishop of St Andrews. Five lists or indications of Scottish Dominican foundations are found up to 1564, viz. (1) a writ of 7 March 1296/7, ordaining payments to be made from the fermes of burghs to the Friars Preachers (*Rot. Scot.*, i. 39); this record may be taken as indicating the houses then in existence; (2) a list, dated 1510, of religious houses printed as an appendix to the *Scotichronicon* (Goodall's edn., ii. 540); (3) a reference, 14 June 1553 (*ALC*, 1501–54, p. 622) to the Friars Preachers, in which their houses are named; (4) a detailed account of the Scottish houses in a communication from the Provincial of Scotland to the Master General, 26 January 1557 (? 1557/8) (*Analecta F.P.* (1895), p. 484); (5) an account of the Blackfriars' foundations in Scotland, said to have been derived from the account of an octogenarian friar in 1564 (*Extracta*, p. 249). The occurrence of the houses mentioned in these lists may be indicated thus:

|  |  |
|---|---|
| Aberdeen | 1.2.3.4.5 |
| Ayr | 1.2.3.4.5 |
| Berwick | 1.5 |
| Cupar | 2.5 |
| Dundee | 3.4.5 |
| Edinburgh | 1.2.3.4.5 |
| Elgin | 1.2.3.4.5 |
| Glasgow | 1.2.4.5 |
| Inverness | 1.2.3.4.5 |
| Montrose | 1.2.3.4.5 |
| Perth | 1.2.3.4.5 |
| St Andrews | 2.3.4.5 |
| St Monan's | 4.5 |
| Stirling | 1.2.3.4.5 |
| Wigtown | 1.2.3.4.5 |

The Blackfriars' house at Haddington, which was evidently of short duration, does not figure in any of these lists.

That the Friars Preachers had twenty-three houses in Scotland, as indicated in the Appendix to Spottiswoode's *History of the Church of*

*Scotland* (1677 ed.), p. 16 (p. 25 in the Appendix as separately published) is quite incredible. Lists of religious houses are numerous in the seventeenth century and their compilers borrowed uncritically from one another. It is noticeable that the National Library of Scotland MS. 22.1.14, in other respects comparatively accurate, has an extremely confused list of Dominican houses; and it may be that the Appendix to Spottiswoode depends on it. In MSS. of this period, the list of Dominican houses is sometimes followed (through a purely factitious arrangement) by a list of "chori oppidani" containing such names as Linlithgow, Jedburgh, Forres, Selkirk and these have probably, by some copyist's blunder, found their way into lists of houses of Blackfriars. On the other hand, MS. Saunders, which belongs to this period, gives a correct list (excluding Berwick and Cupar) of the thirteen houses existing at the Reformation.

## THE DOMINICAN FRIARS

| Name | County | Dedication | Minimum Income (1561) | Founder | Fd. | Date D. or Sec. |
|------|--------|-----------|------------------------|---------|-----|------------------|
| ABERDEEN | Aberdeen | St John B. | £108 | Alexander II | 1230-49 | 1560-87 |
| AYR | Ayr | St Katherine | | Alexander II | c. 1242 | 1567 |
| BERWICK | | St Peter M. of Milan | | Alexander II | -1240/1 | 15th c.(?) |
| CUPAR | Fife | St Katherine | | Duncan, earl of Fife | 1348 | 1519 |

ABERDEEN. Said to have been founded by Alexander II (i.e. between 1230 and 1249) (*Extracta*, p. 249; *Collns. Aberd. and Banff*, p. 201; *Aberdeen Friars*, p. 12). This house was destroyed by Reformers, 4 January 1560 (? 1560/1) (Lesley, *De Origine*, p. 563; *Abredoniae Utriusque Descriptio*, p. 16; *AF*, p. 97). The possessions of this house were granted to George, earl Marischal, 17 May 1587 (*AF*, p. 108), who bestowed them, as part of its endowment, upon Marischal College (*Ibid.*, p. 112).

AYR. Founded before August 1242 by Alexander II, who gave an endowment when the church was dedicated (*Chs. F.P. Ayr*, xxi–xxii, no. 1). The house, lands, etc., were made over to the burgh of Ayr by a charter of Queen Mary, 14 April 1567 (*RMS*, iv. no. 1782; cf. *Chs. F.P. Ayr*, no. 64).

BERWICK. Founded by Alexander II (*Extracta*, p. 249), who gave it an endowment (*ER*, i. 208). There is a reference to this community in March 1240/1 (*CDS*, i. 277). On 17 June 1285, the Pope gave mandate to the bishop of St Andrews to sell to the Friars Preachers, as their house was too far from the town, the former house of the Friars of Penitence (*CPR*, Letters, i. 482, 494–5; Theiner, *Vet. Mon.*, nos. cccxxxviii, cccix). Payments to this house from the Scottish Exchequer are recorded in 1329 and 1332/3 (*ER*, i. 208, 411). On 10 August 1333, Edward III instructed the provincial of the English Dominicans to remove the Scottish friars in this house to English houses south of the Trent and to substitute English friars (*Rot. Scot.*, i. 258). The grant made to the friars by Scottish kings is confirmed to them by Edward III, 20 March 1336/7 (*Ibid.*, i. 486); and on 15 December 1337, a payment to them from the English Exchequer is recorded (*CDS*, ii. no. 1251). This house is said, in a supplication of 25 February 1436, to have been by accident completely burned (Vat. Reg. Supp., 319, 210 (D) ). But it is mentioned in the fifteenth-century poem (attributed to Dunbar), "the Freiris of Berwik" (*Poems of Dunbar*, ed. W. Mackay Mackenzie (1932), p. 183). On 25 April 1461, the Scots regained possession of Berwick; and Brockie (p. 1121) gives a charter (from the collections of Father Richard Augustine Hay) of James III to the sheriff of Berwick, whereby because Berwick has returned to his obedience and the Friars Preachers still dwelling there have been defrauded of help by the English, he ordains that the friars may have free transit (*liberum transitum*, i.e. liberty of movement) through the Merse and Lothian in order to collect alms and that their former revenues are to be restored to them. The regnal year is given (= 3 August 1467–2 August 1468) but no day or month. It is difficult to say whether this document is genuine. In any case, effect could hardly have been given to such provisions, for Berwick was retaken by the English, 22 August 1482. The later history of this house is obscure.

CUPAR. In 1348, Duncan, earl of Fife, petitioned the Pope for faculty to found a Dominican convent in his castle of Cupar (*CPR*, Pet., i. 144). In the same year, the Pope granted the vicar-general in Scotland of the English provincial permission to receive this land and to build an oratory, etc. (*CPR*, iii. 304). A crown charter of 4 October 1519 records that, at a chapter held in Edinburgh at Michaelmas of that year, the provincial incorporated the Dominicans' place at Cupar with the Dominican house at St Andrews, transferring the friars there (*RMS*, iii. no. 196). The Friars Preachers' lands were granted to the burgh of Cupar by James VI, 14 June 1572 (*Ibid.*, iv. no. 2075).

## THE DOMINICAN FRIARS

| Name | County | Dedication | Minimum Income (1561) | Founder | Fd. | Date D. or Sec. |
|------|--------|-----------|----------------------|---------|-----|-----------------|
| DUNDEE | Angus | ? | £7 (?) | Andrew Abercromby | c. 1521 | 1567 |
| EDINBURGH | Midlothian | Assumption of B.V.M. | £67 | Alexander II | 1230 | 1566/7 |
| ELGIN | Moray | St James | £251 | Alexander II | 1233 or 1234 | –1570/1 |
| GLASGOW | Lanark | St John E. | £73 | Bishop and chapter of Glasgow | –1246 | 1566/7 |
| HADDINGTON | East Lothian | | | | –1471 | 1489–90+ |

DUNDEE. As this house seems undoubtedly to have been founded by Andrew Abercromby, burgess of Dundee, before 4 May 1521 (*RMS*, iii. no. 578; Maxwell, *Old Dundee*, p. 62), it is impossible to accept as authentic the charters of donation to Friars Preachers at Dundee of Robert I, 4 September 1315, and others (in 1345 and 1388) given by Brockie (pp. 1206–8), unless they refer to an earlier foundation of which no other information exists. This house had a brief career. It was sacked by a mob in August 1543 (*Diurnal*, p. 29; *Hamilton Papers*, ii. nos. 11, 14, 30, 116; Maxwell, *Old Dundee*, p. 395 (from burgh archives) ); and it was probably destroyed when the English burned Dundee, in November 1548 (Maxwell, *op. cit.*, p. 113). This house is described in 1557 as "recens natum et erectum" but also very recently destroyed first by heretics and then by the English (*Analecta F.P.* (1895), p. 484). In 1567, its property was bestowed on the burgh by a crown charter; the precept for granting this appears *Chs. etc. of Burgh of Dundee*, p. 41.

EDINBURGH. Founded by Alexander II in 1230 (Moir Bryce, *Blackfriars of Edinburgh*, p. 16). Moir Bryce scouts the story of its destruction by fire in 1518 (*Ibid.*, p. 18) (Spottiswoode (p. 442) gives the date of this as 1528). The friary was partly burned by the English in May, 1544 (*Ibid.*, p. 51). It was destroyed by Reformers in June 1559—*Diurnal* (pp. 269, 53) gives two different dates, 14 and 28 June; Knox's account of the destruction of the "frearis places" by the "rascheall multitude" (*History*, i. 362) seems to support the former date; Moir Bryce (*op. cit.*, pp. 56–7) does not make it clear why he accepts the latter date. The lands and possessions of this house were granted to the magistrates and Town Council, 13 March 1566/7 (*Ibid.*, p. 94).

ELGIN. Founded by Alexander II in 1233 or 1234 (Spottiswoode, p. 444); *c.* 1233 (Brockie, p. 1196; where it is mentioned that the foundation charter is lost); *c.* 1235 (Cramond, *Recs. of Elgin*, i. 8). Its lands, etc., were alienated before 1570/1 (?1567) (*RMS*, iv. no. 1955). Property formerly belonging to it is granted under the privy seal, 4 March 1573/4 and 9 January 1575/6 (RSS, xlii. 26v; xlvi. 52v).

GLASGOW. Said to have been founded by the bishop and chapter (*Extracta*, p. 249). A bull of 10 July 1246 grants an indulgence to all the faithful who contribute to the completion of the church which the Friars Preachers of Glasgow have begun to build (*Mun. F.P. Glasgu*, no. 2). The Blackfriars' place with its endowments was bestowed upon the municipality by Queen Mary, 16 March 1566/7 (*Ibid.*, lxxviii). The conventual church existed till *c.* 1670, when it was destroyed by lightning.

HADDINGTON. The existence of a house of this order at Haddington is attested by references on 8–9 August 1471 and 7 May 1482 (*Yester Writs*, nos. 167, 202); and a payment of wheat to it is recorded in the Exchequer account of 1489–90 (*ER*, x. 224). Part of a charter to the Blackfriars here, apparently by John, Lord Hay of Yester, 30 June 1513, appears in Brockie (p. 1234); also a charter to them by Henry Sinclair of Herdmanston, 29 May 1528 (1234–5). The date of the extinction of this house is as uncertain as the date of its foundation. Brockie's statements (p. 1236) that it was devastated by the English and, *c.* 1558, reduced to ashes "by the rage of fanatics" are entirely without confirmation. It is not mentioned among the Dominican houses surviving in 1557 (*v.* p. 96 *supra*). The likelihood is that it has a somewhat brief existence. Brockie (p. 1236) declares that it stood at the West Port of the burgh.

## THE DOMINICAN FRIARS

| Name | County | Dedication | Minimum Income (1561) | Founder | Fd. | Date D. or Sec. |
|------|--------|-----------|-----------------------|---------|-----|------------------|
| INVERNESS | Inverness | St Bartholomew | £38 | Alexander II | −1240 | −1566/7 |
| MONTROSE | Angus | Nativity of B.V.M. | £107 | Alan Durward | −1275 | 1570/1 |
| PERTH | Perth | St Andrew | £93 | Alexander II | 1231 | 1569 |

INVERNESS. The date of the foundation of this house by Alexander II (*Extracta*, p. 249) is not known; but that king confirmed to it a donation (not made by himself), 20 May 1240 (Hutton's Collns., xi. 68). A charter of 20 June 1559 records the "geir" (property) placed by the friars in the custody of the magistrates of Inverness (*Rose of Kilravock*, pp. 226–7). This is mentioned as one of the houses still undemolished, 13 February 1561/2 (*PCR*, 1st Ser., i. 202), but the friary was disbanded, −19 January 1566/7 (*RMS*, iv. no. 2760).

MONTROSE. Said to have been founded by Sir Alan Durward (†1275) (*Extracta*, p. 249). On 14 November 1516, James V with the consent of John, duke of Albany, the Governor and the estates of parliament, empowered Patrick Panter, abbot of Cambuskenneth and master of St Mary's house [hospital] near Montrose, the king's secretary, to institute a new foundation of the latter house in favour of the Friars Preachers (*RMS*, iii. no. 113; *APS*, ii. 389–92). Hence a mandate of the provincial of the Scottish Dominicans, 18 December 1519, calls him the "true founder" of this house (Brockie, p. 1202).[1] A petition of the duke of Albany, on behalf of James V, to Pope Leo X for the bestowal of the hospital and its lands on the Dominicans, whose house is said to have been burned during war more than a century ago, is granted, 18 May 1517 (*Letters of James V*, p. 45). Another letter (or perhaps another version of the foregoing petition) to this Pope, in 1518 supplicating for the grant of the hospital to the Dominicans, speaks of the latter's house as having been "burned by the enemy upwards of two hundred years ago" and lying neglected (*Epp. Reg. Scot.*, i. 290–2; *Letters of James V*, p. 60). A bull confirming this petition is dated 9 June 1518 (*Letters of James V*, p. 60); and the Dominican General Chapter, in the same year, approved the translation of the house to the hospital (*Mon. ord. F.P. Hist.*, ix. 173). But a charter of 10 May 1524 relates that the king had ordained the return of the friars to their former house, as the situation of the hospital in the public street gave rise to disturbance of the friars' services and devotions (*RMS*, iii. no. 1725; *APS*, ii. 395–6). On 1 January 1570/1, James VI granted the revenues and other properties of the Friars Preachers to the burgh of Montrose (*RMS*, iv. no. 1953).

PERTH. Founded by Alexander II in 1231 (Milne, *Blackfriars of Perth*, xviii). The church was dedicated 13 May 1240 (A. O. Anderson, *Early Sources*, ii. 520). Various councils of the Scottish church were held here. The friary was attacked by a mob, 14 May 1543, (Fittis, *Eccles. Annals of Perth*, p. 189) and, 11 May 1559, destroyed along with the other religious houses at Perth (Lesley, *History*, p. 272 (where the date is given erroneously as 1558); Knox, *History*, i. 322–3; Pitscottie, *Cronicles*, ii. 146; Fittis, *op. cit.*, p. 190). Its lands, etc., were granted to the burgh by James VI, 9 August 1569 (*RMS*, IV, no. 1874).

---

[1] This document gives the date of Panter's death as 18 November (1519). Cf. *Cambuskenneth*, lxxxiv; *Letters of James IV*, xxxii.

## THE DOMINICAN FRIARS

| Name | County | Dedication | Minimum Income (1561) | Founder | Fd. | Date D. or Sec. |
|------|--------|------------|------------------------|---------|-----|------------------|
| * St Andrews | Fife | Assumption and Coronation of B.V.M. | £67 (with Cupar) | *V.* notes | *V.* notes | 1567 |

St Andrews. Said to have been founded by William Wishart, bishop of St Andrews (1273–79) in 1274 (Spottiswoode, p. 446; *Extracta*, p. 249, says simply "be the bischop thairof"); and, as late as 1525, Archbishop James Beaton speaks of himself and his predecessors as "first and principall foundatouris of the forisaid place of Freiris Predicatouris within our cietie forisaid" (Herkless and Hannay, *Archbps. of St Ands.*, iii.168–9), a statement which may indicate at least a tradition that the foundation of this house was due to one of the bishops or archbishops. Brockie (p. 1213) gives a charter of Alexander III, 10 March 1285/6, taking under his protection the monastery for Friars Preachers recently erected by William, bishop of St Andrews (who may be William Wishart (1273–9) or William Fraser (1279–97); the charter seems to suggest the latter). There are difficulties in accepting a thirteenth-century date of foundation, e.g. St Andrews does not appear among the eleven Dominican houses granted payment from their respective burghs, 7 March 1296/7 (*Rot. Scot.*, i. 39). It has, however, been assumed that the sixteenth century saw the restoration of a thirteenth-century house which had become impoverished, dilapidated and reduced in *personnel* (*v.* D. Henry, "Dominican Friars at St Andrews", *Trans. Aberdeen Ecclesiol. Socy.* (1893), pp. 18 ff.; *Hist. Mon. Comm. Rep. (Fife and Kinross)*, p. 250). The first reference to a prior of this house occurs, 22 November 1464 (*Aberbrothoc*, ii. 160). But its status about that time is shown by a bull of Pope Sixtus IV, 18 March 1476/7, which, in response to a petition of the vicar-general of the order in Scotland, grants that the places of the Friars Preachers in St Andrews and St Monan's, hitherto known as oratories or hospitals, shall be named conventual houses and the friars shall have liberty to erect churches and monastic buildings; a concession to which the archdeacon of St Andrews, as executor deputed by the Pope, gave effect, on 24 December of that year (St Andrews Chs., no. 75). According to *CPR*, xiii. 571, James III was also a party to this petition. A payment of alms to the St Andrews Blackfriars is recorded, 30 September 1504 (*LHT Accts.*, ii. 264). On 16 November 1514, provision is made for the bestowal by his executor of the residue of the estate of William Elphinstone, bishop of Aberdeen (†25 October 1514), upon the provincial and the order for the building of a convent within the university of St Andrews (*REA*, ii. 310); and a provincial chapter at Stirling, 21 September 1516, decided on the utilization of this sum "for the fabric of the new convent of St Andrews, so that there, by the grace of God, there will be a convent of friars living according to rule and engaged continually in the study of sacred letters where formerly one friar and seldom two were dwelling" (*Ibid.*, ii. 311–12). It is thus evident that the incentive of the development or revival of the convent at St Andrews was the presence of the university. Again, in 1518, the Dominican General Chapter signified its approval of the arrangement between the dean of Dunkeld and the provincial of Scotland for the foundation "for five or six students in the convent of the university of St Andrews" (*Mon. ord. F.P. Hist.*, ix. 173). Moir Bryce (*Blackfriars of Edinburgh*, p. 28) regards the dean of Dunkeld as establishing this foundation; and this is a possible interpretation of the statement of Myln (*Vitae Episc. Dunkeld*, pp. 55–6) concerning this dean [George Hepburn]: "When the order of Preachers in Scotland underwent a reformation by ... John Adamson, professor of sacred letters, provincial of the order, he was of great assistance; he founded their place in St Andrews, whence he deservedly bears the title of their founder, and endowed it for the sufficient maintenance of five friars." Hannay (*Rentale Dunkeldense*, p. 321) takes the latter part of the statement as referring to Adamson. In 1519 the priories of Cupar (*supra*) and (in part) St Monan's (*infra*) and, in 1529, the hospital of St Nicholas (*q.v.*) were united to the St Andrews friary. This house was burned by Norman Lesley, in 1547 (*RSS*, iii. nos. 2345, 2515); and destroyed by Reformers probably on 14 June, 1559 (the date lies between 11 June, when Knox preached in St Andrews (*History*, i. 349) and 21 June, when a charter describes the prior and convent as "violently expelled from their destroyed place" (GRH. Cal. of Chs., no. 1788)). On 17 April 1567, Queen Mary granted the property to the municipality of St Andrews (Reg. of Evidents of the City of St Ands., Inventory, no. 4, 15).

## THE DOMINICAN FRIARS

| Name | County | Dedication | Minimum Income (1561) | Founder | Fd. | Date D. or Sec. |
|------|--------|-----------|----------------------|---------|-----|-----------------|
| ‡ St Monan's | Fife | St Monan | | James III | 1471 | *c.* 1557 |
| Stirling | Stirling | St Laurence (or, according to Brockie, St Kentigern) | £2 (?) | Alexander II | 1233 | 1567 |
| Wigtown | Wigtown | Annunciation of B.V.M. | | Devorgilla | 1267 or −1287 | 1560–70(?) |

St Monan's. Erroneously called St Ninian's (*Extracta*, p. 249). The church of St Monan was originally founded by David II as a chapel with an unspecified number of chaplains, 3 April 1370 (*RMS*, i. no. 304). On 15 November 1471, James III refounded it for "a certain number of Friars Preachers", to whom he transferred its endowments (*Ibid.*, ii. no. 1047). *Extracta* (p. 249) and Spottiswoode (p. 445) allege that in this the king was instigated by John Muir, vicar-general of the order, so that the number of Dominican houses would justify the formation of a separate Scottish province. Whatever basis there may be for this statement, it is certainly true that the General Chapter, at the petition of the king, erected Scotland in 1481 into a separate province, of which Muir was the first provincial (*Mon. ord. F.P. Hist.*, iii. 369). By a bull of Pope Sixtus IV, 18 March 1476/7, procured by the vicar-general and James III, this house was given conventual status (St Andrews Chs., no. 75; *CPR*, xiii. 571). At Michaelmas 1519, the provincial chapter incorporated it in the house at St Andrews, with provision for the maintenance of two friars of advancing age at St Monan's (*RMS*, ii. no. 196). It is stated in 1557 that this house had never more than two friars, but at that date it had none, as its revenues were insufficient to maintain a single friar (*Analecta F.P.* (1895), p. 484).

Stirling. Founded by Alexander II (*Extracta*, p. 249; Spottiswoode, p. 444). Spottiswoode gives 1233 as the date of foundation. A charter of Robert de London (†*c.* 1227), the king's stepbrother, to the Friars Preachers of Stirling, which is given by Brockie (p. 1179), can hardly be regarded as genuine as it refers to the year in which the Galloway rebels were overcome, i.e. 1235. The friary is said to have been destroyed by Reformers in June 1559 (Pitscottie, *Cronicles*, ii. 160); and there is a retrospective reference, 12 September 1559 to the "violent ejection" (of the prior) from this place and its "total destruction" (*RMS*, iv. no. 1373). A precept under the privy seal, 10 May 1560, ordained a charter to be made confirming a grant by the prior and convent of their lands to Alexander Erskine of Cangnoir (*Chs. rel. to Stirling*, 90 (no. xliv) ). On 15 April 1567, the grant by Queen Mary to the municipality of ecclesiastical properties within the burgh included the lands and revenues of the Friars Preachers (*Ibid.*, 94 (no. xlv) ); but it has been pointed out that Erskine clung to the Blackfriars' lands and it was not till 1652 that the burgh obtained possession of them (*Trans. Stirling Nat. Hist. and Archaeol. Socy.*, 1890–1, p. 50).

Wigtown. Founded by "the Maiden of Galloway" (*Extracta*, p. 249), i.e. Devorgilla, daughter of Alan of Galloway, who married John de Balliol, *c.* 1233. Spottiswoode (p. 445) assigns the foundation to Devorgilla to 1267, a date which is probable though not otherwise attested. This house may be taken as having been in existence, −28 January 1289/90, the date of Devorgilla's death (*CDS*, ii. no. 405), and it is mentioned 7 March 1296/7, among the houses in receipt of payments from the fermes of burghs (*Rot. Scot.*, i. 39). One of its priors, Ninian Shanks, appears, 10 May 1490 (*RMS*, ii. no. 2056). The revenues of this house (*v. MB*, i. 140 *n.*) were probably made over to the burgh at the Reformation, like those of other friaries, but of this no record has been found.

## THE DOMINICAN FRIARS

### SUPPOSED FOUNDATIONS

*Coupar Angus.* Listed in the Appendix to Spottiswoode's *Hist. of the Ch. of Scotland* (1677 ed.), 16 (25). Brockie (p. 1236) declares that the founder and date of foundation are unknown, though at another point (p. 1241) he mentions Thomas, commendator-abbot of Coupar and dean of Dunkeld as the probable founder and (p. 1237) gives *c.* 1480 as a possible date. He also supplies transcripts of charters concerning this house from 26 February 1487/8 (p. 1238) onwards. Thus, he exemplifies a charter of James Ogilvy of Airlie to the Friars Preachers of Coupar, 28 March 1488 (p. 1237). This document speaks of his donation as made at the "instigation and request" of Thomas, "Cistercian abbot of Coupar", who also attests the charter; but the contemporary abbot was John Schanwell (1480–1560) (*Coupar Angus*, ii. 274). Again, it refers to Ogilvy's wife, in 1488, as Elizabeth Douglas, but this is almost certainly erroneous (*v. SP*, i. 114). There are good grounds for regarding this and other charters (pp. 1238–40) said to pertain to this house as spurious, while the account which Brockie quotes (pp. 1240–1) ostensibly "from the papers of James Ramsay", of the expulsion of the thirty "monks" of this house by Donald Campbell, abbot of Coupar, at the Reformation, is entirely incredible. Although Brockie distinguishes this alleged house from the house at Cupar, Fife, he appears to have taken over a supposition that there was a Blackfriars' house at Coupar Angus which is based on a confusion with the Cupar foundation. It may safely be stated that the house at Coupar Angus is fictitious.

*Crail.* Brockie (p. 1254) has a charter of Elizabeth Hepburn, abbess of the Cistercian nuns of Haddington, granting the Friars Preachers a site for erecting a church and monastery in the burgh of Crail, 28 September 1448. This charter is not genuine. The head of the Cistercian nunnery at Haddington was a prioress and this office was held from –1440 to *c.* 1463 by Mariota de Douglas (*Trans. East Lothian Antiq. Socy.*, v. 7–8). Other charters (Brockie, pp. 1255–7) to this alleged house must likewise be rejected as unauthentic. There is no reliable evidence of a Dominican monastery at Crail.

*Dumfries.* Included among the Dominican houses listed in NLS. MS. 22.1.14, 153 f., and in the Appendix to Spottiswoode's *Hist. of the Ch. of Scotland* (1677 ed.), 16 (25). This entry is erroneous, as is the reference to the lands of the Friars Preachers (*rectius* Friars Minor) in Dumfries, 1 May 1579 (*RMS*, iv. no. 32).

*Dysart.* Included in the lists cited for Dumfries. Brockie (p. 1229) has a charter of William Sinclair of Dysart granting the Friars Preachers a site for the building of a monastery, of which the church is to be dedicated to St Cuthbert, 27 March 1466 or 1467 or 1468 (the latter part of the date is blotted and uncertain). One of the witnesses is James, bishop of St Andrews, who, however, died in 1465 (Dowden, *Bishops*, p. 32). This charter, of which the style itself raises suspicions, cannot be accepted as genuine. The statement is also made, on the authority of the *New Statistical Account*, that "the chapel at Dysart (dedicated to St Denis) belonged to a priory of Dominicans" (Mackinlay, *Ancient Ch. Dedications* (non-Scriptural), p. 327). No reliable evidence of a Dominican house here can be found.

*Forres.* Included in the lists cited for Dumfries. Other evidence is entirely wanting. This foundation can be rejected.

*Inverkeithing.* Included in the lists cited for Dumfries and given by Maitland (*History*, i. 262). Brockie (p. 1224) has an undated charter of Hugh de Lundey [*sic*], lord of the burgh of Inverkeithing, granting a site for a Blackfriars' monastery here, with the consent of "the illustrious king of Scots Robert de Bruis my lord". The latter phrase, in itself highly suspect, would date the charter 1306+. But among the witnesses are Walter, abbot of Inchcolm (1258–1277+) and Roger de Moubray (†–23 January 1268/9). This charter must be regarded as unauthentic. Stephen (*Hist. of Inverkeithing and Rosyth*, p. 301) declares that "of the existence of a religious house of the Black Friars the evidence is by no means conclusive". There is a reference to Blackfriars here in the index of *LHT. Accts.*, ii; but the corresponding entry in the text (*Ibid.*, ii. 264) refers merely to the "Freris of Inverkethin", i.e. almost certainly the Greyfriars.

*Jedburgh.* Included in the lists cited for Dumfries. The name "Blackfriars" is used locally but inaccurately (*v.* Watson, "Hist. of Franciscan Friary of Jedburgh", *Trans. BNC*, 1906, p. 82). There is also an erroneous reference to a Dominican convent at Jedburgh "whereof the Lairds of Fairnihurst were patrons" (*Macfarlane's Geog. Collns.*, iii. 158). No such convent existed here.

*Kinghorn.* Included in the lists cited for Dumfries. Brockie, who gives (p. 1228) a vague account of this alleged foundation, has a charter (*loc. cit.*) of James de Kirkcaldy making a donation to the Friars Preachers at Kinghorn, 28 September 1388. This charter, witnessed by an abbot (Bernard) of Coupar Angus not otherwise known, is very probably spurious. The existence of a monastery here is not otherwise attested in records and may be regarded as very dubious.

*Kirkcudbright.* There is a reference in 1512 to the Friars Preachers of Kirkcudbright (*ER*, xiii. 472). This is evidently an error for Friars Minor.

*Linlithgow.* Included in the lists cited for Dumfries. Brockie (p. 1219), who says that the name of the founder and the date of foundation are unknown, gives a charter (pp. 1219–20) of John [Balliol], king of Scots, who, "since for the same friars (i.e. the Blackfriars) a new house has been erected in our town of Linlithgow", takes it under his protection, 19 March 1294/5. This charter can hardly be genuine—Alan, bishop of Caithness and chancellor of Scotland, who died in October–November 1291, appears among the witnesses. Again, an indenture between William More, lord of Abercorn, and the Friars Preachers of Linlithgow, 20 May 1348 (Brockie, pp. 1221–3) is said to be attested by the vicar-general of Scotland and sixteen priors (attending a chapter at St Andrews); this detail suggests that the document is a fabrication. References, however, are found in 1451 and 1453 to a croft held on lease by the Friars Preachers of this town (*ER*, v. 457, 544); while, on 29 October 1503, a payment is recorded "to the Blak Freris of Linlithqw" (*LHT. Accts.*, ii. 255). The existence of a Dominican house here, perhaps for a brief period, cannot be ruled out; but it is difficult to resist the conclusion that the references in the above records are errors for the White Friars of Linlithgow.

*St Ninian's.* Given in *Extracta*, p. 249, clearly in error for St Monan's.

*Selkirk.* Included in the lists cited for Dumfries. Brockie (p. 1242) gives a charter (from Tweedie) of James Tweedie of Drumelzier, who has granted the Friars Preachers a site for building a "new monastery" and a church, which on the instructions of David II, is to be dedicated to St Ninian, 28 September 1358. This charter purports to bear the seal of Alexander Maxwell, archdeacon of Tweedale (Tuuedaliae). There was no such archdeaconry and even if we take this as referring to Teviotdale, no mention of an archdeacon of this name has been found (Henry de Smalham was appointed to the archdeaconry of Teviotdale in 1354 (*CPR*, iii. 516) ). The authenticity of this charter is very questionable; and apart from Brockie, there seems to be no evidence of a house of Friars Preachers here.

## THE FRANCISCAN FRIARS
### (I) The Friars Minor Conventual

The Friars Minor are said to have entered Scotland for the first time in 1231 (*Chron. Mailros*, p. 142).

In the accompanying notes reference is frequently made to W. Moir Bryce, *The Scottish Greyfriars*. This work has some unsatisfactory features; but its writer made a close investigation of the public records of Scotland and it includes a useful collection of Scottish Franciscan documents.

| Name | County | Minimum Income (1561) | Founder | Fd. | Date D. or Sec. | |
|---|---|---|---|---|---|---|
| BERWICK | | | Alexander II (?) | 1231 | ? | |
| DUMFRIES | Dumfries | £34 | Alan of Galloway or | 1234 | | |
| | | | Devorgilla de Balliol | −1266 | 1569 | |

BERWICK. According to Moir Bryce (i. 6, following *Chron. Mailros*, p. 142; *Scotich.*, lib. ix, cap. xlviii (ii. 59) ), this house was founded in or about 1231, the year in which the Friars entered Scotland. Brockie (p. 1274), however, gives a charter of Alexander II, who has granted the Friars Minor a "sufficient place" in the burgh of Berwick for building a convent and has constructed for them a church and other buildings, with an annual endowment of twenty merks from the fermes of Berwick, 28 September 1231. This charter may well be genuine. The church was dedicated by David de Bernham, bishop of St Andrews, 6 May 1244 (A. O. Anderson, *Early Sources*, ii. 525). A mandate of Edward III, 10 August 1333, ordered the Scottish friars to be removed and English friars substituted for them. (*Rot. Scot.*, i. 258). On 15 December 1337, a payment from the English Exchequer to the friars is authorized (*CDS*, iii. no. 1251). No further record evidence concerning this house has been found, but it is mentioned in the fifteenth-century poem, "The Freiris of Berwik" (*Poems of Dunbar*, ed. Mackay Mackenzie, p. 183); and it may have been one of the three or four houses of friars near Berwick reported as still standing, 10 March 1539/40 (*L. & P. H. VIII*, xiv[1]. no. 494).

DUMFRIES (St Mary). Brockie (p. 1286) gives a charter of foundation by Alan of Galloway, 20 April 1234. Some of its phraseology and the lack of witnesses make this document somewhat dubious. But Alan may have been the founder. The date of its foundation is given by Moir Bryce (i. 199) as *c.* 1262 without any apparent justification. Little (*Franciscan Papers, etc.*, p. 221) makes this date −1264; but the reference which he gives, viz., *ER*, i. 27, must be dated 1264-6. A. O. Anderson's suggested date, −1305 (*Early Sources*, ii. 479 *n.*) is evidently much too late. Spottiswoode (p. 448) attributes its foundation to Devorgilla de Balliol. John Duns (Scotus) is said to have been admitted to the Franciscan order here in 1278, his uncle, Elias Duns, being warden of the house (Brockie, pp. 1298 ff.). But *v.* p. 12 *supra*. The friars' church was the scene of the slaying of John Comyn by Robert Bruce, 10 February 1305/6. On 9 September 1427, the Pope granted an indulgence in favour of the repair of the conventual buildings (Vat. Reg. Supp., 215, 73 (D) ). The burgh had a grant of the revenues, lands, etc., of the Greyfriars (with other ecclesiastical properties), 23 April 1569 (*RMS*, iv. no. 1848). By 1570, the Town Council had entered into possession of the friary (*MB*, i. 214).

## THE FRANCISCAN FRIARS
### (I) THE FRIARS MINOR CONVENTUAL

| Name | County | Minimum Income (1561) | Founder | Fd. | Date D. or Sec. |
|------|--------|------------------------|---------|-----|------------------|
| DUNDEE | Angus | £52 | Devorgilla de Balliol | –1289 | c. 1560 |
| HADDINGTON | East Lothian | | | –1242 | 1566/7 |

DUNDEE. Moir Bryce (i. 219) accepts 1284 as the date of the foundation. Little (*Franciscan Papers, etc.*, p. 221, citing *Docs. Illust. of Hist. of Scotland*, ii. no. 484) gives –1296, but this is too vague. This house is also said to have been founded by Devorgilla (*Scotich.*, lib. viii, cap. xxv (i. 474) ; Spottiswoode, p. 449) (*v. MB*, i. 218 and *n.* on the alleged foundation charter); and, if this was the case, the foundation must have taken place not later than 1289, the year of her death. Brockie (p. 1435) gives a charter of John [Balliol], king of Scots, confirming and amplifying his mother's foundation, 30 March 1294/5. It was in the friars' church that the Scottish clergy, 24 February 1309/10, attested their support of Robert Bruce's claims to the Crown (*APS*, i. 100). In 1335, the friary is stated to have been partly burned (as well as much of the town) by "ships of Newcastle" (*Chron. Lanercost*, p. 282). Again, according to Froissart, it was totally destroyed by fire during Richard II's invasion in 1385 (*MB*, i. 223), but there is no other evidence that the English penetrated north of the Forth. In 1543, the friary was sacked by Reformers (*Hamilton Papers*, i. no. 11; ii. no. 187; Maxwell, *Old Dundee*, p. 395); and, in all probability, it was burned, with the other ecclesiastical buildings of Dundee, by the English, in November 1548 (Maxwell, *op. cit.*, p. 113). The magistrates were in possession of the land and buildings in 1560 (*MB*, i. 227). On 11 September 1564, Queen Mary gave permission for the use of the place and yard formerly belonging to the friars as a public burying-ground (*Chs. and Docs. rel. to Dundee*, p. 40). Moir Bryce, who describes this as "by far the most wealthy Franciscan community in Scotland" (i. 229), gives its revenues for 1560 as £135 (*Ibid.*, i. 236).

HADDINGTON. The *Chronicle of Lanercost* (p. 50) refers to the burial of Patrick of Athole at the place of the Friars Minor at Haddington in 1242. Hence Moir Bryce (i. 168) declares that "as early as 1242 we find [the friars] in possession of a regular friary" there. Brockie (p. 1446), on the other hand, cites a charter (from the Tweedie MS. to which he frequently refers) of Patrick, earl of Dunbar, granting the Friars a site for a church and convent, 30 September 1252. This charter, which has no witnesses, is not above suspicion; and the date of foundation (as well as the identity of the founder) remains uncertain. The Greyfriars' church is said, e.g. by Major (*Hist. of Greater Britain*, p. 297) to have been called "the Lamp of Lothian", though this has been contested. The friary was burned by the English in 1355 (Major, *loc. cit.*; *Scotich.*, lib. xiv, cap. xiii (ii. 354) ). Moir Bryce (i. 193–4) shows that there were eight friars, with the warden, in 1478; six, with the warden, in 1539 and 1543; three, with the warden, 1557–9. This house was again burned by the English in May 1544 (*L. & P. H. VIII*, xix[1]. no. 533). Its alienation to the magistrates, 10 October 1555 (Burgh Recs.) and later (*MB*, i. 187), was intended to be provisional ("during the present calamity that has fallen upon the religious and churchmen"); and, in 1561, stringent orders were issued against the demolition of the friary church (*Ibid.*, i. 173). But on 24 March 1566/7, the burgh had from Queen Mary a charter of the ecclesiastical properties, including those of the Friars Minor (*RMS*, iv. no. 1776); and in 1572, the Town Council decided upon the demolition of the friars' church (*MB*, i. 173).

## THE FRANCISCAN FRIARS
### (I) The Friars Minor Conventual

| Name | County | Minimum Income (1561) | Founder | Fd. | Date D. or Sec. |
|---|---|---|---|---|---|
| § Inverkeithing | Fife | | Philip de Moubray(?) | 1268(?) or –1384 | 1559 |
| § Kirkcud- bright | Kirkcud- bright | £14 | James II | 1455 | 1569 |
| Lanark | Lanark | £7 | Robert I | 1328–9 (?1325–6) | –1566 |

INVERKEITHING. Brockie (p. 1455) supplies a charter of Philip de Moubray, lord of Barn-bougle, narrating his erection of a church and convent for the Friars Minor at Inverkeithing with an endowment from the lands of Barnbougle, 28 October 1268. The authenticity of this charter is uncertain. Moir Bryce (i. 248), whose account is unsatisfactory, refers to a bull of Pope Clement VI, 29 November 1346 (ii. 149), permitting David II to erect Lanark friary and another "far from the attacks of enemies" and suggests (not too plausibly) that the latter proviso may have been applied] to the foundation of Inverkeithing friary. A specific reference to it is found, 10 March 1384/5, when the bailies of Inverkeithing, in accordance with a grant of Robert II, remitted to the Friars Minor a sum due "from a certain tenement in Inverkeithing which the said friars inhabit" (*ER*, iii. 127 ff., where the date is erroneously given as 1364). The friary and its garden were conveyed to John Swinton, 4 July 1559 (*MB*, i. 249; ii. 165). The hospitium of the friary remains. *V.* further Stephen, *Hist. of Inverkeithing and Rosyth*, pp. 301–3.

KIRKCUDBRIGHT. Brockie (pp. 1431–2) has a charter (from Tweedie) purporting to record the foundation of a house here by Roger de Quincy, earl of Winchester, lord of Gallo-way and constable of Scotland, 16 September 1239. This charter has no witnesses and it is difficult to say whether it is genuine. A reference to an offering made by Edward I on the altar of the priory of Kirkcudbright is regarded by Moir Bryce (i. 36–7) as applying to the [Augustinian] priory of St Mary's Isle. The same writer (i. 36) dates this foundation in or about 1455, and attributes it to James II, on the ground of a reference, 12 July 1458, to a payment to "the Friars Minor of the said burgh newly founded by the present king" (*ER*, vi. 406–7), and of mentions of the Friars Minor of Kirkcudbright, 17 September 1456, and 15 July 1457 (*Ibid.*, vi. 201, 353). According to Moir Bryce, "active Franciscanism in Kirkcudbright was brought to a peaceful termination in the autumn of 1560" (i. 254). On 6 December 1569, James VI gave a charter of the place and church of the Greyfriars, "which for a long time past have been destroyed and now lie waste", to Thomas Mac-Lellan of Bombie (*Ibid.*, ii. 170), who in turn conveyed these properties to the Town Council, the friars' church to become the parish church, 24 March 1570/1 (*Ibid.*, ii. 171).

LANARK. The founder was Robert I. Brockie (p. 1459) has a charter of that king granting the Friars Minor a site for a convent, with a sum for its endowment. The date of this charter (which has only the regnal year) lies between 27 March 1325 and 26 March 1326. Moir Bryce (i. 240) dates the foundation, 11 November 1328–15 May 1329. The lands granted for a site are mentioned, 7 August 1329 (*ER*, i. 163). From Pope Clement VI David II obtained a bull of erection, 29 November 1346 (*MB*, ii. 149; GRH. Vat. Trans., i. 14), in terms of which there were to be twelve friars, though it is doubtful whether that number was ever attained. Before the Reformation (the date is unrecorded), the place and lands of the friary were leased to James Lockhart of Lee (*MB*, i. 243; ii. 158). It is not known when the friary was abandoned, but the removal of its stonework had been going on –1566, when it was checked by the Lords of Council (*Ibid.*, i. 243).

## THE FRANCISCAN FRIARS
### (I) The Friars Minor Conventual

| Name | County | Minimum Income (1561) | Founder | Date Fd. | D. or Sec. |
|---|---|---|---|---|---|
| ROXBURGH | Roxburgh | | Alexander II(?) | 1232 or 1232–4 | 1547+ |

ROXBURGH. Brockie (pp. 1281–2) exemplifies a charter of Alexander II which narrates that the king has granted the Friars Minor a site at Roxburgh and erected for them a church and other buildings, 18 October 1232. This charter is probably genuine. Moir Bryce (i. 161) gives the date of foundation as 1232–4. The friars' cemetery was dedicated, 4 May 1235 (*Calchou*, no. 418). There were four friars here in 1336–7 (*MB*, i. 164). This house ("the friars near Kelso") was burned by the English, 14 September 1545 (*L. & P. H. VIII*, xx². nos. 456, 533) and was evidently abandoned; in November 1547, it was partially roofed over for military purposes by English troops (*Cal. of Scottish Papers*, i. no. 98).

### INCOMPLETE FOUNDATION

*Elgin.* About 1281 William, earl of Ross, gave certain lands for the upkeep of the Friars Minor, "who for the time or in the future may be in occupation of their house in Elgin beside the cathedral". If the friars had not taken up residence or were unwilling to remain there, the income of these lands was to be used for the maintenance of two chaplains in the cathedral (*REM*, no. 220). The settlement of the friars at this time must have been temporary, as the latter alternative came into operation. *V.* under Observants.

### SUPPOSED FOUNDATIONS

*Banff.* A Franciscan convent, its church dedicated to St John, is mentioned here (*Collns. Aberd. and Banff*, p. 205). This is a confusion with the Carmelite house.

*Forfar.* According to *CDS* (ii. no. 856), Edward I, on 23 November 1296, ordered his treasurer in Scotland to examine the rolls of King Alexander [III] and King John [Balliol] regarding the claims of the Friars Minor in the towns of Berwick, Roxburgh, Haddington, Dumfries and Forfar. But reference to *Docs. Illust. of Hist. of Scotland* (ii. no. ccclxxxiv) shows (under 23 November 1297) that this is an error. The king's mandate is concerned with the friars of Dundee, who have 10 l. sterling and 20 l. of wax yearly from the ferme of Forfar. There were no Greyfriars at Forfar.

*Inverness.* The idea that there were Greyfriars here is due to confusion with the Blackfriars.

## THE FRANCISCAN FRIARS
### (II) The Observant Friars

In a letter to Pope Julius II, 1 February 1506/7, James IV declares that, forty-two years previously, his grandmother (Mary of Gueldres) introduced the Observants to Scotland, while he himself "completed and furnished for them house after house" (*Letters of James IV*, no. 76). Both parts of this statement are questionable. Moir Bryce (*Greyfriars*, i. 58) has shown that King James had in mind the bull of Pope Pius II, 9 June 1463, addressed to the vicar-general of the ultramontane province of the Observants, in these terms: "We have learned that, on account of the devotion of Mary . . . illustrious queen of Scotland and of that people, at the request or certain merchants, you have lately sent your brethren as preachers to that kingdom, in which no house of the Observance of your order has been built. . . . We therefore grant you power to erect, found and build and likewise to receive in that kingdom three or four houses, if you find any who graciously proffer a foundation or erection of this sort" (*Ibid.*, ii. 276). But there is evidence that the Edinburgh friary was in existence before 1462–3 (*v.* Edinburgh *infra*). Again, while King James is mentioned as founder of the friaries of Ayr, Elgin and Stirling (*q.v. infra*), only the last may fairly be regarded as of his foundation.

No particulars of the incomes of the Observant houses are available.

K

## THE FRANCISCAN FRIARS
### (II) The Observant Friars

| Name | County | Founder | Fd. | Date D. or Sec. |
|---|---|---|---|---|
| ABERDEEN | Aberdeen | Richard Vaus of Many and others | 1469 | 1559 |
| AYR | Ayr | Inhabitants of the burgh | 1472–74 | 1567 |

ABERDEEN. Brockie (p. 1479) gives a letter of the provost, bailies and community of Aberdeen, 28 June 1450, to the vicar of the Observants in Scotland, intimating that as Richard Vaus of Many has informed them that the vicar is agreeable to sending friars to that burgh if these can obtain an "honest house" to dwell in; and since Vaus has given a site and the community (i.e. of the burgh) has erected a cloister, church, etc., requesting the vicar to supply friars. According to another entry in Brockie (pp. 1480–1), this foundation was confirmed by Pope Nicholas V, 5 December 1450. From references in the Aberdeen Obituary Calendar, Moir Bryce (i. 307) concludes that the friary was "a foundation of gradual growth dating from . . . 1461", when the Observants reached Aberdeen. It is not till 1 May and 20 July 1469 that we find Richard Vaus giving charters of his land to the friars (and it is not mentioned that this was the site of the friary) (*MB*, ii. 212, 216), while this donation was confirmed by James III, 9 May 1469 (*Ibid.*, p. 217) and Thomas, bishop of Aberdeen (who speaks of this land as "for the structure and fabric of the [friars'] church" which may indicate the grant of an endowment rather than a site), 23 May 1469 (*Ibid.*, ii. 217–18). That the burgh was associated with Vaus and others in providing for this friary, though their respective contributions are not made clear, is shown by a crown charter of confirmation of the land included in its site, 21 December 1479 (*Ibid.*, ii. 195). The statement of Father John Hay (*Ibid.*, ii. 176) that this house was constituted in 1470 by the bishop of Aberdeen, who erected a convent beside the University, cannot be accepted. But if the friars were earlier in Aberdeen, it was evidently about this date that their house was built. A new and enlarged church was constructed for the friars, 1518–32, by Bishop Gavin Dunbar (*Ibid.*, i. 314–16). Moir Bryce regards 12–16 as the maximum number of friars (*Ibid.*, i. 318). On 29 December 1559, the friars resigned their entire possessions to the Town Council (*Ibid.*, ii. 233; *Aberdeen Friars*, p. 97), who, on 11 March 1559/60, resolved to maintain the Greyfriars' church and place for the town's use (*Aberdeen Friars*, p. 97). James VI granted to the Town Council, 30 December 1567, the place of the Friars Minor to be converted into a hospital (*Ibid.*, p. 100). It is said that the church stood derelict until 1624, when the citizens began to "reedifie" it (*Abredoniae Utriusque Descriptio*, p. 11); and it remained in use as a parish church till its removal in 1903. The remaining buildings passed to George, earl Marischal, 22 September 1593 (*MB*, i. 328) and were bestowed by him upon Marischal College (*Collns. Aberd. and Banff*, p. 200; *MB*, *loc. cit.*).

AYR. Father John Hay attributes the foundation to the inhabitants of the town in 1474 (*MB*, ii. 176); and a similar statement is made by Spottiswoode (p. 452), who gives the date as 1472. Brockie (pp. 1491–2) has a charter of the provost, bailies and rest of the community to the vicar-provincial of Scotland narrating their foundation of a church and convent for the Observants, 28 October 1472, and also (p. 1493) a bull of Pope Sixtus IV confirming the erection, 18 June 1474. Moir Bryce regards it as one of the friaries sanctioned by the bull of this pope, on the petition of James, bishop of Dunkeld, 19 March 1481/2 (i. 352; ii. 250); and it is also stated to have been founded by James IV (1488–1513) (*Diurnal*, p. 4), though this is very probably erroneous as it may well have been a foundation by the townsmen. It is asserted by Moir Bryce that the friary was sacked at the Reformation (i. 356), though he admits elsewhere that there is no record of this (i. 147); and the same writer assumes, from the fact that there is no record of pensions paid them, that the friars "quitted the burgh in a body" (i. 356). A precept for the grant of the lands and possessions of the Greyfriars (and others) to the burgh was given, 14 April 1567 (*MB*, ii. 255).

## THE FRANCISCAN FRIARS
### (II) THE OBSERVANT FRIARS

| Name | County | Founder | Fd. | Date D. or Sec. |
|------|--------|---------|-----|-----------------|
| EDINBURGH | Midlothian | James Douglas of Cassillis and citizens | 1455 or 1458 | 1562 |
| ‡ ELGIN | Moray | John Innes of Innes | 1479 | c. 1559(?) |
| GLASGOW | Lanark | John Laing, bishop of Glasgow and master Thomas Forsyth, rector of Glasgow | 1473–6 | 1566/7 |

EDINBURGH. This was the earliest of the Scottish Observant houses. Six friars are said to have come from Holland in 1447 (*MB*, i. 47; ii. 174). Their house, with its land, was bestowed upon them by James Douglas of Cassillis and the citizens (*Ibid.*, ii. 195), and was occupied, according to Father John Hay, in 1455 (or perhaps, more correctly, in 1458) (*Ibid.*, i. 56 and *n.*), after the property had been incorporated by apostolic letters in the Roman Church (*Ibid.*, ii. 174). A payment to the friars is entered in the Exchequer account 27 July 1462–27 July 1463 (*ER*, vii. 211) and another, for the repair of their place, appears in the account of 27 July 1463–12 July 1464 (*Ibid.*, vii. 284). On 21 December 1479, they were confirmed in possession of their property by James IV (*MB*, ii. 195). The friars were given the church of St John the Baptist "outside the burgh", 20 November 1464 (*Reg. S. Egid.*, no. 81), and they held it till *c.* 1490 (*MB*, i. 272). The friary was destroyed by Reformers, 14 June 1559 (*Diurnal*, p. 269; Lesley, *History*, p. 275). On 17 August 1562, the Town Council petitioned the Queen to grant the yards of the Greyfriars as a burying-ground (*Edin. BR, 1557–71*, p. 146).

ELGIN. There was a temporary settlement of Greyfriars here in the thirteenth century. *V.* under Conventual Friars. The Observantine house, according to Father John Hay, was founded by John Innes of Innes, in 1479 (*MB*, i. 362; ii. 176). The attribution of the foundation to Innes is supported by a document given by Brockie (p. 1498), viz., a bull of Pope Sixtus IV which, in response to Innes's petition, confirms his foundation in 1479 (no day or month mentioned). Moir Bryce regards it as one of the "two or three" friaries sanctioned by the foregoing Pope, 19 March 1481/2 (ii. 250). The foundation is also attributed (no doubt in error) to James IV (1488–1513) (*Diurnal*, p. 4). At an unascertained date (probably *c.* 1559), the buildings passed into the possession of the burgh and, from 1563, were used as a court of justice (*MB*, i. 364). The Greyfriars' lands were leased by James V to Robert Innes of Invermarky, 20 April 1573 (*RMS*, iii. no. 2133).

GLASGOW. This house according to Father John Hay was founded in 1472 (*MB*, ii. 176). He attributes its foundation, mistakenly, to the archbishop. Brockie (p. 1476), however, supplies a bull of Pope Sixtus IV, 1 December 1476, according to which William [Turnbull], bishop of Glasgow (1448–54), introduced the Observants there. But as their place was too small for a complete (*integrum*) convent, John [Laing], bishop of Glasgow (1473/4–1482/3), wished to build them a house, of which Thomas Forsyth, canon of Glasgow cathedral and rector of Glasgow, was also a benefactor. The Pope signifies his consent to this erection. Bishop Laing appears as granting the site and Forsyth likewise as a donor in the charter of confirmation given by James III, 21 December 1479 (*MB*, ii. 195). It is stated by Brockie (p. 1477) that the friars' church was dedicated (to the Blessed Virgin Mary), on the 8th Sunday after Trinity [3 August], 1477. What happened to this friary at the Reformation is unknown, but Moir Bryce (i.147) suggests it was destroyed in the autumn of 1559. Properties of the Friars Minor were among those granted to the Town Council, 16 March 1566/7 (*Chs. and Docs. rel. to Glasgow*, Pt. II, no. lix). But although these were bestowed upon the college (university) by the magistrates, 6 January 1572/3 (*Ibid.*, no. lxiii), the friary appears to have passed into the private ownership of Sir John Stewart of Minto (*MB*, i. 348).

## THE FRANCISCAN FRIARS
### (II) THE OBSERVANT FRIARS

| Name | County | Founder | Fd. | Date D. or Sec. |
|------|--------|---------|-----|------------------|
| JEDBURGH | Roxburgh | Border nobles or inhabitants of the burgh | −1505 | ? |
| PERTH | Perth | Lord Oliphant | 1460 | 1559–60 |

JEDBURGH. Father John Hay declares that this house was erected in 1513 by the nobles of the Border (*MB*, ii. 178). The year of foundation is also given as 1513 by Father Richard Augustine Hay, who attributes its erection to the inhabitants of Jedburgh (Scotia Sacra, p. 554); and Spottiswoode (p. 453) makes a similar statement. But the friars here are mentioned, 27 March 1505 (*LHT. Accts.*, iii. 508). The bull of erection was issued by Pope Adrian IV, 31 January 1521/2 (*MB*, ii. 262). This house had a brief and chequered career. Although it is not specifically mentioned, the friary was probably involved in the destruction of the town by Suffolk's forces, 24 September 1523 (*L. & P. H. VIII*, iii². no. 3360); and it was burned by Eure, 9 June 1544 (*Ibid.*, xix¹. no. 762) and by Hertford, in September 1545 (*Ibid.*, xx². no. 456). The statement is made by Moir Bryce that "at the Reformation the site and buildings passed into the possession of the magistrates" (i. 379), but the crown grant of ecclesiastical properties (mainly chaplainries) to the burgh (*RMS*, iii. no. 1897) does not explicitly mention those of the Greyfriars. *V*. Watson, "Hist. of the Franciscan Friary of Jedburgh", *Berwickshire Nat. Club*, xx (1910).

PERTH. Fittis (*Eccles. Annals of Perth*, p. 267) erroneously states that a payment is made to Greyfriars of Perth in 1358 (the entry to which he refers (*ER*, i. 557) is a payment merely to "Friars", in this case evidently the Blackfriars). The foundation of this friary is said by Father John Hay to have been made by Lord Oliphant, in 1460 (*MB*, ii. 175). Brockie (p. 1488) has a charter of the provost, bailies and community of Perth to the vicar-general of the Observants in Scotland, in view of his sending friars to occupy the monastery built by Sir Laurence Oliphant of Aberdalgie, making provision for the furnishing and upkeep of their house and church, 28 April 1460; and also (p. 1487) a bull of Pope Pius II, 26 July 1460, confirming the erection of this friary by Sir Laurence Oliphant (who became Lord Oliphant in 1458). On 29 March 1466, the Pope appointed a mandatory on the petition of the vicar and friars of the Order of the Friars Minor in Scotland, containing that Henry, bishop of St Andrews [i.e. Henry Wardlaw, 1403–40], granted them the house of "Bertheon", in the diocese of St Andrews, after which the friars had a house with a church, etc., built there and "have therein for more than forty years served the most high"; and supplicating papal confirmation of this grant, permission that they may receive this house anew and absolution for inhabiting it without papal licence (*CPR*, xii, 539–9). If "Bertheon" is Perth, there is no record of friars there in the time of Bishop Wardlaw and certainly not in 1426. This transaction also appears in what Moir Bryce (i. 57) calls an "obscure paragraph" of the *Annales Minorum* (xii. 606). No satisfactory explanation of it can be given. The Perth friary was destroyed by Reformers in May 1559 (Lesley, *History*, p. 272; Knox, *History*, i. 323; Pitscottie, *Cronicles*, ii. 146), and its site became a burying-ground in 1580 (Fittis, *op. cit.*, p. 269; *MB*, i. 302).

## THE FRANCISCAN FRIARS
### (II) The Observant Friars

| Name | County | Founder | Fd. | Date D. or Sec. |
|------|--------|---------|-----|-----------------|
| St Andrews | Fife | James Kennedy, bishop of St Andrews | 1458 | 1559–67 |
| Stirling | Stirling | James IV | 1494 | 1559–67 |

St Andrews. According to Father John Hay, the founder was James Kennedy, bishop of St Andrews, in 1458 (*MB*, ii. 175). Brockie (p. 1471) gives a bull of Pius II, 24 November 1458, confirming the erection of a house of Observants by this bishop and (p. 1472) states that Patrick Graham, Kennedy's successor, granted them a larger house. The endowment by Kennedy and Graham was confirmed by a charter of James IV, 21 December 1479 (*MB*, ii. 195). It is significant that the foundation by Bishop Kennedy of the friary at St Andrews followed on the founding by him of St Salvator's College (*q.v.*) (*v.* A. I. Dunlop, *Life and Times of James Kennedy*, p. 297). There are references to the burning of this house by Norman Leslie in July 1547 (*RSS*, iii. nos. 2345, 2363). The friary was resigned to the magistrates, 18 May 1559 (*MB*, ii. 202). On or about 14 June following, it was destroyed by Reformers (Lesley, *History*, p. 273) or, according to Knox (*History*, i. 349–50) by the magistrates; and when, on 21 September of that year, the magistrates were invested in the property, the site was described as wasted and the buildings as ruined (*MB*, ii. 202). Along with other ecclesiastical properties, the former possessions of the friars were granted to the burgh by Queen Mary, 17 April 1567 (Reg. of Evidents of the City of St Ands., Inventory, no. 4).

Stirling. This house is said by Father John Hay to have been founded by James IV, in 1494 (*MB*, ii. 177). *Diurnal* (p. 4) and Brockie (p. 4510) likewise give James IV as founder. On that king's petition, Pope Alexander VI issued a bull of erection (*MB*, ii. 257; GRH. Vat. Trans., ii. 370); while grants towards the building are recorded, 9 and 12 May 1498 (*LHT. Accts.*, i. 390, 391). The friary was destroyed by Reformers in 1559 (Lesley, *History*, p. 274). On 15 April 1567, the former possessions of the friars, along with other ecclesiastical property, was granted to the magistrates (*MB*, ii. 259).

## THE CARMELITE FRIARS

| Name | County | Minimum Income (1561) | Founder | Fd. | Date D. or Sec. |
|---|---|---|---|---|---|
| ABERDEEN | Aberdeen | £96(?) | | c. 1273 | 1560–83 |
| BANFF | Banff | | Robert I | 1321–4 | 1574 |
| BERWICK | | | Sir John Gray | 1270 | ? |
| EDINBURGH, GREENSIDE | Midlothian | | Town Council (?) | 1520–5 | –1563 |
| INVERBERVIE | Kincardine | £94 | | –1443 | –1570 |

ABERDEEN. In 1273, Reginald le Chen made a grant to the Carmelites here "till their buildings be ready" (*Aberdeen Friars*, p. 12). Spottiswoode (p. 455), however, declares that this house is said to have been founded by Philip de Arbuthnot of that ilk in 1350; while Brockie (p. 1549) has a charter in the form of a letter by Arbuthnot to the provincial of the Carmelites in Scotland, narrating his foundation of a Carmelite house at Aberdeen "in the place where the castle of that town formerly stood" and dated "the third week-day after the Assumption of the Blessed Virgin Mary" [i.e. 18 August] 1354. This and other features of its style raise suspicions regarding the authenticity of this document. Arbuthnot was undoubtedly a benefactor of the Carmelites; but his grant to them, on 25 April 1355, of an annual rent of 13s. 4d. from the land of Arbuthnot "for the repair of the fabric of their church" (*RMS*, i. 259) would seem to imply an earlier foundation. This house is said to have been destroyed in 1560 by the Reforming barons of the Mearns (Lesley, *De Origine*, p. 563). Its lands were granted to the Town Council by James VI, 26 October 1583 (*RMS*, v. no. 618).

BANFF. Our Lady chapel near Banff was bestowed upon the Carmelites by Robert I, 21 April 1321 (*RMS*, i. App. 1, 91); and it was confirmed to them by that king, 1 August 1324, along with land for the erection of a church and monastery (*Antiqs. Aberd. and Banff*, ii. 114–15). On 10 September 1574, James VI granted the lands, buildings and revenues formerly belonging to this house to King's College, Aberdeen (*RMS*, iv. no. 2304; RSS, xlii. 76).

BERWICK. Said to have been founded in 1270 by Sir John Gray (Dugdale, *Monasticon*, vi. 1574). On 25 September 1296, the Carmelites here were granted lands by Edward I (*Rot. Scot.*, i. 34). Payments to them are also recorded "from the gift of the [Scottish] king", 21 January 1327/8 (*ER*, i. 63) and from the fermes of Berwick, 16 March 1330/1 to 22 February 1332/3 (*Ibid.*, i. 311, 411). On 10 August 1333, Edward III gave mandate to the prior provincial of the order in England to remove the Scottish friars here to English houses and to substitute English friars (*Rot. Scot.*, i. 258). This house received a further payment from the English Exchequer, 15 December 1337 (*CDS*, ii. no. 1251). The Carmelites are mentioned in the fifteenth-century poem, "The Freiris of Berwik" (attributed to Dunbar) (*Poems of Dunbar*, ed. W. Mackay Mackenzie (1932), p. 185).

EDINBURGH, GREENSIDE. On 5 December 1520, the Town Council granted a site at Greenside to the friars of Queensferry, with the permission of the king and the bishop of St Andrews (*Edin. BR, 1403–1528*, p. 203). Not till 11 October 1525 were they given possession of the site and had the keys of the Rood Chapel there handed over to them (*Ibid.*, p. 222; *Prot. Bk. of John Foular*, iii. no. 641). According to a record of 21 March 1529/30, there was friction with Holyrood abbey, resulting in the "downcasting" of the house where the friars lived (*ALC, 1501–54*, p. 325). The friars had ceased to occupy the church and buildings and the croft of Greenside, –23 July 1563 (*Edin. BR, 1557–1571*, p. 168).

INVERBERVIE (BERVIE). Brockie (p. 1552) transcribes a charter purporting to record the foundation of this house by David II in 1358 (no day or month are given) and another charter by Mark Rait of Halgreen to the Carmelites of Bervie, 12 November 1388 (pp. 1554 ff.). It is impossible to say whether these charters (which have no witnesses) are genuine. In 1443, this house is said to have been "recently established" (*Aberdeen Friars*, p. 30). One of its priors, Christianus Bryssone, is mentioned, 20 November 1487 (GRH. Chs., no. 534). It appears to have continued till the Reformation (*v. Thirds of Benefices, passim*); and, on 15 October 1570, a grant was made of lands and other properties formerly belonging to the friars (*RMS*, iv. no. 1932).

## THE CARMELITE FRIARS

| Name | County | Minimum Income (1561) | Founder | Date Fd. | Date D. or Sec. |
|------|--------|-----------------------|---------|----------|-----------------|
| IRVINE | Ayr | | One of the Fullartons of Fullarton | -1399 | 1572 |
| KINGUSSIE | Inverness | | George, earl of Huntly | -1501 | ? |
| LINLITHGOW | West Lothian | £33 | Sir James Douglas of Dalkeith | *c.* 1401 | -1567/8 |
| ¶ LUFFNESS | East Lothian | | | -1335-6 (? 13c) | ? |

IRVINE. On 24 August 1399, Reginald Fullarton made a grant to the friars here for the repairs of the conventual buildings and church (*Macfarlane's Geneal. Collns.*, ii. 336); and, in 1412, the forebears of Rankin Fullarton are described as founders and patrons of this house (*Ibid.*, ii. 336–7). It may thus have been founded in the fourteenth century or earlier by one of the Fullarton family. On 8 June 1572, James VI granted its property to the Royal School of Irvine (*RMS*, iv. no. 2071).

KINGUSSIE. Founded by George, earl of Huntly (†1501) (*Macfarlane's Geneal. Collns.*, ii. 416; *RSS*, ii. xxiv and no. 797). Payments of alms to the friars are recorded, 7 November 1501 and 10 September 1506 (*LHT. Accts.*, ii. 76, 281). The prior and convent had a royal protection, 12 January 1530/1 (*RSS*, ii. no. 797). The subsequent history of this priory has not been traced.

LINLITHGOW. Spottiswoode (p. 455) attributes the foundation of this house to the citizens in 1290; while Brockie (p. 1540) gives a letter of the provost, bailies and the rest of the community of the burgh to Henry Hann de Brunham, provincial of England and vicar and visitor of the order in Scotland, narrating their foundation of a Carmelite house, 28 September 1280. This document is in all probability spurious.[1] On 18 May 1401, an indenture between Sir James Douglas of Dalkeith and the provincial of the Carmelites testifies that the former has granted to the chapel of the Blessed Virgin Mary of Linlithgow and the brethren of the Carmelite order who will celebrate divine service there land for the construction of conventual buildings and a garden (*Reg. Hon. de Morton*, ii. no. 210; cf. *ibid.*, no. 211). This house is said to have been pulled down by Reformers in 1559 (Lesley, *History*, p. 274). There is a reference to land formerly belonging to the priors, 25 February 1567/8 (*Prot. Bk. of Thomas Johnsoun*, no. 533).

LUFFNESS. The first definite reference to this house is in 1335–6, when it is recorded that the friars of "Lufnok" receive from the lands of "Lufnok" ten marks yearly, in virtue of a long-standing endowment (*CDS*, iii, 338). The foundation may thus have taken place in the previous century. This house is also on record, 7 May 1361 (*RMS*, i. App. 2, no. 1230 (Index B (2)) *n.*; cf. *Aberdeen Friars*, p. 17). John Heryng, prior of Luffness, appears 1 March 1497/8 (*Prot. Bk. of James Young*, no. 1004). The priory is mentioned from 1504/5 to 1512 as in receipt of alms from the king (*LHT Accts.*, ii. 268; iv. 186). No further references to it have been found but lands formerly belonging to it were leased by the Crown, 4 January 1609 (*RMS*, vi. no. 3).

---

[1] Cf. its reference to the king as "Alexandro *III* rege".

## THE CARMELITE FRIARS

| Name | County | Minimum Income (1561) | Founder | Fd. | Date D. or Sec. |
|---|---|---|---|---|---|
| ‡ QUEENSFERRY | West Lothian | | James Dundas of Dundas | 1440/1 | –1564/5 |
| TULLILUM | Perth | £16 | Richard, bishop of Dunkeld | 1262 | 1559+ |

QUEENSFERRY. According to Spottiswoode (p. 455), this house was founded by the laird of Dundas in 1330. Brockie (p. 1554) likewise gives what purports to be a letter of James Dundas, laird of Dundas, to the provincial and vicar-general of the Carmelites in Scotland, intimating his foundation of a house at Queensferry, 28 November 1333. Again, the editor of *Dundas of Dundas* declares: "There can be no doubt that the family of Dundas of Dundas, as their charter-chest unfolds, introduced the Carmelite order at the present site about A.D. 1330" (*op. cit.*, xlvii). But a confirmation charter of James II, 5 November 1459, incorporates a charter of James Dundas of Dundas, 1 March 1440/1, granting the Carmelites a piece of ground in Queensferry "for the church of St Mary the Virgin and for the construction of certain buildings there in the form of a monastery (*in modum monasterii*)" (Dundas Chs.); and the latter charter was confirmed by Archibald de Dundas, with an additional endowment, 22 June 1455 (Ibid.). The monastery thus appears to have been a fifteenth-century foundation. Cf. also *HMC. 3rd Rep.*, App., 413. The community was apparently no longer in existence when, on 27 February 1564–5, the prior granted a lease of the monastic buildings (*RMS*, iv. no. 1607). After 1583, the priory church was let by Sir Walter Dundas to the bailies and Town Council of Queensferry for use as a parish church, with an obligation on their part to remove from it when required. This arrangement lasted for about fifty years (*Dundas of Dundas*, xlvii–xlviii).

TULLILUM. Said to have been founded in 1262, when Richard, bishop of Dunkeld, granted the friars a chapel here; this was the first settlement of the Carmelites in Scotland (*Scotich.*, lib x, cap. xiv (ii. 97); Major, *Hist. of Greater Britain*, bk. IV, ch. xii (p. 188); Fittis, *Eccles. Annals of Perth*, p. 201). There is evidence that building (additions or repairs) was in progress at the monastery, *c.* 1514 (*Rent. Dunkeldense*, pp. 238, 315). It is said to have been destroyed by Reformers in 1559 (Lesley, *History*, p. 272; Fittis, *op. cit.*, p. 208) though Pitscottie states that Lord Ruthven saved Tullilum from being cast down but abolished the friars (*Cronicles*, ii. 146).

### SUPPOSED FOUNDATIONS

*Brechin.* According to the account given by Brockie (p. 1559), a house was founded here in the time of Stephen Dempster, bishop of Brechin, who held the see in 1376, by Malcolm Dempster, baron of Careston and nephew of that bishop. This statement cannot be accepted. The bishop of Brechin at that period was Patrick de Locrys (1351–83) (Dowden, *Bishops*, pp. 182–3). Brockie (p. 1559) also gives a charter of Robert de Carnegie making a grant to this alleged house, 30 November 1388. But this charter is spurious; for the contemporary Carnegie was John de Carnegie of that ilk who appears 1375–1430 (*Carnegies*, i. 5). This house is apocryphal.

*Drumtochty.* No house of Carmelites existed here. In 1403 the Carmelites of Aberdeen were granted the lands of Glensaucht (*Aberdeen Friars*, p. 24), and these are mentioned when leased by the prior to James Keith of Drumtochter, as "the lands of Easter Glensaucht *alias* the Friars' Glen" (*Ibid.*, p. 99). Alleged references to a Carmelite house here, when not merely imaginary, are references to *lands*.

*Dunbar.* Said by Spottiswoode (p. 455) to have been founded in 1263 by Patrick, earl of March. Brockie (p. 1538) gives what purports to be a charter of foundation by this earl, 28 January 1263. This charter, which adduces the consent to the foundation of William Wishart, bishop of St Andrews (the bishop of St Andrews in 1263 was Gameline (1255–71)) cannot be regarded as genuine. A much later reference—in 1576 (*RMS*, iv. no. 2543)— probably rests on a confusion with the Trinitarian foundation at Dunbar (*q.v.*). Dunbar is not mentioned in the list appended to the *Scotichronicon* (ii. 540).

*Elgin.* There is a reference in 1581 (*RMS*, v. no. 303) to lands and rents "belonging from of old to the White . . . Friars of Elgin". The reference properly applies to another order, probably the Greyfriars.

*St Andrews.* Spottiswoode (p. 456) tentatively rejects Dempster's assertion that there were Carmelites here. On the other hand, Brockie (p. 1556) narrates the foundation of a house at St Andrews by Bishop William de Laverdale [*sic*] in 1370. There was no such bishop, though William de Landallis (1341/2–1385) may be meant. Brockie (pp. 1557–8) also gives two charters of alleged benefactors of this house in 1370 and 1378. Both of these documents must be regarded as dubious (e.g. their style of dating is very unusual and they have no witnesses). This foundation appears to be suppositious.

## THE AUGUSTINIAN FRIARS

| Name | County | Fd. | Date D. or Sec. |
|------|--------|-----|-----------------|
| BERWICK | | −1329 | V. notes |

BERWICK. Payments are recorded to the friars of the order of St Augustine of part of £20 granted them by the [Scottish] king for the fabric of their church, in 1329 and 1330 (*ER*, i. 173, 279). On 10 August 1333, Edward III gave mandate to the prior provincial of the Augustinian hermits in England to remove the Scottish friars here to English houses and to substitute English friars (*Rot. Scot.*, i. 258). It is highly probable that this house was none other than Sedgen, which appears, from the thirteenth century onwards, as an Augustinian hospital at or near Berwick. V. Segden under Hospitals.

### INCOMPLETE FOUNDATIONS

*Haddington.* A MS. inventory of the burgh charters includes a sasine in favour of the "Augustinian friars" of an annuity of 13s. 4d., 24 April 1464. This entry is inaccurate; for the document, which has been inspected, is an instrument of that date referring to the Augustinian canons of St Andrews. An undated letter of James IV to Pope Julius II requests that the hospital of St Laurence, Haddington, should be converted into a house of Augustinian friars (*Letters of James IV*, no. 471; the date suggested for this letter—July 1512—is too late); and, on 13 October 1511, the Pope suppressed the hospital and erected a house of friars (or hermits) of this order (*L. & P. H. VIII*, i². 1522). But a letter of James V to Pope Leo X, 1513–14, which states that as none of these took up residence, he has conferred it on his chaplain, Walter Ramsay, seeks confirmation of this appointment and the severance of the incorporation of the hospital in this order (*Epp. Reg. Scot.*, i. 193–4; *Letters of James V*, p. 8). Payments are recorded, 1511–12, to a master of the hospital who is designated "friar" (*ER*, xiii. 396, 496) and who may have been an Augustinian. But other friars, to whom payments are made on behalf of this hospital (e.g. *Ibid.*, xiv. 206; xv. 76 and later) can be shown to have been Franciscans (v. Haddington, St Laurence under Hospitals); and it is clear that it did not come into the permanent possession of the Augustinian friars.

*Linlithgow.* From September to December 1503 royal donations to the Augustinian friars here are recorded, e.g. two grants of £7 "to thair bigging [building]" (*LHT. Accts.*, ii. 254, 255, 256). No evidence, however, is forthcoming to show that this order settled here. That it did not do so seems to be suggested by the attempt, soon after, to place friars at Manuel in the same vicinity.

*Manuel.* On the petition of James IV, the Pope, on 16 June 1506, provided for the suppression of the Cistercian nunnery here and the introduction of Augustinian friars Observantines (GRH. Vat. Trans., iii. no. 32). This did not take place. V. Manuel under Cistercian Nuns.

## THE FRIARS OF THE SACK

| Name | Founder | Fd. | Date D. |
|------|---------|-----|---------|
| BERWICK | | 1267 | *c.* 1274 |

BERWICK. A charter of Roger, prior of Coldingham, 18 May 1267, declares that his monastery has conceded to the Friars of Penitence of Jesus Christ that they may erect buildings and an oratory within Coldingham's appropriated parish of Holy Trinity of South Berwick [i.e. Berwick-on-Tweed]. The friars have pledged themselves to do nothing to the prejudice of Coldingham (*N. Durham*, App. no. dclii). But, on 17 June 1285, the bishop of St Andrews is instructed, as papal mandatory, to sell to the Friars Preachers of Berwick the place in that town "late held but now left by the Friars of Penitence" (*CPR*, Letters, i. 482; cf. *Ibid.*, i. 494–5). This house presumably was dissolved on the suppression of the order in 1274.

## THE CRUTCHED FRIARS

Mr R. Neville Hadcock has brought to my notice mentions (mainly in catalogues dated 1552–1635) of a house of this order at a site given as "Pful", "Pfall", "Faill', "Fayl in Scotia" (Hermans, *Ann. can. reg. S. Aug. ord. S. Crucis*, ii. 189, 194, 197). This place is presumably Fail, in Ayrshire. But the religious house at Fail (*v.* p. 91) was Trinitarian. Again, although friars of this order have been located at Dunkeld and Hamilton (Chettle, "Friars of the Holy Cross", *History*, xxxiv (1949), 205), no reliable evidence of these alleged foundations has been found. There is a reference to the appointment of a visitor "of the convents of the kingdoms and lands of England, Scotland, Ireland and Wales" (Hermans, *op. cit.*, ii. 388), but the inclusion of Scotland may be no more than "common form". It is highly probable that this order was not represented in Scotland.

## THE BENEDICTINE NUNS

| Name | County | Founder | Fd. | Date Supp. |
|------|--------|---------|-----|------------|
| * LINCLUDEN | Kirkcudbright | Uchtred of Galloway | –1174 | 1389 |

LINCLUDEN. Spottiswoode (p. 459) as well as MS. and other lists ascribe this foundation to Uchtred, son of Fergus, lord of Galloway (†1174). This writer and another in Hutton's Collns. (I) assign the foundation to the reign of Malcolm IV (1153–65). The community is generally described as of black nuns; in one source, a papal letter of 7 May 1389, the nunnery is designated "of the Cluniac order" (GRH. Vat. Trans., i. 288 ff.). In 1296, the prioress swore fealty to Edward I (*CDS*, ii. no. 823). The nunnery was suppressed in 1389 and a college of secular canons substituted for it (GRH. Vat. Trans., *loc. cit.*). *V*. Lincluden under Secular Canons (II).

### SUPPOSED FOUNDATIONS

*Holystone.* As "Halyston, near Berwick", this house is included by Spottiswoode (p. 459) under Benedictine nunneries. This is erroneous. The supposition that there was a house of that name near Berwick may be due to confusion with the Cistercian nunnery, which was in the vicinity of Halidon; or to the fact that the "prioresse of Halistan del counte de Berewyk" appears among those who swore fealty to Edward I, in 1296 (*CDS*, ii. no. 823). The only house of this name was the Augustinian nunnery of Holystone, in Coquetdale, in the north of England.

*Kilconquhar.* This place is said to be in Galloway. It is in fact in Fife; and the suggestion that it was the site of a nunnery is due to a misinterpretation of the fact that the parish church was held by North Berwick nunnery.

### THE CISTERCIAN NUNS

By way of confirmation of the number of houses included in the following list, it may be noted that a document which records the proposed visitation of Scottish houses by a commissary of Cîteaux in 1516 mentions that there were at this date seven houses of nuns of the Cistercian order (*RSS*, i. no. 2833); and an inhibition by Archbishop Forman of the visitation of these nunneries, *c.* 1516, gives their names as Haddington, North Berwick, Eccles, Coldstream, St Bothan's, Manuel, Elcho (*Formulare*, i. no. 47). A MS. of slightly later date (1524–41(?)) in Edinburgh University Library (MS. Dc. 7. 63) gives a list of nine Scottish nunneries. These, with the exception of Iona, are the Cistercian houses—South Berwick, North Berwick, Eccles, Coldstream, Haddington, St Bothan's, Manuel and Elcho. South Berwick, i.e. Berwick-on-Tweed, is probably mentioned in this list retrospectively, as the nunnery was extinct by this time. St Evoca's, which was extinct about the beginning of the fifteenth century, does not appear.

## THE CISTERCIAN NUNS

| Name | County | Minimum Income (1561) | Founder | Fd. | Date D. or Sec. |
|---|---|---|---|---|---|
| BERWICK | | | David I | −1153 | 1390/1 |

BERWICK. Usually called the nunnery of South Berwick (to distinguish it from North Berwick). It figures as "[the house] of the Blessed Mary and St Leonard of South Berwick", *c.* 1284 (*Dryburgh*, xv *n.*), and is evidently identical with the nunnery of St Leonard outside Berwick, mentioned, e.g. 12 April 1296 (*Rot. Scot.*, i. 23). *Scotichronicon* (lib. v, cap. xlviii (i. 301) ) as well as later writers (e.g. Spottiswoode (p. 460)) and lists (except EU. MS. Db. 6.19, which attributes it to a countess of March) describe it as a foundation of David I (†1153). That the nunnery went back to his reign is borne out by a reference, in 1336, to a grant made to it by that king from the ferme of the burgh (*Rot. Scot.*, i. 416). The nuns appear on record, −1177 (*Melros*, no. 142). A number of lists (*Scotich.*, ii. 451; NLS. MSS. 22.1.14, 33.2.12; Bisset, *Rolment of Courtis*, ii. 128, and others) speak of black nuns here and the list given by Gervase of Canterbury (A. O. Anderson, *Scottish Annals*, p. 327) has white (i.e. Cistercian) monks. But in Henry of Silgrave's list (*c.* 1272) (*Scalacronica*, p. 241; Haddan and Stubbs, *Councils*, ii[1]. 181, etc.) and in EU. MS. Db. 6.19, it appears as a house of white (i.e. Cistercian) nuns; and in papal documents of 28 September 1219 and 2 June 1232 (*Dryburgh*, nos. 37, 270) as well as later Vatican records (e.g. 13 May 1420 (*Supplics.*, p. 196) ), the nuns are designated Cistercian. A charter of Edward III, 28 July 1333, making a grant, in commemoration of his victory at Halidon, to "the nuns beside Berwick" (whose house was situated near the scene of the battle), refers to the conventual church and buildings as destroyed and burned and to the nunnery's possessions as largely wasted (*Rot. Scot.*, i. 257); and although he ordered the sheriff of Berwick to undertake repairs, it appears that the nunnery never recovered from the ravages of war. On 9 March 1390/1, Robert III, since the nunnery was destitute of divine service and regular observance and the nuns were only two in number, granted its lands and possessions to Dryburgh abbey (*RMS*, i. no. 832). The Pope made provision of this house, which had long been void, to Agnes Bron, nun of St Bothan's, 22 and 29 January 1420 (*Supplics.*, pp. 152, 159); but, on 13 May following, the abbot and convent of Dryburgh obtained papal confirmation of their possession of it (*Ibid.*, p. 196). On 31 August 1429, the Pope granted a petition of all the prioresses and nuns of the Cistercian order in St Andrews diocese stating that, although the nunnery was founded by King David, the prioress and nuns, on account of wars, were driven of necessity to leave it and that the abbot and convent of Dryburgh had had it united to their house and supplicating accordingly that this annexation should be cancelled, the house restored to its pristine state and Agnes Bron provided to it (Vat. Reg. Supp. pp. 243, 101 (D) ). Dryburgh still held it when, 23 July 1466, the Pope appointed mandatories, on the petition of Alexander Lumsden, clerk of St Andrews diocese, for the administration of the priory, "since all that region in which the nuns' monastery is situated, was returned to the obedience and fealty of James, King of Scots" (*CPR*, xii. 256). There is no evidence that the nunnery, which is said, in 1420, to be so destroyed that scarcely any traces of the buildings remain (*Supplics.*, p. 196) was reinstated. This house has sometimes been confused with Holystone (*v. Trans. SES*, 1940-1, p. 36).

## THE CISTERCIAN NUNS

| Name | County | Minimum Income (1561) | Founder | Fd. | Date D. or Sec. |
|---|---|---|---|---|---|
| COLDSTREAM | Berwick | £503 | Earl Gospatric | –1166 | 1621 |
| § ECCLES | Berwick | £650 | Earl Gospatric or his wife, Derdere | 1156 | 1609 |

COLDSTREAM. Founded by Earl Gospatric, –1166. The so-called foundation charter is given, *Coldstream*, no. 8. From its phrase, "Be it known to you that I have given and granted to God and the sisters of Witehou serving God there", it has been alleged (e.g. by Spottiswoode (p. 461)) that "the nuns of this place were brought from Withow in England". But "Witehou" (? Whitehowe) was probably the place where the nunnery was established (*v. Coldstream*, viii *n.*). A bull of Pope Honorius III confirmed to Coldstream the churches of Lennel and Hirsel and the chapel of Bassendean. (This bull is mentioned in a list of documents sold in Edinburgh, in December 1934 (*v. Scotsman*, 20 December 1934). Its whereabouts are unknown.)[1] The priory is described as a house of black nuns by Gervase of Canterbury (A. O. Anderson, *Scottish Annals*, p. 327) and Henry of Silgrave (*Scalacronica*, p. 241, etc.); Scottish lists unanimously call it Cistercian. This nunnery suffered some spoliation and damage by the English, March 1296 (*CDS*, ii. no. 723); and it is said in a letter of William de Greenfield, archbishop of York, 12 August 1315, that, because of war and the destruction of their property by the Scots, the nuns were dispersed (*Hist. Papers and Letters from Northern Regs.*, p. 197 *n.*). An account of the burning of this house by the English is given, 30 November 1542 (*Hamilton Papers*, i. xciii; *L. & P. H. VIII*, xvii. no. 1157); and it was again burned, during Hertford's invasion, in 1545 (*L. & P. H. VIII*, xx². no. 633). The subprioress and ten nuns take part in the election of a prioress, 13 February 1537/8 (*Coldstream*, pp. 83 ff.). The last prioress had died or demitted office. –12 May 1588 (*RMS*, v. no. 1538). In 1621, this nunnery was erected into a temporal lordship for Sir John Hamilton of Trabroun, son of the earl of Melrose (*APS*, iv. 647–9).

ECCLES. Said to have been founded in 1156, when a convent of nuns came there for the second time (*Chron. Mailros*, p. 75). (Other dates are given: 1145 (mentioned by Hay, Scotia Sacra, p. 213); 1154 (Spottiswoode, p. 461, citing Hoveden); 1155 (*Ibid.*, citing the Book of Coupar).) The foundation is attributed to (1) Earl Gospatric (Spottiswoode, p. 461; Lawrie, *Annals*, pp. 19 *n.*, 109 *n.*); (2) an unnamed countess of March (perhaps, Derdere, wife of Earl Gospatric) (lists in *Scotich.*, ii. 541; EU. MS. Db. 6.19; NLS. MS. 22.1.14); (3) David I (Hay, Scotia Sacra, p. 213). The last is not admissible if 1156 is the correct date. This nunnery suffered in sixteenth-century English invasions. It was threatened with burning by Dacre, in 1523 (*L. & P. H. VIII*, iii². no. 3098). In October 1543, the corn in the abbey [*sic*] was burned (*Ibid.*, xix². no. 33); in September 1544, the church of Eccles (not certainly the nunnery church) was "won by assault" and eighty men slain in the nunnery and town (*Ibid.*, xix². no. 625; xx¹. no. 395). The nunnery was among the places "brent, rased and cast downe" by the English in September 1545 (*Ibid.*, xx². nos. 456, 633). It was erected into a temporal lordship for Sir George Home, 24 June 1609 (*HMC, 12th Rep.*, App., Pt. VIII, p. 131).

---

[1] This document is described (*Scotsman, ut supra*) as: "Papal bull of Honorius III in the 8th year of his pontificate (1235)." This cannot be correct as Honorius was Pope 1216–27. The date may be 1223–4. On the other hand, if 1235 is the true date, it must be a bull of Pope Gregory IX (1227–41).

## THE CISTERCIAN NUNS

| Name | County | Minimum Income (1561) | Founder | Fd. | Date D. or Sec. |
|---|---|---|---|---|---|
| ELCHO | Perth | £193 | David Lindsay of Glenesk | –1241 | 1610 |
| HADDINGTON | East Lothian | £2710 | Ada, countess of Northumberland and Huntingdon | –1159 | 1621 |
| MANUEL | West Lothian | £284 | Malcolm IV | –1164 | 1599+ |

ELCHO. This foundation is attributed to David Lindsay of Glenesk (†1241) (e.g. MS. lists, *Lives of the Lindsays*, i. 26). Spottiswoode (p. 463) associates Lindsay's mother (Lady Marjory) with the foundation. In an undated charter, Lindsay refers to his obligation to pay annually to Dunfermline abbey half a stone of wax "as a quitclaim of that parcel of land in which the monastery of Elcho is situated" (*Dunfermelyn*, no. 191). Again, a charter regarding a controversy between Lindores abbey and this nunnery, 25 January 1281/2, indicates that the latter was in existence thirty-four years previously, i.e. in 1247 (*Lindores*, no. cxxv). In December 1547, this house was burned by the English (*Cal. State Papers rel. to Scotland*, i. 74). A charter of 26 September 1559, attested by the prioress and six nuns, refers not only to the devastation by the English but also to a later attack by Reformers, who drove out the nuns and completely destroyed their house (*Wemyss*, ii. no. 120). On 6 November 1570, the nunnery is described as ruinous and uninhabited (*Ibid.*, i. 138; *RMS*, iv. no. 1939). Its erection into a temporal lordship for Lord Scone, afterwards Viscount Stormont, is mentioned, 1606 (*APS*, iv. 339) and is the subject of a charter, 1610 (*RMS*, vii. no. 248).

HADDINGTON. Founded by Ada, countess of Northumberland and Huntingdon (*Scotich.*, lib. viii, cap. xxv (i. 475) ); *RMS*, ii. no. 611 and lists). The foundation took place –1159 (*v. Trans. East Lothian Antiq. Socy.*, v (1952), 3). Its prioresses swore fealty to Edward I, in 1291 and 1296 (*CDS*, ii. nos. 508, 823). The nunnery was burned by the English in February 1335/6 (*Scotich.*, lib. xiv, cap. xiii (ii. 354) ), and again in May 1544 (*L. & P. H. VIII*, xix[1]. no. 533) and (perhaps) 1545 (*Chron. of John Smyth*, in *Kinlos*, p. 10). This was one of the largest Scottish nunneries. It is said to have twenty-four nuns, 21 April 1461 (*CPR*, xii. 115); and there were eighteen in 1560 (*Trans. East Lothian Antiq. Socy.*, v. 18). This nunnery was erected into a temporal lordship for John Maitland, master of Lauderdale, in parliament, 1621 and by charter, 1622 (*APS*, iv. 645–7; *RMS*, viii. no. 306).

MANUEL. Founded by Malcolm IV –1164 (*Scotich.*, lib. viii, cap. vii (i. 453) ); his endowment was confirmed by his successor, William the Lion, 1165–71 (*SHS Misc.*, iv. 305). On 16 June 1506, the Pope granted the supplication of James IV who, on the ground that the nuns were scarcely five in number, and led a life alien to the Cistercian rule, sought the suppression of the nunnery, the removal of the nuns to another house and the introduction of Augustinian Friars Observantines (GRH. Vat. Trans., iii. no. 32). This did not take place. In 1552 there were still four nuns along with the prioress (Linlithgow Burgh Recs.). There appears to be no extant record of the erection of this nunnery into a temporal lordship. On 13 April 1599, James VI renewed the lease of the lands formerly pertaining to it in favour of Alexander, Lord Livingstone (*RMS*, vi. no. 890), and they probably passed into the latter's possession.

## THE CISTERCIAN NUNS

| Name | County | Minimum Income (1561) | Founder | Fd. | Date D. or Sec. |
|------|--------|------------------------|---------|-----|------------------|
| ¶ NORTH BERWICK | East Lothian | £1880 | Duncan, earl of Fife | c. 1150 | 1587/8 |
| ST BOTHAN'S | Berwick | £380 | Uncertain | 13 c. | 1622 |

NORTH BERWICK. There seems to be no doubt that the founder was Duncan (I), earl of Fife (1136–54). He is mentioned in a charter of Earl Duncan (II), his successor, as having made a donation of land to the nuns (*N. Berwic*, no. 3). A number of writers (*Scotich.*, lib. ix, cap. xxxi (ii. 38) and ii. 541; *Extracta*, p. 91; Major, *Hist. of Greater Britain*, p. 179; Bisset, *Rolment of Courtis*, ii. 128; Spottiswoode, p. 463) attribute the foundation to Malcolm, earl of Fife (1203–30); but although Malcolm, before succeeding to the earldom, granted the nunnery a charter confirming its possessions, *c.* 1199 (*SHS Misc.*, iv. 308–9), he cannot be regarded as founder. A wide disparity appears in the dates given for the foundation, e.g. *c.* 1136 (Lawrie, *Annals*, p. 15); the third quarter of the twelfth century (*Hist. Mon. Comm. Rep. (East Lothian)*, p. 59); 1216 (Spottiswoode, p. 463); 1218 (*Bk. of Pluscarden*, p. 68). Dr William Angus gives reasons for assigning the foundation to *c.* 1150 (*SHS Misc.*, iv. 334.) This house is described as for black nuns by Gervase of Canterbury (A. O. Anderson, *Scottish Annals*, p. 327) and by Henry of Silgrave (*Scalacronica*, p. 241, etc.); while it is designated Benedictine in papal letters of 1375 and 1384 (*CPR*, iv. 212, 249). But it is called Cistercian in Scottish lists and in a papal bull of 22 February 1258/9 (*N. Berwic*, no. 18) as well as in fifteenth-century Vatican records (*Scottish Benefices*, p. 288 (*anno* 1471), p. 176 (*anno* 1473) ). (There is a curious record (undated but probably 1418+) in which the nuns of North Berwick are declared to be not of the Cistercian order because they do not wear the Cistercian habit (*Copiale*, p. 66.) They are, however, called Cistercian in an associated document of 1405 (*Ibid.*, p. 55).) A bull of the antipope Clement VII, 18 February 1383/4 (*N. Berwic*, no. 37) is directed to the "abbess" and convent; but this is manifestly an error; North Berwick, like all Scottish houses of nuns, was a priory. The church was dedicated by David de Bernham, bishop of St Andrews, 10 October 1242 (A. O. Anderson, *Early Sources*, ii. 523). In Clement VII's bull (*supra*), which is erroneously dated 1529 (*N. Berwic*, xvii), this house is said to have suffered frequent devastation by war and to have had its church burned by hostile action (*Ibid.*, no. 37), but the occasion of the statement is not clear (English invasions took place in April and August 1385, but the reference may be retrospective). There were twenty nuns besides the prioress in the nunnery, in 1544 (*Ibid.*, p. 60). In 1587, the buildings were said to be ruinous (*APS*, iii. 437), and, on 20 March 1587/8, James VI granted to Alexander Home of North Berwick "the place in which the church and cloister . . . of the monastery were formerly situated", with the nunnery's properties, erected into a free barony (*RMS*, v. no. 1492). The hospitals of North Berwick and Ardross (*q.v.*) were attached to this house.

ST BOTHAN'S. The identity of the founder and the date of foundation are alike uncertain. According to Spottiswoode (p. 460), this nunnery "is said to be founded by one of the countesses of March, in the reign of William the Lion" (i.e. 1165–1214). The foundation has been variously attributed to (1) Ada, natural daughter of William the Lion, who married Earl Patrick in 1184 and died in 1200 (*Berwickshire Nat. Club*, 1890–1, p. 92; Lawrie, *Annals*, p. 251); (2) Christiana, who married the same earl, –4 December 1214 (EU. MS. Db. 6.19; NLS. MS. 22.1.14; Bisset, *Rolment of Courtis*, ii. 129); (3) Euphemia, wife of Patrick, sixth earl of Dunbar, who became, by her husband's succession, countess in 1232 and died *c.* 1267 (*Scotich.*, ii. 541). St Bothan's is not mentioned in the lists of Gervase of Canterbury, –1212 and Henry of Silgrave, *c.* 1272. The prioress swore fealty to Edward I in 1296 (*CDS*, ii. no. 823). Little is known of the history of this house. It was burned by the English, 11 August 1544 (*Diurnal*, p. 35). The prioress and three nuns are mentioned, 6 March 1557/8 (*HMC Rep. Milne Home MSS.*, p. 273), and the prioress and one nun appear, 16 June 1565 (*Ibid.*, *12th Rep.*, App. viii. 165), when the whole of its lands were leased to Alexander, Lord Home. It was erected into a temporal lordship for David Lindsay, in 1622 (*RMS*, viii. no. 295).

## THE CISTERCIAN NUNS

| Name | County | Minimum Income (1561) | Founder | Fd. | Date D. or Sec. |
|------|--------|------------------------|---------|-----|------------------|
| St Evoca | Kirkcudbright | | | | -1423 |

St Evoca. All that is known of this house comes from three sources: (1) A supplication to the Pope (granted 22 May 1423) by John de Innerkethyng, canon of Holyrood, for the grant of it to him to be held, ruled and governed by him for the space of ten years. The house is described as the priory of St Evoca the Virgin, of the Cistercian order and diocese of Galloway, wont to be ruled and governed by holy nuns or matrons, now deprived of administration and rule on account of the meagreness of its fruits. It is almost in ruins and at present is not occupied by the nuns or by others in their name. Thus it may be regarded as abandoned by them (GRH. Vat. Trans., Pet., p. 90); (2) A papal letter of 10 January 1463/4 appointing mandatories, on a petition by Robert de Colston, rector of Kirkchrist, in the same diocese, containing that his predecessor held as united to the parish church, the church or chapel of Kyrknok or Kyrkenok (*rectius* Kyrkuoc or Kyrkeuok), situate within the bounds of the said parish, in which church or chapel a nun or religious woman used of old to dwell; and that he had continued this possession and now fears interference with it. No nun or religious woman, it is stated, had for thirty years led a regular life there, its buildings were fallen and it had been so long void that there is no certain knowledge of the true way of its voidance. The mandatories, if satisfied, are to ratify this union (*CPR*, xi. 507); (3) In the eighteenth century, Macfarlane incorporates the following note in his *Geographical Collns.* (ii. 132): "In the parish of Kirkchrist, which is now annexed to Twinam [Twynholm] parish, there was a Nunrie, having the lands called Nuntoun and Nunmill thereunto belonging, but now it is scarce known where the Nunrie was." Its supposed site is mentioned in *Hist. Mon. Comm. Rep. (Kirkcudbright)*, p. 273. *V. Trans. Dumfriesshire and Galloway Nat. Hist. and Antiq. Socy.*, xxiii.

### SUPPOSED FOUNDATIONS

*Elbottle.* Described as a cell of South Berwick (Spottiswoode, p. 460; Bisset, *Rolment of Courtis*, ii. 130; EU. MS. Db. 6.19; NLS. MS. 22.1.14). Evidence of a nunnery here is, however, altogether lacking. The barony of Elbottle, in the medieval parish of Gullane (now Dirleton), included the island of Elbottle (now Fidra) in the Firth of Forth. About 1220, William de Vaux gave to the Premonstratensian canons of Dryburgh serving the church of St. Nicholas in that island the patronage of the church of Gullane "and whatever right I have had . . . in that church . . . saving what the nuns of South Berwick are due to have in the parish of that church" (*Dryburgh*, no. 23). This is the only—and very tenuous —connection of the nunnery of South Berwick with Elbottle. *V.* Gullane (*infra*). The nunnery at Elbottle is apocryphal.

*Gullane.* Spottiswoode (p. 461) and Hay (Scotia Sacra, p. 215) allege this to be a foundation of David I and a cell of South Berwick. These statements, although the latter is repeated by the lists cited under Elbottle (*supra*), are not authenticated. The nuns of South Berwick are mentioned as having a "portion" in the parish of Gullane (*Priory of Coldingham*, cxiv) (*v.* under Elbottle), and, as appears from litigation with the canons of Dryburgh and the rector of Gullane, *c.* 1221, they had claimed the parish church, which had been granted to Dryburgh abbey, as well as certain teinds (*Dryburgh*, nos. 27, 35, 36, 37). In the record of these proceedings, there is no indication of a nunnery at Gullane. It is stated that, in 1369, the prior of Coldingham had submitted to his decision a dispute between the nuns of St Bothan's and the nuns of Gullane regarding the lands of Fenton (Carr, *Coldingham*, p. 283); but the source of this assertion cannot be traced. In any case, the existence of a Cistercian nunnery in each of the contiguous parishes of Gullane and North Berwick is inconceivable.

*Inishail.* "On the island of Inishail are the remains of a building said to have been a Cistercian nunnery, the temporalities of which, it is also said, were at the Reformation given to Hay, the abbot of Inchaffray who embraced the reformed doctrines" (*OPS*, ii. 130). This is based on the *New Statistical Account*, which on points of history is often unreliable. There was a parish church of St Findoca of Inishail, which was appropriated to Inchaffray Abbey, in 1257 (*Inchaffray*, no. lxxxv). But the nunnery is fanciful; and no abbot named Hay is mentioned in the charters of Inchaffray.

*Nunraw.* This has been described as "the site of a settlement of Cistercian nuns" (*v. Trans. East Lothian Antiq. Socy.*, v (1952), 12). On 29 February 1547/8, it is called a "place and fortalice", which the prioress of Haddington undertakes to defend against the English (*ALC*, 1501–54, p. 572). There is no evidence that it was the site of a nunnery.

*Trefontains.* Spottiswoode (p. 460) and others refer to this as a cell of South Berwick. The former mentions David I as founder, while EU. MS. Db. 6.19 and NLS. MS. 22.1.14 attribute its foundation to the countess of March (unspecified). It is impossible to believe that such a house existed about a mile distant from the nunnery of St Bothan's. In the thirteenth century there is a reference to "Trefontaynes, cell of the same" (*Priory of Coldingham*, cxiv), without indication of the house of which it was a dependency. On the other hand, it is designated "the church or hospital of Trefontainys" in a note which states that it was granted to Dryburgh abbey in 1436–7 (NLS. MS. 34.3.12). The lands of Trefontains were, 11 January 1451/2, bestowed upon the collegiate church of Dunglass (*HMC. 12th Rep.*, App., Pt. VIII, p. 127). Then or later, the parish church of Trefontains became a vicarage; it is described in 1627 as "a pendicle of the colledge kirk ) Dunglas" (*Rep. on the State of Certain Parishes*, p. 23).

## THE AUGUSTINIAN NUNS

| Name | County | Minimum Income (1561) | Founder | Fd. | Date D. or Sec. |
|---|---|---|---|---|---|
| ¶ IONA | Argyll | | Reginald, son of Somerled | –1208 | 1574+ |
| PERTH, ST LEONARD | Perth | | | 13c. | c. 1434 annexed to Perth Charterhouse |

IONA. Said to have been founded by Reginald, son of Somerled (†1207 or 1208), whose sister, Bethoc, was the first prioress (Skene, "Notes on the Hist. of the Ruins of Iona", *PSAS*, x (1875), 210; *Highland Papers*, i. 82). Skene notes the statement of the Book of Clanranald that the foundation was for black, i.e. Benedictine nuns. Scottish sources (e.g. *Scotich.*, lib. ii, cap. x (i. 45) and appended list (11. 541); *Bk. of Pluscarden*, p. 406; *Extracta*, p. 9; Bisset, *Rolment of Courtis*, ii. 128; EU. MS. Db. 6.19) as well as Vatican records (e.g. a supplication granted, 26 January 1421/2 (*Highland Papers*, iv. 175–6)) describe them, however, as Augustinian. The suggestion made by Skene that "the nuns may originally have been black or Benedictine nuns . . . but . . . Augustinian nuns may have been substituted" (*art. cit.*, p. 210) seems superfluous. In 1574, the nunnery's lands were granted by the prioress and convent in heritage to Hector McLean of Duart (*OPS*, ii[1]. 296).

PERTH, ST LEONARD. Spottiswoode (p. 464) includes this house among the Cistercian nunneries and is followed by Fittis (*Eccles. Annals of Perth*, p. 277). But in the list of Scottish houses appended to the *Chronicon* of Henry of Silgrave, *c.* 1272 (BM. Cott. MS. Cleop. A, xii. 56, given *Scalacronica*, p. 241; Haddan and Stubbs, *Councils*, ii[1]. 182; cf. A. O. Anderson, *Early Sources*, ii. 699), a "priory of Perth" for "black nuns" appears. (In a similar list given by Gervase of Canterbury –1212 (A. O. Anderson, *Scottish Annals from English Chroniclers*, p. 327), this priory is entered with the manifestly erroneous note, "black monks".) It is uncertain whether this is intended to refer to St Leonard's. But that house is specifically mentioned as Augustinian in a papal letter, 5 February 1292/3 (*CPR. Letters*, i. 548). The prioress swore fealty to Edward I in 1296 (*CDS*, ii. no. 823). About 1434, the nunnery and its hospital (*q.v.*) were annexed to the Charterhouse of Perth (Fittis, *op. cit.*, pp. 219, 278).

## THE DOMINICAN NUNS

| Name | County | Minimum Income (1561) | Founder | Date Fd. | Sec. |
|------|--------|------------------------|---------|----------|------|
| EDINBURGH, SCIENNES | Midlothian | £245 | Dominus John Crawford and others | 1517 | 1569 |

EDINBURGH, SCIENNES. Spottiswoode (p. 458) states erroneously that "this house was founded by the Lady Roslin, countess of Caithness". Brockie, who declares that documentary evidence of the founder's name and the year of erection is wanting (p. 1259) gives a charter of Lady Egidia Douglas, wife of Henry [Sinclair], earl of Orkney and lord of Roslin, purporting to grant a donation to the Dominican nuns "near Edinburgh", 18 October 1404. This charter cannot be accepted as genuine; it has no witnesses; and Egidia Douglas did not marry Henry Sinclair till *c.* 1407 (*SP*, vi. 570). Other charters to this house transcribed by Brockie are spurious, e.g. an alleged charter of Robert Logan of Restalrig making a grant to the nuns, 28 September 1438 (Brockie, p. 1261) is said to have been sealed by George, dean of the collegiate church of Restalrig; but this collegiate church was not erected till 1487 and there was no dean of this name till 1575. A bull of 29 January 1517/8 describes the initiators of the petition to the Pope and founders of the house as the ladies of Seton, Glenbervie and Bass (*Lib. S. Kath. Senen.*, no. 11); but while, as has been pointed out (*Ibid.*, xix), their influence was used to obtain papal authority for the endowment of the house, the foundation was mainly due to "Sir" [dominus] John Crawford, who granted St John's kirk of the Boroughmuir of Edinburgh (which he had founded), with its churchyard, houses and lands, to the sisters "of the order of St Katherine of Siena", 5 January 1516/7 (*EBR, 1403-1528*, pp. 164–5), while Lady Seton contributed to the expense of the building (*Lib. S. Kath. Senen.*, xxi). Further endowment was provided by John Cant, burgess of Edinburgh and Agnes Kerkettil, his wife, according to the charter of foundation, 17 April 1517 (*Ibid.*, no. iii); and Crawford's additional grant of land, of which sasine is given to Josina Henrisoun and the other sisters "of the order of St Dominic, called St Katherine of Senis", 5 December 1517, is witnessed, among others, by the provincial of the Friars Preachers (*Prot. Bk. of John Foular*, ii. no. 60). The erection was for "a monastery of nuns, of the order of St Augustine, under the care of the Friars Preachers, for thirty nuns" (*Lib. S. Kath. Senen.*, no. ii; cf. *Prot. Bk. of John Foular*, iii. no. 655). The annexation of the hospital of St Laurence, Haddington, to this house is recorded, 29 August 1532 (*Lib. S. Kath. Senen.*, no. iv) and, on 26 November of that year, a letter of James V seeks from the Pope ratification of this union (*Letters of James V*, pp. 232–3; from Tyninghame Letter Bk.); it was confirmed by the legate in Scotland, 5 March 1544/5 (*Lib. S. Kath. Senen.*, no. vi). The prioress, sub-prioress and ten nuns subscribe a charter, 18 February 1555/6 (*HMC 14th Rep.*, App., Pt. III, p. 43). On 5 July 1567, the prioress and convent grant a lease of their lands of the Sciennes "in their great need immediately after the destruction of their place . . . and their expulsion from it" (*RMS*, iv. no. 1980). The Town Council, finding that the nunnery had been omitted from the grant to them of the properties of religious houses, took steps to rectify this omission, 1 April 1569 (*EBR, 1557-71*, p. 260). A house at Sciennes is erroneously given as Franciscan (Spottiswoode, *Hist. of the Ch. of Scotland* (1677 ed.), App., 17; Hay, Scotia Sacra, p. 218; Brockie, p. 1524); *v.* under Franciscan Nuns.

### SUPPOSED FOUNDATION (INCOMPLETE)

*Glasgow.* "A Dominican nunnery, dedicated to St Catherine of Siena, was proposed to be erected near the chapel of St Thenew about 1510. Three hundred pounds were bequeathed by Roland Blacadyr, subdean of Glasgow, but no steps were ever taken to carry this bequest into execution" (*OPS*, i. 7). The source of this statement is not given and has not been traced.

## THE FRANCISCAN NUNS

| Name | County | Minimum Income (1561) | Founder | Date Fd. | Sec. |
|------|--------|------------------------|---------|----------|------|
| ABERDOUR | Fife | | James, earl of Morton | 1486 | 1560 |
| DUNDEE | Angus | £2 (?) | James Fotheringham | 1501/2 | 1560 |

ABERDOUR. The hospital (*q.v.*) founded by James, earl of Morton, was placed under the charge of four sisters of the Third Order, 16 October 1486 (*Reg. Hon. de Morton*, ii. 240–2). In the following year (23 June 1487), a bull of Pope Innocent VIII, while confirming the erection of the nunnery, ordained the extinction of the hospital (Theiner, *Vet. Mon.*, no. dccclxxxiv). The nuns continued to be designated the sisters of St Martha (*MB*, i. 395, 397–8). Brockie (p. 1517) has a charter of Joanetta de Crichton, countess of Morton, making donations to the nunnery and purporting to be subscribed[1] by the prioress and six sisters, 4 October 1492; but the *personnel* of the house does not seem to have exceeded a mother and three sisters (cf. *Ibid.*, i. 392, 395). These, on 18 August 1560, leased to the then earl of Morton their house and land (*Ibid.*, ii. 270). The last of the sisters having a liferent of the "sisteris land" of Aberdour is mentioned in 1584 (*Ibid.*, ii. 271). The sisters are erroneously described as of "Aberdene" (Spottiswoode, *Hist. of Ch. of Scotland* (1677 ed.), App., 17).

DUNDEE. Brockie (p. 1520) transcribes a charter of James Graham of Fintry and Claverhouse granting a house in Dundee for a prioress and twelve sisters of the Third Order of St Francis, 28 October 1494. This charter is spurious; for James Graham, at this date, had not attained full age and the contemporary bishop of Brechin was not John (who appears here as a witness) but William Meldrum (1488–*c*. 1515–16) (Dowden, *Bishops*, pp. 188–9). This house was established by James Fotheringham, who granted to two sisters St James's chapel which he had founded, 8 March 1501/2 (*MB*, i. 395–6; ii. 273–4). In August 1560, the house was sold and its land leased by the magistrates (*Ibid.*, i. 397; Maxwell, *Old Dundee*, pp. 69, 183).

### SUPPOSED FOUNDATIONS

*Sciennes*. Brockie (p. 1524) gives a charter (apparently from Tweedie) of Margaret Knox, daughter of Uchtred Knox of Ranfurly and widow of Cuthbert Purves, burgess of Edinburgh, granting her lands of Sciennes, for the erection of a hospital for twelve poor and ailing women, to six sisters from the convent of Aberdour (who, later in the charter, appear along with a prioress), 28 March 1496. This charter, as well as others purporting to deal with this house (Brockie, pp. 1525, 1526, 1527) is spurious (two of these refer to the *abbess* of Sciennes; and one (p. 1526) mentions a preposterous grant to the house of £1000 Scots). The Appendix to Spottiswoode, *Hist. of Ch. of Scotland* (1677 ed.) (p. 17), and Hay (Scotia Sacra, p. 218) also give this as a Franciscan foundation. The only house at Sciennes, however, was one of Dominican nuns (*q.v.*).

*Southannan*. Brockie (p. 1531), quoting from Tweedie, gives a charter of William, Lord Semple, founding at Southannan a house where the poor and sick will be cared for, for twelve sisters from Sciennes (*supra*). ("This house or convent I have constructed and built after the venerable abbess of Sciennes had constituted and decreed twelve sisters of the same foundation (*instituti*) to occupy the same with the venerable Margaret Semple, my daughter, lawfully constituted their prioress . . .".) The date is given as "in festo Sancti *Mungo* Episcopi et Patroni Glasguensis diocesis", 1546; but a medieval charter would undoubtedly have "Sancti *Kentigerni*". This charter is not authentic. Again, the statement (Brockie, p. 1533) that this house was reduced to ashes at the Reformation is absurd. The only ecclesiastical buildings on record at Southannan are a chapel of St Anandi [*sic*] with a chantry in its graveyard, mentioned, 5 June 1509 (*RMS*, ii. no. 3354).

---

[1] That a charter of donation to the nunnery should bear the seal of the convent and the signatures of the prioress and six "senior sisters" suggests that it is not an authentic record. One of the witnesses is James, abbot of Inchcolm, but no such abbot is known in this period.

## SUPPOSED NUNNERIES

### (ORDER UNSPECIFIED)

*Aberdeen.* A convent and church, dedicated to St Catherine, and built by "the Constable of Aberdeen", are said to have stood on St Catherine's Hill here (Hay, Scotia Sacra, p. 218; *Collns. Aberd. and Banff*, p. 205). There is no record evidence of such a foundation.

*Crail. Hist. Mon. Comm. Rep. (Fife, etc.)* (p. 66) notes a site as "nunnery (remains of)". This nunnery is apocryphal. Its supposed existence is due to a misinterpretation of the fact that the nunnery of Haddington held the parish church and certain properties at Crail.

*Edinburgh, St Mary of Placentia.* Dr C. A. Malcolm shows that this alleged nunnery is "completely spurious", an invention of Maitland (*v. History of Edinburgh*, p. 176) to account for the name "Pleasance" (*Hist. Mon. Comm. Rep. (Edinburgh)*, p. 216).

*Inchcailleoch.* The tradition that this island in Loch Lomond was the site of a nunnery "seems to rest on no better foundation than the name, which is said to mean 'the island of old women'" (*OPS*, i. 32). Even the *Scotichronicon*, which has a certain partiality for supposititious foundations on Scottish islands, has the entry: "Inchecalzoch, where [there is] a parish church" (ubi ecclesia parochialis) (lib. ii, cap. x (i. 46)). References to the parish church (a rectory) are found in records (e.g. *REG*, i. lxvii, lxxv; *RMS*, i. App. 2, no. 1144 (10) ). The careful account in *The Lennox* (i. 49–63), which gives details of this parish and its church, does not so much as mention a nunnery.

*Molista.* The suggestion that this was the site of a nunnery (*OPS*, iii. 286) is based on the fanciful explanation of a place-name which is said to mean "the town (or house) of the black old women".

*Murkle.* The supposed nunnery here, at a place locally known as Glosters (*OPS*, ii². 748), cannot be authenticated from Scottish records.

*Nunnery.* This place-name occurs in the parish of Crawford, Lanarkshire (*v. OPS*, i. 166). No explanation of its origin can be given, but it is safe to say that it does not mark the site of a religious house (cf. the place-name Abbey (p. 194)).

*Nuntoun.* At this place in the island of Benbecula, *OPS* (ii¹. 370) reports the former existence of a building "locally believed to have been a nunnery". The sole testimony for this is the statement of the *New Statistical Account*. It need not be taken seriously.

*Papple.* Remains near Papple farm-house in the parish of Whittinghame, East Lothian, have been described as a "convent" (*V. Hist. Mon. Comm. Rep. (East Lothian)*, p. 132). Both the Cistercian nuns of Haddington (*RMS*, ii. no. 610) and the nuns of St Bothan's of the same order (*East Lothian Deeds*, p. 9) held lands in "Popil", but the existence of a "convent" is an unwarranted inference from these facts.

It may be noted that, according to the Wardlaw MS., Hugh, earl of Ross, intended to build a nunnery at Dingwall, "if the towne had not hindered it" (*Chrons. of Frasers*, p. 81). There is no other evidence of a projected foundation at Dingwall. Again, in the context of the narrative, *Hugh*, earl of Ross (who held the earldom 1322/3–33) is almost certainly an error.

## THE KNIGHTS TEMPLARS

The lack of records makes the history of the Templars in Scotland difficult to trace. David I is said to have introduced the order into Scotland. The date is given variously (and without record authority) from *c.* 1128 (Edwards, "Knights Templars in Scotland", *Trans. SES,* iv[1] (1913), 37) to 1153 (*Abstracts of Chs. in Chartulary of Torphichen,* p. 6). But there is no evidence of their presence in Scotland during this reign except a vague reference which may point to their holding land in St Andrews, 1126/7–1158/9 (*RPSA,* p. 124). The number of Templar houses in Scotland is generally much exaggerated, e.g. by Spottiswoode (p. 435), whose account of them is inaccurate and misleading. While the Knights held lands and other property in many parts of Scotland, it is clear that they had only two houses. This is attested by the record of the proceedings against them in Scotland (in 1309), according to which one of the Templars states in examination that he has lived "in various houses" of the order in England since his reception into it, also at "Culthur" and at "Blancrodoks" in Scotland (*Spottiswoode Socy. Misc.,* ii. 11), i.e. at Maryculter and Balantrodoch, the only Scottish houses. The Templars' revenues in Scotland are said to have amounted to three hundred marks (*Kts. Hospitallers in England,* p. 201).

| Name | County | Founder | Date Fd. | Supp. |
|---|---|---|---|---|
| ⁋ BALANTRODOCH (TEMPLE) | Midlothian | Probably David I | –1175–99 (–1153(?)) | *c.* 1309 |
| MARYCULTER | Kincardine | Walter Byset | 1121–36 | *c.* 1309 |

BALANTRODOCH (TEMPLE). Spottiswoode (p. 435) gives "the Temple" and Balantrodoch as separate houses, attributing the foundation of the former to David I. He was apparently unaware that the later medieval and modern Temple is identical with Balantrodoch. This was the principal seat of the Templars in Scotland. There is no record of its foundation, though it is commonly assumed that this was due to David I. The earliest reference is probably in 1175–99, when Brother Raañ (? Ranulphus) Corbet, "master in the land of the king of Scots of the House of the Temple", grants a charter with the consent of "our brethren of Plentidoc [*sic*]" (*REG,* i. no. 41). "Plentidoc" is almost certainly a garbled form of the name "Balantrodoch". This charter—of a toft in Glasgow granted to the Templars by Bishop Jocelin—is witnessed by a brother-almoner, a brother-preceptor and two other brethren. An explicit reference to the master and brethren of the Temple of Balintrodoch is found in 1237 (*Neubotle,* p. 160). After the suppression of the Templars, "Tempill of Balantrodoch with the kirk" became one of the baronies held by the Hospitallers (*Abstract of Chs. in Chartulary of Torphichen,* p. 8), while, at an unascertained date, the (former) Templars' church became parochial—a vicar of Temple is mentioned, 19 September 1524 (*RMS,* iii. no. 275). That church was in use till the nineteenth century and still exists in ruins.

MARYCULTER. This place in Kincardineshire is frequently confused with Culter in Lanarkshire. The house was founded by Walter Byset, 1221–36 (*Calchou,* no. 233). A controversy with the abbey of Kelso (which held the parish church of Culter) regarding the newly built chapel of the Knights, was settled, 4 November 1287 (*Ibid.,* no. 223; *REA,* ii. 288 ff.). Maryculter also became one of the baronies of the Knights of St John.

### THE KNIGHTS TEMPLARS

#### SUPPOSED FOUNDATIONS

There are numerous references to alleged houses of Templars in Scotland. These are exaggerated accounts of what were merely Temple lands such as are found in many parts of the country (*v.* lists in *Abstract of Chs. in Chartulary of Torphichen*, pp. 7–55) or, in some cases, of appropriated churches. Those which are patently absurd have been ignored.

*Aberdeen.* Under the heading "Templars or Red Fryers [*sic*]" appears the statement: "Their convent and church stood in the northwest corner of the Castlegait" (*Collns. Aberd. and Banff*, p. 203). The "convent and church" are imaginary. The Templars merely had property here.

*Aboyne.* Described by Spottiswoode (p. 435) as a "considerable estate and house belonging to this order". This is an exaggeration. The grant of the church of Aboyne to the Templars at Culter by Walter Byset was confirmed by Ralph, bishop of Aberdeen, 1239–42 (*REA*, ii. 271) and by Alexander II, 15 April 1242 (*Ibid.*, ii. 272). It is mentioned otherwise as a church held by the Templars (*Templaria*, pp. 5, 7; *Abstracts of Chs. in Chartulary of Torphichen*, p. 9).

*Culter.* Morton (*Monastic Annals*, p. 144) and others have confused Maryculter (sometimes called simply Culter) in Kincardineshire, where there was one of the two Templar houses, with Culter in Lanarkshire, which had no such connection with the Templars.

*Forvie.* This church is described as "formerly the Knights Templars now King's College" (*Collns. Aberd. and Banff*, p. 217). There was certainly no Templar house here and the church is not otherwise mentioned as held by the Templars.

*Inchinnan.* This was a parish church held by the Templars and afterwards by the Hospitallers (*Templaria*, pp. 5, 7; *Abstracts of Chs. in Chartulary of Torphichen*, p. 9; *CPR*, viii. 504).

*Ladykirk (Ayrshire).* The mention of the "preceptory" of Our Lady Kirk of Kyle, 28 September 1505 (*RSS*, i. no. 1128) has given rise to the idea that it was a Knights Templars' church. This was in fact a secular chapel, founded *c.* 1446 by John Blair (*CPR*, ix. 548). Offerings made at it and payments to its priests by James IV are recorded frequently from 1488 onwards in the *LHT. Accts.*, i–iv. The term "preceptory" was by no means applied merely to the houses of the Templars and Hospitallers. It is a common synonym for the mastership of a hospital and is also used in connection with a monastic cell (*v.* Gadvan under Cistercian Dependencies). Here it apparently refers to the office of the head of a quasi-collegiate group of priests serving this chapel. It may be noted that the description of Ladykirk as an "old monastrie now ruinous" (*Macfarlane's Geog. Collns.*, i. 409) is entirely misleading.

*Oggerstone.* Given by Spottiswoode (p. 435) as a "fort and barony" belonging to the Knights. But this refers to Ogerston in England (*VCH*. Hunts., iii. 229).

*St Germains.* Spottiswoode (p. 435) speaks of it as belonging to this order. It was, however, a Bethlehemite hospital. *V.* under Hospitals.

*Tullich.* Spottiswoode (p. 435) calls it a residence of the Knights. It was in fact a parish church held by the Templars and latterly by the Hospitallers (*Templaria*, pp. 5, 7; *Abstracts of Chs. in Chartulary of Torphichen*, p. 9).

## KNIGHTS HOSPITALLERS

In regard to the Hospitallers' records it has been stated: "[The archives] of the Scottish commanderies seem absolutely lost and no trace of them exists" (*Cartulaire général des Hospiteliers de S. Jean de Jérusalem*, i (1890), clx). But there are more incidental references to the Hospitallers than to the Templars and sixteenth-century rentals supply considerable particulars of their lands and possessions in Scotland, including those which came to them on the suppression of the Templars. In 1338, the normal revenues of the order in Scotland are given as two hundred marks (*Kts. Hospitallers in England*, p. 129).

| Name | County | Founder | Date Fd. | Sec. |
|------|--------|---------|---------|------|
| *‡ Torphichen | West Lothian | David I (?) | –1153(?) | 1563/4 |

Torphichen. This was the only house of Hospitallers in Scotland (*v.* list in *Scotich.*, ii. 540). It is said by Spottiswoode (p. 438) to have been founded by David I. The Hospitallers are recorded as having received from Malcolm IV a full toft in every burgh of his realm, *c.* 1153 (*RMS*, ii. no. 1791); and their possessions were confirmed by Alexander II on 30 June 1231 and 12 June 1236, and by Alexander III, on 17 January 1283/4 (*Ibid.*). In 1338 their lands and possessions (like those of the Templars) are described as destroyed and burned during the long-continued war (*Kts. Hosp. in England*, p. 129). The Pope, on 10 February 1355/6, issued letters conservatory of the Hospitallers in Scotland (GRH. Vat. Trans., i. 35). They are said to have held in the sixteenth century the baronies of Torphichen, Thankerton, Denny, Kirkliston, Balantrodoch [Temple] and Maryculter, with a large number of smaller lands and five parish churches (Aboyne, Inchinnan, Kinbethock [Towie], Maryculter and Tullich) (*Abstract of Chs. in Chart. of Torphichen*, pp. 8–55). On 25 January 1563/4, Queen Mary granted to John, Lord St. John, the lands and baronies belonging to Torphichen, these having been incorporated in one barony (*RMS*, iv. no. 1499).

### SUPPOSED FOUNDATIONS

*Ancrum.* The Knights of St John are said to have had a preceptory or hospital here (Mackinlay, *Place Names*, p. 368). This is mere conjecture. Ancrum Spittal (*q.v.*) was a secular foundation.

*Edinburgh.* The "Preceptory" mentioned *Hist. Mon. Comm. Rep.* (*Edinburgh*) (1951), 126, no. 75, is an exaggerated description of property held by the order.

## HOSPITALS

The compilation of a list of medieval Scottish hospitals involves considerable difficulties; and although the list which follows includes a few items not previously noted, nothing like finality can be claimed for it. "Border-line" cases are inevitable and some items which have been listed are barely admissible, while certain others relegated to the "uncertain" category are placed there with hesitation. In framing such a list, it is necessary to be wary of the suggestion that where the name "Spittal" survives, a medieval hospital must have existed. Not infrequently it can be verified that "Spittal" indicates a medieval site; but the name may also indicate a site which is post-Reformation. In certain cases, it has apparently become attached to hospital lands at a distance from the establishment to which they belonged. In a number of instances, its occurrence admits of no explanation. It may be noted that "Maison Dieu" appears likewise as a name attached to land or property in places where no hospital of such a designation is recorded.

Dedications. The following abbreviations have been used:

| | | |
|---|---|---|
| St John B. | = | St John the Baptist |
| St John E. | = | St John the Evangelist |
| St Mary M. | = | St Mary Magdalene |
| St Mary V. | = | St Mary the Virgin |

Types. The following abbreviations are used:

| | | |
|---|---|---|
| L = for Lepers. | A = | Almshouse, in most cases for resident poor people. |
| P = for the Poor. | | |
| S = for the Sick. | Am = | As last, for bedesmen. |
| T = for Travellers and Pilgrims. | Aw = | As last, for bedeswomen. |

A hospital was sometimes of dual or mixed type, e.g. for the Poor and the Sick (indicated thus: PS).

A hospital sometimes changed its type, e.g. from Lepers to the Poor (indicated thus: L–P).

RULES. Some hospitals were in charge of religious orders or of brethren (in one case, sisters) under a rule. Thus the Trinitarians originally held several hospitals, others were in some sense Augustinian, one was Bethlehemite (i.e. in the hands of the order of *Cruciferi cum Stella*, not the fifteenth-century order of St Mary of Bethlehem), and another of the order of St Anthony of Vienne. These orders are shown thus: (Trinitarians) . . . (Vienne).

Some hospitals attached to monasteries were clearly secular, e.g. St Leonard's, attached to Holyrood abbey.

The contraction "Contd." signifies that the hospital remained in existence after the Reformation.

| Name | County | Dedication or Designation | Founder | Fd. | Date Termd. or Sec. | Type | Dependent on or Rule |
|------|--------|---------------------------|---------|-----|---------------------|------|----------------------|
| ABERDEEN | Aberdeen | St Anne (Leper house) | | −1363 | 1573 | L | |
| ,, | ,, | St Mary | Gavin Dunbar, bishop of Aberdeen | 1531/2 | Contd. | Am | |
| ,, | ,, | St Peter | Matthew, bishop of Aberdeen | −1179 | 1427 | S | |
| ,, | ,, | St Thomas the Martyr | Master John Clat | 1459 | Contd. | PS | |
| ADNISTON (AULDENESTUN) *v.* LEGERWOOD | | | | | | | |
| ALDCAMBUS | Berwick | | Probably David de Quickswood | −1214 | ? | L | |

ABERDEEN, LEPER HOUSE. Mentioned as "the houses of the lepers", 1 July 1363 (*REA*, ii. 263). A chapel, dedicated to St Anne, is said to have been added to it in 1519 (*Abredoniae Utriusque Descriptio*, p. 19). On 18 August 1574, the magistrates and council were ordered by the Regent to collect a rent of land belonging to the lepers "betuix New and Auld Aberdeen" and with the proceeds to have the leper house thatched and repaired; provision is also made for the maintenance of the house and the support of the lepers (*PCR*, 1st Ser., i. 391). The house was in ruins in 1661 and in 1718 its lands were sold to King's College (McPherson, *The Kirk's Care of the Poor*, p. 169).

ABERDEEN, ST MARY. Founded by Gavin Dunbar, bishop of Aberdeen, outside (to the west of) the cathedral burial ground, 23 February 1531/2; for twelve old men (*REA*, i. 401–6; *RMS*, iii. no. 1145). Payments to this hospital are recorded till at least 1600 (*ER*, later vols. to xxiii. 352); and it continued to exist till the eighteenth century (*Abredoniae Utriusque Descriptio*, p. 22; *Collns. Aberd. and Banff*, p. 156).

ABERDEEN, ST PETER. Founded by Matthew, bishop of Aberdeen (1172–79); for "infirm brethren" (*REA*, i. 11). In 1266, there is also a reference to "the sisters living therein" (*Ibid.*, ii. 39). The revenues were diverted in 1427 to the endowment of two chaplainries in the cathedral (*Ibid.*, ii. 226, 228). It is stated in a supplication of 18 January 1436 that Henry, bishop of Aberdeen, founded these chaplainries considering that for forty years and more the hospital had been assigned to secular clerks (Vat. Reg. Supp., 318, 95 (D) ).

ABERDEEN, ST THOMAS THE MARTYR. Founded by master John Clat for reception of the poor and the infirm, with a master, 26 May 1459 (*Cart. S. Nich.*, i. no. lxxiv). Payments to the bedesmen are recorded till at least 1596–7 (*Spalding Club Misc.*, v. 120); and it was apparently still in use after 1660 (*Abredoniae Utriusque Descriptio*, p. 16).

ADNISTON (AULDENESTUN). *V.* LEGERWOOD.

ALDCAMBUS. David de Quickswood's donation to this hospital and the lepers dwelling there was confirmed by William the Lion (1165–1214) (*N. Durham*, App., no. clxxxvi). It is also mentioned in a thirteenth-century inventory (*Priory of Coldingham*, lxxxix).

## HOSPITALS

| Name | County | Dedication or Designation | Founder | Fd. | Date Termd. or Sec. | Type | Dependent on or Rule |
|------|--------|--------------------------|---------|-----|---------------------|------|----------------------|
| ANCRUM | Roxburgh | | | ? | 1545 | ? | |
| ANNAN | Dumfries | | | −1258 | ? | ? | |
| ARBROATH | Angus | St John B. | | −1352 | ? | A | Arbroath abbey |
| ARDROSS | Fife | | Duncan, 4th earl of Fife | −1154 | ? | PT | North Berwick nunnery |
| AYR | Ayr | St Leonard | | −1420 | ? | ? | |
| BALGOWNIE | Angus | St Mary(?) | | −1418 | Contd. | ? | |

ANCRUM. *Macfarlane's Geog. Collns.* (ii. 158) refers to a hospital beside "Ancram". The only evidence of a hospital here comes from a list of places "brent, rased and cast downe" during Hertford's invasion in 1545: one of the three "spitelles and hosbitalles" destroyed is given as "Angeram Spittel", burned on 14 September (*L. & P. H. VIII*, xx². nos. 456, 533). References to the Mains (*terrae dominicales*) of Spittal, "called Ancrum-Spittal", are found from 6 July 1566 to 31 May 1670 (e.g. *RMS*, iv. no. 1737; *HMC 12th Rep.*, App., Pt. VIII, 151; *Roxburgh Retours*, nos. 126, 253). (The statement that "there appears to have existed [here] an establishment of the Knights Templars the remembrance of which is preserved in the name 'Ancrum-Spittell'." (*OPS*, i. 304) is entirely unwarranted.)

ANNAN. The hospital of Annan appears in a charter of donation to St Bees priory, *c.* 1258 (*Reg. St Bees*, p. 254). (For this reference I am indebted to Mr R. C. Reid.) There is also a mention, 15 February 1609, of hospital lands in Annan parish "which formerly belonged to the preceptory of Trailtrow and the hospital within the parish of Annan" (*RMS*, vii. no. 21). The history of this hospital is otherwise obscure.

ARBROATH, ST JOHN BAPTIST. First mentioned in 1352 (*Aberbrothoc*, i. no. 352). This was the monastery's almshouse (*Ibid.*, ii. no. 160). It had a chapel dedicated in 1485 (*Ibid.*, ii. no. 267).

ARDROSS. At Earlsferry, the north end of the ferry on the Firth of Forth (*v,* North Berwick, *infra*). Founded by Duncan, fourth earl of Fife, −1154, for poor people and travellers; and granted by Duncan, fifth earl, to the nuns of North Berwick, −1177 (*N. Berwic*, no. 3). *V. SHS Misc.*, iv. 334-5.

AYR, ST LEONARD. A charter of James II refers to the union of this hospital with the lands of Collinhatrig in Dumfriesshire, as made by Robert, duke of Albany (†1420) and William, bishop of Glasgow (1408–25) (*REG*, ii. no. 347). The hospital or chapel of St Leonard near the burgh of Ayr is associated with an indulgence, *c.* 11 July 1425 (Vat. Reg. Supp., 189, 24 (D)). This is evidently the same as the hospital of St Leonard of Doonslee beside the burgh of Ayr, which appears, 25 May 1506 (*RSS*, i. no. 1266).

BALGOWNIE (EASSIE). The hospital or chapel of Balgony, in St Andrews diocese, is mentioned, 20 August 1418 (*Supplics.*, p. 16). This is almost certainly the hospital of Balgownie, in the parish of Eassie, Angus, which appears frequently at a later date (Eassie was in the diocese of St Andrews). There is a reference to a chapel of the Blessed Virgin Mary, Balgownie, in the parish of Eassie, 5 August 1450 (*Reg. Panmure*, ii. 236). From 4 October 1499 (*RSS*, i. no. 418), numerous presentations to the mastership of this hospital are recorded. That office was apparently held by a succession of members of the family of Lyon; and there are references to it (as the preceptorship) till 1695 (*Forfar Retours*, no. 536). This hospital was clearly at Balgownie in Angus and not at Balgonie in Fife. It is specifically described as in the sheriffdom of Forfar, 17 May 1529 (*RSS*, ii. no. 97).

## HOSPITALS

| Name | County | Dedication or Designation | Founder | Fd. | Date Termd. or Sec. | Type | Dependent on or Rule |
|---|---|---|---|---|---|---|---|
| BALLENCRIEFF | E. Lothian | St Cuthbert | | −1291 | −1481 | ? | |
| BARA | ,, | | | mentioned *c.* 1340 | | ? | |
| BERWICK | | Maison Dieu | | −1287 | 14 c. | P | |
| ,, | | St Edward | | −1234 | ? | PS | Trinitarians |
| ,, | | St Leonard | | −1297 | ? | ? | |

BALLENCRIEFF (RED SPITTAL). The master or warden of this hospital swore fealty to Edward I in 1291 and 1296 (*CDS*, ii. nos. 508, 823). It was, however, of considerably earlier date; there is a somewhat indefinite reference in 1296 to its foundation by the ancestors of Robert de Pinkeny (*Ibid.*, ii. no. 857). The patronage of this hospital, commonly called the Red Spittal, is mentioned 20 April 1421 (*Douglas Bk.*, iii. nò. 60) and 6 March 1422/3 (GRH. Chs. no. 258). But it was apparently defunct and part of its lands granted to the collegiate church of Dunglass by 13 June 1481, since on that date "Redspetall" was one of the prebends constituted in that church (Ibid., no. 496; cf. *Thirds of Benefices*, p. 28; *APS*, iv. 663, etc.). The lands of "Eister and Wester Spittell alias Reid-Spittell" mentioned 15 March 1553/4 (*RSS*, iv. no. 2569) and later (e.g. *Earls of Haddington*, i. 25; *Haddington Retours*, no. 12) were evidently former properties of the hospital.

BARA. A hospital (*domus hospitalitatis*) is mentioned, *c.* 1340 (*Yester Writs*, no. 24).

BERWICK, MAISON DIEU. Miss R. M. Clay gives Philip de Rydale as the founder in 1286 (*Med. Hosps. of England*, p. 311). His generous benefactions to the master, chaplains and poor of this hospital are confirmed by Edward I, 24 November 1300 (*CDS*, ii. no. 1176), but he is not named as founder. This hospital is mentioned in 1287 and 1291, when the master was engaged in a suit concerning its lands of Bowsden (*Docs. Illust. of Hist. of Scotland*, i. nos. xviii, cxii). It appears, in 1328, as having its Scottish possessions restored (*CDS*, iii. no. 962). At the end of 1333 a petition of the master, poor brethren and sisters of the Maison Dieu to the English king and his council shows that their church and house were destroyed during the siege of the town (*Ibid.*, iii. no. 1105). So far the indications are that this was a secular foundation. A grant of it by James I to his chaplain, Thomas de Lawedre, is provisionally dated 8 June 1425 (*HMC 12th Rep.*, App., Pt. VIII, 174). The "Mason Dew" is mentioned in the fifteenth-century poem "the Freiris of Berwik" (*Poems of Dunbar*, ed. W. Mackay Mackenzie, p. 183). *V.* next entry.

BERWICK, ST EDWARD. "The hospital of the Bridge of Berwick." Charters deal with the grant, −1234, of the church of Kettins to this hospital for the maintenance of the sick (*Yester Writs*, nos. 9, 12) or the poor (*Ibid.*, no. 11) dwelling there. Soon after its foundation it came into the possession of the Trinitarians (*q.v.*). Later references show that the designation "Maison Dieu" was applied to the Trinitarians' hospital. Thus, Robert III (1390–1406) granted to that order's lately founded hospital of Dundee the church of Kettins "annexed of old to the Domus Dei of Berwick" (*RMS*, i. no. 838). Again, a letter under the privy seal, 1 July 1529, mentions "the hous of God that wes possedit [possessed] thare [i.e. at Berwick] of the said religioun be the ministeris and brether thairof that is distroyit and put down" and goes on to refer to the "translatioun and applicatioun of the rentis . . . of the . . . place [i.e. of the Trinitarians] and hous of God of Berwik and Kytternis [Kettins] to the . . . place of Peblis [Peebles]" (*RSS*, ii. no. 203). This "translation" was made by James III, −1488 (*Ibid.*). It is difficult to say what is implied by the phrase "the place and hous of God of Berwik". It appears that the Maison Dieu (*supra*) and St Edward's hospital were originally separate foundations, the one under secular supervision, the other placed under regulars. Was the latter also known as a "Maison Dieu" or did the Trinitarians' hospital take over that designation after the destruction of the secular institution? This problem remains insoluble.

BERWICK, ST LEONARD. In 1297(?), the master and brethren petition Edward I and his council for the restitution of land in Liddesdale of which they have been dispossessed (*Docs. Illust. of Hist. of Scotland*, ii. no. ccccxx). This is the only reference to this hospital which has been found.

## HOSPITALS

| Name | County | Dedication or Designation | Founder | Date Fd. | Termd. or Sec. | Type | Dependent on or Rule |
|---|---|---|---|---|---|---|---|
| BERWICK | | St Mary M. | | −1296 | 1395+ | P | |
| BIGGAR | Lanark | Almshouse | Malcolm, Lord Fleming | 1545/6 | ? | Am | Biggar collegiate church |
| ,, | ,, | St. Leonard | | −1470 | −1545 | ? | |
| BRECHIN | Angus | Maison Dieu | William de Brechin | −1267 | Contd. | P | |
| CARNWATH | Lanark | | Thomas de Somerville | 15 c. | ? | Am | Carnwath collegiate church(?) |
| CAVERS *v.* RULEMOUTH | | | | | | | |
| COCKBURNSPATH | Berwick | | | −1511 | 1581+ | ? | |
| CREE | Kirkcudbright | | | mentioned 1306 | | ? | Held by Dundrennan abbey |

BERWICK, ST MARY MAGDALENE. The master of this hospital had restitution of lands from Edward I in 1296 (*Rot. Scot.*, i. 25). On 6 June 1356, it is mentioned as a poor's hospital which has been destroyed by the Scots; Edward II, who has had it in his hands, restores it (*Ibid.*, i. 794). Appointments to the mastership are recorded till 1395 (*Ibid.*, ii. 128).

BIGGAR, ALMSHOUSE. According to the foundation charter of the collegiate church, 16 January 1545/6, six bedesmen, with a house assigned to them, are to be attached to it, while the fourth prebendary is to act as their preceptor (*Spalding Club Misc.*, v. 300, 302). This provision was made *de novo* and had no relation to the older hospital (*infra*).

BIGGAR, ST LEONARD. The church of Biggar and the hospital of the same are mentioned, 28–9 May and 12 July 1470 (*Yester Writs*, nos. 155, 157, 160; *RMS*, ii. no. 995). The latter was extinct or extinguished, 16 January 1545/6, when, by a somewhat curious arrangement, the founder of the collegiate church grants the lands of Spittal, which had apparently formed the hospital's endowment, to the first prebendary of the college, who, though designated prebendary of the hospital of St Leonard, is to be master of the college's song school (*Spalding Club Misc.*, v. 299).

BRECHIN, MAISON DIEU. Founded −1267 (probably 1261–7) by William de Brechin whose charter refers to St Mary's chapel of his foundation, and to the master, chaplains and the poor people serving God continually there (*REB*, i. no. 3; *Reg. Panmure*, ii. 205). On 20 June 1572, ecclesiastical endowments in Brechin were vested in the burgh authorities (*RMS*, iv. no. 2079); but bedesmen were evidently still being maintained in 1582 (*Ibid.*, v. no. 597) and there are references to the preceptory (mastership) till at least 1636, when the office was conjoined with a mastership in the grammar school (*Reg. Panmure*, ii. 321–2).

CARNWATH. A hospital for eight bedesmen is said to have been founded here by Sir Thomas Somerville at the beginning of the fifteenth century (*OPS*, i. 126, which does not give the source of this statement). If the place still called Spittal, at some distance from Carnwath, marks its site, it is difficult to regard it as having a connection with the collegiate church there. From 1524 onwards, Spittal appears as in lay possession (*Court Bk. of the Barony of Carnwath, passim*); this would suggest that the hospital was extinct before that date.

COCKBURNSPATH. A hospital is mentioned here from 26 August 1511 (*RMS*, ii. no. 3634) to 16 June 1581 (*Ibid.*, v. no. 218).

CREE. The hospital of "Crithe" appears among the possessions of Dundrennan abbey, 18 October 1305 (*CDS*, ii. no. 1702). Nothing is known of its history, but the site is probably indicated by the name Spittal, in the parish of Kirkmabreck (*v. RMS*, vi. no. 1122 (25 December 1600); *Kirkcudbright Retours*, no. 256 (30 September 1652)).

## HOSPITALS

| Name | County | Dedication or Designation | Founder | Date Fd. | Termd. or Sec. | Type | Dependent on or Rule |
|---|---|---|---|---|---|---|---|
| CROOKSTON | Renfrew | | Robert Croc | –*c.* 1180 | ? | S (?) | |
| DALHOUSIE (=LASSWADE; POLTON) | Midlothian | St Leonard | | –1500 | Contd. | ? | |
| DALKEITH | ,, | Maison Dieu | Sir James de Douglas | 1396 | ? | P | Dalkeith collegiate church |
| DOONSLEE *v.* AYR, ST LEONARD | | | | | | | |
| DUMBARTON | Dunbarton | | | 15 c.(?) | 16 c.(?) | Am | Dumbarton collegiate church |
| DUNBAR | E. Lothian | Maison Dieu | | ? | 16 c. | P | Dunbar collegiate church or Trinitarians. *v.* notes. |
| DUNDEE | Angus | Leper house | | –1498 | –1552 | L | |

CROOKSTON. A charter of the prior and convent of Paisley, *c.* 1180, concedes to the infirm brethren of the hospital which Robert Croc has built in his land that they may have a chaplain and a chapel (*Passelet*, p. 77). This hospital is said to have stood on the west side of the Levern water, between Old Crookston and Neilston (*OPS*, i. 68).

DALHOUSIE. References to the patronage of the chapel and hospital of St Leonard, within the barony of Dalhousie, are found from 20 May 1528 (*RMS*, iii. no. 590) to 27 July 1666 (*Ibid.*, xi. no. 939). This is evidently the same as the hospital of St Leonard "besid the brig of Laswaid", mentioned 20 July 1500 (*RSS*, i. no. 551), and also identical with the hospital of St Leonard of Polton, situated near the bridge of Lasswade, the chapel of which appears, 7 May 1505 (*Prot. Bk. of James Young*, no. 1530).

DALKEITH. Founded by Sir James de Douglas, beside the chapel of St Nicholas (later the collegiate church) as a "domus dei sive hospitale" for six poor people, 27 June 1396 (*Reg. Hon. de Morton*, ii. no. 208).

DOONSLEE, *v.* AYR, ST LEONARD.

DUMBARTON. Charters of 12 March 1551/2 and 1 February 1552/3 (*RMS*, iv. nos. 683, 747) refer to a hospital for bedesmen attached to the collegiate church. This was probably transferred here from Polmadie (*q.v.*).

DUNBAR. A "massindiew [Maison Dieu] or hospitall", said to be associated with the collegiate church, is mentioned in an undated (probably sixteenth century) record (BM. Harl. MS. 4637C, f. 189). As, however, "Lie Masondew" appears among lands leased by the minister and convent of the Trinitarian house of Peebles, 1 June, 1558 (*RMS*, iv. no. 3037), it may have been originally connected with the house of that order at Dunbar.

DUNDEE, LEPER HOUSE. Mentioned 20 June 1498 (*RMS*, ii. no. 2446). It stood on the river bank at the east end of the town (Maxwell, *Old Dundee*, p. 68). There is a reference to the hospital or houses of the lepers, 30 August 1540 (*Chs. etc. of Burgh of Dundee*, p. 30); but, in 1552, the building had become ruinous and uninhabitable (Maxwell, *op. cit.*, p. 68); and although, in 1556, the Town Council ordained its repair, this does not seem to have taken place. In 1564, its land was being leased for agricultural purposes (Maxwell, *loc. cit.*).

## HOSPITALS

| Name | County | Dedication or Designation | Founder | Date Fd. | Termd. or Sec. | Type | Dependent on or Rule |
|---|---|---|---|---|---|---|---|
| DUNDEE | Angus | Maison Dieu | Sir James Lindsay | *c.* 1390 | 1553+ | PS | Trinitarians *v.* notes. |
| DUNFERMLINE | Fife | St Leonard | | Uncertain | Contd. | Amw | |
| DUNGLASS | E. Lothian | St Mary and St John B | Sir Alexander Home | –1480 | – | P | Dunglass collegiate church |
| DUNKELD | Perth | St George | George Browne, bishop of Dunkeld (revived foundation) | –1506 | Contd. | P | |
| DUNS | Berwick | | | –1274 | ? | ? | |
| EARLSTON | ,, | | | mentioned 12 c. | ? | ? | |

DUNDEE, MAISON DIEU. About 1390, Sir James Lindsay granted a tenement in Dundee to the Trinitarians for a hospital and Maison Dieu. This grant is incorporated in and confirmed by an undated charter of Robert III (1390–1406), who also bestows upon the hospital (which is described as for the infirm, aged and ailing) the church of Kettins "annexed of old to the Domus Dei of Berwick", to be held by it while Berwick remains in the hands of the English (*RMS*, i. no. 838). It is impossible to say for how long the Trinitarians held this hospital, but for some time before the Reformation the Town Council appointed the master and chaplain (Maxwell, *Old Dundee*, p. 65). It was burned by the English in 1548 (*Ibid.*, p. 113) and various property of the Almshouse and its chapel, hidden during the English invasion, was restored in 1551 (*Ibid.*, p. 66). There is a reference in 1553 to the Almshouse and "the puir and sick men thereof" (*Ibid.*, p. 67).

DUNFERMLINE, ST LEONARD. At the south end of the town. The chapel of the hospital of St Leonard is mentioned in a bull of 1184 (*Dunfermelyn*, no. 239), but it is not certain that the reference is to a hospital of this dedication in Dunfermline. Again, a hospital of Dunfermline, which cannot positively be identified with St Leonard's, appears in a charter of 1227 (*Ibid.*, no. 214). There is little doubt that this was a medieval foundation, but specific references to it seem only to be found after the Reformation. Thus, several appointments to widowships are recorded from 1590 (Webster and Duncan, *Regality of Dunf. Court Bk.*, p. 187), while St Leonard's hospital and its almoner, widows and bedesmen appear, 9 November 1615 (*Laing Chs.*, no. 1736). The chapel is said to have been wrecked by Cromwell's soldiers after the battle of Pitreavie, July 1651 (Beveridge, *BR of Dunf.*, xxix). The hospital is mentioned till 1 April 1651 when it was evidently in a state of disrepair, and its lands till 1732 (Webster and Duncan, *op. cit.*, p. 191).

DUNGLASS. A bull of Pope Sixtus IV, dated 5 August 1480, refers to the poor's hospital, which, with a chapel of St Mary and St John Baptist, Sir Alexander Home had built near the collegiate church (Theiner, *Vet. Mon.*, no. dccclxxi; *CPR*, xiii. 271).

DUNKELD, ST GEORGE. George Browne, bishop of Dunkeld (1484–1514/5), revived and augmented an earlier foundation (Myln, *Vitae Dunkeld. Episc.*, pp. 41–2). The hospital, which was for a master (a canon of Dunkeld) and seven poor folk (*Ibid.*, p. 42), is first mentioned in diocesan accounts in 1506 (*Rentale Dunkeldense*, p. 80). There are references to the master of the hospital of St George in 1606 (*HMC 7th Rep.*, Pt. II, App., 716) and 1608 (*RMS*, vii. no. 416).

DUNS. Mentioned only in "Bagimond's Roll", 1274–5 (*SHS Misc.*, vi. 33) and in a taxation-roll of the same century (*Priory of Coldingham*, cx).

EARLSTON. Mentioned only in a charter of Walter de Lyndesay to Kelso, *c.* 1166 (*N. Durham*, App., no. clxiv).

## HOSPITALS

| Name | County | Dedication or Designation | Founder | Date Fd. | Termd. or Sec. | Type | Depen dent on or Rule |
|---|---|---|---|---|---|---|---|
| EDINBURGH | Midlothian | Kirk o' Field | | mentioned 16 c. | 1544–7 (?) | ? | Probably attached to St Mary in the Fields collegiate church |
| ,, | ,, | Leper house | | mentioned 1522–9 | ? | L | |
| ,, | ,, | St John B. | | mentioned 1392 | ? | ? | |
| ,, | ,, | St Leonard | | –1261–7 1493 (recon- stituted) | ? | Am | Holyrood abbey |
| § ,, | ,, | St Mary M. | Michael MacQueen and Jonet Rhynd, his wife | –1537 | Contd. | P | |

EDINBURGH, KIRK O' FIELD. A hospital attached to this collegiate church is said to have been burned and destroyed by the English 1544–7 (*CCM*, cccvii).

EDINBURGH, LEPER HOUSE. There are references to lepers at St. Ninian's chapel, 1522–1529 (*Reg. S. Egid.*, nos. 126, 130, 141).

EDINBURGH, ST JOHN BAPTIST. There are references to the tenement of the hospital of St John Baptist in charters, one of 1392 and another undated (*Reg. S. Egid.*, nos. 19, 157), but no further information on this foundation is forthcoming.

EDINBURGH, ST LEONARD. "The brethren of the hospital of St Leonard of Edinburgh" are parties to a controversy, 1261–7 (*Dunfermelyn*, no. 220). David II (1329–1370/1) granted this hospital to Holyrood abbey (*RMS*, i. App. 2, Index A, no. 1668; *CPR*, xii. 734). There was evidently a proposal, approved by a papal bull of 2 May 1472, to dissolve the union with Holyrood (*Scottish Benefices*, p. 172); but, on 18 July 1493, the hospital was reconstituted by Robert Ballantyne, abbot of Holyrood, for six poor or aged men, in the almshouse on the south side of St Leonard's chapel (*Lib. S. Crucis*, pp. 234 f.) and on 3 September 1494, the abbot duly gave six inmates of this almshouse sasine of two crofts and an annual rent (*Prot. Bk. of James Young*, no. 730). A preceptor of this hospital appears in 1591/2 and 1592 (*Yester Writs*, nos. 896, 903).

EDINBURGH, ST MARY MAGDALENE. A chapel and hospital for a chaplain and seven poor men were founded by Michael Macqueen, burgess of Edinburgh (†1537) and his wife, Jonet Rhynd, whose confirmation charter is dated 1547 (*Hist. Mon. Comm. Rep.* (Edinburgh), pp. 41–4, *q.v.* for a good account of this foundation; cf. also *RMS*, iii. nos. 2262, 2513; *RSS*, ii. no. 4325). The number of poor men is given as four, 19 July 1554(?) (*RMS*, iv. no. 950).

M

## HOSPITALS

| Name | County | Dedication or Designation | Founder | Date Fd. | Termd. or Sec. | Type | Dependent on or Rule |
|------|--------|--------------------------|---------|----------|----------------|------|----------------------|
| EDINBURGH | Midlothian | St Mary V. | Provost and community of Edinburgh | –1438 | 1583+ | Aw | |
| ,, | ,, | St Paul | Archibald Crawford, abbot of Holyrood or Thomas Spens, bishop of Aberdeen | 1469 | Contd. | Am | |

EDINBURGH, ST MARY, ST MARY'S WYND. This was not a nunnery, as has sometimes been assumed (e.g. by Spottiswoode, p. 464), but an almshouse for poor women. Cf. references to "the hospital of the Blessed Virgin Mary in the Wynd commonly called St Mary's Wynd and the poor dwelling therein" (in 1484) (*RSS*, ii. no. 1600); "the poor sisters of the hospital of St Mary's Wynd outside the gates" (in 1535) (*Reg. S. Egid.*, no. 135). Spottiswoode (p. 464) states that "in the chartulary of St Giles", the nuns of St Mary's Wynd are recorded". But the "sisters" mentioned there are clearly not nuns but bedeswomen. (The use of the term "sister" for a bedeswoman is illustrated by a reference to the granting of sasine to "Marion Cockburn, sister of the Virgin Mary in St Mary Wynd, in name of the other sisters, bedeswomen of the said hospital" (*Prot. Bk. of John Foular*, iii. no. 346).) On 30 May 1438, James [II], king of Scots, supplicates for an indulgence for this hospital, which has been founded (with accommodation for forty-eight inmates) by the provost and community of Edinburgh (Vat. Reg. Supp., 348, 28v (D) ). Appointments of bedeswomen are recorded till at least 1583 (*EBR, 1573–89*, p. 314). In 1585, the magistrates provided for using its chapel as a poor children's shelter (*Ibid.*, p. 479). The latest reference to it—the payment of a deceased bedeswoman's due—occurs, 19 December 1589 (*EBR, 1589–1603*, p. 11).

EDINBURGH, ST PAUL. In Leith Wynd. There are divergent accounts of the foundation of this hospital. It is described, 3 February 1469/70, as a poor's hospital which Archibald Crawford, abbot of Holyrood, had newly erected with a chapel dedicated to St Paul (*CPR*, xii. 761). On the other hand, a Town Council minute attributes its foundation to Thomas Spens, bishop of Aberdeen (*c.* 1459–80) (*EBR, 1573–89*, pp. 137–8), who, it is said, founded it for twelve poor men, in 1479, not many months before his death (Arnot, *Hist. of Edinburgh*, p. 247 cited Dowden, *Bishops*, p. 127). It has a variety of designations, e.g. "the hospital of St Mary of St Paul", 7 October 1488, 20 March 1490/1, 6 July 1514 (*Prot. Bk. of James Young*, nos. 127, 414, 2042); "the hospital of the Blessed Virgin, called St Paul's, situated near Trinity College, at the end of Leith Wynd", 6 September 1501 (*Ibid.*, no. 1159); "the hospital of St. Mary the Virgin and St Paul", in 1508 (*Prot. Bk. of John Foular*, i. no. 469). Again, it is described as St Paul's "Werk" [building], which is specifically identified with Our Lady Hospital, e.g. in 1518, when it appears as "the place or hospital of the Virgin Mary and St Paul called St Paul's werk" (*Ibid.*, ii. no. 111); in 1579, when it is designated "the hospitall of Oure Lady, callit Sanct Paullis Wark" (*EBR, 1573–89*, pp. 137–8), with other similar mentions till 1608 (e.g. *Ibid., 1573–89*, p. 564; *ibid., 1604–26*, p. 43). New statutes for the master and bedesmen were made by the Town Council in 1582 (*Ibid., 1573–89*, p. 564). The hospital was apparently rebuilt in 1619 and developed in the seventeenth century as a workhouse or house of correction; it is said to have continued thus till 1750. *V. EBR, passim; Hist. Mon. Comm. Rep. (Edinburgh)*, p. 184. The building of 1619, however, survived; in it, in 1805, James Ballantyne established his press and there the Waverley Novels were printed.

## HOSPITALS

| Name | County | Dedication or Designation | Founder | Fd. | Date Termd. or Sec. | Type | Dependent on or Rule |
|---|---|---|---|---|---|---|---|
| EDINBURGH | Midlothian | St Thomas | George Crichton, bishop of Dunkeld | 1541 | Contd. | Am | |
| ,, | ,, | Trinity College | Mary of Gueldres, queen of Scots | –1460 | 1567 | Am | Trinity College |
| EDNAM | Roxburgh | St Leonard | Ada, countess of Northumberland and Huntingdon (?) | –1178 | –1627 | Am | |

EDINBURGH, ST THOMAS. In the Watergate. This hospital is said to have been founded in 1541 by George Crichton, bishop of Dunkeld (1526–1543/4) and formerly abbot of Holyrood, for two chaplains and seven bedesmen (Maitland, *Hist. of Edinburgh*, pp. 154–5 cited Dowden, *Bishops*, p. 87). There are references to the lands of St Thomas, in the Canongate, 23 December 1489 (*Prot. Bk. of James Young*, no. 289) and later; and St Thomas's chapel in the Canongate is mentioned, 19 May 1500 (*Ibid.*, no. 1034). The hospital may have been attached to this chapel, which is said to have been founded by Gavin Crichton (*Laing Chs.*, no. 1911). There is a record of a presentation by the then bishop of Dunkeld to a bedesmanship in 1564 (*Prot. Bk. of Gilbert Grote*, no. 265) and of the appointment of a master in 1560 (RSS, xlvi. 131). This hospital survived the Reformation. Thus, the "bedrellis" or hospitallers of the hospital of SS Thomas and Andrew in the almshouse founded by George, bishop of Dunkeld, appear in a charter of 2 November 1622 (*Laing Chs.*, no. 1911).

EDINBURGH, TRINITY COLLEGE. Founded by Mary of Gueldres, widow of James II, for thirteen poor people. This hospital was part of the establishment of the collegiate church of the Holy Trinity, the foundation of which preceded a bull of 23 October 1460 (*CCM*, p. 58). The queen's foundation charter is dated 25 March 1462 (*Ibid.*, pp. 46 ff.). The inmates were endowed in part from the hospital of Uthrogle (*q.v.*). On 12 November 1567, Sir Simon Preston, provost of Edinburgh, had a grant (evidently on behalf of the burgh) of the college church and hospital, with the proviso that this should not prejudice the bedesmen (*RMS*, iv. no. 1802). At the same time the Town Council made provision for the erection of a new hospital (*EBR, 1557–71*, pp. 243–4). In 1578, the Council made preparations for housing in it twelve aged and sick people (*Ibid., 1573–89*, p. 77). The new hospital was apparently completed before 1587, when the older building, which was in a ruinous condition, was to be devoted to some "profitable use" (*Chs. and Docs. rel. to Trinity College, 1460–1661*, no. xx).

EDNAM. There is a reference to a donation to the master and congregation by Ada, countess of Northumberland and Huntingdon (†1178) (*Dryburgh*, no. 161). The suggestion of Spottiswoode (p. 475) that the hospital was founded by the Edmonstons of Ednam is probably unwarranted. Payments are recorded to the master, in 1327 (*ER*, i. 67) and later. The English burned this hospital, 26 October 1542 (*L. & P. H. VIII*, xvii. nos. 998 (2), 1136). Brockie (p. 1105) is wide of the mark in describing it as "reduced to ashes by the fury of fanatics [i.e. Reformers]". The patronage of it is mentioned, 16 January 1543/4 (*RMS*, iii. no. 2987) and as late as 22 November 1649, when there is also a mention of the lands of Spittle, "called from of old the lands of the place of the hospital of St Leonard of Ednam" (*Roxburgh Retours*, no. 197). In 1627, however, there were no bedesmen at the hospital (*Rep. on State of Certain Parishes*, p. 196).

## HOSPITALS

| Name | County | Dedication or Designation | Founder | Fd. | Date Termd. or Sec. | Type | Dependent on or Rule |
|---|---|---|---|---|---|---|---|
| ELGIN | Moray | Leper house | | mentioned 1391 | | L | |
| ,, | ,, | Maison Dieu | Andrew, bishop of Moray | –1237 | 1594/5 | P | |
| FAIRNINGTON | Roxburgh | | | –1511 | 1585+ | ? | |
| FORTUNE | East Lothian | | | –1270 | ? | ? | |
| GLASGOW | Lanark | Blacader's | Roland, Blacader, subdean of Glasgow | c. 1524–5 | –1605 | P | |

ELGIN, LEPER HOUSE. About 1391 "land called Spetelflat, beside the houses of the lepers of Elgin" is mentioned (*REM*, no. 117).

ELGIN, MAISON DIEU. Founded by Andrew, bishop of Moray (1222–42), –1237 (*REM* nos. 39, 116, 117; NLS. MS. 34.7.2). In 1390, this was one of the buildings burned by the "Wolf of Badenoch" (*REM*, no. 303). It is described, in 1445, as having been long void and wont to be assigned to secular clerks as a perpetual benefice, though originally founded for the maintenance of poor brothers and sisters (*CPR*, ix. 480). On 17 November 1520, James, bishop of Moray, granted it to the Blackfriars of Elgin (NLS. MS. 34.7.2). But although, 1561–72, its revenues appear as pertaining to the Blackfriars, there is about this time a record of payment to three bedesmen (*Thirds of Benefices*, pp. 32, 109, 133), and, in 1567, a gift of the preceptory to Robert Douglas (RSS, xxxvii, 8v). Finally, James VI, because the lands and rents of the hospital, since the Reformation, have been applied to the particular uses of certain persons without respect to the poor for whom it was founded, grants the hospital to the provost and council for the provision of a preceptor who will teach music and other liberal arts and for placing in it as many poor as are provided for by the first foundation, 22 March 1594/5 (*RMS*, vi. no. 249).

FAIRNINGTON. Early references are apparently to a chapel here. Not till 27 August 1511 is there a reference to the lands of "Fermyngtoun" with the hospital of the same (*RMS*, ii. no. 3635). There are later mentions of the hospital in 1581 and 1585 (*RMS*, v. no. 218; *APS*, iii. 257, 259, 409).

FORTUNE. In the parish of Athelstaneford, East Lothian. "The whole land that was of the hospital of Fortun" was among the lands bestowed, c. 1270, by Cristiana de Mubray upon the Trinitarian monastery of Houston (*q.v.*), which she had founded. Her donation was confirmed by Alexander III, 26 January 1271/2 (*PSAS*, 1887–8, p. 28). This grant may imply that the hospital was extinct. It cannot be taken to indicate a connection of the hospital with the monastery. "The lands of the hospital of Fortoun" appear in a much later confirmation of Cristiana's donation—by James V, 8 January 1541/2 (*RMS*, iii. no. 2569); but the reference is of course retrospective.

GLASGOW, BLACADER'S HOSPITAL. Roland Blacader, subdean of Glasgow cathedral, founded a chaplainry in the nave of the church of Glasgow (the cathedral), at the altar of St John Baptist and St Nicholas, the chaplain to be master of the hospital for casual poor and indigent people founded by Blacader in the city of Glasgow, near the Stablegreen, c. 1524–5 (*REG*, ii. no. 495; *Chs. and Docs. rel. to Glasgow*, i. Part I, 13). (It is said also that Blacader bequeathed £100 for the erection of a hospital beside the collegiate church of St Mary and St Anne (Our Lady College); but the bequest apparently was not carried into effect (*OPS*, i. 7). The source of this statement has not been traced.) In 1605, the decayed hospital was acquired for rebuilding for the use of poor craftsmen (*Chs. and Docs. rel. to Glasgow*, i. Pt. I, 54).

## HOSPITALS

| Name | County | Dedication or Designation | Founder | Date Fd. | Termd. or Sec. | Type | Dependent on or Rule |
|------|--------|---------------------------|---------|----------|----------------|------|----------------------|
| GLASGOW | Lanark | St Nicholas | Andrew de Durisdere, bishop of Glasgow | 1471 | Contd. | Am | |
| ,, | ,, | St Ninian | | c. 1359 or 15 c. | 1636 | L | |
| HADDINGTON | E. Lothian | Almshouse | John Haliburton, vicar of Greenlaw | c. 1478 | ? | A | |
| ,, | ,, | Leper house | | –1470 | ? | L | |

GLASGOW, ST NICHOLAS. Founded by Andrew de Durisdere, bishop of Glasgow (*c.* 1456–73), for a priest and twelve old men, in 1471 (*Chs. and Docs. rel. to Glasgow*, i. Pt. II, 96; *RMS*, v. no. 2015). The statement that it was founded by Roland Blacader, subdean of Glasgow (*RSS*, iii. no. 1401) seems to be erroneous. It received bequests in 1567 (*Chs. and Docs. rel. to Glasgow*, i. Pt. I, 22); and although the "back almshouse" was deserted before 1600 (*Ibid.*, ii. 562 *n.*), the hospital continued till the eighteenth century and its revenues are still administered by the Town Council. *V. Chs. and Docs. rel. to Glasgow*, i. Pt. I, xlvi ff.

GLASGOW, ST NINIAN. At the south end of Glasgow bridge. Said to have been founded *c.* 1359 (*OPS*, i. 19); but probably the foundation took place in the following century. The earliest records found mention men and women lepers in the hospital and poor lepers dwelling there, 30 June and 1 July 1485 (*Chs. and Docs. rel. to Glasgow*, ii. 465–8). On 31 May 1494, William Stewart, canon and prebendary of Killearn (in Glasgow cathedral) founded a chaplainry in St Ninian's chapel, "constructed by him and built anew" at the lepers' hospital beside the bridge of Glasgow (*REG*, no. 469). This chapel is also mentioned as newly built, 16 August 1491 (*Chs. and Docs. rel. to Glasgow*, ii. 472). The hospital was granted to the city by Charles I, 16 October 1636 (*Ibid.*, i. Pt. II, 387).

HADDINGTON, ALMSHOUSE. On 11 June 1478, an indenture is made between the Greyfriars of Haddington and John Haliburton, vicar of Greenlaw, concerning an almshouse erected by him in the Poldrait of Haddington (Moir Bryce, *Greyfriars*, ii. 13). Its history is "wholly unknown" (*Ibid.*, i. 180).

HADDINGTON, LEPER HOUSE. In terms of the refoundation of St Laurence's hospital, 1470–2, a chalder of victual is to be given by its master, at the two yearly terms, to the lepers of Haddington, dwelling in the leper house (Haddington Burgh Writs). This perquisite of the lepers passed to the burgh; an act of parliament of 1592 empowered the provost and magistrates to uplift it (*APS*, iii. 580).

HOSPITALS

| Name | County | Dedication or Designation | Founder | Date Fd. | Termd. or Sec. | Type | Dependent on or Rule |
|------|--------|--------------------------|---------|----------|----------------|------|----------------------|
| HADDINGTON | E. Lothian | St Laurence | | −1327/8 1470−2 (refounded) | *v.* notes | A | |
| „ | „ | St Mary | | mentioned 1319 | | ? | |
| HELMSDALE | Sutherland | St. John B. | | −1362 | ? | ? | Kinloss abbey |

HADDINGTON, ST LAURENCE. A payment to the master of the hospital of Haddington is recorded, 26 February 1327/8 (*ER*, i. 73); and "St Laurence's hospital beside Haddington" is described as in receipt of fixed alms "from of old", 29 September 1337 (*CDS*, iii. no. 1247). On 20 November 1469, master Richard Guthrie, the king's almoner general, was appointed (*APS*, ii. 97) to put into operation an act of 9 October 1466 for the reformation of hospitals (*Ibid.*, ii. 86); and his visitation and reconstitution of this hospital are recorded in an undated charter among the burgh writs. (Its date can be determined by the fact that Guthrie appears in it as abbot of Arbroath, an office to which he was appointed, 3 November 1470 and which he demitted between 20 May 1471 and 29 July 1472 (*Aberbrothoc*, ii. nos. 186−8).) A letter of James IV to Pope Julius II, *c.* 1511, asked that this hospital, said to have been founded and endowed by his ancestors for the use of the poor,[1] should be converted into a house of Augustinian Friars Observantines (*Letters of James IV*, no. 471; the date suggested for this letter—July 1512—is too late); and the Pope, on 13 October 1511, suppressed the hospital and erected a house of this order (*L. & P. H. VIII*, i². 1522). But, because these friars did not take up residence, James V bestowed the hospital upon a secular clerk, who appears as master, 1513−14, and requested of Pope Leo X the severance of the hospital from incorporation in that order of friars (*Epp. Reg. Scot.*, i. 193−4; *Letters of James V*, p. 8; *ER*, xiv. 62). It is possible that Friar James Wyndiyettis, who appears as master, 1 July 1511−20 July 1512 (*ER*, xiii. 396, 496) was an Augustinian; but the friars who appear between 1515−16 and 1544−45 as receiving payments on behalf of the hospital were wardens of the Franciscan house at Haddington (*Ibid.*, xiv. 206−xviii. 74). On 29 August 1532, the hospital was annexed to the Dominican nunnery of Sciennes, Edinburgh (*Lib. S. Kath. Senen.*, no. iv). A master of the hospital, whose office presumably continued to receive a payment from the burgh till 1558−9 (*ER*, xix. 86). The lands of the hospital were leased, 15 February 1555/6 (*HMC 14th Rep.*, App., Pt. III, 42−3) and 15 February 1562/3 (*Lib. S. Kath. Senen.*, no. ix) and thereafter became permanently secularized. *V. Trans. East Lothian Antiq. and N.H. Socy.*, vi. (1955) 9−18.

HADDINGTON, ST MARY. A warden of this hospital was nominated, 30 July 1319 (*CDS*, iii. no. 657). No other reference has been found.

HELMSDALE. William, earl of Sutherland, is said to have bestowed upon Kinloss abbey the hospital of St John Baptist at Hebnisden, 21 May 1362 (Ferrerius, *Hist. Abbatum de Kynlos*, pp. 27−8; *Kinlos*, xxxix−xl). This has been identified with the hospital of St John at Helmsdale, the master of which is mentioned in 1471 (Fors Chs., cited *OPS*, ii². 731), and which is said to have been "subsequently" a canonry and prebend of the cathedral (at Dornoch) (*op. cit.*, p. 731). There is a reference, in 1578, to a chaplainry in the chapel of St John Baptist at Helmsdale (*Ibid.*).

---

[1] This statement cannot be confirmed and may be rhetorical.

## HOSPITALS

| Name | County | Dedication or Designation | Founder | Date Fd. | Termd. or Sec. | Type | Dependent on or Rule |
|---|---|---|---|---|---|---|---|
| HOLYWOOD | Dumfries | St John B. | Archibald de Douglas, lord of Galloway | –1372 | ? | Am | Lincluden collegiate church |
| HORNDEAN | Berwick | St Leonard | Robert Byseth of Upsettlington | c. 1240 | ? | A | Kelso abbey |
| HOUSTON | East Lothian | | | –1296 | ? | ? | Trinitarians |
| HUTTON | Berwick | St John | | –1296 | 1542 | ? | |
| INVERKEITHING | Fife | | | mentioned 1196 | | ? | Dryburgh abbey |
| JEDBURGH | Roxburgh | Maison Dieu | | –1296 | Contd.(?) | P | |

HOLYWOOD. The foundation of a poor's hospital within the enclosure or limits of the Premonstratensian monastery of Holywood, previously contemplated by Edward de Bruce, was made by Archibald de Douglas (Archibald "the Grim"), lord of Galloway, before 2 June 1372, when it was confirmed by Robert II (*RMS*, i. no. 483). On the petition of the founder, it received papal confirmation in 1378 (*CPR*, Pet., i. 538). This hospital, governed by a secular priest and with eighteen poor bedesmen, and situated near the nunnery of Lincluden "at [a distance of] a mile or thereabout", was annexed to the collegiate church erected on the suppression of the nunnery, the number of bedesmen increased to twenty-four and the master of the hospital made provost of the college, on the petition of Archibald de Douglas, 7 May 1389 (GRH. Vat. Trans., i. 288 ff.). A papal letter of 19 November 1434 refers to the hospital of St John Baptist in Lincluden, annexed to the provostship (*CPR*, viii. 493).

HORNDEAN. About 1240, Robert Byseth, lord of Upsettlington, granted to Kelso abbey the hospital of St Leonard, founded in his territory beside Tweed, opposite Horwerden (*Calchou*, no. 240). The hospital of Horndean is mentioned, c. 1300, as held by Kelso, with provision for a chaplain and two poor people (*Ibid.*, p. 467).

HOUSTON. In 1296, the master of the hospital of the Holy Trinity of Houston, in the county of Haddington, swore fealty to Edward I (*CDS*, ii. no. 823) and had restitution of its lands from him (*Rot. Scot.*, i. 25). This hospital was an adjunct of or identical with the Trinitarian house of Houston (*q.v.*).

HUTTON. The warden of this house came to Edward I's peace in 1296 and had its lands restored (*Rot. Scot.*, i. 25). The fact that it is described, on that occasion, as the hospital of St John of "Hoton" has given rise to the absurd idea that it belonged to the Hospitallers (cf. *BNC*, xvi (1896–8), 12). The hospital was granted with the church of Hutton to Dunglass collegiate church, 26 April 1451 (*HMC 12th Rep.*, App., Pt. VIII, 127). Hutton Spittal appears in a list of places burned by the English in 1542 (*Hamilton Papers*, i. xci).

INVERKEITHING. A bull of 15 March 1196 confirms, among other possessions of Dryburgh abbey, "the hospital of Innerkethyn" (*Dryburgh*, no. 250). No other reference to this hospital has been found. The hospital land near Inverkeithing, mentioned c. 1400 (*Dunfermelyn*, no. 397), belonged to the hospital of North Queensferry (*q.v.*).

JEDBURGH, MAISON DIEU. In 1296, the master of this hospital had restitution of lands from Edward I (*Rot. Scot.*, i. 25). The suggestion that there were other hospitals here (*OPS*, i. 372) is probably without warrant; the use of the term "hospitals" (*Rot. Scot.*, ii. 172) may be regarded merely as "common form". The patronage of this hospital is mentioned in 1684 and 1696 (*Roxburgh Retours*, nos. 282, 318).

## HOSPITALS

| Name | County | Dedication or Designation | Founder | Date Fd. | Termd. or Sec. | Type | Dependent on or Rule |
|------|--------|---------------------------|---------|----------|----------------|------|----------------------|
| KINCARDINE o' NEIL | Aberdeen | | Alan Durward | 1244+ | ? | P | |
| KINGCASE | Ayr | St Ninian | | 14 c. (?) | Contd. | L–A | |
| KINGGHORN | Fife | St James | | –1478 | ? | P | |
| LANARK | Lanark | St Leonard | | –1249 | Contd. | A | |
| LASSWADE, ST LEONARD *v.* DALHOUSIE | | | | | | | |

KINCARDINE O' NEIL. Founded by Alan Durward, justiciar of Scotland (1244+), for a master and an unspecified number of poor men (*REA*, i. 83; ii. 273). In 1296, the master swore fealty to Edward I (*CDS*, ii. no. 823). No later reference has been found.

KINGCASE. Despite the traditional connection of this hospital with Robert I, the terms and date of the foundation are unknown. A copy of the foundation charter is said (*ALC*, 1501–54, p. 201) to be in the register of Paisley, but does not appear there. The earliest reference to it seems to be in a charter of James II, granting to Hugh Wallace and his heirs, "hospitallers" of the house of "Kilcase", the lands of Spitalshiels, "even as the hospitallers of the said house were endowed and infeudated therein from of old by the king's predecessors", 14 February 1451/2 (*RMS*, ii. no. 328). The term "hospitaller" here has nothing to do with the Knights Hospitallers. It is used (*v.* Soutra) of an inmate of a hospital. In the case of the Wallaces, it implies that they had come to hold the hospital as a heritable possession (*v. Recs. of Prestwick*, p. 128). That the hospital "is of auld foundit for lepir men" (*ALC*, 1501–54, p. 201) and that it had been "usit be thame sen the deces of king Robert the Bruce" (*Ibid.*, p. 207) are assertions quoted in 1524 by way of resisting claims to bedesmanships in the hospital. But the proceedings in this case show that bedesmen had been customarily admitted to it, a practice which, on 30 July 1535, the Lords of Council sought to check by instructing commissioners of the archbishop of Glasgow to visit the hospital with powers to remove the non-leprous and to put lepers in their place (*Ibid.*, p. 443). But although "seik lipper folkis in Kingcais" are mentioned in 1603 (*Recs. of Prestwick*, p. 129), this foundation became, with the disappearance of leprosy, a hospital for the sick and poor and, as such, was in existence till the eighteenth century (*Ibid.*, pp. 127, 129). The head of this hospital is frequently called prior; e.g. on 26 January 1538/9, there is a reference to the prior of the hospital of St Ninian of Kinkais (*RSS*, ii. no. 2871).

KINGHORN. A charter of Robert Peirson, burgess of Kinghorn, 20 July 1478, makes, in supplement of the maintenance of the poor in the new hospital and a chaplain in the chapel of St James, a grant of the land on which the chapel and hospital are built (*RMS*, ii. no. 1407).

LANARK. The land of the brothers of the hospital appears in a charter which is evidently of the reign of Alexander II (1214–49) (not of the time of William the Lion, as in *OPS*, i. 48) (*Dryburgh*, no. 216), while payments to the master of the hospital of Lanark, described from 1365 as St Leonard's, are recorded from 1327 (*ER*, i. 71) till 1559 (*Ibid.*, xix, 87). There is a reference, in 1482, to a hospital of St Laurence at the burgh of Lanark (*RMS*, ii. no. 1531), but this would appear to be an error for St Leonard's. On 9 November 1392, Robert III granted the hospital and its lands heritably to Sir John de Dalziel (*Ibid.*, i. no. 864); but a precept of sasine by James IV, for infefting Archibald, earl of Angus, in the barony of Braidwood, 8 May 1497, includes the patronage of this hospital (*Douglas Bk.*, iii. no. 149). On 20 February 1632, Charles I gave the patronage of the preceptorship to the burgh authorities (*Extracts from Recs. of Burgh of Lanark*, pp. 325–6); and, on 15 November 1636, its lands were acquired by the magistrates and Town Council for the poor of the burgh and parish (*Ibid.*, p. 370).

LASSWADE, ST LEONARD, *v.* DALHOUSIE.

| Name | County | Dedication or Designation | Founder | Date Fd. | Termd. or Sec. | Type | Dependent on or Rule |
|------|--------|--------------------------|---------|----------|----------------|------|----------------------|
| LASSWADE | Midlothian | St Mary V. | Master Robert Blackadir, rector of Lasswade | 1478 | ? | PST | |
| LAUDER | Berwick | St Leonard | Richard de Moreville | *c.* 1170 | ? | Am | |
| LEGERWOOD | Berwick | | | −1177(?) or −1296(?) | ? | L(?) | |
| LEITH | Midlothian | St Anthony | Uncertain | 1418 | 1591 | PS | Vienne |

LASSWADE, ST MARY. On 11 March 1477/8, the Pope, on the petition of master Robert Blackadir, rector of the parish church of Lasswade, who proposed to institute a hospital at his church, under the invocation of St Mary of Consolation, for the poor, pilgrims and the infirm, gave faculty for building it (Theiner, *Vet. Mon.*, no. dccclxv). An indulgence was granted, 4 April 1478, to those who visit the church and assist the construction of the hospital (*Ibid.*, no. dccclxiv). Cf. *Scottish Benefices*, p. 193.

LAUDER. This hospital was founded by Richard de Moreville, constable of Scotland, *c.* 1170 (*Dryburgh*, pp. 267–9; *HMC 5th Rep.*, App., 613). The idea that it was a hospital for leprous monks is fanciful. The foundation was for "infirm brothers", "brother" and "sister" being a usual designation of beneficiaries of hospitals. The master of this hospital had restitution of lands from Edward I in 1296 (*Rot. Scot.*, i. 25). It is not known how long this hospital survived. But there appears to have been another and much later hospital in this parish. *V.* Thirlestane *infra.*

LEGERWOOD. The warden of this hospital swore fealty to Edward I in 1296 (*CDS*, ii. no. 823). This appears to be the only clear reference to it. An undated charter of Walter, son of Alan, steward of the king of Scots (†1177), grants an endowment of land "to God and St Mary and the hospital of Auldenestun and the infirm brethren dwelling there" (*Melros*, i. no. 80). The charter does not name the abbey of Melrose as participating in this grant but the donor gives warrandice "to the aforementioned [prenominatis] [*sic*] monks". By another undated charter, which makes no mention of the hospital, the steward conveys "to God and the church of St Mary of Melrose" the identical lands and privileges specified in the foregoing charter (*Ibid.*, no. 81). No satisfactory explanation of these transactions can be given. It has been assumed that Melrose abbey held this hospital; but this remains uncertain and no further mention of it is made in the Melrose charters. Again, Walter's first charter (no. 80) is endorsed "charter of the lepers of Moricestun [Morriston]"; and part of the endowment is "the easement of the wood of Birkenside [now Birkhillside] and the wood of Liggardewude [Legerwood]". These place-names, as well as "Auldenestun" (Adniston, in a map of 1831), are found in the parish of Legerwood, and it is tempting to identify the hospital mentioned −1177 with that which appears in 1296. This identification, while probable, is, however, unverified.

LEITH, ST ANTHONY. Said to have been founded by Sir Robert Logan of Restalrig in 1430 (Rogers, "St Anthony's Mon. at Leith", *Trans. RHS*, v. 384, citing NLS. MS. 34.3.12, 11); while a papal letter, 8 February 1443/4 (*CPR*, ix. 405), declares that James I began to build it about fourteen years previously. But a supplication for an indulgence, granted on 30 July 1418, describes the hospital as newly founded (*Supplics.*, p. 12). The identity of its founder remains uncertain. It was erected for canons of the Augustinian order of St Anthony of Vienne—a preceptor and four canons are mentioned in 1443/4 (*CPR*, ix. 406)—and designed for the poor and those suffering from St Anthony's disease (erysipelas). In 1505, a letter of the preceptor to the General of the order declares that pestilence had carried off all the brethren except himself and another and refers to the destitution of this house (*Letters of James IV*, no. 19). On 28 March 1591, the preceptory was suppressed and granted with the place, lands and other possessions of St Anthony's to Mr John Hay (*RMS*, v. no. 1850).

HOSPITALS

| Name | County | Dedication or Designation | Founder | Date Fd. | Termd. or Sec. | Type | Dependent on or Rule |
|---|---|---|---|---|---|---|---|
| LINCLUDEN *v.* HOLYWOOD | | | | | | | |
| LINLITHGOW | W. Lothian | St Mary M. | | –1335 | –1591 | P | |
| LOCH LEVEN | Kinross | St Mary V. | William de Malvoisin, bishop of St Andrews | *c.* 1214 | | P | Trinitarians |
| MONTROSE | Angus | St Mary V. | | *c.* 1245; refounded 1516 for Friars Preachers | 1524 | L–P | |

LINCLUDEN, *v.* HOLYWOOD.

LINLITHGOW, ST MARY MAGDALENE. Spottiswoode (p. 467) declares that this hospital was "formerly governed by the Lazarites". Of this there is no evidence. There are references, *c.* 1251, to land held by this order in the territory of "Kathlac" (*RPSA*, pp. 292, 294) (possibly Cathlaw, south of Linlithgow); but no connection between this land or this order and St Mary Magdalene's hospital is indicated. The hospital is first mentioned 26 December 1335, when Edward III claimed to appoint a warden (*Rot. Scot.*, i. 392). The suggestion that it provided for pilgrims is apparently mere guesswork, based on the fact that there was a "Pilgrims' Hill" in the vicinity. According to a charter of 12 June 1528, this was a poor's hospital, with a chapel and cemetery (*RMS*, iii. no. 721). A master of this hospital is mentioned, 28 February 1563/4 (*Prot. Bk. of Nicol Thounis*, no. 181), but its lands were alienated before 1 June 1591 (*RMS*, v. no. 1875).

LOCH LEVEN, ST MARY. Founded by William de Malvoisin, bishop of St Andrews (1202–38), for the reception of the poor and needy (GRH. Chs., no. 48). The hospital was in existence, *c.* 1214, when the founder granted it the church of Moonzie (*Ibid.*, no. 23). This donation was confirmed 1225–36, by the prior of St Andrews (*RPSA*, p. 175), who also exempted it from the payment of teind (except certain teinds due to the church of Portmoak); it is here described as the hospital "beside the bridge of Lochleven" (*Ibid.*, p. 176). This foundation became known as Scotlandwell. On 2 October 1244, its chapel was dedicated by David de Bernham, bishop of St Andrews (A. O. Anderson, *Early Sources*, ii. 535), who, 2 January 1250/1, granted the hospital with its appropriated churches of Moonzie and Carnock, to the Trinitarians (GRH. Chs., no 48). *V.* Scotlandwell.

MONTROSE. A hospital here is mentioned *c.* 1245 (*Aberbrothoc*, i. 337). It is said to have been a royal foundation and for lepers (*Epp. Reg. Scot.*, i. 290), but both these statements may be queried. In a letter of James IV to Pope Julius II, asking an indulgence for those who visit it, it is described as for the poor (*Letters of James IV*, no. 334; cf. *ibid.*, no. 417). On 18 August 1512, the same king empowered his counsellor and secretary, master Patrick Panter, mentioned in 1507 as preceptor of this hospital (*RMS*, ii. no. 3121), to alter the foundation because Panter had redeemed the hospital out of the hands of "secular potentates", recovered its alienated lands and rebuilt the church and buildings (*Ibid.*, ii. no. 3765). We find James V, 14 November 1516, granting Panter authority to institute a new foundation of the hospital in favour of the Friars Preachers (*Ibid.*, iii. no. 113); and a petition of the duke of Albany (on behalf of James V) to Pope Leo X for the grant of the hospital and its lands to the Dominicans is granted, 18 May 1517 (*Letters of James V*, p. 45) (*v.* Montrose under Dominican Friars). But, on 10 May 1524, because the situation of the hospital in the public street proved disturbing to the friars, the king ordained their return to their old location (*RMS*, iii. no. 1725).

## HOSPITALS

| Name | County | Dedication or Designation | Founder | Fd. | Date Termd. or Sec. | Type | Dependent on or Rule |
|---|---|---|---|---|---|---|---|
| MUSSELBURGH | Midlothian | St Mary M. | | −1419 | ? | P | |
| NENTHORN | Roxburgh | | | mentioned 1542 | | ? | |
| NEWBURGH | Aberdeen | | Alexander Cumyn, earl of Buchan | c. 1261 | ? | A | |
| NORTH BERWICK | E. Lothian | | Duncan, earl of Fife | −1154 | 1560+ | PT | North Berwick nunnery |
| PEEBLES | Peebles | St Leonard | | −1327 | Contd. (?) | P | |
| PERTH | Perth | St Anne | | ? | 1586 | P | |
| ,, | ,, | St Katherine | John Tyrie, provost of the collegiate church of Methven | 1523 | 1567(?) | PT | |
| ,, | ,, | St Leonard | | ? | c. 1434 | ? | Annexed to Charterhouse |

MUSSELBURGH, ST MARY MAGDALENE. Mentioned, 6 September 1419 (*Supplics.*, p. 119). There are references to its rector, 28 February and 21 March 1428, when it is described as a poor's hospital (*CPR*, viii. 26, 19).

NENTHORN. Nenthorn Spittal appears in the list of places burned by the English in 1542 (*Hamilton Papers*, i. xci; *L. & P. H. VIII*, nos. 998 (2), 1136 (2) ).

NEWBURGH (ABERDEENSHIRE). Founded by Alexander Cumyn, earl of Buchan, for six poor men, with a chaplain, c. 1261 (*REA*, ii. 276; *Collns. Aberd. and Banff*, pp. 371–2).

NORTH BERWICK. At the south end of the ferry on the Firth of Forth (*v*. Ardross, *supra*). Founded −1154, by Duncan, fourth earl of Fife, for poor people and pilgrims, and granted by Duncan, fifth Earl of Fife to the nuns of North Berwick, −1177 (*N. Berwic*, no. 3). *V. SHS Misc.*, iv. 334–5. In 1560 an appointment is recorded to the chaplainry of the hospital of the "poor brethren" (*N. Berwic*, pp. 76–7).

PEEBLES, ST LEONARD. In the west end of the burgh, Payments to the master are recorded from 1327 (*ER*, i. 71). This was a poor's hospital (*Chs. and Docs. rel. to Peebles*, pp. 170–1). It appears, 1396–8, as St Laurence's hospital (*ER*, iii. 392, 419, 450), but it is mentioned as St Leonard's hospital till 1395 (*Ibid.*, iii. 365) and from 1406 (*Ibid.*, iv. 24). The appointment of a "perpetual preceptor", 26 June 1558 (*Chs. and Docs. rel. to Peebles*, p. 248), seems to mark the secularization of this hospital; yet a charter of James VI, in 1621, appears to contemplate the continuance of payments to a master (*Ibid.*, pp. 99–100).

PERTH, ST ANNE. This hospital is not mentioned till 1580 (*PCR*, 1st Ser., iii. 289). But it was apparently in existence earlier as a poor's hospital, associated with St Anne's chapel, with an endowment "of auld" for their maintenance (*Ibid.*). The chapel was destroyed in 1559, but the use of the hospital was apparently revived in July 1580 (Fittis, *Eccles. Annals of Perth*, p. 283). In 1586, the inmates were removed to a new hospital (*Ibid.*).

PERTH, ST KATHERINE. Founded 18 June 1523, by John Tyrie, provost of the collegiate church of Methven, for poor travellers (Fittis, *Eccles. Annals of Perth*, p. 291). It was associated with St Katherine's chapel and was probably included with the lands, houses, etc., of that chapel disponed to Patrick Murray of Tibbermuir, in 1567 (*Ibid.*, p. 292).

PERTH, ST LEONARD. This hospital was evidently attached to St Leonard's nunnery (*q.v.*). Its master is mentioned in 1403 and 1411 (Fittis, *Eccles. Annals of Perth*, p. 278). By 1434, this hospital was transferred, with the nunnery, to the Carthusians, and, on 24 April 1438, the prioress of St Leonard's resigned all claim to it (*Ibid.*, pp. 278–9).

HOSPITALS

| Name | County | Dedication or Designation | Founder | Fd. | Date Termd. or Sec. | Type | Dependent on or Rule |
|---|---|---|---|---|---|---|---|
| PERTH | Perth | St Mary M. | | −1327 | 1434 | P | Annexed to Charterhouse |
| ,, | ,, | St Paul | John Spens of Glendouglas | 1434 | 1559(?) | PTS | |
| POLMADIE | Renfrew | St John or St Mary M. | One of the earls of Lennox(?) | −1285 | 1427/8 or 1453/4 | Amw | Perhaps transferred to Dumbarton and attached to the collegiate church |
| PORTINCRAIG | Angus | | Gillebride, earl of Angus | −1187-9 | ? | ? | |

PERTH, ST MARY MAGDALENE. Persistently described as a nunnery, but clearly designated in records as a hospital of which the master had payments made to him from 1327 (*ER*, i. 66). On 24 November 1425, it is described as a poor's hospital, wont to be governed "by secular laymen" (per laicos seculares) (Vat. Reg. Supp., 191, 72v (D). It was suppressed and annexed to the Carthusian priory in 1434 (Fittis, *Eccles. Annals of Perth*, p. 275).

PERTH, ST PAUL. Founded, 25 December 1434, by John Spens of Glendouglas, burgess of Perth, for strangers, the poor and the infirm (Vat. Reg. Supp., 308, 16 (D); Fittis, *Eccles. Annals of Perth*, p. 288). On 6 July 1435, the founder supplicates for an indulgence (Vat. Reg. Supp., *loc. cit.*, ) which was granted, on the following 17 September, to all who visit and give alms for the chapel of the hospital (*CPR*, viii. 552). The chapel and hospital may have been destroyed at the same time as the Perth religious houses, in 1559. This seems to be implied by the statement that "after the Reformation, [they] remained in ruins for a considerable time" (Fittis, *op. cit.*, p. 289). An attempt to re-establish a hospital on this site in 1583 did not succeed (*Ibid.*).

POLMADIE. On 28 May 1316, Robert I conceded to the master, brethren and sisters that they might freely enjoy the privileges they were wont to use in the reign of Alexander III (1249-1285/6) (*REG*, no. 265). This hospital is said to have been dedicated to St John (*OPS*, i. 18) and also to St Mary Magdalene (*Copiale*, p. 389). In 1394, the Pope was petitioned to appropriate the hospital, "in which for a long time nothing has been done for the poor", to the choir of Glasgow cathedral for the maintenance of a music master and choristers (*CPR*, Pet., i. 614). On 12 January 1427/8 John, bishop of Glasgow, erected the hospital and its appropriated church of Strathblane into a prebend of Glasgow and had papal consent, 5 December 1429 (*REG*, no. 338). During the fourteenth century the earls of Lennox had asserted their right to present to the hospital and had formally renounced this, 16 February 1440/1 (*Ibid.*, no. 344). But, on 3 January 1453/4, the Pope appointed mandatories on the petition of Isabel, countess of Lennox, to erect a collegiate church at Dumbarton and to transfer to it this hospital, founded by her predecessors and described as "neglected and forgotten and turned from its original purpose" (*CPR*, x. 623-4). This transference appears to have taken place. *V.* Dumbarton, *supra*.

PORTINCRAIG (BROUGHTY FERRY). Founded by Gillebride, earl of Angus (†1187-9), who gave land to build a hospital here (*Aberbrothoc*, i. nos. 52, 53). This hospital does not seem to be mentioned later than 1214-26, when the grant of land was confirmed by Malcolm, earl of Angus (*Ibid.*, i. no. 53).

## HOSPITALS

| Name | County | Dedication or Designation | Founder | Date Fd. | Termd. or Sec. | Type | Dependent on or Rule |
|------|--------|--------------------------|---------|----------|----------------|------|----------------------|
| PORTMOAK | Kinross | St Thomas | | Mentioned −1184 | | P | Probably = Loch Leven, St Mary |
| QUEENSFERRY (NORTH) | Fife | | Malcolm IV (?) | −1165 | ? | ? | Attached to Dunfermline abbey |
| RATHVEN | Banff | | John Byseth | 1224–6 | Contd. | L-Am | |
| ROXBURGH | Roxburgh | Maison Dieu | | c. 1145 (?) | Contd. (?) | P | |
| ,, | ,, | St John | | −1330 | ? | ? | |
| ,, | ,, | St Peter | | mentioned 1426 | | | |

PORTMOAK, ST THOMAS. Described as "at the bridge of Portmoak" and "for the reception of poor people", −1184 (*RPSA*, p. 146). This seems to be the only reference. This hospital is very probably identical with Loch Leven, St Mary (*supra*).

QUEENSFERRY (NORTH). The hospital here, which belonged to Dunfermline abbey, had an endowment of lands from Malcolm IV (1153–65) (*Dunfermelyn*, no. 250). Whether it was one of the "dwellings" for pilgrims and the poor said by Turgot to have been built by Queen Margaret "upon either shore of the sea that separates Lothian and Scotland" (i.e. the Firth of Forth) (A. O. Anderson, *Early Sources*, ii. 77) is impossible to say. It does not seem to be mentioned later than 14 July 1233 (*Dunfermelyn*, no. 268), but its land near Inverkeithing "called the land of the hospital", which is mentioned, 30 December 1211 (*Ibid.*, no. 250), is the subject of a charter, c. 1400 (*Ibid.*, no. 397).

RATHVEN. Founded by John Byseth for a chaplain, seven lepers and a servant, 1224–6 (*REM*, no. 71). In a charter of 19 June 1226 the head of this house is called "prior" (*Ibid.*, no. 72). There is some indication that the revenues of the hospital as well as of the church of Rathven were appropriated to Aberdeen cathedral by Robert I (1306–29) (*REA*, ii. 150) and that they formed part of the endowment of a prebend in 1425 (*Ibid.*, ii. 253). But the hospital undoubtedly continued, latterly as an institution for the poor. Its bedesmen's pensions are mentioned, c. 1563 (*Antiqs. Aberd. and Banff*, ii. 145) and its existence is noted till the nineteenth century (*Ibid.*, ii. 143–4 *nn.*). It is, in fact, stated that the last bedesman died in 1859 and the house was demolished −1886. *V.* Cramond, *History of the Bede House of Rathven* (Buckie, 1890), p. 13; this work traces its post-Reformation history.

ROXBURGH, MAISON DIEU. About 1145, David I granted land to the hospital of Roxburgh (*Calchou*, no. 372). It is impossible to say whether this was identical with the Maison Dieu. In Edward I's parliament of 28 February 1305/6, a petition of the master of the Maison Dieu (that he and his brethren might enjoy its rents and possessions) was presented (*Mem. de Parl*, no. 368); and a payment to the master of part of the Scottish king's grant for the fabric of the hospital's church is recorded in 1327 (*ER*, i. 67–8). This hospital was situated some distance north-east of Roxburgh. The description of it as for pilgrims and for the diseased and the poor (*OPS*, i. 462) is exaggerated. "Massendew" is mentioned as one of the places burned by Hertford's forces, 17 September 1545 (*L. & P. H. VIII*, xx². nos. 456, 533). This place is given as on the Kale water; but the location may be erroneous, as no hospital is known with certainty to have existed there and the Maison Dieu is probably that of Roxburgh. Mentions of the patronage of this hospital continue till at least 1696 (*Roxburgh Retours*, no. 318).

ROXBURGH, ST JOHN. There is a reference to this hospital, 1330 (*Calchou*, no. 491). It may have been associated with St John the Evangelist's church in Roxburgh castle.

ROXBURGH, ST PETER. This hospital is mentioned, 28 June 1426 (*CDS*, iv. no. 403).

HOSPITALS

| Name | County | Dedication or Designation | Founder | Date Fd. | Termd. or Sec. | Type | Dependent on or Rule |
|---|---|---|---|---|---|---|---|
| RULEMOUTH (SPITTAL-ON-RULE) | Roxburgh | St Mary(?) | | –1425/6 | 1545 | L | |
| RUTHERFORD | ,, | St Mary V. or St Mary M. | | –1276 | ? | ? | Granted to Jedburgh abbey |
| ST ANDREWS | Fife | St Leonard | Robert, bishop of St Andrews | 1144 | 1512 | PT–Amw | Erected into St Leonard's College |
| ,, | ,, | St Nicholas | | –1127 | 1583+ | L–P | Granted to the Friars Preachers |

RULEMOUTH, SPITTAL-ON-RULE. "There is another hospital for lepers at the mouth of the water of Rule called Rule Hospital" (*Macfarlane's Geog. Collns.*, iii. 158). On 5 March 1425/6, an inquest on an alleged case of leprosy was held in the chapel of the hospital of "Roulmouth" (Minto Chs., cited *Trans. Hawick Archaeol. Socy.*, 1903, p. 43). This was probably the hospital of St Mary in Teviotdale, mentioned, 28 December 1510 (*RSS*, i. no. 2171). "Rowle Spittell" was one of the places burned by Hertford's forces, 16 September 1545 (*L. & P. H. VIII*, xx². nos. 456, 533).

RUTHERFORD. This hospital is said to be mentioned in 1276 (*OPS*, i. 298). Its dedication is given as St Mary the Virgin, in 1296 (*Rot. Scot.*, i. 25), and as St Mary Magdalene, in 1395 and 1444 (*RMS*, i. no. 933; *Melros*, no. 566). It was granted by Robert III to Jedburgh abbey, 2 May 1395 (*RMS*, i. *loc. cit.*), but there is an appointment to the mastership, 18 May 1426 (*Ibid.*, ii. no. 52).

ST ANDREWS, ST LEONARD. In 1144, Robert, bishop of St Andrews, assigned the hospital of the Culdees to the canons of the newly founded priory and endowed it for the reception of visitors and pilgrims (*RPSA*, p. 123). Later, it is described as for the reception of visitors, the poor and pilgrims (*Ibid.*, p. 58). In 1183 (*Ibid.*) and later, it is called the hospital of St Andrew (or probably of St Andrews), and, 1158–62, the new hospital (*Ibid.*, p. 127). It is first mentioned as St Leonard's in 1248 (*Ibid.*, p. 103). That these designations apply to one and the selfsame hospital is shown by Herkless and Hannay (*Coll. of St Leonard*, pp. 10, 12). It is said to have been occupied eventually by old women and also by poor men (*Ibid.*, pp. 16–17). On 20 August 1512, Alexander Stewart, archbishop of St Andrews, erected the hospital and church of St Leonard into the college of that name (*Ibid.*, pp. 16–17, 128 ff.). *V*. St Leonard's College.

ST ANDREWS, ST NICHOLAS. A donation was made to this hospital by Roger, bishop of St Andrews, –1127 (*RMS*, iii. no. 2032). It was a leper hospital (*Ibid.*, iii. *loc. cit.*; v. no. 883); but it is also described as a poor's hospital, 12 May 1438 (Vat. Reg. Supp., 348, 157 (D)). In 1529, St Nicholas's was united to the Dominican house at St Andrews (*Macfarlane's Geneal. Collns.*, ii. 186); and there is a reference, 1568–72, to an annual rent paid to the Blackfriars for the "crypellis, lamyt, blynd and pouir" of this hospital (*Thirds of Benefices*, p. 241). It was apparently still in use in 1583, when an endowment of victual was made to the "poor folk, present and to come" (St And. Univ. Chs., cited *Copiale*, p. 409).

## HOSPITALS

| Name | County | Dedication or Designation | Founder | Date Fd. | Termd. or Sec. | Type | Dependent on or Rule |
|------|--------|--------------------------|---------|----------|----------------|------|----------------------|
| St Germains | E. Lothian | St German | | –1219 | 1577+ | P | Bethlehemite. Granted to King's College, Aberdeen |
| St Magnus | Caithness | St Magnus | | –1476 | Contd. | ? | |
| St Nicholas (Boharm) | Banff | St Nicholas | Muriel de Polloc | –1235 | Contd. | PT | |

St Germains (St German's). This was the only Scottish foundation of the Bethlehemite order. Ralph, prior of this house, is mentioned, –1219 (*Dunfermelyn*, no. 155). On 9 February 1495/6, a bull of Pope Alexander VI, which describes the hospital except the chapel as ruinous, while its fruits are secularized, grants, at the instigation of James IV, its revenues to the newly erected university of Old Aberdeen (later King's College), with provision for the maintenance of one religious and three poor people at the hospital and likewise of three poor students in the university (*Fasti Aberd.*, no. 4). A charter of 12 August 1507 is granted by William, bishop of Aberdeen, chancellor of the university and "master of the house of the hospital of St German's . . . annexed to the new college of the Blessed Virgin Mary in the said university" (*RMS*, v. no. 868). There is a reference to the chaplain or preceptor of the chapel of St German's, 12 August 1577 (*Ibid.*, iv. no. 2744). It should be noted that a papal latter of 11 December 1474 (*CPR*, xiii. 462) refers to "the hospital of St German in the diocese of Aberdeen, which has been from of old in the presentation of the priory of St Germanus at St German's . . . in the diocese of St Andrews". This statement which seems to indicate a second foundation under the same invocation in the diocese of Aberdeen undoubtedly involves a blunder. Cf. *Scottish Benefices*, p. 181. The only hospital of St German's was in the diocese of St Andrews.

St Magnus (Caithness). This hospital is first recorded, 14 December 1476 (*RMS*, ii. no. 1267). There was attached to it a church mentioned as "the rectory of the church of [Spittal] called the hospital of St Magnus in Caithness", 27 March 1547 (*RSS*, iii. no. 2228). It was leased, with its revenues, by the master, 5 and 24 March 1580/1 (*Cal. of Writs of Munro of Foulis*, no. 97). The patronage of the hospital is mentioned till 1633 (*APS*, v. 154). *V. OPS*, ii². 757–8; *Hist. Mon. Comm. Rep.* (*Caithness*), no. 89.

St Nicholas (Boharm). "Beside the bridge of Spey." Founded by Muriel de Polloc for the reception of poor travellers (*REM*, no. 106). In 1232, Alexander II made provision for a chaplain and clerks serving in the chapel of St Nicholas (*Ibid.*, no. 110). The hospital does not appear in a dated record till 1235 (*RPSA*, p. 326), but must have been in existence previously. The master is mentioned in a charter, 10 June 1471 (*Thanes of Cawdor*, p. 53). The buildings are said to have survived the Reformation and "in considerable extent" until removed for the rebuilding of the bridge (*Antiqs. Aberd. and Banff*, ii. 277–8).

## HOSPITALS

| Name | County | Dedication or Designation | Founder | Fd. | Date Termd. or Sec. | Type | Dependent on or Rule |
|------|--------|--------------------------|---------|-----|---------------------|------|----------------------|
| SEGDEN | Berwick(?) | St Mary | | 13 c. | −1437 | Am (?) | Augustinian |
| SHOTTS | Lanark | St Catherine | James de Hamilton | −1476 | | ? | P |
| SMAILHOLM | Roxburgh | | | | mentioned 1542 | ? | |

SEGDEN. This house has been erroneously located at Seggieden, near Perth. Thus, Spottiswoode (p. 479) speaks of it as "situated upon the River Tay in the shire of Perth". (The only connection of that place with a religious house was that the lands of Seggieden were granted to the Friars Preachers of Edinburgh, 11 February 1546/7 (*RSS*, iii. no. 2143).) This was an Augustinian hospital at or near Berwick. It appears in a thirteenth-century taxation roll (*Priory of Coldingham*, p. cxvi). In 1296, the master of the house of St Augustine of Seggeden, in the sheriffdom of Berwick, swore fealty to Edward I and had its lands restored (*CDS*, ii. no. 823; *Rot. Scot.*, i. 25). A reference is found 20 December 1333, to a tenement of Berwick acquired from the brethren of Seggedene (*Cal. Inquis., Miscell.*, ii (1307–49), no. 1402); and, on 21 March 1354, it is stated that two chaplains "of the order of the house of Segden in Scotland" used to have a chantry on an island in Windermere (*Ibid.*, iii (1348–77), no. 167). There is a record, 11 September 1367, of a tenement in Berwick pertaining to the master and brethren and of four acres adjoining the hospital, belonging to its enclosure and within the churchyard of that town (*Ibid.*, iii. no. 647). A chapel of Segden is mentioned, 5 March 1335/6 and 27 May 1379 (*Rot. Scot.*, i. 352; ii. 15). On 6 February 1431/2, there is a reference to the hospital of St Mary, Segden, near Berwick, along with the free chapel of St Mary Magdalene (*Cal. Pat. Rolls, H. VI (1429–36)*, p. 131); and on 4 November 1437 and 16 May 1453, it is called the hermitage of Segden, annexed to that chapel (*Ibid., H. VI (1436–41)*, p. 97; *CDS*, iv. no. 1251). The designation "the house of St Augustine of Seggeden" (*supra*) refers to the order not to the dedication. Is this house to be identified with the house of Augustinian friars at Berwick (*q.v.*)?

SHOTTS (BERTRAMSHOTTS). On 30 April 1476, a bull of Sixtus IV confirms the erection and measures for the endowment of the chapel of St Catherine (created by the ordinary a parish church) and the poor's hospital founded by James de Hamilton at Bertramshotts (*HMC 11th Rep.*, App., Pt. VI, 48; *CPR*, xiii. 489–90). No later references to this hospital have been found.

SMAILHOLM. "Smalham Spettell" appears in a list of places burned by the English in 1542 (*Hamilton Papers*, i. xci; *L. & P. H. VIII*, xvii, nos. 998 (2), 1136 (2) ). There are also mentions of Smailholm Spittal in rentals of Dryburgh abbey, *c.* 1540 onwards (*Dryburgh*, pp. 340 etc.) and elsewhere as late as 17 March 1637 (*Roxburgh Retours*, no.165), but the reference in these cases is to land so designated.

## HOSPITALS

| Name | County | Dedication or Designation | Founder | Date Fd. | Termd. or Sec. | Type | Dependent on or Rule |
|---|---|---|---|---|---|---|---|
| § SOUTRA | Midlothian | Holy Trinity | Malcolm IV | 1164 | 1583/4 | T–P | Augustinian |
| SPITTAL (CAITHNESS) *v.* ST MAGNUS | | | | | | | |
| STIRLING (OVER HOSPITAL) | Stirling | Almshouse | | –1296 (?) | Contd. (to –1610) | P | |

SOUTRA. Said to have been founded by Malcolm IV, in 1164, for lodging travellers (*Scotich.*, lib. viii, cap. vii (i. 453) ). But the foundation was probably somewhat earlier; there is a charter of King Malcolm to Soutra, 1161–4 (*CCM*, p. 3), which is not the foundation charter. In a bull of Pope Gregory IX, 20 September 1236, specific mention is made that the rule of St Augustine, instituted in the hospital, shall be observed in perpetuity (*Ibid.*, p. 36), and the fact that it is designated the house or hospital of the Holy Trinity from –1164 (*Ibid.*, p. 3) merely indicates its dedication and gives no support to the suggestion that it should be regarded as Trinitarian. Cf. the supplications of the master and brethren for confirmation of the privileges granted by Pope Gregory IX (*supra*), 27 May 1420 (*Supplics.*, p. 199) and for the right to wear rochets "after the manner of other canons of the same order", 10 June 1420 (*Ibid.*, p. 207). But, in 1444, its deterioration was such that doubts were expressed whether it was a Trinitarian or an Augustinian house and the opinion was given that it was more likely to have been founded as a hospital than as a religious place (Vat. Reg. Supp., 400, 34 cited A. I. Dunlop, *James Kennedy*, p. 408). On 20 November 1450, the Pope appointed a mandatory to deal with the petition of Melrose abbey for the appropriation to it of Soutra hospital (*CPR*, x. 501), but this did not take place. It is said to have been annexed, by authority of Pope Nicholas V (1447–55), to the chancellorship of St Andrews cathedral (*CCM*, p. 58), though this can hardly be accurate. But, on the petition of Mary of Gueldres, the widowed queen of James II, Pope Pius II united it by his bull of 23 October 1460 (*Ibid.*, pp. 58–61) to her new foundation of Trinity College and hospital, Edinburgh. The queen's charter of 25 March 1462 provides that the provost of Trinity College, who is to hold the church of Soutra, will maintain three poor people living there (*Ibid.*, p. 65); references to the "hospitallers" (i.e. residents in the hospital) of Soutra are found in 1531 and as late as February 1583/4 (*Ibid.*, pp.102, ciii). In the following (i.e. the seventeenth) century the hospital of Soutra is described as "alluterlie [completely] ruyned" (Bisset, *Rolment of Courtis*, ii. 123). Although Soutra is said to have been founded as a hospital for travellers (*supra*) there are many indications, from the thirteenth century onwards (e.g. the appropriation of churches to it for the maintenance of the poor (*CCM*, pp. 13, 15, 17) ), that it was a poor's hospital; and while its career as a well-endowed regular hospital was terminated in the fifteenth century, the maintenance of "hospitallers" was no doubt a continuance of its traditional association with the poor. The description of it as a "hospice" on the tablet affixed to the remaining fragment of its buildings is hardly accurate.

SPITTAL (CAITHNESS) *v.* ST MAGNUS.

STIRLING, ALMSHOUSE (THE OVER HOSPITAL). A poor's hospital (with a chaplain), on the east side of the parish church, beside the burial ground, is mentioned, 17 February 1540/1 (*Chs. rel. to Stirling, 1124–1705*, no. xlii), and again 28 February and 1 May 1610, when it was ruinous and proposed to be rehabilitated (*Ibid.*, no. lii). This may be the hospital at Stirling mentioned in 1296 (*Trans. Stirling Nat. Hist. and Archael. Socy.*, 1891–2, p. 5) and 1327 (*ER*, i. 67).

N

## HOSPITALS

| Name | County | Dedication or Designation | Founder | Date Fd. | Termd. or Sec. | Type | Dependent on or Rule |
|------|--------|---------------------------|---------|----------|----------------|------|----------------------|
| STIRLING (NETHER HOSPITAL) | Stirling | | | ? | ? | ? | |
| STIRLING | ,, | St James | | –1402/3 | –1606 | ? | Granted to Cambuskenneth abbey |
| STRATHBLANE | ,, | | | –1429 | ? | P | |
| TEVIOTDALE, ST MARY IN, v. RULEMOUTH | | | | | | | |
| TORRANCE | Stirling | St Leonard | | –1296 | 1546+ | ? | |
| TRAILTROW | Dumfries | St James | | –1455 | 1574+ | P | |

STIRLING, THE NETHER HOSPITAL. Commonly called Spittal's Hospital, from its supposed foundation by Robert Spittal, tailor to James IV, in 1530. Shirra, who examines the alleged evidence of local inscriptions (*Trans. Stirling Nat. Hist. and Archaeol. Socy.*, 1891–2, pp. 9 ff.) declares: "I can find no proof that Robert Spittal ever founded an hospital in Stirling or that he had any part in the establishment of the one which now bears his name." The same writer has "no hesitation in placing it prior to the Reformation" (*Ibid.*, p. 15); but it does not occur in pre-Reformation records of the burgh.

STIRLING, ST JAMES. First mentioned, 10 March 1402/3, when Robert III granted the hospital of St James, "at the end of the causeway of the bridge of Stirling", to Cambuskenneth abbey (*Cambuskenneth*, no. 108). The patronage of this hospital was bestowed upon the magistrates and community by James II, 24 June 1456 (*Chs. rel. to Stirling, 1124–1705*, no. xxiii). But it apparently continued to be held by Cambuskenneth, for, with its lands, it is included among the properties of that abbey incorporated, by act of parliament, 1606, in a temporal lordship (*APS*, iv. 345). It is said to have been destroyed at the Reformation and never rebuilt (*Trans. Stirling Nat. Hist. and Archaeol. Socy.*, 1891–2, p. 5); and the Town Council made regulations regarding the removal of the stonework of St James's chapel, 2 November 1567 (*Chs. rel. to Stirling*, p. 210).

STRATHBLANE. There are several references, in 1429, to a poor's hospital here (*CPR*, viii, 101, 102; *Scottish Benefices*, p. 97). It does not seem to be otherwise on record.

TEVIOTDALE, ST MARY IN, v. RULEMOUTH.

TORRANCE. The warden of this hospital swore fealty to Edward I in 1296 and had its lands restored (*CDS*, ii. no. 823; *Rot. Scot.*, i. 26). It was associated in some way with the church of Torrance. Thus, it is designated the hospital of the chaplainry of Torrens, 30 June 1439 (Vat. Reg. Supp., 359, 108v (D) ); and the hospital of the church of Torrance, 29 September 1512 (*RSS*, i. no. 2435). Again, a presentation to the rectory, chaplainry and hospital of Torrance is recorded, 5 August 1531 (*Ibid.*, ii. no. 977), and another to the rectory and preceptory of Torrance, 5 May 1546 (*Ibid.*, iii. no. 1648). Brockie (p. 1096) mistakenly locates this hospital near Peebles.

TRAILTROW. There is a reference to a poor's hospital here, 20 April 1455 (*CPR*, xi. 261). Preceptors of it are mentioned till 27 September 1574 (*RMS*, iv. no. 2311); one of these is designated (in 1501) preceptor of St James of Trailtrow (*HMC 15th Rep.*, App., Pt. VIII, 59). It was evidently extinct before 15 February 1609 when there is a mention of lands formerly held by this hospital (*RMS*, vii. no. 21); and although this hospital and hospital lands are mentioned till 1696 (*Dumfries Retours*, no. 346), obviously these had long been secularized.

## HOSPITALS

| Name | County | Dedication or Designation | Founder | Fd. | Date Termd. or Sec. | Type | Dependent on or Rule |
|------|--------|--------------------------|---------|-----|---------------------|------|----------------------|
| TURRIFF | Aberdeen | | Alexander Cumyn, earl of Buchan | 1272/3 | 1412 | A | |
| UPSETTLINGTON *v.* HORNDEAN | | | | | | | |
| UTHROGLE | Fife | St John B. | | −1394 | 1462 | ? | Annexed to Trinity College, Edinburgh |
| WHEEL | Roxburgh | | | mentioned 1348 | | ? | |

TURRIFF. Founded by Alexander Cumyn, earl of Buchan, for a master, six chaplains and thirteen poor people, 6 February 1272/3 (*REA*, i. 30–4). A reference to "the prebend of Turriff otherwise the hospital founded by the earl of Buchan" suggests that its revenues were merged with those of the church of Turriff, when the latter was made a prebend of Aberdeen cathedral, in 1412 (*REA*, i. 213–14; ii. 253).

UPSETTLINGTON *v.* HORNDEAN.

UTHROGLE. This hospital, mentioned in 1394 (*CPR*, Pet., i. 615) and 1420, when it is described as "the hospital of St John, Ouctherogale" (*Supplics.*, p. 228), was granted to Trinity College, Edinburgh, for the maintenance of the bedesmen there, in 1462 (*CCM*, pp. 64, 67). Its nature is not specified. It was evidently associated with a chapel, united likewise, in 1462, to Trinity College (*Scottish Benefices*, pp. 142, 240, 278) and designated the chapel of St John the Baptist, 16 October 1543 (*CCM*, p. 109).

WHEEL. This site is in south-west Roxburghshire and is described as "between the Wheel causeway and Peel burn, one mile south of the hill known as Wheelrig Head" (Watson, "Wheel Kirk, Liddesdale", *Trans. Hawick Archaeol. Socy.*, 1914, p. 20). The chapel, "del Quele" in Scotland is mentioned, 5 August 1347 (*CDS*, iii. no. 1500) and it is designated the hospital or free chapel "del Whele", 26 May 1348 (*Ibid.*, iii. no. 1532).

### INCOMPLETE FOUNDATION

*Aberdour, St Martha.* Called St Mary's (*Scottish Benefices*, p. 221). Founded, 9 July 1474, by James, earl of Morton, for the maintenance of the poor and the entertainment of pilgrims and wayfarers; and on 22 July following, the abbot and convent of Inchcolm intimated that they had given permission to John Scot, vicar of Aberdour and canon of that abbey, to take over the care and administration of the proposed hospital (*Reg. Hon. de Morton*, i. no. 231). As the project had not been realized, the earl granted the lands for the building of a hospital to four sisters of the Third Order of St Francis, 16 October 1486 (*Ibid.*, i. no. 233); but a bull of 23 June 1487 extinguished the name and rights of the hospital (Theiner, *Vet. Mon.*, no. dccclxxxiv).

### UNCERTAIN AND UNAUTHENTICATED FOUNDATIONS

*Aberdeen, Maison Dieu.* On 1 September 1459, there is a reference to *land* called "Masyndow" (*Cart. S. Nich.*, ii. 329). This was in the vicinity of the house of the Trinitarians, who may have had a hospital on this site (I owe this suggestion to Mr John Mackintosh, Aberdeen). Evidence, however, is wholly lacking. A later hospital for decayed burgesses was founded (in 1632) on the site of the Trinitarian monastery (McPherson, *The Kirk's Care of the Poor*, p. 164).

*Aberdeen, St Anthony.* A papal letter, dated in *CPR* (ix. 412) 8 January 1443/4, which is said to record a petition of the abbot and convent of St Anthony, Vienne, and the preceptor of St Anthony's, Leith, containing that "the brethren of the houses of Dundee and Aberdeen (and others) . . . on account of certain churches, chapels, oratories, etc., of theirs, dedicated to St Anthony, ask and receive alms", and which nominates mandatories to check this practice, has been taken to indicate that there were houses of the order of St Anthony at the places named. This was not the case. A supplication of the above abbot and convent and preceptor, 6 January 1444, shows that the alleged offenders were the Friars Minor of Dundee and the Friars Preachers of Aberdeen (Vat. Reg. Supp., 394. 77 (D) ).

*Arnbeg.* Land called the Spittal of Arnbeg, in the parish of Kippen, is mentioned, 26 January 1686 (*Perth Retours*, no. 943). There is, however, no evidence of a hospital here.

*Arngibbon.* There is a reference to land called the Spittal of Arngibbon, 7 September 1550 (*RMS*, iv. no. 517). Cf. *OPS*, i. 38. This land may have belonged to a hospital. There is nothing to show that it was the site of one.

*Auchintorlie.* Although the lands of Spittal are mentioned along with those of Auchintorlie, e.g. 14 October 1550 (*RMS*, iv. no. 530), no evidence of a hospital in this locality is forthcoming.

*Auchterderran.* From 30 April 1511 (*RMS*, ii. no. 3567), there are references to the lands of "Innerlochty alias Spittale", in this parish. Cf. also *Fife Retours*, no. 129 (20 April 1603); *RMS*, vii, no. 1058 (13 March 1627). No evidence of a hospital here can be found.

*Balfron.* The occurrence of the name Spittal in this parish permits of no specific explanation.

*Banff.* The hospital or bedehouse for eight poor women (*Antiqs. Aberd. and Banff*, ii, 114) was, in all likelihood, a post-Reformation foundation.

*Blairspittal.* The lands so named along with the Spittal in the barony of Buchanan(?) 18 February 1685 (*Perth Retours*, no. 936) can hardly be regarded as the site of a hospital.

*Cairnwell.* There is said to have been a hospital called Sheen Spidell or Old Hospital, on the road over the Grampians (*Collns. Aberd. and Banff*, p. 642; *Antiqs. Aberd. and Banff*, ii. 84). No record attesting its existence has been found.

*Cambuslang.* "It is said that two miles east from the church was an hospital, to which some lands, still called Spittal and Spittal-hill, seem to have been attached" (*OPS*, i. 61). Spittal, in the vicinity of Cambuslang, appears, 5 August 1668 (*Lanark Retours*, no. 308). But the occurrence of this place-name is quite inadequate evidence of the existence of a hospital.

*Crailing.* "An hospital and church or chapel existed at an early though unknown date at a place called Spital in Nisbet, now occupied by the modern mansion of Monteviot" (*OPS*, i. 387). But the sources cited for this statement (viz. *APS*, iv. 500, 538 and *Retours*) do not bear it out. *APS* refers to the joining of the churches of Crailing, Nisbet and Spittell in one parish, 9 July 1606. There is no indication of the location or nature of "Spittell". Again, the references to Spittal in the Roxburgh retours (nos. 126, 253) do not apply to this site, but to Ancrum Spittal, which was, in fact, the only hospital in the locality.

*Cullen.* "There was a hospital at Cullen which may have been associated with the collegiate church" (*Antiqs. Aberd. and Banff*, ii. 136–7). This connection, however, is highly improbable. There may have been more than one bedehouse at Cullen; but such foundations were post-Reformation. Thus, William Lawtie (†1657) endowed a bedehouse for poor men and women (decayed farmers and farmers' widows) (McPherson, *The Kirk's Care of the Poor*, p. 165). Again, a hospital is said to have been founded for men by the family of Findlater, while another was founded for women "by the present earl of Findlater his deceast Countess" (*Antiqs. Aberd. and Banff*, ii. 135–6). In the Old Statistical Account is a reference to a bedehouse for eight old men, which is said to be ruinous and removed (*Ibid.*, ii. 137 *n.*). The fact that the earldom of Findlater was not founded till 1638 suggests that foundations by this family were not earlier than the seventeenth century. We may assume that any hospital existing at Cullen was one of the fairly numerous bedehouses endowed in the north-east of Scotland after the Reformation.

*Dalnaspidal.* The existence of a hospital here is merely a surmise from the place-name ("the field of the hospital"). Nothing is known of any such foundation.

*Drymen.* The lands of Spittal of Drymen called Craginschedrach are mentioned, 12 July 1548 (*RMS*, iv. no. 227) and 18 November 1646 (*Stirling Retours*, no. 186), while other references to Spittal lands in this parish occur till 13 February 1685 (*Ibid.*, no. 295; cf. *OPS*, i. 38). No explanation of these place-names can be given, as evidence of a hospital here is wholly lacking.

*Dundee, Hospice.* "For cases of severe or protracted sickness the abbey [of Coupar Angus] owned a hospital at Dundee where medical aid could always be obtained" (*Cupar Angus* (ed. Rogers), i. xlvii). In this statement, imagination runs riot. It is true that the entry in the Rental Book of Coupar Angus, on which it purports to be based, is translated: "At Pentecost, 1469, the hospital of Dundee is let to William Tullach . . ." (*Ibid.*, i. 145); but reference to the original (GRH Registrum Assedationum, etc., B. Marie de Cupro (1443–1458), 12v) reveals that the phrase is "Hospitium Dunde". Likewise, the alleged mention of the garden of the hospital of Dundee in 1464 (*Cupar*, i. 147) is in fact a mention of the garden of the *hospitium* there (Registrum, 13v). There is no doubt that the so-called hospital was simply the abbot's lodging in Dundee. It is correctly mentioned as "hospitium nostrum" (*Cupar*, ii. 205). Oddly enough, in a reference to the abbot's lodging at Perth (*Ibid.*, ii. 64), the word *hospitium* is given and correctly translated.

*Dundee, St Anthony, v.* Aberdeen, St Anthony.

*Dundee, St John Baptist.* Although there is a reference to the chapel or hospital of St John Baptist, 4 July 1443 (*REB*, i. no. 53), St John's chapel, otherwise called the Rood chapel, is not elsewhere associated with a hospital. It stood considerably to the east of the leper house outside the burgh boundary and there is no evidence of a connection between them. The chapel seems to have become derelict by 6 March 1561/2 (Maxwell, *Old Dundee*, pp. 16 *n.*, 54, 177).

*Eckford.* There is a local tradition of the existence of a leper hospital in this parish, and a rivulet flowing into the Kale water is known as the Spittal or Spittalend burn. *OPS* (i. 397) also refers to a place called Spittalbank or Hospital Lands. No evidence of such a hospital has been found. "Massendew" is mentioned as one of the forty-four places on the "river of Kale" burned by the English, 17 September 1545 (*L. & P. H. VIII*, xx². nos. 458, 533). But it is difficult to accept this as a reference to a hospital at Eckford. It is more likely to be an erroneous reference to the Maison Dieu of Roxburgh.

*Edinburgh, Maison Dieu.* "There was an hospital likewise at Edinburgh, founded at Bell's Wynd. It was called, 'The Maison Dieu'." This statement of Spottiswoode (p. 475) has commonly been accepted, but no specific reference to a hospital here is available. "Le Masondew" appears as a place-name, 9 September 1477 (*RMS*, ii. no. 2014; *Reg. S. Egid.*, no. 86), and there is a mention of "the garden or land formerly called Maison Dieu . . . beside the place of the Friars Minor Observantines", 22 January 1489/90 (*RMS*, ii. no. 1923). If such a hospital existed here, it must have been defunct in or before the fifteenth century. Attempts to identify it with the later Magdalen Hospital seem to be based merely on the fact that both were near the Grey Friars.

*Edinburgh, St Andrew.* On 4 February 1560/1, the Town Council ordered their treasurer to make a payment to the bedesmen of "St Andros hospitale" (*EBR*, 1557–71, p. 98). This may be the hospital otherwise designated St Thomas's (*q.v.*), which is described, in a charter of 1622, as the hospital of St Thomas and St Andrew (*Laing Chs.*, no. 1911). In 1666, there is a reference to the patronage of the hospital of St Andrew and St Katherine, near Holyroodhouse (*Edinburgh Retours*, no. 1152), and this may be the same foundation.

*Edinburgh, St Giles.* A charter of 2 July 1566 is headed: "the hospital of Sanct Geils kirk sett in feu farm" (*Reg. S. Egid.*, no. 152). The text of the charter, however, reveals that this was "the hospice (hospitium) of the provostry within the cemetery of the said church"; and that, having been burned by the English, it was ruinous and in need of repair. It was in fact a residence for the provost and curate of St Giles for whom, in terms of the above charter, accommodation is to be reserved in it.

*Elgin.* In 1360, John, bishop of Moray, gave to four chaplains in the cathedral a "piece of land . . . held of the brethren of St Lazarus outside the walls of Jerusalem" (*REM*, no. 236). There is likewise a reference to "Lazarus Wynd" as a boundary of land, 25 June 1590 (*RMS*, v. nos. 1742, 1743). The Lazarites apparently held land at Elgin; but there is no evidence that they had a house there.

*Fala.* A charter of 13 May 1513 refers to "the lands of Edmonstoun and Ednam, with the gift of churches and chaplainries and the right of patronage of the hospital of Fawlo" (*RMS*, ii. no. 3844). There is said, in 1627, to have been a foundation of four bedesmen in Fala, which was apparently defunct and of which no information was available (*Rep. on State of Certain Parishes*, p. 65). This statement may point to the existence of a hospital here, though it may also be due to confusion with the neighbouring hospital of Soutra (*q.v.*). On the other hand, the church of Fala was held by the hospital of Ednam (*Ibid.*, p. 65), and it is possible that "hospital", in the 1513 charter, is an error for "church."

*Forda (Fordam).* In the narrative of the endowments of Holyrood abbey in David I's "Great Charter", 1128–53 (*Lib. S. Crucis*, no. 1), the phrase appears: "Hamere and Forda (or Fordam) with their proper marches and the hospital with a carrucate of land" (Hamere et Fordam cum suis rectis divisis et hospitale cum una carrucata terre). Lawrie annotates this as follows: "*Fordam*: Forda, a land in Whitekirk, where, it seems, there was a hospital for travellers." (*ESC*, p. 385). But there are two points of dubiety here. The hospital is an item separate from Hamere and Forda; and when these are mentioned elsewhere (e.g. *Lib. S. Crucis*, nos. 2, 27 and p. 169), there is no reference to a hospital. Further, there is nothing to bear out the statement that this was a hospital for travellers. This hospital can only be regarded as unidentified.

*Fyvie.* The idea that there was a hospital here is due to a wrong entry in the index of *REA* (ii. 374). "Hospitale S. Petri" clearly does not refer to Fyvie, but to the hospital of that dedication at Aberdeen (*Ibid.*, ii. 226–7). A charter of 20 June 1427 refers to the appropriation of the vicarage to the "monks in the religious house built on the land of Ardlogy, beside the *church* of the Blessed Peter of Fyvie" (*Ibid.*, ii. 225); but there is no mention in this or any other record of a hospital under this invocation at Fyvie.

*Glendye.* The occurrence of the place-name Spittal in this locality admits of no explanation. Evidence of a hospital is entirely lacking.

*Glenmuick.* There is said to have been a hospital at the east end of Loch Muick, where there is a pass, called the Caiple Month, to the hills of Clova (Angus) (*Collns. Aberd. and Banff*, p. 640). Its existence cannot be verified.

*Glenshee.* The earliest reference found is to the lands of "Spittale of Glensche" in a charter of sale by David Wemyss, lord of Strathardill [Strathardle], etc., 10 October 1542 (*Wemyss*, ii. no. 197). The possibility that there was a chapel in Glenshee is suggested by the mention of the Chapel-crofts in 1615 (*RMS*, vii. no. 1156) and 1641 (*Perth Retours*, no. 498). No evidence of a hospital here has been discovered.

*Gosford.* The supposition that there was a hospital here is due to the mention of the lands of Gosford along with those of Ballencrieff (where there was a hospital), e.g. 20 April 1421 (*Douglas Bk.*, iii. no. 60). Cf. references to the lands of Ballencrieff, Gosford and Spittall (i.e. land formerly belonging to the hospital) in 1551/2 and 1607 (*RMS*, iv. no. 151; vi. no. 1961). There was no hospital at Gosford.

*Hamilton.* "The land of St Mary of Bethlehem, mentioned as a burgh boundary, indicates an hospital endowed by the family of Hamilton and others in the lower part of the town. It appears to have belonged to the short-lived order of Our Lady of Bethlehem, founded by Pope Pius II in 1459" (*OPS*, i. 156). This remains conjectural. The only recorded bequests to a hospital here, e.g. in 1627–9, are post-Reformation.

*Harehope.* The fact that, in 1296, the master of the house of St Lazarus of Harop had letters from Edward I, directed to the sheriff of Edinburgh, for restitution of his house's lands (*Rot. Scot.*, i. 25) has given rise to the supposition that this house was situated in Scotland. It has thus been located at Harehope, in the parish of Eddleston in Peeblesshire (*OPS*, i. 211). This, however, is erroneous; the house in question was undoubtedly the hospital of Harehope in Northumberland. On 15 June 1376, Robert II granted to his son John, earl of Carrick, the lands of Prestisfelde, St Giles' Grange and Spetelton, in the sheriffdom of Edinburgh, which were in the king's hands by reason of the forfeiture of the brethren of Harehope, these brethren being at the faith and peace of the king of England and against the faith and peace of the king of Scots (*RMS*, i. no. 582). From this charter it appears not only that the brethren belonged to an English house but also that the lands held by them in Scotland were not those of Harehope in Eddleston parish. The assertion that this was a foundation of David I (*OPS*, i. 211) is likewise unwarranted; it is recorded that Waldeve, son of Edward, gave Harehope (in Northumberland) to the brethren of St Lazarus (1178+) (*CDS*, i. no. 1712; Hodgson, "The Hospital of St Lazarus and the Manor of Harehope", *Archaeol. Aeliana*, 3rd Ser., xix (1922), 77). There is, again, no ground for the statement: "It is sufficiently certain [*sic*] that the 'Harehope' of this charter (i.e. *RMS*, i. no. 582) is the . . . monastery of Holmcultram . . . which was commonly called also by the name of 'Harihop'" (*OPS*, i. 212). *OPS* relies unduly on a confused account in the *Scotichronicon* (ii. 161): "The monks of Harehope, otherwise Holme, founded by a grant of . . . King David . . . to which had been annexed certain lands in Lothian, near the royal town of Edinburgh, namely, Spitalton and 'Sant Gilysis' Grange." *V. Medieval Religious Houses: England and Wales*, p. 275.

*Hassendean.* Morton, referring to the settlement of a controversy between Jocelin, bishop of Glasgow, and William the Lion regarding the patronage of Hassendean church, declares: "They agreed that the revenues and property of the said church shall be devoted to some work of charity. The bishop therefore, with the consent of the king, conferred the patronage thereof, with its lands, tithes and dues, upon the convent of Melrose, to be used in founding and maintaining a house of hospitality at Hastenden [Hassendean] for the reception and entertaining of the wayfaring poor and pilgrims journeying to Melrose abbey. The hospital was afterwards called Monks' Tower" (*Monastic Annals*, p. 272). But Bishop Jocelin's charter (*Melros*, no. 121) says nothing about a "house of hospitality" at Hassendean. The bishop grants this church to Melrose "for the reception of the poor and of pilgrims coming to the house of Melrose"; and, again, "for the perpetual uses of the poor and of pilgrims". In other words, the bishop's donation was not intended to supply a hospice *at Hassendean*; its motive was to augment *at Melrose* the provision for the poor and pilgrims coming *there*. Further, the building known as "Hassendean Tower otherwise Monks' Tower" was a secular building, viz., a tower or fortalice (*OPS*, i. 318).

*Killearnan.* "At Spittal there is said to have been a religious foundation belonging to the Knights Hospitallers. The lands of Spittal occur in a record of 1599" (*OPS*, ii². 525). But Killearnan does not appear among the Hospitallers' properties listed in *Chs. etc. in the Chartulary of Torphichen*. The lands of "Kilernane and Spitle" are mentioned, 12 October 1693 (*Ross and Cromarty Retours*, no. 156), but there is nothing to show that this was the site of a hospital.

*Kintore.* There is a reference, in 1551, to four roods of land called the Hospital of Kintore (*REA*, i. 454). This land was so called because, as appears from a charter of 1499, it was held by the hospital of St Thomas the Martyr at Aberdeen (*Antiqs. Aberd. and Banff*, iii. 239).

*Kirkcowan.* The place-name Spittal occurs in this parish, but no explanation of it can be given.

*Lanark.* Spottiswoode (p. 477) says of the Lazarites that "Lanark belonged likewise to this sect [*sic*]." There is, however, no evidence of property held by this order at Lanark.

*Leith, St Nicholas.* "The fort of Leith had a chapel dedicated to St Nicholas. . . . The precise date of its erection is not known, but it is believed to have been founded after A.D. 1493. Adjoining it was the hospital of St Nicholas. The chapel and the hospital were much damaged in 1544 when the English attacked Leith" (Mackinlay, *Dedications* (*NS*), p. 434). This chapel, described as on the north side of the water of Leith (*Prot. Bk. of James Young.* no. 844), is frequently mentioned from 23 September 1488 (*Ibid.*, no. 123). But no mention of a hospital associated with it has been found and such a foundation must be regarded as very probably conjectural. The earliest indication of a hospital (apart from St Anthony's) at Leith would appear to be on 11 November 1657 (*EBR, 1655-65*, p. 70; cf. *Ibid.*, p. 181) and this was evidently post-Reformation.

*Linlithgow.* On 14 May 1496, Henry de Levingstoun of Middle Binning granted a tenement "to the chapel to be built anew in the place of his seven perches at the east end of the burgh of Linlithgow, in the Middleraw . . . with an almshouse (cum una domo hospitali elemosine)" (*RMS*, ii. no. 2333). This donation was confirmed under the great seal, 18 November 1496 (*Ibid.*), but no further evidence concerning the proposed almshouse has been discovered.

*Mauchline.* There are references to a *hospitium* here, 2 March 1533/4 and 1 September 1535 (*RMS*, iii. nos. 1369, 2569). On both occasions it occurs in the phrase "the place, houses and hospice of Mauchline"; and there are apparently no other references to it. What this *hospitium* was is entirely uncertain. It may have been a lodging for visiting representatives of Melrose abbey or for the "master" who probably supervised that abbey's property in this neighbourhood (*v.* Mauchline, under Cistercian Houses). It may have been an inn for travellers.

*Maybole.* A reference to *lands* called the "Masonedew", 9 October 1574, may point to the existence of a hospital, perhaps connected with the collegiate church. But of this there is no definite evidence. (The reference is *RMS*, iv. no. 2746.)

*Monymusk.* This is given in the heading of a charter (perhaps taken from the endorsement) *REA*, ii. 264) which reads: "Ad reformandum hospitale siue Kildey de Monymusk" ("Kildey" is a mutilated form of "Keledei", i.e. Culdees, with whom the charter is concerned); and also in the index to *REA*. There is, however, no reference to a hospital in the text of the charter and no mention elsewhere of a hospital at Monymusk. "Hospitale" is a blunder.

*Obsdale.* In the parish of Roskeen. The lands of Hospitill in the earldom of Ross, mentioned 1597, have been identified with those of Obstuill or Obsdale (*OPS*, ii. 469). But this identification is doubtful and leads nowhere. There is no evidence of a medieval hospital here. The only foundation connected with Obsdale which is on record is a chaplainry in Fortrose cathedral, mentioned 6 November 1547 (*RSS*, iii. no. 2529), 21 July 1570 (*Cal. of Writs of Munro of Foulis*, no. 84), 10 May 1583 (*RMS*, v. no. 588).

*Papa Stour.* The structures of which the foundations remain on Brei Holm, an islet fifty feet distant from Papa Stour, and which are known locally as the "leper houses" (*v. Hist. Mon. Comm. Rep.* (*Orkney and Shetland*), iii. 156) have been supposed to be of medieval origin. Dr Gordon Donaldson informs me that while an eighteenth-century leper settlement (rather than a hospital) here is well documented, he has found no reference to a medieval hospital.

*Peebles, Almshouse* (1). On 25 October 1462, land was granted for an almshouse of which the chaplain of Our Lady Chapel was to be "tutour and sursear" (*Chs. and Docs. rel. to Peebles*, pp. 146-7). There is no evidence that this almshouse was erected.

*Peebles, Almshouse* (2). On 1 October 1464, land was granted by the magistrates, at the request of the master of the Cross Kirk (the Trinitarian priory) for the building of an almshouse (*Chs. and Docs. rel. to Peebles*, p. 151). There is no evidence that this project matured.

*Perth, Hospice.* V. Dundee, Hospice (*supra*).

*Rutherglen.* The lands of Spittal and Spittalquarter, in the vicinity of Rutherglen, mentioned, 21 November 1607 (*RMS*, vi. no. 1991) and 20 December 1617 (*Lanark Retours*, no. 118), were probably associated with the hospital of Polmadie (*q.v.*). No evidence of a hospital at Rutherglen is forthcoming.

*Sanquhar.* The supposition that there was a hospital here (which may have originated with Spottiswoode (pp. 478-9)) is based on a reference to the warden of the "New Place of Senerwar", who, in 1296, swore fealty to Edward I (*CDS*, ii. no. 823). But it is not at all certain that this is an indication of a hospital (though the warden is described as a chaplain); and, as Spottiswoode (pp. 478-9) admits, the identification of this site with Sanquhar in Dumfriesshire is at best conjectural. A local historian (Brown, *Hist. of Sanquhar*, pp. 53-4) purports to give the situation of this hospital, but this needs verification. Brockie's statement (p. 1097) that there was a hospital of Sanquhar erected "as is supposed", by the ancient lords (reguli) of Galloway, is mere romancing.

*Selkirk.* According to Brockie (p. 1092), David, prince of Cumbria and earl of Northumberland (i.e. the future David I) wished to convert the former site of the monastery at Selkirk (*v.* under the Order of Tiron) into a hospital for the poor and sick and this hospital, governed by the monks of Kelso, remained till the Reformation. These statements would seem to be unfounded. No mention of a hospital here has been traced.

*Snawdon.* V. Thirlestane (*infra*).

*Spittal* (in the parish of Penicuik). This place-name survives, but evidence of a hospital is entirely lacking. H. F. Brown ("Newhall on the North Esk", *SHR*, xvi (1919), 178) mentions an alleged *hospitium* for travellers here, but does not attempt to authenticate it.

*Stewarton.* There are references to the lands of "le Spetale" (also called le Spittalis and Spittale) in the lordship of Stewarton (with some variants), 30 June 1452 and later (*RMS*, ii. nos. 583, 751, 1876, 3371). The significance of this place-name does not transpire. No evidence of a hospital in this vicinity has been found.

*Stonehouse.* "On the eastern side of the parish . . . at a place still called Spittal, stood formerly an hospital which is said to have been endowed with the lands of Spittal" (*OPS*, i. 109). These lands are mentioned as in the barony of Stonehouse, 10 March 1657 (*Lanark Retours*, nos. 266, 267; cf. *ibid.*, no. 328). No reference to a hospital here has, however, been discovered. It may be noted that James Hamilton of Stonehouse had a charter of the lands of Spittalshiels and other lands near Lanark, which belonged to St Leonard's hospital there (*RMS*, iii. no. 2838); and these lands are mentioned as being held by a later individual of the same name and designation, 6 August 1611 (*Lanark Retours*, no. 95). It does not seem possible, however, to infer that the lands of Spittal in Stonehouse parish were connected with St. Leonard's hospital.

*Stoneykirk.* The place-name Spittal occurs in this parish, but no explanation of this can be given.

*Tarves.* The hospital here for four poor men (*Collns. Aberd. and Banff*, p. 330) was very probably post-Reformation. The foundation is attributed to William Forbes of Tolquhon (*floruit, c.* 1584(?) ) (*Ibid.*, p. 330).

*Thirlestane.* A ruined building to the east of the farmhouse of Thirlestane has been identified with a hospital, evidently for poor men and women, to which references are found, 1674–1701, in the Lauderdale estate account books (*BNC*, xvi (1896–8), 23–4). It has been stated that "there is a strong probability that it dates from pre-Reformation times" (*Ibid.*, p. 23). In support of this is adduced a reference to "Spittle Snawdoun" near Thirlestane, 12 April 1557 (*Ibid.*, p. 24), though an earlier mention might have been cited, viz., in a charter, 15 April 1541,[1] which refers to the incorporation by the abbot of Dryburgh of this and other lands in the tenandry or lordship of Spittale (*RMS*, iii. no. 2332). The lands of Spittale Snawdoun are also mentioned as lying near the burgh of Lauder, 23 February 1562/3 (*Dryburgh*, pp. 298, 299). But it is impossible to say what this place-name signifies. It may indicate the existence of a pre-Reformation hospital at or near Thirlestane. On the other hand, there is nothing to suggest an association of the lands of Snawdon with the older hospital at Lauder (*q.v.*).

*Trefontains.* There is a mention here of a church or hospital (*v.* under Cistercian Nuns). But the existence of a hospital must be regarded as unconfirmed.

The place-name "Spittal" occurs in other localities where, for lack of evidence, it cannot be explained.

---

[1] This charter as printed (*RMS*, iii. no. 2332) gives "Spittle, Snawdoun", i.e. as two separate items. But it has been confirmed that the comma has been inserted in error and is not in the original.

SECULAR CANONS (I): CATHEDRALS

Information regarding the history, constitution and *personnel* of the Scottish cathedrals is very unequal and, in some instances, e.g. Lismore, altogether meagre. For only four of the medieval bishoprics—Aberdeen, Brechin, Glasgow and Moray—is a chartulary available; for others we have to be content with random references. Again, the foundation or restoration of a see is often difficult to date with precision[1] and may precede by a considerable interval the establishment of a cathedral and the setting up of a chapter. In certain cases *infra*, the foundation (or restoration) of the see is indicated by "S"; the foundation of the cathedral by "C". Where bishops and archdeacons held canonries, these are included in the figures given for "canons". It is virtually impossible to distinguish between chaplains and vicars and the numbers of these are mainly given as identical. Deacons and subdeacons (except when given as vicars) as well as acolytes, etc., are included with choristers under "other clergy". Where there are isolated references to cathedral *personnel*, especially in the case of chaplains and vicars, the date is given in brackets. Only at Dunkeld and Kirkwall can an accurate number of chaplains be mentioned at a specific date.

The following contractions are used: v. = vicars; ch. = chaplains; d. = deacons; sd. = subdeacons; ac. = acolytes; chr. = choristers; sac. = sacrist.

---

[1] The complex subject of the origins of the Scottish bishoprics has recently been discussed by Dr G. Donaldson ("Scottish Bishops' Sees before the Reign of David I", *PSAS*, lxxxvii (1952–3). 106–117). This article to which reference is made *infra*, re-examines the "conventional" attribution to David I of the establishment of most of the Scottish sees.

## SECULAR CANONS (I): CATHEDRALS

| Name | County | Minimum Income (1561) | Date of Foundation | Canons | Vicars, chaplains, etc. | Other clergy, choristers, etc. |
|---|---|---|---|---|---|---|
| *‡ ABERDEEN | Aberdeen | £5170 | –1157 | 13–28 | 20 (1506) 24 (1540) | 2 d. 2 sd. 2 ac. (1506) 6 chr. a sac. 8 chr. (1540) |
| *‡ BRECHIN | Angus | £1250 | –1150 S uncertain C (1150+(?)) | 11–13 (14?) | 17 (1453) | 6 chr. (1429) |
| ‡ DORNOCH | Sutherland | £1166 | 1146–50(?)S 1224–45 C | 10 | 10 (c. 1225(?)) 4 (1497) 3 (1561) | |

ABERDEEN. The traditions that a see was founded at Mortlach (*q.v.*) by Malcolm II, in 1011 (as given e.g. *Scotich.*, lib. iv, cap. xliv (i. 227)) or by Malcolm III in 1063 (as given *REA*, i. 3) and that the see was transferred by David I to Aberdeen in 1125 (*Ibid.*, ii. 247) are discussed *Ibid.*, i. xi ff.; Skene, *Celtic Scotland*, ii. 378; Lawrie, *ESC*, pp. 230, 354; cf. Donaldson, "Scottish Bishops' Sees before the Reign of David I", *PSAS*, lxxxvii (1952–3), p. 115. While early charters which support these traditions are spurious or suspect and the evidence of the *Book of Deer* (to which Dowden (*Bishops*, pp. 97–8) attaches considerable weight) is of somewhat uncertain value, there may well have been at Mortlach a bishopric of later Celtic (or pre-medieval) type. On 10 August 1157, Pope Adrian IV gave Edward, bishop of Aberdeen (1150–71) authority to institute monks or (secular) canons, at his will, in his cathedral (*REA*, i. 6). In 1256, there were thirteen canonries, including that of the dean and that held by the bishop (*Ibid.*, ii. 39–40). In 1526, twenty-eight (excluding the bishop's canonry) are named (*Ibid.*, ii. 254–5). The cathedral building was restored during the episcopate of Alexander de Kyninmund (†1380) (*Ibid.*, i. xxxi).

BRECHIN. According to Dowden (*Bishops*, p. 173), "it has been generally accepted that [the foundation of the bishopric] may be placed about 1150"; but its origins, though uncertain, are probably earlier (*v.* Donaldson, *op. cit.*, pp. 113–14). This was the site of a community of Culdees (*q.v.*), who formed the original chapter and were gradually superseded by secular canons, 1219–50. *V.* Skene, *Celtic Scotland*, ii. 400–2. According to a record of 1372, the canonries were originally eleven in number (*REB*, no. 15), but two were added, in 1384/5 and 1474 respectively (*Ibid.*, pp. 17, 94), while the prebend of Guthrie was probably extinguished, *c.* 1480 (*v.* Guthrie, under Secular Canons (II) ). Seventeen vicars and chaplains of the choir appear, 17 November 1453 (*Ibid.*, ii. no. 52), but, judging from the chaplainries and altars mentioned in the episcopal records, there were probably more. *V.* Brechin, under Secular Canons (II).

DORNOCH. That the see of Caithness was placed here was in all probability due to the previous existence of a Celtic foundation. The see is said to have been founded by David I, between 1146 and 1150 (Lawrie, *ESC*, p. 408) and Dr Donaldson is of opinion that, of the Scottish sees, Caithness "has by far the strongest claim to be regarded as a new foundation by David" (*PSAS*, lxxxvii, 116). It was not till the time of Bishop Gilbert (?1224–1244 or 1245) that a constitution was made for the cathedral, which he proposed to rebuild. Hitherto, it is said, the church had been served by a single priest. Following apparently the pattern of Moray, he provided, *c.* 1225, for a chapter of ten canons, one of whom, was the bishop and another the abbot of Scone. The bishop and the dignitaries were bound to provide priests as their vicars (i.e. in the cathedral) and the simple canons vicars in deacon's orders (*Bannatyne Misc.*, iii. 11–14, 17–21). *V.* also *Origine Parochiales*, ii². 601 ff.; Skene, *Celtic Scotland*, ii. 382–4.

## SECULAR CANONS (I): CATHEDRALS

| Name | County | Minimum Income (1561) | Date of Foundation | Canons | Vicars, chaplains, etc. | Other clergy, choristers, etc. |
|---|---|---|---|---|---|---|
| ‡ DUNBLANE | Perth | £640 | c.1150(?) S 1237+C | 9(1296) −14+ | 9(1522) 12(1532/3) | ? |

DUNBLANE. There was an early Celtic foundation here, but the presence of Culdees (*q.v.*) cannot be authenticated. Dowden suggests that the bishopric was founded, *c.* 1150 (*Bishops*, p. 193), though this may have been a reconstitution rather than a foundation (Donaldson, *op. cit.*, p. 116). A canon is mentioned, *c.* 1190 (*Inchaffray*, no. 1). But a bull of Pope Gregory IX, 11 June 1237, describes the decay of the church of Dunblane as this is portrayed by Bishop Clement (1233–1256 or 1258)—the church's property has long been alienated to laymen; for ten years it has been bereft of a pastor; there is no *collegium*; the service is maintained by "a certain rural chaplain"; and the bishop's income is hardly sufficient to maintain him for half a year. The papal mandatories are now enjoined to make provision for the bishop from the fourth part of the teinds of the parishes of his diocese, out of which also he is to assign portions for the dean and canons whom the mandatories are to institute. Alternatively, they are to assign to the bishop the fourth part of all churches of the diocese held by laymen and to transfer the see to the monastery of St John [Inchaffray], the canons of which are to have power to elect the bishop when the church of Dunblane is vacant (*Lib. Ins. Missarum*, xxx = *Aberbrothoc*, i. no.176 = Theiner, *Vet. Mon.*, no. xci). The latter course was not followed; for, soon after (1 July 1238), we find the church of Kippen assigned for a prebend to the dean (*Lib. Ins. Missarum*, xxxi) and, on 29 January 1239/40, the dean, precentor and archdeacon attest a charter (*Inchaffray*, no. lxvii). On the latter date also, the abbot of Cambuskenneth is granted a canonry of Dunblane (*Cambuskenneth*, no. 125). About the same time, the abbot of Inchaffray was given the precentorship (*Inchaffray*, xxxvii), while the abbot of Arbroath became a canon, *c.* 1239 (*Aberbrothoc*, i. no. 241). In 1296, an episcopal election had been made by these abbots (as canons),[1] the dean, archdeacon, chancellor, treasurer and two other canons (*CPR*, Letters, i. 567). In fifteenth and sixteenth century records there are mentions of prebends of Aberfoyle, Abernethy, Balquidder, Comrie, Crieff, Kippen, Logie and Monzie, but how many of these represent additions to the chapter –1296 it is difficult to say. A subdean is mentioned, 18 January 1532/3 (*RMS*, iii. no. 1257). Nine chaplains are recorded, 14 May 1522 (*HMC Rep.*, *Var. Collns.*, v. 70) and twelve chaplains (of the choir), 18 January, 1532/3 (*RMS*, iii. no. 1257).

---

[1] The abbot of Inchaffray appears here as "preceptor", a not uncommon blunder for "precentor".

## SECULAR CANONS (I): CATHEDRALS

| Name | County | Minimum Income (1561) | Date of Foundation | Canons | Vicars, chaplains, etc. | Other clergy, choristers, etc. |
|---|---|---|---|---|---|---|
| *‡ DUNKELD | Perth | £3400 | 12 c.(?) S –1337 C | 9–22 | 13 | 6 chr. |
| * ELGIN | Moray | £5000 | –1124(?)S 1208–15 (Spynie) C c.1224 (Elgin) | 8–24 | 17 ch.(1350) 25 ch.(1350+) 17–18 v.(1489) 14 ch.(1566–72) | some |

DUNKELD. This was the site of a Celtic bishopric. *V.* Skene, *Celtic Scotland*, ii. 370 ff. The bishopric is said to have been revived by Alexander I (1106/7–1124) (Dowden, *Bishops*, p. 47), but this is a supposition based on "the first, casual, isolated mention of the name of a bishop" (Donaldson, *op. cit.*, p. 112). Originally the diocese included the territory of the diocese of Argyll, which was separated from it *c.* 1200 (Dowden, *op. cit.*, p. 51; Myln, *Vitae*, p. 8). Myln declares that the building of the cathedral was begun by Bishop William Sinclair (1309/10–1337) (*Vitae*, p. 13); this church was dedicated by Bishop Thomas de Lawder in 1464 (*Ibid.*, pp. 22–3). About 1220, the archdeacon, precentor and seven canons are mentioned (*Coupar Angus*, i. no. xxviii; cf. *Lib. S. Crucis*, p. 53; *Inchaffray*, no. xlviii; *Inchcolm*, no. xiv). According to Myln, Bishop Geoffrey (1236–49) reconstituted the cathedral after the pattern of Sarum, provided for a dean, added to the canons' endowments and erected an additional prebend (*Vitae*, p. 10). (There is a reference to the dean and chapter of Dunkeld, in 1236 (*CPR, Letters*, i. 157), but as they are associated with the postulation of Geoffrey as bishop, the mention of them may be no more than "common form"). In 1238, we find on record the dean (a former canon), precentor, archdeacon, treasurer, subdean, succentor and one canon (*Inchaffray*, no. lxv). In the episcopate of Bishop George Browne (1485–1514/5), when Myln wrote his account of the bishops, there were, on the latter's statement, a dean, precentor, chancellor, treasurer, archdeacon, subdean, succentor and fifteen canons (*Vitae*, pp. 2, 55–68); and this is confirmed as the state of the chapter, in 1564 (*Rentale Dunkeldense*, pp. 346–51).

ELGIN. Lawrie declares: "It would be rash to say positively that there was not a bishop of Moray before 1124, but it is permissible to say that there is no good evidence that there was" (*ESC*, p. 283). *V.* Donaldson, *op. cit.*, p. 115. According to a charter, 1208–15, of Bishop Brice, his predecessors had no fixed place for their see, but alternated between Birnie, Spynie and Kinnedar. This bishop now fixed his see at Spynie (*REM*, no. 46). But, in 1224, the see was transferred to Elgin (*Ibid.*, nos. 26, 57, 58; Theiner, *Vet. Mon.*, no. lii (10 April 1224)), where the cathedral was founded on 19 July of that year (*REM*, no. 58). On 17 June 1390, it was burned, along with the canons' and chaplains' houses, by the "Wolf of Badenoch" (*Ibid.*, no. 303). Bishop Brice's foundation was for eight canons, including the dean, precentor, treasurer, chancellor and archdeacon. The constitution of the cathedral was modelled on Lincoln (*Ibid.*, no. 46). "It is an interesting fact", says Dowden,"'that the earliest account of the constitution of Lincoln that now appears anywhere is to be found in the document supplied [i.e. *Ibid.*, no. 48] . . . at request by the dean and chapter of Lincoln to the dean and chapter of Moray" (*Medieval Ch. in Scotland*, p. 65). It was, however, ordained, in 1242, that the use of Sarum should be followed in the services of the church (*REM*, no. 93). During the episcopate of Andrew de Moravia (1222–42), the bishop was assigned an existing canonry and fifteen new canonries were added (*Ibid.*, no. 81); not until 1542 was another canonry erected (*Ibid.*, p. 474). Bishop Andrew also made provision for seventeen vicars of whom seven (priests) were to be provided by the chancellor, treasurer, archdeacon, subdean and succentor and two canons; five (deacons) by five of the canons; and five (subdeacons) by the five remaining canons. The eighth canon (of Croy) is to act as bishop's vicar and the subdean and succentor are apparently regarded as vicars of the dean and precentor (*Ibid.*, no. 81). This number seems to have varied little; in 1489, arrangements are made for the payment of eighteen vicars (stallers) and a sacrist (*Ibid.*, no. 210). How far these correspond with the seventeen resident chaplains mentioned, 1331–50 (*Ibid.*, no. 227), it is impossible to say. The chaplainries numbered twenty five shortly after this date (*Ibid.*, no. 278). The number of boy-choristers is not given but provision was made, in 1489, for their instruction (*Ibid.*, no. 210).

## SECULAR CANONS (I): CATHEDRALS

| Name | County | Minimum Income (1561) | Date of Foundation | Canons | Vicars, chaplains, etc. | Other clergy, choristers, etc. |
|---|---|---|---|---|---|---|
| * FORTROSE (ROSEMARKIE) | Ross and Cromarty | £2100 | temp. David I (1124–53)(?) | 8 (1226) –18(?) | 5+v.(1255) 3 ch.(1543–6) | some |
| ‡ GLASGOW | Lanark | £4400 | –1197 | 7(9?)–33 | 11–numerous | 4+chr. |

FORTROSE (ROSEMARKIE). There was apparently a Celtic foundation here but the presence of Culdees (*q.v.*) is not authenticated. The see of Ross "emerges in the reign of David I" (Dowden, *Bishops*, p. 209), but may have antedated it (Donaldson, *op. cit.*, p. 116). Little information is forthcoming on the development of the chapter. A charter of 1 February 1226/7 is signed by the bishop of Ross (as canon), the, dean treasurer, archdeacon (who is also a canon), two canons of Ross, a canon who is also parson of Ardersier and another canon of Ross who is also a canon of Moray (*REM*, no. 65). On 27 May 1236, Pope Gregory IX conceded the bishop's petition that he might increase the meagre revenues of the prebends and institute new ones (Theiner, *Vet. Mon.*, no. lxxx); and a letter of Pope Alexander IV, 9 February 1255/6, specifies a deanery, precentorship, chancellorship, treasurership, archdeaconry, and other prebends, as well as a subdeanery and succentorship (*Ibid.*, no. clxxxii). According to this document, the dean is to be elected "as in the church of Sarum", but there is no further suggestion that Salisbury is the model of the cathedral constitution. A papal letter, 5 January 1324/5, shows that the abbot of Kinloss was a canon of Ross (*Kinlos*, p. 120); and a rental of 1574 indicates that the abbey paid for a "staller" in the cathedral (*Ibid.*, p. 159). Bisset gives the number of members of the chapter as eighteen, including dean, precentor, chancellor, treasurer, subdean, succentor and archdeacon (*Rolment of Courtis*, ii. 40). Dowden declares that "eventually the prebends reached some nineteen or twenty in number" (*Med. Ch. in Scotland*, p. 63). It is difficult to check these figures.

GLASGOW. The see is said to have been "revived" by Earl David (afterwards David I), *c.* 1115 (Dowden, *Med. Ch. in Scotland*, p. 8). Cf. Donaldson, *op. cit.*, pp. 114, 116. There seems to be no suggestion of Culdees at Glasgow; and, apart from its legendary association with St Kentigern, its connection with the Celtic church, if such there was, is difficult to define. The church of Glasgow was dedicated, 7 July 1136 (*Chron. Holyrood*, p. 119) and the church of Govan was granted it as a prebend, 1147–64 (*REG*, no. 7). During the episcopate of Bishop Jocelin (1174–99), there is a reference to a dean and six canons, 1188–98 (*Melros*, no. 121; cf. *Ibid.*, no. 43), and that bishop dedicated the cathedral which he had built anew, 6 July 1197 (*Chron. Mailros*, p. 103). The constitution of the cathedral of Salisbury was, with certain modifications, adopted as a model for Glasgow in 1258 (*REG*, i. nos. 207, 208, 211, 213–14). In 1266, the dean, precentor, chancellor, treasurer and subdean are mentioned, and they, with the other canons (whose number is not specified), are to provide for their vicars (*Ibid.*, i. no. 212), for whom, with the deacon and subdeacon, a house is supplied in 1270 (*Ibid.*, i. no. 220). In 1325, there are ten canons, besides the dignitaries and the two archdeacons (*Ibid.*, i. no. 273); in 1401 twenty-three prebends are listed; and, *c.* 1430, six new prebends were added by Bishop John Cameron (*Ibid.*, ii. no. 340). On 17 February 1501/2, the chapter consisted of the dean, precentor, chancellor, treasurer, subdean, the two archdeacons, and twenty six canons (*Ibid.*, ii. 611–2). Glasgow was erected into an archiepiscopal and metropolitan see by a bull of Pope Innocent VIII, 9 January 1491/2 (*Ibid.*, ii. no. 459).

## SECULAR CANONS (I): CATHEDRALS

| Name | County | Minimum Income (1561) | Date of Foundation | Canons | Vicars, chaplains, etc. | Other clergy, choristers, etc. |
|---|---|---|---|---|---|---|
| ‡ KIRKWALL | Orkney | £1100 | –1137 S 1137 C | 6(–1544) 14(1544) | 6(–1544) 13(1544) | 6 chr. (1544) |
| ‡ LISMORE | Argyll | | *c.* 1200 S uncertain C | 9(?) | ? | ? |

KIRKWALL. On the early bishops of Orkney, *v.* Dowden, *Bishops*, pp. 253 ff. Orkney was made a suffragan bishopric of Nidaros by a bull of Pope Anastasius IV, 1 December 1154. On 17 August 1472, Pope Sixtus IV brought it under the jurisdiction of the archbishop of St Andrews (Dowden, *op. cit.*, pp. 255, 261). The see is said to have been first at Christ's Kirk, Birsay, from which it was moved to Kirkwall on the erection of the cathedral founded by Earl Rognvald in 1137 (J. Anderson, *Orkneyinga Saga*, lxxiv, lxxxvii–lxxxviii). Of the constitution of the cathedral little is known until the sixteenth century. On 28 October 1544, a charter of Bishop Robert Reid declares that there are six canons and as many chaplains and proceeds to establish a provost, archdeacon, precentor, chancellor, treasurer, subdean and succentor, seven other prebendaries, thirteen chaplains and six boy-choristers (*RMS*, iii. no. 3102).

LISMORE. The diocese of Argyll or Lismore was formed by subdivision from Dunkeld. *V.* Dowden, *Bishops*, p. 377. Its history is obscure. The view that the see was first located at Muckairn, on the south side of Loch Etive (*v.* Skene, *Celtic Scotland*, ii. 408) seems to be based merely on the interpretation of the place-name Killespeckerrill as "the church of Bishop Harold" and is entirely conjectural. There are said to have been Culdees (? in Lismore) (*q.v.*), but of this evidence is wanting. A reference to the dean and chapter of Lismore, in 1203 (*CPR, Letters*, i. 15) may be no more than "common form". On 7 July 1236, the bishopric, which had been in the charge of the bishop of the Isles, is said to be in great poverty (Theiner, *Vet. Mon.*, no. lxxxiv); and, on 2 January 1249/50, the Pope empowered the bishops of Glasgow and Dunkeld to transfer the see of Argyll from the island of Lismore to a safer and more convenient place (*CPR, Letters*, i. 251). But no such step was taken. There is a mention of a canon of this church, in 1250 (*Passelet*, p. 134), likewise of the dean and "all the chapter", in 1251 (*RMS*, ii. no. 3136). Sporadic record evidence attests that the chapter consisted of the four dignitaries, with the archdeacon and an uncertain number of canons. At least four prebends are mentioned in the fifteenth century (*CPR, passim*): Glassary, Kilchousland (St Constantine in Argyll), Kilcolmkil (St Columba in Argyll) and Kilmodan (St Modan of Glendaruel), and these seem to have been held by simple canons. The archdeacon and two canons attest a charter, in 1557 (GRH. Chs., no. 1691). In 1512, James V proposed to the Pope that, as the cathedral of Lismore was ruinous and deserted, the see should be transferred to Saddell in Kintyre and a new cathedral erected there (*Letters of James IV*, no. 446). This did not take place. *V.* Saddell, under Cistercian Abbeys.

### NOTE ON "MONASTIC" CATHEDRALS

ST ANDREWS. For the history of the bishopric of St Andrews during the "Celtic" period, *v.* Skene, *Celtic Scotland*, ii. 323 ff. It is evident that already in this period, the bishopric was approximating to its later pattern and status. The last of the Celtic bishops, Fothad, died in 1093. In 1109, Turgot began the line of medieval bishops. On the foundation of the Augustinian priory in 1144, the canons formed the chapter of the cathedral. There was also a body of Culdees attached to this church which, despite David I's provision for their eventual replacement by regular canons, persisted and later made repeated assertions of their right to participate in episcopal elections. *V.* Skene, *op. cit.*, ii. 324 ff., and especially Barrow, "the Cathedral Chapter of St Andrews and the Culdees in the Twelfth and Thirteenth Centuries", *JEH*, iii (1952), 23 ff.

WHITHORN. This see was revived probably by Fergus of Galloway during the reign of David I (1124–53). The first bishop was elected *c.* 1125 and consecrated 1128 or later. The cathedral is said to have had canons regular who were "changed into Premonstratensians" during the episcopate of Bishop Christian, 1154–86. *V. Trans. Dumfriesshire and Galloway Nat. Hist. and Antiq. Socy.*, 3rd Ser., xxvii, 104, 139.

*Iona.* According to Dowden (*Bishops*, p. 289) it was *c.* 1430 that "bishops were appointed to Man as a diocese under York and also to the Scottish Sodor or the Isles". Iona abbey became the cathedral of the Isles as a Scottish diocese, 1498-9. *V.* under Iona and St German's (Isle of Man). This can hardly be called a monastic cathedral as there is no evidence that the monks of Iona formed the chapter. No indication of a chapter, indeed, exists.

As appears *supra* (pp. 167-68), Aberdeen and Inchaffray might have (but did not) become the sites of monastic cathedrals.

SECULAR CANONS (II): COLLEGIATE CHURCHES

With such exceptions as Restalrig and St Mary on the Rock, St Andrews (destroyed by the Reformers), St Mary in the Fields, Edinburgh and Peebles (destroyed by the English) and the Chapel Royal at Stirling (rebuilt in 1594), the Scottish collegiate churches (i.e. their buildings) survived the Reformation and more than half their number, in whole or in part, are still extant. No column appears in the following list to show the date at which these churches ceased to function in their collegiate capacity because it may be assumed that, in general, their career as secular colleges was closed with the abolition and outlawry of the mass by the acts of parliament of 1563 and 1567 (*APS*, ii. 535; iii. 22). Many of these churches continued as parish churches; some which had not previously been parochial became so. It should be noted that for some time after the Reformation presentations to prebends and chaplainries in collegiate churches continued to be made. This was due to the act of parliament of 1567 (*Ibid.*, iii, 25) which ordained that such benefices might be granted, as bursaries, to students at the universities.

| Name | County | Minimum Income (1561) | Founder | Date of Foundation | No. of clergy Prebendaries etc. | Chaplains | Others |
|------|--------|------------------------|---------|--------------------|------------------|-----------|--------|
| ‡ ABERDEEN, KING'S COLLEGE | Aberdeen | £390 | William Elphinstone, bishop of Aberdeen | –1500 | 32–36 | | 4–6 |

ABERDEEN, KING'S COLLEGE. On the petition of James IV the erection of a *studium generale* at Old Aberdeen was sanctioned by a bull of Pope Alexander VI, 9 February 1494/5 (*Fasti Aberd.*, p. 1). The foundation of a college is first mooted in an instrument of 22 May 1497 when certain sums are "to be applied to the support of the collegiate church, to be founded by the bishop in the said university" (Rait, *Univs. of Aberdeen*, p. 29); and an inscription over the west door of King's College chapel indicates that building was begun in the spring of 1500 (*Ibid.*, p. 30). The founder, William Elphinstone, bishop of Aberdeen, provides by his charter of 17 September 1505, for thirty-six persons: a master or licentiate in theology, who is to be principal; a doctor of canon law; a doctor of medicine; a master of arts, regent in arts, who is to be subprincipal; a second master of arts, who is to be grammar regent—these, except the M.D., are prebendaries; five masters of arts, students of theology; thirteen scholars or poor clerks; eight prebendaries, of whom one is to be cantor, the other sacrist; and four choristers (*Fasti Aberd.*, p. 46). On 18 December 1529, a charter of Gavin Dunbar, bishop of Aberdeen, extended the foundation to provide for forty-two persons: four doctors—of theology, canon law, civil law and medicine—the first to be principal; eight masters of arts, the first to be subprincipal, another to be grammar regent, the remaining six to be students of theology; two masters of arts, bachelors or students one in civil law, the other in canon law; a student of civil law; thirteen scholars; eight prebendaries, the first to be cantor, the second sacrist; and six choristers (*Ibid.*, p. 68). St Germains hospital (*q.v.*), with certain reservations, was appropriated to the college. *V.* further *Fasti Aberdonenses* (Spalding Club, 1854); Rait, *The Universities of Aberdeen* (1895).

O

## SECULAR CANONS (II): COLLEGIATE CHURCHES

| Name | County | Minimum Income (1561) | Founder | Date of Foundation | No. of Clergy Prebendaries etc. | Chaplains | Others |
|------|--------|----------------------|---------|--------------------|--------------------------------|-----------|--------|
| ‡ ABERDEEN, ST NICHOLAS | Aberdeen | | | 1540 | 22–16–? | | |
| ABERNETHY | Perth | £240 | One of the Abernethies of Abernethy | –1345 | 6–11–6 | | |
| ‡ BIGGAR | Lanark | | Malcolm, Lord Fleming | 1545/6 | 9 | | 4 |

ABERDEEN, ST NICHOLAS. This large parish church, the rectory of which was assigned to the sixth prebend of the cathedral in 1256 (*REA*, ii. 40), had, in the fifteenth century, a considerable body of chaplains. For these, regulations were made by Ingeram de Lyndesay, bishop of Aberdeen (1441–59) (*Cart. S. Nich.*, i. no. cxxii), a step which has been regarded as "nothing less than the constituting of St Nicholas' a collegiate church" (*Ibid.*, ii. xxvi); but this is an exaggeration. In 1491, when there were twenty-two chaplains (*Ibid.*, i. no. cxxiv), the church is prematurely described as collegiate (*RMS*, ii. no. 2033). About this time, the number of chaplains was apparently reduced to sixteen (*Cart. S. Nich.*, i. no. cxxv). New statutes made on 14 July 1519 (*Ibid.*, i. no. cxxvi), contemplate, however, a quasi-collegiate organization; while thirty-four stalls were ordered for the new choir (*Ibid.*, ii. 346), which was evidently completed early in the sixteenth century. But it was not till 28 March 1540 that William Gordon, bishop of Aberdeen, with the consent of the dean and chapter, gave the vicarage of St Nicholas' to "the College of the Chaplenis of the said Sanct Nicolas kirk . . . for sustentatioun of ane prouest" (*Ibid.*, ii. 381), thus completing the collegiate constitution of the church.

ABERNETHY. Erroneously stated to have been founded by George, earl of Angus, *c.* 1450 (*CCM*, iv). The community of Culdees (*q.v.*) here was succeeded by Augustinian canons, who are said to have formed a priory in 1272 or 1273 (*Scotich.*, lib. x, cap. xxxiii (ii. 120)). *V.* under Augustinian Canons. This priory appears in turn to have been transformed, in the earlier fourteenth century, into a college of secular canons, the head of which for some time retained the title of prior (*RMS*, i. App. 1, no. 141 (*anno* 1359); *CPR*, Pet., i. 579 (*anno* 1394)), though that title had been changed to provost by 31 May 1456 (*Ibid.*, xi. 306). A canon of Abernethy, who may have been regular, is mentioned in 1325 (*Ibid.*, ii. 243), but a secular canon appears in 1345 and 1349 (*Ibid.*, Pet., i. 89, 145). We find Margaret, countess of Angus (eldest daughter and co-heiress of Sir Alexander Abernethy, who married John Stewart, earl of Angus, *c.* 1328), described in 1364 as "patron of the church, lineal descendant of the original founders, lords of Abernethy" (*Ibid.*, iv. 215), but it is not clear whether these were founders of the priory or of the collegiate church. The collegiate foundation was initially for a prior and five canons; and the number of the latter was raised to ten on the prospective increase of the church's income. But as this augmentation did not take place, the bishop of Dunblane, 8 February 1364/5, reduced the number to the original five (*Ibid.*, pp. 214–15). As the result of a petition of the prior and chapter, the Pope commissioned the bishop of St Andrews to inquire into the circumstances of the college, 8 April 1373 (GRH Vat. Trans., i. 102), and, on 31 October 1375, confirmed the reduction (*CPR*, iv. 214–15).

BIGGAR. Founded in the parish church by Malcolm, Lord Fleming, 16 January 1545/6, for a provost, eight prebendaries, and four choristers (*Spalding Club Misc.*, v. 296 ff.). An almshouse was attached to it. *V.* under Hospitals.

## SECULAR CANONS (II): COLLEGIATE CHURCHES

| Name | County | Minimum Income (1561) | Founder | Date of Foundation | Prebendaries, etc. | No. of Clergy Chaplains | Others |
|------|--------|------------------------|---------|--------------------|--------------------|------------------------|--------|
| § BOTHANS | E. Lothian | £162 | Sir William Hay, Thomas Boyd, Eustace de Maxwell, and Dougal McDowal | 1421 | 5–7 | | |
| ‡ BOTHWELL | Lanark | £423 | Archibald, earl of Douglas | 1397/8 | 7–8 | | 2 |
| § CARNWATH | Lanark | | Thomas de Somerville | 1424 | 7 | | |
| ‡ CORSTORPHINE | Midlothian | £434 | Sir John Forrester | 1429 (–1436/7) | 5–9 | | 4 |

BOTHANS. Spottiswoode (p. 466), whose account of the foundation is inaccurate and confused (*v.* Yester *infra*), gives this erroneously as "Botham". It is also mistakenly called "St Bothan's" (e.g. *CCM*, iii)—this is the name of a Cistercian nunnery in Berwickshire; but Bothans in East Lothian had no connection with this saint; its patron was St Cuthbert. The erection by Henry, bishop of St Andrews, of the college in this parish church is dated 22 April 1421, following on a petition of Sir William Hay, sheriff of Peebles, Thomas Boyd, Eustace de Maxwell, and Dougal McDowal, co-lords of the lordship of Yester and patrons in turn of this church, made, 1 August 1420, and with provision for a provost and four chaplains (*Yester Writs*, nos. 53, 55). Two additional chaplainries were added, 30 July 1443, and 23 January 1535/6 (*Ibid.*, nos. 85, 522).

BOTHWELL. The petition of Archibald, earl of Douglas, for the erection of this parish church to collegiate status, with a provost and six prebendaries, was granted by the Pope, 21 February 1397/8 (GRH Vat. Trans., ii. 30 ff.). Spottiswoode (p. 466) and *OPS* (i. 54) give the date of foundation as 10 October 1398 and the number of prebendaries as eight. On 30 January 1477(/8), the Pope appointed a mandatory to confirm the erection of an additional prebend, with provision for two boy clerks (*CPR*, x. 340–1; cf. *OPS*, i. 54).

CARNWATH. The list appended to the *Scotichronicon* (ii. 541), MS. lists and Spottiswoode (p. 466) ascribe this foundation to Thomas de Somerville. Spottiswoode also states that the foundation was for a provost and six prebendaries and gives the date as 1424 (this is followed by *OPS* (i. 126) ). The date is also given as 1425–30 (*Memorie of the Somervilles*, i. 166). Apart from a reference to a prebendary (*OPS*, i. 126), this college does not seem to be mentioned in records, but an aisle is extant. *V.* Carnwath under Hospitals.

CORSTORPHINE. This collegiate church originated in a chapel beside the parish church; the foundation of three chaplainries there was confirmed under the great seal, 25 February 1425/6 (*CCM*, pp. 293–5). Two more chaplains and two clerks were added, 20 May 1429 (*Ibid.*, p. 295); and an inscription in the church attributes the foundation to that year. The foundation charter is not extant, but a college of a provost, four other priests and four choristers had been founded by Sir John Forrester before 7 January 1436/7 (*CPR*, viii. 595), while, on 30 October 1444, in terms of a bull of Pope Eugenius IV, the bishop of St Andrews sanctioned the addition of four chaplains (instead of five as originally proposed) (*CCM*, pp. 298–303; cf. *CPR*, viii. 595; x. 476).

SECULAR CANONS (II): COLLEGIATE CHURCHES

| Name | County | Minimum Income (1561) | Founder | Date of Foundation | No. of Clergy Prebendaries, etc. | Chaplains | Others |
|---|---|---|---|---|---|---|---|
| ‡ CRAIL | Fife | | William Myrton, vicar of Lathrisk, and others | 1517 | 11 | | probably some |
| ‡ CRICHTON | Midlothian | £233 | William, Lord Crichton | 1449 | 9 | | 2 |
| ‡ CULLEN | Banff | | Alexander Ogilvy of that ilk, Alexander Dick, Archdeacon of Glasgow, John Duff of Muldavit and others | 1543 | 7 | | 2 |

CRAIL. The first indication of the proposed erection of a college in the parish church is apparently a charter recording the vicar's consent to the erection of the vicarage into a provostry, 3 March 1516/7 (*Reg. Coll. Ch. of Crail*, no. 102). The erection was initiated by a petition, dated 7 and 8 June 1517, and directed to Andrew [Forman], archbishop of St Andrews, by Jonet, prioress of the Cistercian nunnery of Haddington (which held the church of Crail) and William Myrton, vicar of Lathrisk, for the confirmation of their proposals for a provostry, ten prebends (seven of which originate in seven chaplainries founded by Myrton) and a clerkship, of which the endowments are set forth (*Ibid.*, no. 101). On 20 June following, the archbishop ratified the collegiate foundation (*Ibid.*, no. 103). In the version of the archbishop's charter given in *Formulare* (i. no. 288), the bailies, councillors and community of Crail and the parishioners of the church are named among the petitioners. These are mentioned (*Reg. Coll. Ch. of Crail*, no. 101) in respect of their consenting to the erection of two existing chaplainries into prebends as the prioress of Haddington nunnery appears consenting to the annexation of the vicarage to the provostry (*Ibid.*, nos. 47, 101). But in an undated charter of the above archbishop of St Andrews, confirming additional statutes for the college, Myrton is designated its "first and principal founder" (*Formulare*, i. no. 290). The archbishop's charter of 20 June 1517 provides for instituting four choristers (*Reg. Coll. Ch. of Crail*, no. 103), and although there is no further mention of these, one of Myrton's charters of endowment, 22 October 1520, assigns the charge of the song school to the second prebendary (*Ibid.*, no. 47) and another, 9 November 1525, makes provision for a grammar school (*Ibid.*, p. 12). On 10 May 1587, James VI grants to the bailies and councillors of Crail, for the maintenance of the church, school and hospital of the burgh, the collegiate church, with its benefices and properties (*RMS*, v. no. 1197).

CRICHTON. Founded in the parish church by William, Lord Crichton, chancellor of Scotland, 26 December 1449, for a provost, eight prebendaries and two boy-choristers (foundation charter as in *CCM*, pp. 306 ff.). *V. CCM*, lxxvii–lxxxii, 305–12.

CULLEN. Founded in the parish church by Alexander Ogilvy of that ilk, Alexander Dick, archdeacon of Glasgow, John Duff of Muldavit, the bailies, councillors and community of Cullen, and the parishioners of the church, 23 April 1543, for a provost, six prebendaries and two boy-choristers (foundation charter as in Cramond, *Church and Churchyard of Cullen*, pp. 34 ff.).

## SECULAR CANONS (II): COLLEGIATE CHURCHES

| Name | County | Minimum Income (1561) | Founder | Date of Foundation | No. of Clergy Prebendaries etc. | Chaplains | Others |
|---|---|---|---|---|---|---|---|
| ‡ DALKEITH | Midlothian | | Sir James de Douglas | 1406 | 6–11 | | 3 |
| DIRLETON | E. Lothian | | Sir Walter Haliburton | 1444 | Only a provost mentioned | | |
| DUMBARTON | Dunbarton | £340 | Isabel, duchess of Albany, countess of Lennox | c. 1454 | 7 | | |
| DUNBAR | E. Lothian | £690 | Patrick, earl of Dunbar | 1342 | 10 | | some(?) |

DALKEITH. On 21 June 1406, six chaplains, one of whom was to be provost, were endowed in the chapel of St Nicholas by Sir James de Douglas, lord of Dalkeith (*CCM*, p. 313; *Reg. Hon. de Morton*, ii. 324). Three prebendaries and three clerks or choristers were added, 17 May 1477 (*Reg. Hon. de Morton*, ii. 230, which gives details omitted in *CCM*, p. 319), and two further chaplains, 20 July 1503 (*CCM*, p. 323). This collegiate church became the parish church of Dalkeith, 1 October 1467 (*Ibid.*, cxvi). As early as 1396, a hospital was attached to St Nicholas' chapel. *V.* under Hospitals.

DIRLETON. This church is said to have been founded by Sir Walter Haliburton in 1444 (Spottiswoode, p. 467). A similar statement is made in the list appended to *Scotichronicon* (ii. 541), where it is added: "Here he established a provost, but nothing was done for the project" (hic constituit praepositum sed nihil factum ad propositum). The name of a provost (John Burgon) is given in that year (Wallace-James's MS. Notes on the Parishes of Dirleton and Dunbar, GRH.), and others appear in 1464 (Hutton's Collns., v. 12) and 1579 (Prot. Bk. of Thomas Steven, iii. 182²). There are also references to the provostry from 1539 (*Rentale S. And.*, p. 55) to 1600 (*APS*, ii. 215); in 1561, it is described as "the provostry of the chapel of the castle of Dryltoun, situated near the castle of the same" (*N. Berwic*, p. 82). This was obviously a small foundation. There is no mention of other clergy than the provost, a title which may have been borne by a single priest serving the chapel.

DUMBARTON. A papal mandate was issued, following on the petition of Isabel, duchess of Albany and countess of Lennox, for the erection of the chapel of St Mary (not of St Patrick, as given by Spottiswoode (p. 468)) into a collegiate church, with a provost and a sufficient number of chaplains, 3 January 1453/4 (*CPR*, x. 623–4). It is said to have been endowed for a provost and six prebendaries (*OPS*, i. 24–5). The hospital of Polmadie was proposed to be transferred to it (*CPR*, loc. cit.), and a hospital (at Dumbarton) is found attached to it in the sixteenth century. *V.* under Hospitals.

DUNBAR. Patrick, fifth earl of Dunbar, is said to have founded a collegiate church here in 1218 (*Scots Peerage*, iii. 252), while Spottiswoode (p. 467) attributes the foundation to George, earl of March, in 1392. Both statements are erroneous. The foundation charter shows that the college was founded in the parish church by Patrick, ninth earl of Dunbar, and second or fourth earl of March, 21 September 1342, for a dean, an archpriest and eight prebendaries (*SHS Misc.*, vi. 89–97). In 1501, the archpriestship and five prebends were appropriated to the Chapel Royal of Stirling (*Reg. Cap. Reg. Striv.*, pp. 4, 14). *V. SHS Misc.*, vi, 81–109.

## SECULAR CANONS (II): COLLEGIATE CHURCHES

| Name | County | Minimum Income (1561) | Founder | Date of Foundation | No. of Clergy Prebendaries etc. | Chaplains | Others |
|---|---|---|---|---|---|---|---|
| * DUNGLASS | E. Lothian | £160 | Sir Alexander Home | 1443/4(?) | 3–13(?) | | 4 |
| DUNROSSNESS | Shetland | | ? | ? | several | | |
| ‡ EDINBURGH, ST GILES | Midlothian | | Magistrates and community | 1466–9 | 17 | numerous | 4 |

DUNGLASS. On 30 November 1423, Alexander Home made certain donations to the chapel of St Mary of Dunglass and "the presbyters there serving God" (*HMC 12th Rep.*, App., Pt. VIII, 123); and this chapel was the nucleus of the collegiate church. The date of the collegiate foundation is given as 1403 (*CCM*, iii) and also as 1450 (Spottiswoode, p. 468). The former date appears in the foundation charter but is clearly an error. On 22 August, 1450, James II, confirming the charter granted in 1423 by Alexander Home, father of Sir Alexander Home, refers to the chapel as lately founded as a collegiate church (*HMC 12th Rep.*, App., Pt. VIII, 123–4). The date of the founder's charter, 12 March 1403, may thus be intended for 12 March 1443 (1443/4). According to this writ, the college was founded by Sir Alexander Home in the chapel of St Mary of Dunglass for a provost, two chaplains and four boy-choristers (*Ibid.*, pp. 124–6). It is difficult to ascertain the eventual number of prebends. Nine are mentioned in 1481 (GRH Chs., no. 496), another was endowed in 1503 (*HMC 12th Rep.*, App., Pt. VIII, 177–8) and at least three others are indicated (*HMC Rep. Milne Home MSS.*, pp. 55, 75, 181). A hospital was attached to this church, which also held the hospital of Hutton (*v.* under Hospitals). *V. Trans. East Lothian Antiq. Socy.*, iv (1948), 15–17.

DUNROSSNESS. Dr Gordon Donaldson has given me a reference to the gift of a prebend, called the Cross Stouk, in the "college kirk" of Dunrossness, 21 June 1590 (RSS, lx. 141). Though there are no pre-Reformation references, the foregoing seems to show that this was a collegiate church. The "Croce stowk" is mentioned as a benefice separate from the vicarage of Dunrossness, 1561+ (*Thirds of Benefices*, pp. 2, 48). Dr Donaldson has also suggested that other "stowks" mentioned in Shetland, e.g. the "small Stowk in Northmavin callit St Michaelis Stowk" and the "lytil Stowk callit Osta" (Goudie, *Celtic and Scandinavian Antiquities of Shetland*, p. 157) were probably prebends of this church.

EDINBURGH, ST GILES. On 19 July 1419, Pope Martin V appointed a mandatory to deal with the petition of the provost, bailies and community of Edinburgh for the erection of this parish church to collegiate status (*CPR*, vii. 136). This had no result. But, on 21 October 1466, James III assented to a similar proposal (*RMS*, ii. no. 887); and on 26 February 1468/9, Pope Paul III granted the petition of the magistrates and community for its erection for a provost, sacrist and minister of the choir, fourteen prebendaries and four choristers (Theiner, *Vet. Mon.*, no. dcccxxxvii). Forty-nine altars in this church are listed (*Reg. S. Egid.*, xciv–xcv), but this figure is probably not entirely accurate.

## SECULAR CANONS (II): COLLEGIATE CHURCHES

| Name | County | Minimum Income (1561) | Founder | Date of Foundation | No. of Clergy Prebendaries, etc. | Chaplains | Others |
|---|---|---|---|---|---|---|---|
| EDINBURGH, ST MARY IN THE FIELDS | Midlothian | | Holyrood abbey | c. 1510 | 11 | | |
| EDINBURGH, TRINITY COLLEGE | ,, | £532 | Mary of Gueldres, queen of Scots | –1460 | 9–11 | | 2 |

EDINBURGH, ST MARY IN THE FIELDS. This collegiate church is said to have been founded by master David Vocat (EU. MS. Db. 6.19; NLS. MS. 22.1.14). This may be regarded as improbable. Vocat was a chaplain in this church in 1509 (*CCM*, cxi) and appears as provost in 1527 (*Ibid.*); he is also frequently mentioned as master of the burgh's grammar school (e.g. *LHT. Accts.*, iv. 240, 242; *RMS*, iii. no. 918; *Lib. S. Crucis*, p. 257). In litigation between the abbey of Holyrood and the provost of this church in 1523, it was claimed that the abbey, which held the patronage of St Mary's in the Fields, had had it erected into a collegiate church (*ALC., 1501–54*, p. 178). The date of the foundation is indicated by the facts that, on 21 March 1510/11, there is a reference to the prebendaries (*CCM*, p. 261), that, on 19 September 1511, lands passed to its possession for the building of houses for the "master" and chaplains (*Ibid.*, pp. 261–2), and that, on 23 October 1512, there is a further mention of the provost and prebendaries (*Ibid.*, pp. 262–3). The foundation is said to have been for a provost and ten prebendaries (NLS. MS., 31.3.13). The prebendaries' houses and the hospital attached to it (*q.v.*) are stated to have been destroyed by the English, 1544–7 (*CCM*, xxxvii). On 21 June 1563, a contract is recorded between the provost of Kirk o' Field and the Town Council for the sale to the latter of the buildings (*Edin. BR., 1557–71*, p. 163); and, on 9 August 1564, the council arranged for the purchase of the stonework, which was being taken down, "owther [either] for the hospitall or for ane vniuersite to be maid in the said Kirk of Feild [sic]" (*Ibid.*, p. 182). This became the site of the college which developed into Edinburgh University. *V. CCM*, xxxiii–xlii, 261–272.

EDINBURGH, TRINITY COLLEGE. A bull of Pope Pius II, 23 October 1460, annexes the hospital of Soutra (*q.v.*) to the college and hospital of the Holy Trinity, founded by Mary, queen of Scotland [Mary of Gueldres, widow of James II] (*CCM*, p. 57; *Chs. Trin. Coll.*, no. 1). The foundation had taken place somewhat before this date; and the queen's charter, 25 March 1462 (which is no doubt the foundation charter), ordained the constitution of the college and assigned the endowments (*Ibid.*, pp. 64 ff.; *ibid.*, no. 11). Provision was made for a provost, eight chaplains and two choristers as well as for thirteen bedesmen (*v.* Trinity College Hospital). Two additional prebendaries, one of whom was to be called dean, were provided, 14 November 1502 (*Chs. Trin. Coll.*, no. vi). A letter of James V to Pope Clement VII, 23 March 1531/2, desired an indulgence for penitents visiting Trinity College, where the provost had planned to bring the rest of the church into keeping with the nobly constructed choir (*Letters of James V*, p. 217, from Tyninghame Letter Bk.). The prebendaries' houses are said to have been destroyed by Reformers in 1559 (Lesley, *History*, p. 275). On 12 November 1567, James VI granted the church and hospital to Sir Simon Preston, provost of the city and the provost, bailies, councillors and community, as his successors (*Chs. Trin. Coll.*, no. x), and again, to the latter, 26 May 1587 (*Ibid.*, no. xiv). This church, "the last and finest Gothic fragment in Edinburgh", was made parochial *c.* 1580 and continued in use till 1848, when it was removed to make a site for the Waverley Station (*v. CCM*, xxix–xxxi; Cockburn, *Memorials* (1909 ed.), p. 414 *n.*). *V. CCM*, xii–xxxii; *Chs. Trin. Coll.*, pp. 57–258.

SECULAR CANONS (II): COLLEGIATE CHURCHES

| Name | County | Minimum Income (1561) | Founder | Date of Foundation | No. of Clergy Prebendaries etc. | Chaplains | Others |
|------|--------|------------------------|---------|--------------------|--------------------------------|-----------|--------|
| ‡ Fowlis (Easter) | Angus | | One of the Lords Gray | –1538 | 8 | | |
| Glasgow, Our Lady College | Lanark | | James Houston, subdean of Glasgow | 1525 | 9–12 | | 3 |
| Guthrie | Angus | | Sir David Guthrie of Guthrie | c. 1479 | 5 | | |
| ‡ Haddington | E. Lothian | | Magistrates and community | c. 1540 | | numerous | |

FOWLIS (EASTER). An inscription in this church indicates that it was built in 1453, probably by Andrew, Lord Gray, who is frequently regarded as the founder of the college (e.g. *Scotich.*, ii. 541; NLS. MS. 33.2.12, 9; Spottiswoode, p. 468). This building may have replaced an earlier parish church. But a note in NLS. MS. 34.3.11 attributes the collegiate foundation to a later Lord Gray, viz., Patrick, who succeeded to the title in 1514 and died in 1541, as well as the confirmation of this foundation and the consecration of the church to James Beaton, archbishop of St Andrews (1522–39). The sixteenth-century erection of the college gains credence from the fact that the first mention of a provost, along with seven prebendaries, is found in 1538 (Prot. Bk. of Thomas Ireland, f. 3). *V.* Dalgetty, *Hist. of the Ch. of Fowlis Easter* (1933).

GLASGOW, OUR LADY COLLEGE. Founded by James Houston, subdean of Glasgow. There are indications from 20 February 1522/3 that this foundation was contemplated (*Lib. Coll. Nostre Domine*, xii, 79, 80, 83 *n.*). On 29 April 1525, the archbishop of Glasgow approved the foundation of this church, the building of which had begun (*Chs. and Docs. rel. to Glasgow*, ii. 494–7). The original foundation was for a provost, eight prebendaries (one of whom was archpriest), and three choristers; and three prebendaries were later added (*Lib. Coll. N.D.*, xv and *passim*). The building was in use as a parish church from 1592 to 1793, when it was destroyed by fire. *V. Lib. Coll. Nostre Domine, passim*; *Chs. and Docs. rel. to Glasgow*, i. Pt. I, lix–lxi.

GUTHRIE. The date of foundation has been given as *c.* 1456 (*CCM*, iv), but this is too early. Spottiswoode (p. 468) describes Sir David Guthrie of that ilk as founder and the latter is thus designated in a charter which also shows that his death took place before the proposed foundation was complete (*RMS*, ii. no. 2910). On 19 May 1479, the Pope, in response to a petition of Sir Alexander Guthrie, Sir David's son and successor, containing that his late father enlarged and adorned the parish church of Guthrie, then a prebendal church of Brechin cathedral, with a view to its erection into a collegiate church, consented to the extinction of the prebend and the erection of the church for a provost and four canons (*CPR*, xiii. 137). There is a reference to annates to be paid in the name of the provost and chapter of Guthrie, "newly erected into a collegiate church", 24 July 1483 (*Scottish Benefices*, p. 207). Only three prebends, besides the provostry, were at first endowed; but provision was made for a fourth canonry, 30 September 1505 (*RMS*, ii. no. 2910).

HADDINGTON. About 1540, the priests of this large parish church, already mentioned, 20 May 1537, as "the college kirk of Haddington" (Wallace-James's MS. Notebooks, GRH., Miscell., i. 77), were, on the initiative of the bailies, councillors and community, formally constituted as a college, under a president (*Formulare*, ii. no. 435). There is a reference to the "prebendars of the College kirk", 5 December 1540, and another to the "president of the College kirk", 22 May 1541 (Wallace-James's MS. Notebooks, GRH., Miscell., i. 83, 85 (from burgh records) ).

## SECULAR CANONS (II): COLLEGIATE CHURCHES

| Name | County | Minimum Income (1561) | Founder | Date of Foundation | No. of Clergy Prebendaries etc. | Chaplains | Others |
|------|--------|------------------------|---------|--------------------|----------------------------------|-----------|--------|
| HAMILTON | Lanark | | James, Lord Hamilton | 1450/1 | 7 | | |
| § INNERPEFFRAY | Perth | | John, Lord Drummond (?) | 1506–42 | some | | |
| § KILMAURS | Ayr | | William Cunningham, lord of Kilmaurs | 1413– | 9 | | 2 |
| § KILMUN | Argyll | | Sir Duncan Campbell of Lochawe | 1441 | 6 | | |

HAMILTON. The foundation in the parish church by James, Lord Hamilton, confirmed by Pope Nicholas V, 4 January 1450/1 (Theiner, *Vet. Mon.*, no. dcclvii), was for a provost and six chaplains. *V. OPS*, i. 106.

INNERPEFFRAY. This church is not noted by Spottiswoode nor in MS. and other lists. A chapel of St Mary is mentioned, 28 November 1365 (*Inchaffray*, p. 128) and 10 May 1483 (*Oliphants*, no. 37); and, on 3 February 1506/7 (or 4 February, according to *Oliphants*, no. 77), four chaplainries were endowed there by John, Lord Drummond (*RMS*, ii. no. 3048). It thus appears to have been a chantry which acquired a collegiate form. On 25 October 1542, this is called a collegiate church (*Ibid.*, iii. no. 2825); and there are references to provosts in 1562 and 1567 (NLS. MS. 16.1.1; *RMS*, iv. no. 2378), and to a "provost or principal chaplain of the church of the Blessed Mary of Innerpeffray" (Macfarlane's Notes (NLS. MS.), p. 34). The provostry is mentioned, 11 February 1548/9 (*ALC, 1501–1554*, p. 581) and in 1566 (*Thirds of Benefices*, pp. 15, 255).

KILMAURS. The date of foundation is given as 13 May 1403 (Spottiswoode, p. 469; NLS. MS. 35.4.16, 9), but this is too early. The foundation charter is not extant, but the endowment of three chaplainries in the parish church by William Cunningham, lord of Kilmaurs, 14 May 1413 (Hutton's Collns., vii. 101; McNaught, *Kilmaurs Parish and Burgh*, pp. 325–6) was probably the origin of the college. This is said by Spottiswoode (p. 469) to have been founded for a provost, eight prebendaries and two boy-choristers, but evidence is lacking.

KILMUN. The document entitled "Fundatio Collegii de Kilmun" (NLS. MSS. 22.1.14, 217; 34.3.11, 156; printed *RMS*, ii. no. 346) and dated 4 August 1442, is a charter of endowment rather than of foundation. On 5 August 1441, the Pope granted the petition of Sir Duncan Campbell of Lochawe for the confirmation of the erection of the parish church of St Mund into a collegiate church for five chaplains, one of whom will be provost (Vat. MS. Reg. Supp., pp. 375, 124). *OPS* (ii¹. 71) says a provost and seven prebendaries. Annates paid in the name of the provost and five chaplains "to be constituted in the parish church of St Mund ... on its erection into a collegiate church" are recorded, 5 October 1441 (*Scottish Benefices*, p. 129).

### SECULAR CANONS (II): COLLEGIATE CHURCHES

| Name | County | Minimum Income (1561) | Founder | Date of Foundation | No. of Clergy Prebendaries etc. | Chaplains | Others |
|------|--------|------------------------|---------|---------------------|-------------------------------|-----------|--------|
| * LINCLUDEN | Kirkcudbright | £540 | Archibald de Douglas, lord of Galloway | 1389 | 9–11 | | |
| * MAYBOLE | Ayr | | John Kennedy of Dunure | 1383/4 | 3–4 | | 1 |
| § METHVEN | Perth | £790 | Walter Stewart, earl of Athole, Caithness and Strathearn | 1433 | 6 | | 4 |
| § PEEBLES | Peebles | | Magistrates and John Hay of Yester | 1543 | 13 | | 2 |

LINCLUDEN. Originally a Benedictine nunnery. *V.* under Benedictine nuns. On 7 May 1389, the Pope, on the petition of Archibald de Douglas, lord of Galloway, commissioned the bishop of Glasgow to suppress the nunnery and to erect a collegiate church for a provost, eight priests and twenty-four bedesmen (GRH. Vat. Trans., i. 288 ff.). The date of foundation is given erroneously as 1413 (*CCM*, iv). An additional chaplainry was founded, 22 September 1429 (*RMS*, ii. no. 123), and apparently another prebend was added, 1525/6–1541 (*Formulare*, ii. no. 358). On 3 June 1508, the Pope consented to the annexation of the provostry of Lincluden to the Chapel Royal at Stirling (GRH. Vat. Trans., iii. 163 ff.; *Hist. C.R. of Scotland*, cxlv); but the union was dissolved before 27 October 1529 (*Letters of James V*, p. 161; cf. *RSS*, ii. no. 210). A hospital was attached to this church. *V.* Holywood Hospital. On Lincluden, *v. Trans. Dumfriesshire and Galloway Nat. Hist. and Antiq. Socy.*, xxiii. 190–5.

MAYBOLE. On 29 November 1371, a chapel was founded by John Kennedy of Dunure beside the churchyard of the parish church, for three chaplains and a clerk (*RMS*, i. nos. 378, 428). A college was founded there by Kennedy, 1 March 1383/4, for a provost, two chaplains and a clerk (*Crosraguel*, i. no. 21)., and a third chaplainry was endowed, 18 May 1451 (*RMS*, ii. no. 446). The date of foundation is given erroneously as 1441 (Spottiswoode, p. 470; *CCM*, iv).

METHVEN. Founded in the parish church by Walter Stewart, earl of Athole, Caithness and Strathearn, for a provost, five chaplains and four boy-choristers, 1 May 1433 (*CPR*, viii. 460–1). The date is given erroneously as 1439 (*CCM*, iv). About 1516, there was a "new erection" (*RSS*, i. nos. 2782, 2798), but details of it are lacking.

PEEBLES. On 8 June 1543, Mary, queen of Scots, ratified the foundation in the parish church by the bailies, councillors and John Hay of Yester of a college consisting of a provost, twelve prebendaries (ten, according to *OPS*, i. 229) and two choristers (*Chs. and Docs. rel. to Peebles*, pp. 61–4). On 17 December 1560, this church is said to have been "brint and distroyit be Yngland xii yeris syne or thairby" (i.e. *c.* 1548) (*Ibid.*, p. 264).

## SECULAR CANONS (II): COLLEGIATE CHURCHES

| Name | County | Minimum Income (1561) | Founder | Date of Foundation | Preben-daries etc. | No. of Clergy Chap-lains | Others |
|---|---|---|---|---|---|---|---|
| § RESTALRIG | Midlothian | £530+ | James III | 1487 | 9 (10(?)) | | 2 |
| ‡ ROSLIN | ,, | | Sir William Sinclair | *c.* 1521 | 5 | | |

RESTALRIG. A bull of 13 November 1487 confirms the foundation by James III (not James II, as in Spottiswoode (p. 471)) of a collegiate church, the building of which has been begun, for a dean and an unspecified number of prebendaries (*CCM*, pp. 273 ff.). Eight prebendaries were instituted by James IV and James V, with provision for a further prebend (*Ibid.*, pp. 280 ff.). In 1487, the church is called "the king's chapel beside the parish church of Restalrig" (*ER*, ix. 540), and in 1497, the dean is designated as of "the chapel royal of Restalrig" (*Ibid.*, xi. 2). On 9 April 1512, James IV asked for the renewal and confirmation by Pope Julius II of the privileges granted to this church, founded by his father (*Letters of James IV*, no. 440). According to a charter of 1552, the prebendaries' houses had been "burned and almost destroyed" by the English (*HMC Rep., MSS. in Various Collns.*, v. 68). In 1560, the church was ordered by the Reformed General Assembly to be demolished (*CCM*, lix). *V. CCM*, xlii–lxiv, 272–92.

ROSLIN. The suggestion that this celebrated church, founded by William, earl of Caithness of Orkney, in 1446, was from the outset collegiate, is frequently made (e.g. Spottiswoode, p. 471; Hay, *Genealogie of the Sainteclaires*, p. 26); Spottiswoode adds that the foundation was for a provost, six prebendaries and two choristers. It is described, in 1456, as a "college kirk" (*Bannatyne Misc.*, iii. 96). Again, charters of 10 December 1476 and 5 January 1491/2 refer to the "preses" or "presidens" and prebendaries (*RMS*, ii. nos. 1270, 2076; Hay, *Genealogie*, p. 83). No provost, however, is mentioned till 5 February 1523/4 (*CCM*, p. 328). It appears that hitherto the collegiate organization had been incomplete; the head of the group of priests bore the title of "preses" or president. In the *Formulare* (i. no. 389), the formal erection of this church to collegiate status is attributed to Andrew Forman, archbishop of St Andrews (†11 March 1520/1), whose undated charter purports to erect it, on the petition of Sir William Sinclair, into a "perpetual college" for a provost and four prebendaries. The editors of the *Formulare*, however, point out (*Ibid.*, i. 348 *n.*) that as this document cannot have been issued before 18 May 1521, it must have been given by Archbishop James Beaton, Forman's successor. It was probably granted about the same time as Sinclair's charter providing manses for the provost and prebendaries, 5 February 1523/4 (*CCM*, pp. 328–31).

## SECULAR CANONS (II): COLLEGIATE CHURCHES

| Name | County | Minimum Income (1561) | Founder | Date of Foundation | No. of Clergy Prebendaries etc. | Chaplains | Others |
|---|---|---|---|---|---|---|---|
| St Andrews, St Mary on the Rock | Fife | £500 | Continuation of Culdees | c. 1250 | 11(?) | | |
| ‡ St Andrews, St Salvator | ,, | | James Kennedy, bishop of St Andrews | 1450 | 3–10 | numerous (*v.* Cant, *College of St Salvator,* pp. 21 ff.) | 6(?) |
| * Semple, or Lochwinnoch | Renfrew | | John, Lord Semple | 1504 | 7 | | 3 |

St Andrews, St Mary on the Rock (Kirkheugh). This college was a development of the community of Culdees (*q.v.*), whose head and members are thus described, 5 November 1250: "Master Adam de Malkarviston conducting himself as provost of the church of St Mary of the city of St Andrews and the Culdees conducting themselves as canons" (NLS. MS. 15.1.18, 30); while a bull of 7 April 1251 refers to the "provost and secular chapter" of St Mary's (*Inchaffray*, p. 154). In 1344, it is still designated "St Mary of the Culdees" (*CPR*, iii. 150, 152). This church had the dignity of a chapel royal. It is difficult to say when it acquired this status, but it may have been so regarded from the time of its inception as a secular college. Thus there is a reference in a mandate of Edward I, 10 September 1298, to the "provostry of the king's free chapel of St Andrews" (*CDS*, ii. no. 1017). On 24 January 1385/6, Pope Urban VI granted a petition of Robert II, who desired that the provost of the chapel royal should, like the archdeacons of St Andrews, be given a stall, a place in the cathedral chapter and a voice in elections (GRH. Vat. Trans., i. 250 ff.). Attempts were made in the fifteenth century to have the revenues of the priory of Coldingham annexed to this church (*v.* Coldingham). In 1501, the provostry of St Mary's was united to the deanery of the Chapel Royal of Stirling, but this arrangement was revoked in 1504 (*Reg. Cap. Reg. Striv.*, p. 82). This church is said to have had a provost and ten prebendaries (Spottiswoode, p. 469; NLS. MS. 35.4.16); Martine says "at least nine" (*Reliquiae Divi Andreae*, p. 217). But, on 5 April 1425, Henry, bishop of St Andrews, "having regard to the fewness of persons in the Chapel Royal of St Mary . . . who are seven in number and not more", endows a new prebend (*RPSA*, p. 407); while a petition granted by Archbishop Forman (†1520/1), for the erection of another prebend, states that there are only eight (*Formulare*, i. no. 131). The charter of erection of a third additional prebend, also granted by Forman, is given in *Formulare* (i. nos. 121, 122), but it is uncertain whether this took place. This church is said to have been pulled down by Reformers in June 1559 (Lesley, *History*, p. 273). *V.* Barrow, "Cathedral Chapter of St Andrews and Culdees", *JEH*, iii. 23–9.

St Andrews, St Salvator. The date of foundation is given as 1458 (*CCM*, iv); this, however, is the date of the revised charter of foundation (Cant, *Coll. of St Salvator*, p. 80). The original foundation charter was granted by James Kennedy, bishop of St Andrews, 27 August 1450, providing for a provost, who is to be a master of theology, a licentiate and a bachelor of theology, four masters of arts and six poor clerks (*Univ. Comm. Rep., St And.*, pp. 270 ff.; Cant, *op. cit.*, pp. 1, 54 ff.; A. I. Dunlop, *Life and Times of James Kennedy*, pp. 274–5). The foundation was confirmed by Pope Nicholas V, 5 February 1450/1 (Theiner, *Vet. Mon.*, no. dcclix). There were at least seven additions to the three original prebends (including that of the provost), though it is not certain that all of these were permanent (Cant., *op. cit.*, pp. 28–30).

Semple, or Lochwinnoch. Founded by John, Lord Semple, 21 April 1504, for a provost, six chaplains, a sacrist and two choristers (*REG*, ii. no. 483).

## SECULAR CANONS (II): COLLEGIATE CHURCHES

| Name | County | Minimum Income (1561) | Founder | Date of Foundation | No. of Clergy Prebendaries, etc. | Chaplains | Others |
|---|---|---|---|---|---|---|---|
| * SETON | E. Lothian | | George, Lord Seton | 1470–92 | 7 | | 3 |
| STIRLING, CHAPEL ROYAL | Stirling | £1270 | James IV | 1501 | 19–32(?) | | 6 |

SETON. On the petition of George, Lord Seton, Pope Paul II gave a mandate for the erection of this parish church, on its voidance by the present rector, into a collegiate church for a provost, six canons, a clerk and two choristers, 13 April 1470 (*CPR.*, xi. 346). On 22 December 1492 Pope Alexander VI, on the petition of George [II], Lord Seton, appointed mandatories to carry out the erection as the church was now vacant (NLS. MS. 15.1.19, 15).

STIRLING, CHAPEL ROYAL. The attempt to endow a chapel royal from the revenues of Coldingham priory (*q.v.*), 1472–87, did not succeed. On 2 May 1501, Pope Alexander VI, on the petition of James IV, sanctioned the erection of the Chapel Royal of St Mary and St Michael, Stirling, into a collegiate church for a dean, subdean, sacrist, sixteen canons and six choristers. The provostry of St Mary on the Rock, St Andrews, was to be erected into the deanery of the Chapel Royal, Stirling, to form a joint dignity, the holder having pre-eminence in both churches. Provision was also made for the partial appropriation of the revenues of Restennet priory (*q.v.*), of certain prebends of the collegiate church of Dunbar (*q.v.*), and of some fifteen parish churches (*Reg. Cap. Reg. Striv.*, no. 1). In 1502, one of the canonries was erected into a precentorship (*Ibid.*, no. 2) and, in 1504, a treasurership and ten lesser canonries were added (*Ibid.*, no. 8). A succentorship is mentioned in 1506 (*RSS*, i. no. 1341), in 1507 an archdeaconry was adumbrated (*Ibid.*, i. no. 1560), and in 1527 a chancellor appears (*RMS*, iii. no. 497). On 3 July 1504, on the petition of James IV, Pope Julius II revoked the union of St Mary on the Rock and the Chapel Royal and united the deanery to the bishopric of Galloway [Whithorn], so that the bishop of that diocese would be dean of the Chapel Royal (*Reg. Cap. Reg. Striv.*, nos. 15, 17). On 3 October 1506 and 6 April 1507, James IV is found asking the Pope and the Cardinal of St Mark that the dean should have his title altered to bishop and that the priory of Inchmahome (*q.v.*) should be annexed to the episcopal *mensa* (*Letters of James IV*, nos. 52, 53, 101). These requests had apparently been granted before 1 March, 1507/8, when the king intimates his desire that besides Inchmahome priory, the priory of Restennet (which evidently had not yet been appropriated) and the provostry of Lincluden should be annexed to it (*Ibid.*, no. 156). The Pope, 3 June 1508, consented to these appropriations (GRH. Vat. Trans., iii. 168–9), but, on 8 November following King James is found mentioning, in a letter to the Cardinal of St Mark's, that the annexation of Restennet had not taken effect (*Letters of James IV*, no. 195; cf. no. 201). On 1 March 1507/8, the king had asked that the bishop of Galloway and the Chapel Royal should be inferior to no other (*Ibid.*, no. 156) and, on 1 August 1511, requested the Pope to confirm the privileges of the bishop of the Chapel Royal, conferring upon him jurisdiction over the king and his household, as well as over annexed churches of royal patronage and their parishioners and to declare that the Chapel Royal, in this respect, covered all the palaces of his kingdom (*Ibid.*, no. 209). A further letter to the Pope, 9 April 1512, mentions that the suit of the archbishop of Glasgow against the Chapel Royal and its privileges had been quashed by the Pope and asks that a suit involving the provostry of Lincluden should be dealt with similarly (*Ibid.*, no. 241). Before 27 October 1529, despite King James's efforts to the contrary (*ADC*, xxxvii, 151), Inchmahome and Lincluden had been disjoined from the Chapel Royal (*Letters of James V*, p. 161; cf. *RSS*, ii. no. 210). There is a reference to the union of the abbey of Tongland to the bishopric of Galloway and of the Chapel Royal, by bulls of Pope Clement VII, 14 January 1529/30 (Brady, *Episc. Succession*, i. 208); and, from 1529 to 1541, James V appears as attempting to secure this (*Letters of James V*, pp. 162, 425; *Epp. Reg. Scot.*, ii. 115–19). The Chapel Royal because it was "ruinous and too little" was decided to be "utterly rased" in 1594 and a new chapel erected (*Reg. Cap. Reg. Striv.*, lxxxi). Rogers, *Hist. of the Chapel Royal of Scotland* (Grampian Club, 1882) has a useful collection of documents (to which reference is frequently made *supra*), but is otherwise ill-edited.

## SECULAR CANONS (II): COLLEGIATE CHURCHES

| Name | County | Minimum Income (1561) | Founder | Date of Foundation | No. of Clergy Prebendaries etc. | Chaplains | Others |
|------|--------|------------------------|---------|---------------------|----------------------------------|-----------|--------|
| ‡ STIRLING, HOLY RUDE | Stirling | | Magistrates and community | –1546 | | numerous | |
| STRATHMIGLO | Fife | | Sir William Scott of Balweary | c. 1527 | ? | | 3 |
| § TAIN | Ross | £100 | Thomas, bishop of Ross | 1487 | 8 | | 5 |

STIRLING, HOLY RUDE. This parish church had a new choir built by the magistrates, Town Council and community in the early sixteenth century (*Chs. rel. to Stirling*, no. xxxvii; *Stirling Burgh Recs.*, p. 18); and, before 1546, a college of priests choristers which had been previously founded was constituted with a president and subpresident (*Formulare*, ii. 172).

STRATHMIGLO. On 31 March 1527, mention is made of a proposal by Sir William Scott of Balweary to set up a college in this parish church (*ALC, 1501–54*, p. 257). The patronage of the provostry and prebends is confirmed to him, 5 March 1528/9 (*RMS*, iii. no. 760), and to his son, 30 April 1548 (*Ibid.*, iv. no. 200). The number of prebends is not known, but there is a reference to three choristers (*ALC, 1501–54*, p. 257).

TAIN. By a charter of 10 October 1457, James II endowed a chaplainry in what is designated "the collegiate church of St Duthac of Tain" (*Fraser Papers* (SHS), p. 220); and, in 1467, when this building was destroyed or damaged by fire, it is called "the famous collegiate chapel . . . of St Duthac of Tayne" (NLS. MS. 35.4.12a (Macfarlane's Collns.) ). It may, however, have been no more than a chantry. On 3 December 1487, with the assent of his chapter and at the instigation of James III, Thomas, bishop of Ross, erected it—"for the increase of the divine worship of the chapel or collegiate church of the blessed confessor and bishop Duthac of Tain"—into a collegiate church for a provost, five canons or prebendaries, two deacons or subdeacons, a sacrist and assistant clerk, and three boy-choristers (NLS. MSS. 34.3.11, 198; 34.2.1, i. 57; *RMS*, ii. no. 1694). *V. OPS*, ii². 417 ff. (It may, however, be noted that a transaction took place in the choir of the collegiate church of Tain, 8 October 1487 (*Earls of Cromartie*, ii. 324 (Cromartie Chs., no. 526)).)

### INCOMPLETE FOUNDATIONS

*Darnley.* On 24 February 1421/2, the Pope granted a petition of John Stewart, Lord Darnley, for the annexation of the parish church of Tarbolton to a college of six priests which he proposed to found in the territory of "Derneley" (*Supplics.*, p. 283). The foundation did not take place.

*Douglas.* On 27 March 1423, the Pope was petitioned by Archibald, earl of Douglas, to sanction the erection of the parish church of Douglas into a collegiate church under a dean (GRH. Vat. Trans., Pet., 78); and, again, on 7 August 1448, the Pope granted a petition of William, earl of Douglas, for the foundation of a collegiate church with a provost and thirteen prebendaries (*CPR*, x. 429). Although an indulgence is granted to penitents who give alms for the completion and maintenance of this church, described as "erected by papal authority into the collegiate church of St Bride, Douglas, which William, earl of Douglas, has at great cost caused to be new built", 1 February 1450/1 (*Ibid.*, x. 84), and although there are mentions of a provostry, 31 January 1488/9 (*Douglas Bk.*, iii. no. 119; *RMS*, ii. no. 1827) and 5 July 1499 (*Douglas Bk.*, iii. no. 152), it does not seem to have acquired collegiate status and is mentioned simply as a parish church, 7 March 1483/4 and 16 June 1506 (*RMS*, ii. nos. 1586, 2974).

*Falkirk.* On 24 February 1449/50, the Pope consented on the petition of Alexander Livingstone, to the erection of a collegiate church for a provost and six canons; but, because objection was made by the king and the abbey of Holyrood, which held this (parish) church, the consent was withdrawn, 1 June 1450 (Vat. Reg. Supp., 434, 297; 442, 228v.)

*St Ninian's.* A charter of James V, 28 June 1528, made provision for the erection by the abbot of Cambuskenneth, the sheriff of Stirling and the *generosi*, nobles, knights and parishioners of St Ninian's for the erection of a college in this parish church (*RMS*, iii. no. 601). The project does not seem to have matured.

## UNCERTAIN AND SUPPOSED FOUNDATIONS

*Arbroath.* References are found between 1561 and 1572 to the provostry of Our Lady in Arbroath (*Thirds of Benefices*, pp. 10, 167, 235). There is no other mention of a secular college in Arbroath, but the reference may be to a chantry "beside the bridge" of that town of which a principal chaplain of the Blessed Virgin Mary is mentioned, 4 January 1519/20 (*Aberbrothoc*, ii. no. 583).

*Arbuthnott.* This church, mentioned as collegiate (e.g. MacGibbon and Ross, *Eccles. Archit.*, iii. 235), was simply a parish church.

*Auchterless.* Given by Dempster (*Apparatus* i. 77) as a collegiate church, founded by David Dempster of Auchterless, in 1403. There is no evidence of this and Dempster's statements are notoriously unreliable.

*Brechin.* References to a college (e.g. 4 September 1503 (*RSS*, i. no. 977) ) and to a collegiate church (e.g. 7 November 1512 (*Ibid.*, i. no. 2440) ) are explained by the foundation made by Walter, earl of Strathearn, Athole and Caithness, lord of Brechin and of Cortachy, 22–31 October 1429, of an association of four priests and six choristers serving in the cathedral, for whom a residence is provided (*REB*, i. nos. 33, 34).

*Houston.* Keith declares that this is referred to in the Register of the Privy Seal as a provostry (*Hist. of Affairs of Church and State in Scotland*, iii. 511). But the reference is to the ministry of Houston (*RSS*, ii. no. 1069), i.e. Houston in East Lothian. There is, however, a puzzling reference, in a charter of 1525, to a "pensionary provost in the parish church of Houston" (*REG*, ii. no. 497), i.e. Houston in Renfrewshire. No other indication of a provostry here has been noticed.

*Kennethmont.* Given by Dempster (*Apparatus*, i. 77) and Hay (Scotia Sacra, p. 384) as a collegiate church founded by Andrew Dempster. The parish church was appropriated to Lindores abbey (*Lindores*, no. ii, etc.). No evidence of a college in it or elsewhere is forthcoming.

*Markle.* This place in Prestonkirk parish is given as the site of a provostry by Mackinlay, who states that "Dr J. G. Wallace-James . . . has notes of charters *c.* 1450 in which St Mary . . . is named as the titular of the provostry" (*Ancient Ch. Dedications (non-scriptural)*, pp. 499–500). No mention of this "provostry" has, however, been found in Wallace-James's notes (now in GRH.). Again, it is said of a chapel here: "In its later stages it had a collegiate organisation with a provost and prebends but the erection does not seem to have been confirmed" (*Fasti Ecclesiae Scoticanae*, viii. 110). This statement is conjectural and unfounded. A chaplainry or chapel (dedicated to St Mary) of Markle is on record from 27 August 1511 (*RMS*, ii. no. 3635) to 12 May 1653 (*Haddington Retours*, no. 233); but there is no reference to a provostry or college. As it appears in charters along with the prebend of Hauch (since both were in the patronage of the earls of Bothwell), this juxtaposition may have given rise to the idea of a collegiate foundation at Markle. But Hauch or Linton was a prebend of the college of Dunbar. Markle is also given (even less plausibly) as the site of a monastery (e.g. in the *Ordnance Gazetteer* (1885)).

*Perth.* There is a reference, 11 January 1547/8, to the chaplainry of the altar of St Fillan, founded within the collegiate church of Perth (*RSS*, iii. no. 2601). This is an exaggeration of the status of the parish church of Perth.

*Tullibardine.* Frequently given as a collegiate church. Thus, Spottiswoode (p. 473) declares that it was founded by Sir David Murray of Tullibardine, in 1446, for a provost and several prebendaries; while Hay refers to its foundation as a collegiate church in 1447 (NLS. MS. 35.4.16, 10). But it is described as a chapel, 30 October 1455 (*HMC 7th Rep.* App., 708) and 21 March 1618 (*Perth Retours*, no. 255). There is no record of its being made collegiate.

*Yester.* Given by Spottiswoode (p. 473) as a collegiate church. This is a blunder due to that writer's failure to recognize that the medieval parish of Bothans is identical with the post-Reformation parish of Yester. The statements made by him concerning the suppositious college of Yester are more nearly correct, as applied to the authentic college of Bothans, than those made in the paragraph dealing with the latter (which he calls "Bothan" (p. 466)).

In his *Commentary on the Rule of St Augustine* (SHS, ed., p. 73), Richardinus [Richardson] has a reference to "that most holy and most religious college of the lord of Borthwick", with an indication that it was dedicated to St Kentigern. This college defies identification. The most obvious interpretation of the reference would be that it applies to the church of Lochorwart (now Borthwick), which had St Kentigern as its patron. But this was not a collegiate church. Again, it might be taken to apply to the neighbouring collegiate church of Crichton (to which Lochorwart was appropriated), which was also under the invocation of St Kentigern. But, in that case, it is not clear why the college should be described as "of the lord of Borthwick".

## ACADEMIC SECULAR COLLEGES

The medieval academic colleges of Scotland survived the Reformation and, with the exception of St Leonard's College, St Andrews, have continued to the present day. St Salvator's College, St. Andrews and King's College, Aberdeen, are included under Secular Canons (II), as more nearly akin to the collegiate churches of the period.

| Name | County | Founder | Date Fd. | Personnel |
|---|---|---|---|---|
| ABERDEEN, KING'S COLLEGE, *v.* under Secular Canons (II). | | | | |
| ¶‡ ST ANDREWS ST LEONARD'S COLLEGE | Fife | Alexander Stewart, archbishop of St Andrews; John Hepburn, prior of St Andrews | 1512 | *V.* notes |
| ST MARY'S COLLEGE | | James Beaton, archbishop of St Andrews | 1537/8 | *V.* notes |
| ST SALVATOR'S COLLEGE, *v.* under Secular Canons (II). | | | | |

ABERDEEN, KING'S COLLEGE, *v.* under Secular Canons (II).

ST. ANDREWS, ST LEONARD'S COLLEGE. The charter of Alexander Stewart, archbishop of St Andrews and John Hepburn, prior of St Andrews, erecting the hospital and church of St Leonard into "the college of poor clerks of the church of St Andrews", is dated 20 August 1512 (*Coll. of St Leonard*, pp. 128 ff.). The prior and convent added certain endowments, 1 February 1512/13 (*Ibid.*, pp. 130 ff.) and the foundation was confirmed by James IV, 23 February 1512/13 (*Ibid.*, pp. 134-5). Papal confirmation of this foundation is wanting but it was confirmed by Cardinal David Beaton as legate, 28 November 1545 (*Ibid.*, pp. 177 ff.). The original foundation was for a "master and principal director" (who is to be a canon of the cathedral), four chaplains (two to act as regents), twenty scholars in arts and six in theology (*Ibid.*, p. 129). This college was united to St Salvator's in 1747. *V.* Herkless and Hannay, *College of St Leonard*; Cant, *University of St Andrews*, pp. 28 ff.

ST ANDREWS, ST MARY'S COLLEGE. Founded by James Beaton, archbishop of St Andrews; the bull of foundation by Pope Paul III is dated 12 February 1537/8 (*Univ. Comm. Rep., St And.*, p. 357). The foundation was completed in 1554 by Archbishop John Hamilton, for a provost (a doctor in theology), a licentiate and a bachelor in theology, a canonist, eight priests (students of theology), five regents in arts and sixteen poor students in arts (Cant, *Univ. of St And.*, pp. 35-6). *V.* Cant, *op. cit.*

ST ANDREWS, ST SALVATOR'S COLLEGE, *v.* under Secular Canons (II).

## CELTIC FOUNDATIONS (SURVIVING INTO THE MEDIEVAL PERIOD)

The number of Celtic foundations in existence at or after 1050 is somewhat difficult to determine. Those of which the survival seems sufficiently attested are given in the following list; and it is with some hesitation that Deer and Turriff are classed as uncertain. Most of the surviving establishments were settlements of Culdees. While the nomenclature of the records has been followed in the case of the "hermits" or "brethren" found at Inchaffray, the possibility is that these were of the same type as the Culdees.

The lands of former Celtic monasteries, i.e. monasteries which had disappeared by 1050, are held to be indicated in charters by the term *abthen* or *abthane*, latinized as *abthania* (and occasionally as *abbatia*) and extant in the place-name *Appin*. But it is hardly possible to draw precise conclusions from the occurrence of this term. In certain cases, such lands are found in the hands of hereditary lay abbots. Thus, the abbots of Brechin, Abernethy, Glendochart, etc., mentioned in this period, were evidently laymen holding a title (associated, it would appear, with the holding of secularized property), which had once pertained to the head of a Celtic community. *V.* Skene, *Celtic Scotland*, ii. 383–5, 398–401; Lawrie, *Early Scottish Charters*, p. 223; A. O. Anderson, *Early Sources*, i. 577 *n.*

| Name | County | Recorded until | Type |
|------|--------|----------------|------|
| ABERNETHY | Perth | 1272–3 | House of Culdees |
| BRECHIN | Angus | –1249 | House of Culdees |
| INCHAFFRAY | Perth | 1200 | House of "Brethren" |

ABERNETHY. The Culdees here are mentioned, 1189–99 (*Aberbrothoc*, i. no. 34). The abbot of Abernethy who appears in this record was a layman, holding an office which had become secularized and hereditary. *V.* Skene, *Celtic Scotland*, ii. 399–400. Before 1214 the prior and Culdees are parties to a controversy with Arbroath abbey (*Ibid.*, i. no. 214); and a prior of the Culdees is on record in 1235 and 1239 (*Lindores*, nos. li, liv). The Culdees became, or were replaced by, Augustinian canons in 1272 or 1273 (*Scotich.*, lib. x, cap. xxxiii (ii. 120) ). *V.* under Secular Canons (II).

BRECHIN. The abbots of Brechin, mentioned till *c.* 1219 (*REB*, i. iv–v) were laymen, as in the case of Abernethy (*supra*). On the erection of the episcopal see, *c.* 1150, the prior and members of the Culdee community formed the chapter (cf. *Aberbrothoc*, i. nos. 188, 192, etc.). The transformation of this body into a chapter of secular canons was evidently completed by 18 February 1249/50, when a bull of Pope Innocent IV refers to the fact that "the brethren who have been wont to be in the church of Brechin were called Keledei and now by change of name are styled canons" (*Lindores*, no. xcix).

INCHAFFRAY. This site was originally occupied by "brethren", called, in 1200, "the brethren of St John of Strathearn", the head of whom is designated "hermit" (*Inchaffray*, nos. vii, ix). These apparently formed a community of Celtic type. In 1200, Gilbert, earl of Strathearn, founding the Augustinian house, provides that the "presbyter and hermit", who is head of the Celtic brethren, will administer the new foundation and that those who are associated with him will be instructed in the service of God according to the rule of St Augustine (*Ibid.*, no. ix).

CELTIC FOUNDATIONS (SURVIVING INTO THE MEDIEVAL
PERIOD)

| Name | County | Recorded until | Type |
|---|---|---|---|
| INCHCOLM | Fife | –1123 | Hermitage |
| IONA | Argyll | 1204 | Celtic monastery; Culdees |
| LOCH LEVEN | Kinross | c. 1150 | House of Culdees |
| MONIFIETH | Angus | 1236–42 | House of Culdees |
| MONYMUSK | Aberdeen | early 13 c. | House of Culdees |
| MUTHILL | Perth | 1284+ | House of Culdees |
| ST ANDREWS | Fife | early 14 c. | House of Culdees |

INCHCOLM. It is said that there was a hermit in this island before the foundation of
the Augustinian monastery in 1123 (*Scotich.*, lib. v, cap. xxxvii (i. 287) ).

IONA. The Celtic community in Iona is not mentioned after 1204, when there was possibly some attempt to resist the setting up of a Benedictine house. *V.* Skene, *Celtic Scotland*,
ii. 416–17; A. O. Anderson, *Early Sources*, ii. 363. There is a reference to Culdees here
in 1164 (A. O. Anderson, *op. cit.*, p. 253).

LOCH LEVEN. A number of donations to the Culdees here by early Scottish kings and
bishops of St Andrews are recorded from 1040–57 (*RPSA*, pp. 114–17). The grant by
David I, *c.* 1150, of the island of Loch Leven to the canons regular of St Andrews so
that they may introduce canons there provides that any of the Culdees who wish to live
as canons will remain; those who resist will be expelled from the island (*Ibid.*, pp. 188–9;
*N. Durham*, App., no. xxvi; Lawrie, *ESC*, no. ccxxxii).

MONIFIETH. A charter of Matilda, countess of Angus, grants to Arbroath abbey in
1242–3 the land "on the south side of the church of Monifieth which the Culdees held in
the lifetime of my father" (i.e. Malcolm, earl of Angus (*c.* 1214–42) ) (*Aberbrothoc*, i. no.
115). This may be taken to indicate a comparatively recent disappearance of the Culdees.
Their property had evidently become secularized *c.* 1220, as at that date Earl Malcolm
made a grant of all the land of the *abthein* of Monifieth (*Ibid.*, i. 330–1) to Nicholas, who
witnesses Countess Matilda's charters, 1242–3, as "abbot" (i.e. lay-abbot) of Monifieth
(*Ibid.*, i. nos. 49, 114).

MONYMUSK. The Culdee community was transformed into a house of Augustinian
canons in the early thirteenth century. *V.* under Augustinian Canons. For what is known
of the history of the Culdees here *v.* W. Douglas Simpson, "Augustinian Priory and Parish
Church of Monymusk", *PSAS*, lix (1925), 40–4.

MUTHILL. The prior and two brethren of the Culdees are mentioned, 1178–95 (*N.
Berwic*, no. 5). The latest specific reference to the Culdees (a mention of their prior) seems
to be, 7 May 1236 (*Lindores*, no. li). But a prior of Muthill witnesses a charter of William,
bishop of Dunblane (1284–96(?) ) (*REM*, p. 469).

ST ANDREWS. After the foundation of the Augustinian priory in 1144, a bull of Pope
Eugenius III ordained that as the Culdees died out, their places should be taken by regular
canons, 30 August 1147 (*RPSA*, p. 49); and, about the same date, David I issued a mandate
to the prior and canons providing that these should receive the Culdees of Kilrimont, with
their possessions and revenues, as canons, if such they were willing to become. If they
were unwilling, those now living might hold their possessions for their lifetime and,
after their death, as many canons as there were Culdees were to be instituted in the church
of St Andrews, the Culdees' possessions being converted to the canons' use (*Ibid.*, p. 186).
The Culdee community, however, maintained its existence and entered into agreements
with the priory regarding lands and revenues, –1161 (*Ibid.*, p. 203) and 1198–9 (*Ibid.*,
p. 318). (An abbot of the Culdees appears, 1180–6 (*Ibid.*, p. 353).) About 1250, this community, with its prior, had become a college of secular canons. *V.* under Secular Canons
(II). Mr G. W. S. Barrow shows that, by 1249 at latest, it was the formal transference of
the Culdees into another church, while retaining their rights and privileges, that was
responsible for the mid-thirteenth-century foundation of the collegiate church of St Mary
("Cathedral Chapter of St Andrews and the Culdees", *JEH*, iii. 36). The Culdees are
said to have been finally excluded from participating in episcopal elections in 1273 (*Scotich.*,
lib. vi, cap. xliii (i. 360) ).

The existence of other Celtic foundations within this period is uncertain or doubtful, viz.:

*Deer.* It has been assumed that *notitiae* in the so-called *Book of Deer* and especially a charter of David I to the *clerici* of Deer, the latter dated 1131–44 by A. O. Anderson (*Early Sources*, ii. 181 *n.*) and *c.* 1150 by Lawrie (*ESC*, no. ccxxiii), point to the continuance of a Celtic monastery at Deer till this part of the twelfth century. Lawrie, however, is sceptical of the value of these *notitiae* (*Ibid.*, pp. 220–3) and suspects that David I's charter is a fabrication (*Ibid.*, p. 425). A. O. Anderson, who points out that there is no other evidence of a monastery at Deer in David's reign, gives the more cautious judgment that neither the Gaelic *notitiae* nor David I's charter "can be proved not to be copies of genuine documents" (*Early Sources*, ii. 181 *n.*). The existence of a Celtic monastery at Deer within this period must remain uncertain. It should be added that, although there is nothing to establish a specific connection between the Cistercian monastery founded at Deer in 1218 and an earlier Celtic foundation, it may be significant, as Mr Barrow has suggested, that a number of lands said to have been held by the Celtic community were later in the possession of the Cistercians.

*Dunkeld.* Gervase of Canterbury (–1216) (A. O. Anderson, *Scottish Annals*, p. 327) and Henry of Silgrave (*c.* 1272) (*Id., Early Sources*, ii. 699) give under the bishopric of Dunkeld: "black canons and Culdees". "Black canons" is certainly an error; the canons here were secular. There are other references to Culdees at Dunkeld, e.g. the litany said to have been used by them but which appears only in a fifteenth–sixteenth century version (Haddan and Stubbs, *Councils*, ii. Pt. I, 278 ff.) and cannot be regarded as satisfactory evidence; and the assertion of Myln, writing in the sixteenth century, that David I superseded the Culdees and, *c.* 1127, instituted a bishop and canons, the bishop being for some time abbot of the monastery (*Vitae*, pp. 4, 5), statements on which too much reliance cannot be placed. There does not seem to be sufficient reason for holding with Reeves (*Culdees*, p. 43) that Culdees and secular canons "co-existed for nearly two centuries"; while the contentions in Migne (*Patr. Lat.*, 69, col. 563) regarding the old records preserved by the Culdees here and the persistence of "some trace of the old discipline" (i.e. of the Culdees) till the twelfth century are probably too categorical. We find Ethelred, son of Malcolm III, described as "abbot" of Dunkeld, 1093–1107 (*RPSA*, p. 115); but, despite Lawrie (*ESC*, p. 244), who regards him as an ecclesiastic, it would seem more likely that he was a layman. Likewise, the abbacy of Dunkeld, of which the rights are reserved in a charter of David I, *c.* 1150 (*Dunfermelyn*, no. 2, p. 6) may have been by this date secularized. For lack of definite evidence, the existence of Culdees at Dunkeld, after 1050, can only be held as "not proven".

*Glendochart.* The "abbot of Glendochir (or Glendocheroch)", who is mentioned as a local magnate, along with the earl of Athole, in the reign of William the Lion (1165–1214) (*APS*, i. 50, 239), was apparently a layman. There is no record of a monastery Celtic or otherwise, in Glendochart during this period.

*Kilspindie (Perthshire).* Malcolm, abbot of Kilspindie, witnesses a charter, 1211–25 (*Scon*, no. 84). There is no evidence of a monastery here. His office was probably titular, derived from a former Celtic monastery.

*May.* Lawrie makes the statement: "It is possible that on the Isle of May, in the beginning of the twelfth century, there was a small fraternity of Culdees or monks of the old Scottish church" (*ESC*, p. 387). This remains entirely conjectural.

*Mortlach, v.* p. 195.

*Scone.* The editor of the *Liber de Scon* states that "the monastery of Scone, a foundation of unknown antiquity of the Culdees or followers of St Columba . . . was re-formed by King Alexander I" (*op. cit.*, ix). Likewise, Dr A. O. Anderson, in a note on the entry in the Chronicle of Melrose (*s.a.* 1115): "the church of Scone was given over to canons" (*Chron. Mailros*, p. 65), declares that "the abbey of Scone had formerly been occupied by céli-dé" (*Early Sources*, ii. 160 *n.*). While this is possible, there seems to be no explicit evidence of the presence of Culdees here.

*Turriff.* That there was a Celtic monastery here has been taken as implied by the mention of Cormac, abbot of Turbruaid, in one of the *notitiae* in the Book of Deer, *c.* 1135

(Lawrie, *ESC*, no. cvii). It may be the same individual who, as "Cormac de Turbrud", witnesses a charter of David I, *c.* 1150, marginally recorded in the Book of Deer (*Ibid.*, no. ccxxiii). Apart from the question of the authenticity of these data (*v.* Deer, *supra*), the existence of this foundation can only be regarded as uncertain, as nothing is known of it.

The lists of religious houses given by Gervase of Canterbury (–1216) (A. O. Anderson, *Scottish Annals*, pp. 327–8) and Henry of Silgrave (*c.* 1272) (*Id.*, *Early Sources*, ii. 699–700) show Culdees not only under the bishopric of Dunkeld (*supra*) but also under the bishoprics of Dunblane, Ross, Caithness and Argyll. In none of the latter instances, however, is there definite evidence of the existence of Culdees. *V.* Skene, *Celtic Scotland*, ii. 377–408.

## DOUBTFUL AND REJECTED FOUNDATIONS
### (*Not previously included*)

*Abbey.* Two places in the south of Scotland bear this name: (1) Abbey, to the west of the village of Forth, in the parish of Carstairs, Lanarkshire. The source of this name has not been discovered; but it may definitely be said that there was no religious house on this site. (2) Abbey, on the Cliffhope burn, north of Saughtree, in Liddesdale. Mr George Watson has shown that this was probably not used as a place-name till 1726, and that there is insufficient evidence "to warrant one's assuming that 'the Abbey' was a structure built for ecclesiastical or sacred purposes". *V.* his article, "The Abbey, Upper Liddesdale", *Trans. Hawick Archaeol. Socy.* (1916), pp. 32–3. The name, it has been suggested, is due to the possession by Jedburgh abbey of lands in this area (*Berwickshire Nat. Club* (1887–9), pp. 461–3).

*Buchan.* On 18 October 1221, the Pope grants protection to the prior and canons of St James's, Buchan, with confirmation of their possessions, especially the churches of St James, All Saints, St Andrew, Buchan and Chenigale, with their chapels and appurtenances (*CPR*, Letters, i. 83). There is no known house of regular canons in the district of Buchan, Aberdeenshire, nor are any of the appropriated churches recognizable. "Buchan" here may be an orthographical error for a place-name elsewhere than in Scotland.

*Charterhouse. V.* Makerstoun, under the Carthusian Monks.

*Clova (Aberdeenshire).* A bull of Pope Adrian IV confirming the rights and possessions of the church of Aberdeen, 10 August 1157, includes "the monastery of Cloveth" (*REA*, i. 6, 85). This may have been a Celtic settlement, but there is no other evidence of its existence. The church of Clova and its land appear as granted to Beyn, bishop of Mortlach, in a spurious charter of Malcolm II (1011) (*Ibid.*, i. 3), but this church was not bestowed on Aberdeen cathedral till *c.* 1262 (*Ibid.*, i. 29).

*Holy Island.* Opposite Lamlash, on the east coast of Arran. Monro, in 1549, speaks of this as "ane . . . little ile callit the yle of Molass, quherin there was foundit by Johne, Lorde of the iles, ane monastery of friars which is decayit" (*Western Isles*, p. 15). The alleged founder was probably "the good John of Islay", who died in 1380 (*Bk. of Arran*, ii. 74). But the existence of a house of friars here must be regarded as very doubtful; and there is no evidence of any other form of (medieval) monastic establishment. The island was associated with the Celtic saint, Molaise.

*Inchkenneth.* This island is said to have had a monastery (*OPS*, ii[1]. 316), but of this there is no evidence. Even *Scotichronicon*, which is prone to locate suppositious religious houses in the Isles, does not mention a monastery here; its statement is: "The island of St Kenneth of which and in which there is a parish church" (lib. ii, cap. x (i. 45–6)). Monro (*Western Isles*, p. 21) does not mention a monastery. The whole lands belonged to the nunnery of Iona (*Ibid.*; *OPS*, ii[1]. 316, 317) and the idea of a monastery may have originated in its connection with Iona (*OPS*, ii[1]. 316).

*Inchmarnock.* Of this island, lying between Bute and Kintyre, *Scotichronicon* says: "Inchemernoc or the island of St Mernoch; and there [is] a cell of monks" (lib. ii, cap. x (i. 45)). *Origines Parochiales* (ii. 223) calls Inchmarnock "the site of a chapel or monastery". Monro (*Western Isles*, p. 16) does not mention a monastery here; and there is no evidence of such a foundation. The island, however, had a parish church, which, on 17 January 1390/1, Saddell abbey obtained by exchange from Crossraguel abbey, by which it had been previously held (*Highland Papers*, iv. 142–4).

*Kar.* On 15 February 1220/1, Henry III ordered the justiciar of Ireland to allow the monks of the order of Vaudey, dwelling at Kar in Galloway, to buy corn, etc., in Ireland for their sustenance (*CDS*, i. no. 795). Charters in *Liber de Melros* (i. nos. 192–5) deal with the grant by Thomas de Colville, in the early thirteenth century and certainly –1223, of the land of "Keresban" to the abbey of Vaudey. This land is described as in Galloway (*Ibid.*, i. no. 195), but was probably in south Ayrshire, since it extended to the river Doon. In none of these records is there any suggestion that the monks of Vaudey were resident on this land. In 1223, Vaudey abbey, finding the possession of this land useless and a source of danger, gave it to Melrose Abbey in perpetual lease (*Ibid.*, i. *loc. cit.*).

*Kennethmont.* There is said to have been a cell (the order is not specified) here which was burned down at the Reformation (*Collns. Aberd. and Banff*, p. 200). (Cf. the statement that there was a collegiate church here. *V.* under Secular Canons (II).) But no evidence of any ecclesiastical foundation other than the parish church is to be found. Kennethmont was one of the churches granted by the founder to Lindores abbey, 1188–9 (*Lindores*, no. ii) and is frequently mentioned in the Lindores charters.

*Mortlach.* The monastery of "Murthillach" appears among the possessions of the church of Aberdeen confirmed by a bull of Pope Adrian IV, 10 August 1157 (*REA*, i. 6, 85). This may have been a Celtic establishment, but its existence is unsupported by definite evidence. *V.* Aberdeen, under Cathedrals.

*Rothesay.* MacGibbon and Ross (*Eccles. Archit.*, iii. 418) refer to the ruined church here as "St Mary's abbey". This was not a monastic building but evidently the medieval parish church.

*Texa.* "Helantexa" (the island of Texa), according to *Scotichronicon* (lib. ii, cap. x (i. 45)), had a cell of monks. Monro (*Western Isles*, p. 26) says of "Tigsay" that it has "a kirk in it", but the "cell" is no doubt apocryphal.

*Thirlestane.* A ruinous building east of the farm of Thirlestane has been described as a "convent" (Thomson, *Lauder and Lauderdale*, p. 69; *BNC*, xviii (1901–2), pp. 267, 292); and it is alleged that "to this" Sir Richard Maitland gave all the lands which Walter de Gilling held in his fee of Thirlestane, as well as pasturage there (*BNC*, xviii (1901–2), 267). But Maitland's charter, *c.* 1260, makes no mention of a religious house at Thirlestane. It indicates plainly that his benefaction was made to Dryburgh abbey (*Dryburgh*, no. 124). The "convent" is an antiquary's invention; and the building in question was probably a hospital (*v.* p. 165). *Hist. Mon. Comm. Rep. (Berwick)*, p. 106, refers to it as a chapel.

*Upsettlington.* The site of a "convent chapel" at Chapel Park is listed (*Hist. Mon. Comm. Rep. (Berwick)*, p. 102). There was, however, no religious house in this vicinity.

The pseudo-medieval names of certain mansion-houses may be noted here:

*Crawford Priory.* South-west of Cupar, Fife. This name is attached to a mansion-house built in 1813. There was never a priory on this site and the name appears to be fanciful.

*Inchrye Abbey.* In north Fife, near Newburgh. The mansion-house thus designated was built in the nineteenth century. The name is fanciful.

*Ross Priory.* On the east side of Loch Lomond. It is called "Ross" in 1793 (Ross Estate Muniments, no. 1163). Scott, writing to the proprietor (his friend and colleague, Hector Macdonald Buchanan), addresses his letters, which are unreliably dated, both to "Ross" and "Ross Priory" (*Letters of Sir Walter Scott*, iv. 469; vi. 173; ix. 213). The latter name was probably invented in the early nineteenth century and perhaps after an addition had been made to the building in 1810 (*v.* Smith, *Strathendrick*, p. 277).

*Rossie Priory.* In the Carse of Gowrie, west of Dundee. This name is attached to a mansion-house begun in 1807. There is a reference in a charter of Malcolm IV (1153–65) to the "abbacy" (abbatia) of Rossie (*RPSA*, p. 200), which points to the existence of a (defunct) Celtic religious house; while "Rossinclerach" and its church were granted to the priory of St Andrews by Bishop Ernald, 1160–2 (*Ibid.*, p. 126). But no medieval priory existed at Rossie and the name applied to the mansion-house is without historical justification.

These names, products of the age of Scott, were probably adopted in imitation of English mansion-houses (e.g. Nostell Priory) which had a better claim to such designations.

## RELIGIOUS HOUSES IN THE ISLE OF MAN

The following notes on the Manx houses owe much to the kind and assiduous assistance of Mr B. R. S. Megaw, Director and Librarian of the Manx Museum, Douglas.

The edition of the *Chronicle of Man* cited *infra* is that of P. A. Munch (1860).

### THE CISTERCIAN MONKS

| Name | Rank | Valuation (1540) | Founder | Date Fd. | D. | Dependent on |
|------|------|-----------------|---------|------|------|------|
| MIRESCOG | | | Godred II, king of Man | 1176 | *c.* 1200 (?) | Rievaulx (?) |
| RUSHEN | Abbey | £215 | Olaf I, king of Man | 1134/5 | 1540 | Furness |

MIRESCOG. In Kirk Christ Lezayre parish. Later called Sulby Grange. Mr Megaw informs me that the supposed siting of this house at Ballamona (*v.* Tanner and others) is incorrect. It is stated that, in 1176, "Godred, king of Man, gave as an offering to . . . abbot Silvanus (i.e. of Rievaulx) part of the land of Mirescog. He immediately built a monastery there, but in process of time all the land with the monks was granted to the abbey of St Mary of Rushen" (*Chron. Man*, pp. 13–14). It has been suggested that there was still a monastery here in 1249. But the passage on which this supposition is based speaks of an island in the wood of Mirescog; a monastery at Mirescog is not mentioned in this connection (*Ibid.*, p. 24).

RUSHEN. It is said that, in 1134, Olaf, king of Man, gave to Ivo, abbot of Furness, part of his land in Man for the constitution of an abbey in the place called Russin (*Chron. Man*, pp. 7–8). This date is also found in a list of Cistercian foundations (*JBAA*, xxvi (1870), 358), where it is called "[the abbey] of Mann". Janauschek (p. 101) assigns the foundation to 10 January 1134(/5). In *Furness Coucher Book* (i. 11), the date is given erroneously as 1238. It may be noted that "the abbey of Man" is included with Furness among the abbeys subject to the abbot of Savigny which are confirmed to him by Pope Anastasius IV, 20 April 1154 (*Patr. Lat.*, 188, col. 1054). The abbey is stated to have been transferred in 1192 to Douglas, but the monks returned to Rushen four years later (*Chron. Man*, p. 15). The church was dedicated by Richard, bishop of Sodor, in 1257 (*Ibid.*, p. 27). In 1275, when a Scottish force subdued the island, the abbey suffered considerable spoliation (*Annals of Furness* in *Chrons. of Stephen, etc.*, p. 570); and it was again despoiled in 1316 during an invasion of Man by Richard de Mandeville and his associates from Ireland (*Chron. Man*, p. 28). This house was dissolved by arbitrary act of Henry VIII (since the act of 1539 did not apply to Man), 24 June 1540, when the abbot and six brethren were removed from the abbey (*PRO* Roll of Accounts (Isle of Man—Dissolutions (1540)); *v.* T. Talbot in *Manx Sun*, 24 November 1894, p. 8; A. W. Moore, *Hist. of Isle of Man*, i. 351). It was granted by the Crown to Thomas Hungate of the Household, 18 March 1543/4 (*L. & P. H. VIII*, xviii[1]. 557). The statement that it was the last monastery to be dissolved (as in Tanner and *Manx Society*, xii, 57) should be extended to cover the other Manx houses (*infra*). (The last house to be dissolved in England was Waltham, on 10 April 1540.)

## THE FRANCISCAN FRIARS

| Name | Valuation (1540) | Founder | Date Fd. | D. |
|---|---|---|---|---|
| BEMAKEN | not given | William Montague, earl of Salisbury | 1367 | 1540 |

BEMAKEN. In Kirk Arbory parish. On 7 December 1367, following on the petition of the provincial and brethren of the Friars Minor of the province of Ireland, and William Montague, earl of Salisbury, which contained that, since there was no place of that order in the diocese of Sodor, the earl proposed to assign one to the friars in the *villa* of St Columba in Man. Pope Urban V appointed the bishop of Sodor mandatory to license the provincial and friars to accept this place and to build there a church and the necessary offices, with provision for twelve friars (*CPR*, iv. 75; *Chron. Man* (Appendix), pp. 179–180, where the papal letter is printed *in extenso*). Tanner gives the date of foundation as 1373 (cf. *Manx Society*, xii. 54). The property was apparently seized by Henry VIII in 1540, along with the other religious houses in Man. The friary was granted by the Crown to Thomas Hungate of the Household, 18 March 1543/4 (*L. & P. H. VIII*, xviii[1]. 557).

## THE CISTERCIAN NUNS

| Name | Rank | Valuation (1540) | Founder | Date Fd. | D. |
|---|---|---|---|---|---|
| DOUGLAS | Priory | £58 | Reginald, king of Man | –1226 | 1540 |

DOUGLAS (ST MARY). The supposed dedication of this house to St Bridget is doubtful, unless it was additional to the dedication to St Mary. Reginald, king of Man (1187–1226) is named as founder and the house is described as Cistercian in an inquisition of 1414 (recorded in an abstract of 1511) (*Journal of Manx Museum*, ii. no. 27, p. 21). Robert [Bruce], king of Scots, is said to have stayed at the nunnery, 20 May 1313, on an expedition to Man (*Chron. Man*, p. 27). In 1422, the prioress of Douglas appears as one of the barons of Man called to do fealty (*Lex Scripta of the Isle of Man*, p. 5). The dissolution took place, 24 June 1540, when the prioress and her three sisters "departed" from the priory (PRO Roll of Accounts (Isle of Man—Dissolutions (1540)); *v.* T. Talbot, *Manx Sun*, 24 November 1894, p. 8; A. W. Moore, *Hist. of Isle of Man*, i. 351). Douglas priory was granted to Thomas Hungate of the Household, 18 March 1543/4 (*L. P. & H. VIII*, xviii[1]. 557).

## HOSPITAL

| Name | Dedication | Founder | Date Fd. | D. |
|---|---|---|---|---|
| BALLACGNIBA | uncertain | Olaf I, king of Man (?) | –1153(?) | ? |

BALLACGNIBA. In Kirk Marown parish. Perhaps founded by Olaf I, king of Man, between 1134 and 1153; his wife was a daughter of Fergus of Galloway, and *Chron. Man*, p. 9 (*s.a.* 1142) implies his introduction of Galloway settlers in Man. This hospital is mentioned along with the church of St Ninian of Ballacgniba (St Trinian's) and the church of St Runan (Kirk Marown) as granted by Olaf II to Whithorn priory in Galloway, 1193–1215 (B. R. S. Megaw, "The Barony of St Trinian's in the Isle of Man", *Trans. Dumfries-shire and Galloway N.H. and Antiq. Socy.*, 3rd Ser., xxvii (1950), 176 ff.); and it may have been associated with the former church. Its further history is unknown.

### ADDITIONAL NOTE

Mr Megaw informs me that a place-name found at Peel (at least as early as 1703), viz. Boaly Spittal, is evidently *Boayl y Spital*, i.e. "place of the hospital", but there is no record of a hospital, medieval or otherwise, at this site.

## CATHEDRAL

| Name | Date of Foundation | Personnel |
|------|-------------------|-----------|
| ST GERMAN | –1231 | no information available |

ST GERMAN (PEEL). The inception of the building of the cathedral of St German, in the island of St Patrick, is attributed to Simon, bishop of Sodor (1229/30–1247/8) (*Chron. Man*, pp. 23, 29). It is mentioned in a bull of Pope Gregory IX to that bishop, 30 July 1231 (*SHR*, viii (1911), 259). In the entry *s.a.* 1247/8, it is stated that, after Simon's death, Laurence, archdeacon in Man, was elected bishop "with the common consent and assent of the whole Manx chapter" (*Chron. Man*, p. 23). Munch declares: "As it is certain that no chapter existed before, it is evident that this important institution was founded by Simon, and closely connected with the erection of the new cathedral" (*Ibid.*, App., 142). The chapter is also mentioned in papal letters, e.g. in 1253 (*CPR*, Letters, i. 284) and 1393 (*Ibid.*, Pet., i. 577); but this may be no more than "common form"; in any case, no particulars of the constitution of this chapter can be found. It is to be noted that, in 1134, Olaf I granted the election of the bishop to the church of Furness (*Manx Society*, vii. 1–2) and that, in a papal mandate of 15 February 1244/5, this right is said to belong to the abbot and convent of Furness (*CPR*, Letters, i. 206). But it is impossible to believe that the "chapter" of the chronicler's statement was a monastic one. The term is probably used here not of a cathedral chapter but of the totality of the clergy of the diocese. It is thus possible that Munch has read too much into the chronicler's statement. On 3 January 1363/4, Pope Urban V granted the petition of William, bishop of Sodor, who had represented that his cathedral church and precincts had been occupied as a fortress by the lord of the Isle of Man, during the wars between England and Scotland, so that the bishops had suffered greatly and divine service had ceased and who supplicated that the Pope would require the said lord to restore the cathedral to the bishop (*Ibid.*, Pet., i. 394). Again, the Pope granted licence, on 24 October 1392, to Sir William de Scrope, lord of the kingdom of Man and the Isles, to build a castle in the place called "Patrikysholm" near and belonging to the church of Sodor, whose buildings had been destroyed by invasion and could not, through the slenderness of its means, be repaired, whereby divine worship had been almost entirely diminished and divine offices for long had not been celebrated. Scrope, it is said, intended to repair the church, to which the castle would serve as a defence (*Ibid.*, iv. 432). On the same date, the Pope issued an exhortation for alms for the repair of the church of Sodor (*Ibid.*, iv. 433). From the third decade of the fifteenth century the diocese was resolved into two parts. Iona abbey became the cathedral of the Scottish diocese of Sodor or the Isles, *c.* 1498. *V.* p. 172 *supra.*

### CELTIC FOUNDATION

*St Leoc.* In 1153 a bull of Pope Eugenius III confirms, among other possessions, to Furness Abbey: "In Man, by gift of . . . Olaf, king of the Isles, the lands of Carneclet as far as the monastery of St Leoc . . ." (*Manx Socy.*, vii. 10–11). This monastery, of which nothing seems to be known, was probably a Celtic foundation. The reference here is presumably to its site and does not necessarily imply that it was still in being.

APPENDIX II

# THE INCOME OF THE SCOTTISH RELIGIOUS HOUSES: THE SOURCES

*(Contributed by Dr Gordon Donaldson)*

The records which preserve the figures for the values of the Scottish religious houses arose from the Crown's interest in and management of the ecclesiastical revenues at the Reformation. By arrangements made in 1561, all persons holding benefices retained their fruits with the exception of one-third, which was collected to augment the revenues of the Crown and make payments to the clergy of the reformed church. This "assumption of thirds" involved the gathering in of rentals of all benefices in Scotland, except those in the diocese of Argyll and the Isles and a number which were fraudulently or negligently omitted. The "Books of Assumption", in which these records were recorded, have not survived in a complete form. What may be regarded as the principal volume, in H.M. General Register House, Edinburgh, covers the east coast counties as far north as Moray, with the Borders and Perthshire. It was written in or about 1605, but the rentals in it mostly belong to 1561. Two volumes written at an earlier date, one in the Register House and one in the National Library of Scotland (MS. 31.3.12), together deal with the same parts of the country as that "principal" volume. For a complete set of figures (lacking, however, the details of the rentals), we must turn to the Accounts of the Collectors of Thirds of Benefices, which begin in 1561.

The values given in the present volume are based on the figures printed in the *Accounts of the Collectors of Thirds of Benefices, 1561–1572* (Scottish History Society), with some supplementary information from "The 'New Enterit Benefices', 1573–1586" in *Scottish Historical Review*, xxxii, 93–8. The figures given there for the various revenues in money and kind have been compared with the figures, derived from both the Books of Assumption and the Collectors' Accounts, which were printed by Bishop Keith (*History of Church and State in Scotland* (Spottiswoode Society), iii, 374 ff.), and in a few instances verification has been sought in the MS. Books of Assumption themselves. A money equivalent of the revenues received in kind has been calculated from the figures for the sale of victual and other fruits for the year 1561, as printed in the *Accounts of the Collectors of Thirds*.

The valuation on which the third was assessed represented certain deductions from the gross value—the portions which continued to be paid to the monks, the salaries of officers on the estates and in the precincts of the house, contributions to the College of Justice, and some other items. In the case of the abbey of Dunfermline, such deductions amounted to £714 (*v.*, in general, *Accounts of the Collectors of Thirds*, xiv–xv). Rentals specially prepared for the "assumption" were no more likely to exaggerate the revenues than is an income tax return to-day. With these qualifications, and bearing in mind that Scots money was, by 1561, worth only one-fifth of the corresponding sterling, the figures now printed do afford some indication of the value of the Scottish houses and a basis for comparison among them.

# INDEX OF RELIGIOUS HOUSES

## ABBREVIATIONS FOR ORDERS, ETC.

| | | | |
|---|---|---|---|
| A | Augustinian Canons | H | Hospital |
| B | Benedictine Monks | KH | Knights Hospitallers |
| BC | Cluniac Monks | KT | Knights Templars |
| BT | Monks of the Order of Tiron | NA | Augustinian Nuns |
| C | Cistercian Monks | NB | Benedictine Nuns |
| CA | Carthusian Monks | NC | Cistercian Nuns |
| CE | Celtic Foundations | ND | Dominican Nuns |
| FA | Friars, Augustinian | NF | Franciscan Nuns |
| FC | Carmelite | P | Premonstratensian Canons |
| FCr | Crutched | SA | Secular College (Academic) |
| FD | Dominican | SC(i) | Secular Canons (Cathedral) |
| FF | Franciscan | SC(ii) | (Collegiate Church) |
| FFO | Franciscan Observant | T | Trinitarian |
| FS | of the Sack | U | Uncertain Order |
| G | Gilbertine Canons | V | Valliscaulian Monks |

Numerals, in *italics*, after the abbreviation of Order denote the number of such establishments, if more than one.

Abbreviations shown in *italics* denote incomplete, uncertain, supposed or rejected foundations.

Alternative names are shown in brackets.

| | | Page | | | Page | | | Page |
|---|---|---|---|---|---|---|---|---|
| Abbey | U | 194 | Arbroath | BT | 58 | Beauly | C | 68 |
| Aberdeen | B | 49 | | H | 136 | | V | 70 |
| | FC | 114 | | *SC*(ii) | 187 | Bervie | | |
| | FD | 98 | Arbuthnott | *SC*(ii) | 187 | (Inverbervie) | FC | 114 |
| | FFO | 110 | Ardchattan | V | 70 | Berwick | FA | 118 |
| | H*4* | 135 | Ardross | H | 136 | | FC | 114 |
| | H*2* | 159–60 | Arnbeg | *H* | 160 | | FD | 98 |
| | *KT* | 132 | Arngibbon | *H* | 160 | | FF | 105 |
| | SC(i) | 167 | Auchintorlie | *H* | 160 | | FS | 119 |
| | SC(ii) *2* | 173–4 | Auchterderran | *H* | 160 | | NC | 121 |
| | T | 90 | Auchterless | *SC*(ii) | 187 | | H*4* | 137–8 |
| | U | 130 | Ayr | FD | 98 | | T | 90 |
| Aberdour | *H* | 159 | | FFO | 110 | Biggar | H*2* | 138 |
| | NF | 129 | | H | 136 | | SC(ii) | 174 |
| Abernethy | A | 74 | | | | Blairspittal | *H* | 160 |
| | CE | 190 | | | | Blantyre | A | 74 |
| | SC(ii) | 174 | Balantrodoch | | | Bothans | SC(ii) | 175 |
| Aberuthven | *A* | 84 | (Temple) | KT | 131 | Bothwell | SC(ii) | 175 |
| Aboyne | *KT* | 132 | Balfron | *H* | 160 | Brechin | CE | 190 |
| Adniston (Aulden- | | | Balgownie | H | 136 | | *FC* | 116 |
| estun) *v.* Leger- | | | Ballencrieff | H | 137 | | H | 138 |
| wood | | | Balmerino | C | 62 | | SC(i) | 167 |
| Aldcambus | H | 135 | Banff | FC | 114 | | *SC*(ii) | 187 |
| Ancaria | *C* | 69 | | *FF* | 108 | | *T* | 93 |
| Ancrum | H | 136 | | *H* | 160 | Brough of Birsay | *T* | 93 |
| | KH | 133 | Bara | H | 137 | Broughty Ferry | | |
| | *T* | 93 | Barra | *T* | 93 | (Portincraig) | H | 153 |
| Annan | H | 136 | Barry | *T* | 93 | Buchan | U | 194 |

201